UNITED PROVINCES' POLITICS, 1936 – 1937: FORMATION OF THE MINISTRIES AND START OF CONGRESS GOVERNMENT

Governors' Fortnightly Reports and other Key Documents

United Provinces' Politics, 1936 – 1937: Formation of the Ministries and Start of Congress Government

Governors' Fortnightly Reports and other Key Documents

compiled and edited by

LIONEL CARTER

Former Librarian, Centre of South Asian Studies, University of Cambridge

MANOHAR

2008

First published 2008

ISBN 81-7304-790-1

Published by
Ajay Kumar Jain *for*
Manohar Publishers & Distributors
4753/23 Ansari Road, Daryaganj
New Delhi 110 002

Printed at
Lordson Publishers Pvt Ltd
Delhi 110 007

To the Memory of
Geoffrey Stern, 1935–2005
Academic, Composer and Friend

Contents

Editor's Introduction

This is the first volume in a series on the United Provinces which will parallel the five volumes I have published on the Punjab. (*Punjab Politics,* New Delhi: Manohar, 2004–2007). The aim is to reproduce in full the text of the U.P. Governors' Fortnightly Reports to the Viceroys together with other important documents from the Governors or their Secretaries to the Viceroys or their Private Secretaries. Space considerations do not allow the publication of the Viceroys' replies although these are footnoted where necessary. Enclosures to Governors' letters are only included when they are important. The fortnightly "Official Reports" produced by the Chief Secretary to the U.P. Government are also not printed although a copy was generally enclosed with each Governor's Report. They are more formal documents than the Governors' Reports. When the Congress took over the ministry, the Premier sometimes had a hand in the drafting of the Chief Secretary's Report. (See, for example, No. 121.)

The series of Governors' Reports was started in 1936 because, with the beginning of the new constitution set up under the 1935 Act, both Viceroy and Secretary of State for India felt the need for more confidential and personal assessments of the developing situation in the eleven Indian Provinces than the usual official documents were able to provide. The Viceroy was the first to feel the need for such reports and on 11 October 1936 he asked the U.P. Governor, Sir Harry Haig, to send him a confidential appreciation of local political developments at roughly monthly intervals. (No. 1, note 1.) The Secretary of State for India followed the Viceroy's initiative by asking on 25 March 1937 (Despatch No. 3) for Governors to forward him at short intervals, reports "of the more important events and tendencies, political, administrative and economic, in the Province . . . with an expression of the Governor's personal views upon them".[1] In response to this Haig copied to London his report of 7 April 1937 (No. 23) and thereafter the fortnightly series was fully launched. As I have said in the introduction to my Punjab series we are able through this development to see the working of the late colonial mind in detail and be privy to some of it most confidential thoughts.

* * *

The United Provinces is a Province of major significance in the study of the late British raj. For the Viceroy, Lord Linlithgow, it was of "critical importance . . . in the general scheme of things". (Appendix 11.) It was central to the thinking of the Indian National Congress. Amongst other things it was the home of the Nehrus and other important leaders and was at the forefront of Congress's radical agrarian programme. The U.P. was also the Province where the Muslim League made spectacular advances in the late 1930s and really got going. I recognise that much research has been done on the pre-Independence U.P., particularly in recent years.[2] However I feel that the publication of the documents in the present volume, providing as they do a detailed (sometimes day-to-day) account of developments, allows us to make a fuller and deeper assessment of the actions, attitudes and policies of all the personalities concerned. It was Professor Harold Temperley who criticised the partial use of manuscripts, saying it was as misleading as the partial use of books. "There is an immense difference," he wrote, "between a knowledge of fifty per cent of the material available and a knowledge of ninety per cent of it. For the last part of knowledge matters a good deal more than the first part of it."[3]

The first significant document in this volume (No. 2) is a lengthy survey of the U.P. political scene in the autumn of 1936 written in response to Linlithgow's request of 11 October mentioned above. It reflects Haig's well-known sympathies for the U.P. landlords[4] but the Governor was far too perceptive not to realise the threat which Congress now posed to them (the Congress having greatly increased in strength in the U.P. in the months since August). "The Congress trumpets are sounding," he wrote, "and in many places the walls of Jericho seem only too ready to fall down." Moreover, the landlords' problems were compounded by personal differences and by the beginnings of a Hindu-Muslim split. Nonetheless, Haig reported that the general feeling was that the landlords would win the provincial elections scheduled for the beginning of 1937 although as the weeks went on the estimates of their likely strength were clearly going down. (Nos. 3–4, 6.) Still it came as a shock when Congress won by something approaching a landslide. In the lower house Congress took 133 seats out of a total of 228 thereby possessing a substantial majority.

Congress in the U.P. were now expected to take up office under the Premiership of their local leader, Pandit Govind Ballabh Pant. The general view, however, was that the Congress ministry would not last long before a mass movement was begun. Haig himself felt that "it is not impossible, though I think in this province unlikely, that they will settle down and work what I may call a genuine though radical policy." (No. 12.) However

Pant, in accordance with central Congress policy, refused to form a government until he received assurances that Haig would not use against the ministry the special powers given to him under the 1935 Government of India Act. Negotiations on this point finally broke down on 29 March. (No. 16.)

In the circumstances Haig's first reaction was that he should take over the reins of government himself under Section 93 of the 1935 Act (No. 13) but he was persuaded by Linlithgow that the correct course was to attempt to form a minority ministry. This proved exceptionally difficult in the U.P., in fact more difficult than anywhere else in India. Hopes rested with the veteran Muslim leader, the Nawab of Chhatari, who had been a former Governor of the province. However Chhatari manifested rather a defeatist attitude towards such a task. (Nos. 17-19.) Perhaps he was fearful that the minority ministry would not last long and would bring discredit to the landlords. In the event Haig had to go behind Chhatari's back and secure the support of possible ministers, then presenting Chhatari with a *fait accompli*. (No. 20.) The Chhatari ministry took up office on 3 April 1937.

The record of the minority ministry can be studied in Chapter 2 of the Summaries of Documents. (Nos. 21-54.) At its close the Governor felt able to report that the ministry had handled its charges satisfactorily and that the period was one of comparative rest and tranquillity. (No. 57.) Throughout its tenure Chhatari was clearly uneasy at the ministry's position and he made many suggestions aimed at providing Congress with an early opportunity of taking office. (See Nos. 29–30, 33 and 41.) Still we may say that the minority ministry manoeuvre served the British purpose well enough. No doubt the sight of Indian ministers exercising power had an effect on those elements within Congress which wished to accept office. Following a statement by Linlithgow on 21 June clarifying the position on the use of Governors' special powers, the Congress Working Committee, meeting at Wardha, decided on 7 July to agree to form Ministries even though Linlithgow's assurances fell short of what it had demanded. The Chhattari ministry accordingly resigned and the first members of the Pant ministry were sworn in on 17 July. (No. 54.) The ministry was to be without Muslim League members, negotiations between the Congress and League breaking down around 26 July. (See No. 57, note 3.) These negotiations have been the subject of much historical controversy but the Governor's letters do not shed any light on them.

Haig's first reaction to the ministry as formed by Pant was one of relief. He wrote that: "on the whole [it is] of a comparatively moderate character" and he singled out as its two most important members Pant and Dr K.N. Katju, the Minister of Justice, Development and Agriculture. (No. 63.) In making this assessment Haig failed to recognise (as he failed to recognise throughout 1937) the importance of the Congress Muslim Minister for Revenue and Jails, Rafi Ahmad Kidwai, who appeared to Haig at one point to be not very bright. (No. 75.) In fact Kidwai had been the major organiser and financier of the 1937 Congress election victory in the U.P. and emerged as the most important figure in the state party organisation with a large personal following among the district leaders.[5]

Despite Haig's initial feelings of relief, he was soon faced with a succession of problems. Pant was unhappy with the Governor's functions as laid down in the Rules of Business. (No. 55.) The Premier also did not want Haig to ordinarily preside at cabinet meetings.[6] (Nos. 58 and 65.) There was anxiety at to whether tenants would pay their rents. (No. 121.) As time went on there were doubts over the ministry's ability to tackle law and order issues and to control its supporters in the districts. (Appendices A5–A6, A8, A10 and A13.) Particular concern was felt by the Viceroy over the practice whereby local Congress Committees took up individual complaints and forwarded them to the highest levels of government. Linlithgow saw this as the creation of a parallel government and he strongly objected to the issue of a circular (Appendix A9) by the U.P. Chief Secretary on 10 November (in fact intended to stem local Congress activity in handling complaints) which encouraged district magistrates to cultivate relations of mutual confidence with local Congress leaders. (Appendix A16.) Matters reached a climax in Kanpur where there had been a legacy of strikes and where a Muslim worker was murdered. The murdered man had been prominent in getting the strikers back to work. Here the district magistrate took decisive action on his own authority and arrested seven members of the relevant mill committee and also issued orders against ten communist leaders. Pant subsequently backed the district magistrate's action. (No. 114.)

It was however the question of release of political prisoners, and the aftermath of the releases, which brought about the first two major crises of the Pant ministry. According to Sarvepalli Gopal, "Pant's first act on taking charge in the U.P. was to sit down at his office table to write the order for their [the political prisoners'] discharge."[7] Haig was clear that it would not be practicable to resist this (No. 52) but a crisis arose when receptions started to be organised for the released prisoners and some of their number made speeches. (Nos. 78 and 79.) Haig's initial reaction was to say that he could not agree to further releases but he was eventually persuaded by the cabinet to continue the release programme to avoid the

Ministry's political position being weakened. The cabinet agreed in return that it would firmly oppose the release of dangerous prisoners. (No. 84.) Both the Viceroy and the Secretary of State for India (Lord Zetland) agreed with this course of action.

Problems over the issue of speeches by released prisoners again arose in late November 1937. One particular released prisoner, Pandit Parmanand, made a speech at Dehra Dun "inciting to violent revolution and revolt against the British and seducing of troops". (No. 111.) Haig favoured an immediate prosecution of Parmanand but the Cabinet were not in favour of taking this action without giving Parmanand a prior warning about his conduct. Ignoring their objections Haig ordered the Dehra Dun magistrate to proceed with the prosecution subject to the required legal examination. (No. 111.) Subsequently (following consideration of the matter by a committee of the Congress Working Committee) it became clear that the Ministry might well resign over the Dehra Dun prosecution. A way forward was however suggested by Pant. As it happened Parmanand had been arrested and was being prosecuted in Delhi for a similar offence. Pant suggested that this would allow the U.P. to issue a communiqué stating that it had ordered the prosecution of Parmanand but in view of the Delhi prosecution the U.P. were dropping theirs. At the same time the communiqué would make it clear that the U.P. government would not hesitate to prosecute Parmanand if he repeated his offence in the Province. (Nos. 117, 121 and 122.) Linlithgow was not initially in favour of this course but Haig showed great skill in his handling of the Viceroy and the Secretary of State and he eventually succeeded in persuading them. His crucial telegram of 15 December (No. 126) is a document of great courage particularly when one bears in mind that Haig would have realised from his discussions with Linlithgow in Delhi (only three weeks before) that he faced the probability of dismissal if his actions failed to please. (Appendix A12.) The U.P. communiqué as issued is printed as Appendix A17.

Haig, therefore, was able by the end of 1937 to feel that solid progress had been made. The ministry had taken resolute action in Kanpur; the security situation had improved with the arrest of Parmanand in Delhi; and the communiqué issued by the U.P. government contained a statement that prosecutions for offensive speeches would be made in future without necessarily giving individual warnings. Haig felt able to write to the Viceroy: "The Congress use at once the language of revolution and reform, but there is reasonable and I think growing chance that reform will predominate and the constitution justify itself." (No. 131.) This was not quite how Linlithgow viewed matters. He replied early in January 1938:

> "Pant in my judgment came very badly out of the Parmanand case, even though you, I, and the Secretary of State found it possible to accept the compromise on the basis of which that case was settled. For, in effect, as I see it, although he continues to lay stress on his support of democratic principles and his reluctance to proceed to strong measures against individuals, he has taken refuge behind the District Magistrate of Delhi; while I have reason to believe that his own handling of the situation in the United Provinces has brought him little credit with the Right Wing of the Congress.[8] It is a very depressing state of things that at a time when so much turns on personality, and on the presence at the helm of affairs of individuals of a resolute character and a readiness to take the risks which anyone must take on whom falls the burden of government in this or any other country, we should find that we have to deal with an idealist of the type of Pant, and that we should have to accept the fact that since there is no alternative to him which is even equally satisfactory, we must make the best of what we have got."[9]

* * *

One of the fascinating aspects of these documents is the picture they give of the relationship which grew up between Haig and Pant – a relationship which foreshadows the Mountbatten-Nehru relationship.[10] Haig and Pant were men of very different origins. Haig was a product of Winchester and New College, Oxford who rose in the I.C.S. to become Government of India Home Member in 1932 before his appointment as U.P. Governor in 1934. He was, according to Low, after Lord Hailey, "the most distinguished member of the Indian Civil Service in its final decades".[11] Haig has often been regarded as hostile to Congress during his time as Home Member[12] but this fails to do him proper justice. Even during the civil disobedience movement he wrote to the Viceroy's Private Secretary:

> "There can be no question, at the present time, of conversations with Congress. We must show that civil disobedience has failed. When that is once appreciated, we have no wish to remain in conditions of permanent hostility with Congress. On the contrary, we must look to them coming in immediately or gradually as one of the most important elements, if not the most important, in the working of the new constitution. I do not at all despair of our reaching that position at no very distant date."[13]

Pant by contrast to Haig was born in the Kumaon Hills and grew up in the small town of Almora.[14] A sickly child he was tutored at home and did not go to school until he was ten. At fourteen he suffered a heart attack but he recovered and was admitted to Muir Central College in Allahabad in 1905. After qualifying in law Pant returned to Almora to start a law practice. However in 1922 he gave this up to join in the various Gandhian campaigns for Hindu-Muslim unity and against Untouchability. Pant became a member of the U.P. Legislative Council in 1924 and was elected leader of the Swaraj Party in the U.P. later that year. During the Civil Disobedience movement Pant found himself in jail with Nehru who was to become a life-long co-worker. In 1934 Pant became deputy leader of the Congress party in the Central Assembly and he was elected Congress leader in the U.P. in 1937.

It is important to realise that both Haig and Pant had limitations on their power of manoeuvre. Haig was constrained by the outlook of Linlithgow who considered him to be indecisive and lacking in firmness. The Viceroy took the view that Haig was probably more suited to secretariat work than a Governorship. Twice in the course of the volume Linlithgow came close to recommending Haig's dismissal. (Appendices A1, A11 and A12.) In studying the Linlithgow-Haig relationship one sometimes feels that their differences were more emotional and intellectual than based upon grounds of policy. Pant's problem was that, unlike Kidwai, he had no power base within his own party. Even in Almora he had no power and he had to contest elections in places where he was more respected. As Brass says, he was a parliamentary leader rather than an organisational leader. "He was esteemed by all Congressmen in Uttar Pradesh as a man of intelligence and integrity, but he had no group of his own."[15]

As we shall see in the next volume, a serious difficulty between the British and Congress lay ahead. In February 1938 the ministries in both the U.P. and Bihar submitted their resignations over the non-release of certain prisoners. The subsequent moves which brought the Congress back into office can be viewed as a climb-down on the part of Linlithgow. Whatever may have been the reason, Haig survived as U.P. Governor and the Haig-Pant collaboration was able to continue. We must be thankful that this was the case. For it is questionable whether Linlithgow's choice for Haig's replacement, Sir Maurice Hallett, would have shown the political dexterity which Haig did.[16]

The documents in this volume are British Crown Copyright and are all taken from the following classes of material in the India Office Records:

L/P&J	India Office – Public & Judicial Department files.
L/PO	India Office – Private Office files.
MSS.EUR.F 97	Brabourne papers.
MSS.EUR.F 115	Haig papers.
MSS.EUR.F.125	Linlithgow papers.
R/3/1	Prints of Viceroy's correspondence with the Governors.

I would like once again to express my thanks for help and advice received from Anthony Farrington, formerly head of the India Office Records at the British Library. I am also most grateful to Graham Shaw, Director of Asia, Pacific and Africa Collections at the British Library, for his interest. I owe a special debt to Ram Advani and to Ramesh Dogra, M.B.E. and Urmila Dogra for advice on a wide range of issues. My publisher, Ramesh Jain, has, as ever, extended many kindnesses to me. None of the foregoing bears any responsibility for errors and omissions in the book. The responsibility for these rests solely with me.

Harrow, November 2006 LIONEL CARTER

NOTES

1. Lord Zetland's Despatch is on L/P&J/9/287. This file is on the subject of the 'Supply of Information to the Secretary of State'. Similar papers are on L/P&J/7/989.
2. Key works on the U.P. in this period would include: Paul R. Brass, *Factional politics in an Indian state: the Congress Party in Uttar Pradesh* (Berkeley: University of California Press, 1965); William Gould, *Hindu nationalism and the language of politics in late colonial India* (Cambridge: C.U.P., 2004); Mushirul Hasan, *Legacy of a divided nation: India's Muslims since independence* (London: Hurst, 1997); Gyanesh Kudaisya, *Region, Nation, "Heartland": Uttar Pradesh in India's Body-politic* (New Delhi: Sage, 2006); Visalakshi Menon, *From Movement to Government: The Congress in the United Provinces, 1937-42* (New Delhi: Sage, 2002); Salil Misra, *A Narrative of Communal Politics: Uttar Pradesh, 1937-39* (New Delhi: Sage, 2001); Gyanendra Pandey, *The Ascendency of Congress in Uttar Pradesh: Class, Community and Nation in Northern India, 1920-1940* (London: Anthem, 2002); P.D. Reeves, *Landlords and Governments in Uttar Pradesh: A study*

of Their Relations Until the Zamindari Abolition (Bombay: O.U.P., 1991); P.D. Reeves, 'Landlords and Party Politics in the United Provinces, 1934-7' in D.A. Low (ed.), *Soundings in Modern South Asian History* (London: Weidenfeld and Nicolson, 1968).

The following works contain material which is particularly relevant to this volume: P.N Chopra (ed.), *Towards Freedom, 1937-47*, Vol. 1: *Experiment with Provincial Autonomy, 1 January-31 December 1937* (New Delhi: Indian Council of Historical Research, 1985); D.A. Low, *Britain and Indian Nationalism: The Imprint of Ambiguity, 1929-1942*, especially Chapter 7 (Cambridge: C.U.P., 1997); B.R. Nanda (chief ed.), *Selected Works of Govind Ballabh Pant*, Vol. 7: *[September 1936-December 1937]* (Delhi: O.U.P., 1997).

3. Temperley criticising Lytton Strachey. Cited in the new introduction by Sir Herbert Butterfield to the reprint of Temperley's *The Foreign Policy of Canning, 1822-1827* (London: Frank Cass, 1966, p. xx).
4. The Raja of Mahmudabad recalled a lunch with Haig in 1936 at which he was berated for joining the Muslim League. Haig reminded him that his estate was a gift from the British sovereign and that he should dissociate himself from the 'arch enemy' (i.e. Jinnah) and join the National Agriculturist Party. 'Some Memories' in C.H. Philips and M.D. Wainwright, *The Partition of India: Policies and Perspectives, 1935-1947* (London: Allen & Unwin, 1970, pp. 381-9).
5. Brass, p. 39. Kidwai's biographer records that during the 1937 election campaign all available transport in the U.P. and even Bihar was taken under control by Congress so that opponents could not use it. This action hit the landlords very hard. P.N. Chopra, *Rafi Ahmad Kidwai, His Life and Work* (Agra: Shiva Lal Agarwala, 1960, pp. 45-6).
6. Haig himself feared that if he always presided at Cabinet meetings, the Ministers might gather separately before a Cabinet meeting and decide the line they would take so as to conceal possible differences of approach. The procedure Haig feared was in fact adopted in Bombay. See Moraji Desai, *The Story of My Life*, Vol. 1 (Delhi, Macmillan India, 1974, pp. 160-1). Such pre-Cabinet meetings by Congress were also to take place during the all-India Interim Government of 1946 and 1947.
7. Sarvepalli Gopal, *Jawaharlal Nehru: A Biography*, Vol. 1: *1889-1947* (London, Cape, 1975, p. 229).
8. Cf. Appendix A15.
9. Linlithgow to Haig, 6 January 1938. MSS.EUR.F. 115/3.
10. Anthony Low has pointed out that there were quite a few examples in the late British empire of a coming together of nationalist leaders and colonial rulers of which the Mountbatten-Nehru association is the most notable. *Britain and Indian Nationalism*, p. 119.
11. Anthony Low's entry for Haig in: H.C.G. Mathew and Brian Harrison (eds.), *Oxford Dictionary of National Biography* (Oxford: O.U.P., 2004).

12. See, for example, Gopal, p. 170.
13. Haig to Miéville, 13 April 1932. MSS.EUR.F. 115/1.
14. There are at least five biographies in English of Pant. These are by the following authors: (1) S.R. Bakshi (New Delhi: Anmol, 1990); (2) M. Chalapathi Rau (New Delhi, Allied, 1981); (3) Subhash C. Kashyap and Mahesh C. Shah (New Delhi: National, 1988); (4) M.K. Rastogi (Nainital: Gyanodaya Prakashan, 1987); (5) Shyam Sunder and Savitri Shyam (Lucknow: Shailanil, 1960). Of these the account by Chalapathi Rau is the best but he tends to view matters rather uncritically from the Congress perspective.
15. Brass, p. 40.
16. Hallett, of course, acted as Governor of the U.P. during Haig's period of leave between May and September 1938.

Abbreviations

A.I.C.C.	All-India Congress Committee.
C.-in-C.	Commander-in-Chief.
C.I.D.	Criminal Investigation Department.
Cr.P.C.	Criminal Procedure Code.
D.C.	Deputy Commissioner.
D.I.B.	Director of the Intelligence Bureau.
D.I.G.	Deputy Inspector General.
D.M.	District Magistrate.
D.O.	Demi-Official.
G. of I.	Government of India.
H.E.	His Excellency.
H.M.G.	His Majesty's Government.
I.A.	Indian Army.
I.C.S.	Indian Civil Service.
I.G.P.	Inspector General of Police.
I.P.	Indian Police.
I.P.C.	Indian Penal Code.
M.L.	Muslim League.
M.L.A.	Member of the Legislative Assembly.
M.L.C.	Member of the Legislative Council.
P.S.	Postscript *or* Parliamentary Secretary.
P.S.V.	Private Secretary to the Viceroy.
S. of S.	Secretary of State.
S.D.O.	Sub-Divisional Officer.
S.P.	Superintendent of Police.
U.P.	United Provinces.

Glossary

Anna	One-sixteenth of a rupee.
Babu	A term of respect; often accorded to Indians who were fluent in English.
Bania	Trader, moneylender.
Bigha	A measure of land equal to 5/8th of an acre.
Chaprasi	An office messenger; an orderly in government service.
Crore	One hundred lakhs or ten million.
Dacoity	Robbery with violence committed by a gang.
Dussehra	Hindu festival celebrated in September-October in honour of Durga and Rama.
Fasli	Belonging to the harvest; the harvest year. A method of computing time which was prevalent throughout India and was one of the forms used in public orders and regulations. The era was started by the Emperor Akbar and the year began with the month of Asarn (June/July). It is necessary to add 592 to the *fasli* year to compute the Common Era year (593 if the date is more than halfway through the *fasli* year).
Gaddi	*Lit.:* a cushion. A ruler's throne.
Inqilab	Revolution.
Khadi	*Strictly:* cloth woven by hand from yarn village-spun also by hand.
Kharif	Grain crops sown in summer and reaped by early winter.
Kisan	Peasant, cultivator, tenant.
Kist	Instalment, portion.
Lakh	One hundred thousand.
Lathi	Thick stick, usually bamboo, sometimes bound with iron rings.
Maulvi	Muslim religious teacher.

Mazdur Sabha	Trade union.
Mufti	Plain clothes.
Panchayat	Court of arbitration (properly of five persons) for determination of petty disputes; village council.
Pandal	Large tent, canopy or open-sided temporary building used for ceremonies or meetings.
Patwari	Village accountant.
Rabi	Principal grain harvest sown after the rains and reaped in the spring season.
Sabha	Association, conclave, assembly.
Shia	One of the two main branches of Islam (cf. Sunni); followers of Ali, the son-in-law of Muhammad.
Sunni	The majority in Indian Islam, who regard Caliphs Abu Bakr, Omar and Osman as spiritual descendants of Muhammad.
Swaraj	Self-rule, independence.
Tahsil	Revenue sub-division of a District. Tahsildar: collector of the revenue within a tahsil.
Taluqdar	Large landholder in Oudh; holder of a revenue subdivision.
Vakil	Lawyer; authorised pleader in a court of justice.
Zamindar	Landed proprietor paying land revenue to Government, revenue farmer.
Zindabad	Long live!

Principal Holders of Office, October 1936–December 1937

UNITED KINGDOM

Secretary of State for India	The Marquess of Zetland

INDIA

Viceroy, Governor-General and Crown Representative	The Marquess of Linlithgow
Private Secretary to the Viceroy	Mr Gilbert Laithwaite
Commander-in-Chief, India	General Sir Robert Cassels

UNITED PROVINCES

Governor	Sir Harry Haig
Secretary to Governor	Major D.A. Brett Mr J.C. Donaldson (from 1 April 1937)
Chief Secretary to Government	Mr C.W. Gwynne

Appointments under the 1919 Constitution operative until 2 April 1937

MEMBERS OF COUNCIL

Home Member and Vice-President of Council	Sir Maharaj Singh
Finance Member	Sir Joseph Clay

MEMBERS FOR THE ADMINISTRATION OF TRANSFERRED SUBJECTS

Minister for Local Self-Government	Nawab Sir Muhammad Yusuf

Minister for Education	Sir Jwala P. Srivastava

U.P. LEGISLATIVE COUNCIL

President	Sir Sita Ram
Deputy President	Nawabzada Liaqat Ali Khan

Appointments under the 1935 Constitution operative 3 April–16 July 1937

MEMBERS OF THE COUNCIL OF MINISTERS

Minister of Home Affairs	The Nawab of Chhatari
Minister of Local Self-Government and Health	Nawab Sir Muhammad Yusuf
Minister of Finance and Industries	Sir Jwala P. Srivastava
Minister of Education	The Raja of Salempur
Minister of Revenue and Agriculture	Raja Maheshwar Dayal Seth
Minister of Justice	The Maharajkumar of Vizianagram
Minister of Communications and Rural Development	The Raja of Tirwa

U.P. LEGISLATIVE ASSEMBLY

(No Speaker or Deputy Speaker was elected during this period as the Legislative Assembly did not meet.)

Appointments under the 1935 Constitution operative from 17 July 1937

MEMBERS OF THE COUNCIL OF MINISTERS

Premier and Minister of Home Affairs and Finance	Pandit Govind Ballabh Pant
Minister of Revenue and Jails	Mr Rafi Ahmad Kidwai
Minister of Justice, Development, Agriculture and Veterinary	Dr Kailash Nath Katju
Minister of Local Self-Government and Health	Mrs Vijayalakshmi Pandit
Minister of Education	Pandit Pyare Lal Sharma (from 28 July 1937)

Minister of Communications and Irrigation	Hafiz Muhammad Ibrahim (from 28 July 1937)

U.P. LEGISLATIVE ASSEMBLY

Speaker	Shri Purushottamdas Tandon
Deputy Speaker	Mr Abdul Hakeem

Summaries of Documents

CHAPTER 1 : DOCUMENTS FOR 15 OCTOBER 1936 – 2 APRIL 1937

	Name and Number	*Date*	*Main subject or subjects*
		1936	
		Oct.	
1	Haig to Linlithgow Letter	15	Will send first report on provincial politics when he returns to Lucknow
2	Haig to Linlithgow 1st Report	29	Lengthy survey of the political scene in U.P.
		Dec.	
3	Haig to Linlithgow 2nd Report	2	Political situation has not altered fundamentally since No. 2; line-up of individuals and groups for forthcoming election
		1937	
		Jan.	
4	Haig to Linlithgow 3rd Report	6	Election prospects of the parties; Congress and the services
5	Haig to Linlithgow Letter	26	Explains circumstances in which U.P. government decided to ban Congress independence resolution
		Feb.	
6	Haig to Linlithgow Letter	4	District Officers report that Congress propaganda has been extremely intensive and effective; idle to speculate on results of election
7	Haig to Linlithgow Letter	13	Congress's remarkable successes in elections; views as to spirit in

			which Congress will take office; causes of landlords' defeat
8	Haig to Linlithgow Letter	13	Date on which Governors of Provinces with Congress majorities should announce they have invited Congress leader to form govt.; in event of Congress declining, favours resort to Section 93 after approaching opposition leaders
9	Haig to Linlithgow Letter	17	Effects of election on landlords, Muslim League and Congress; general assumption that Congress will take office; lines of policy Congress are likely to pursue; suggests Conference of Governors of Congress-majority provinces; Enclosure: extracts from speeches by Nehru in Meerut Division
10	Haig to Linlithgow Letter	23	Elaborates his idea of discussions between Governors of Congress-majority provinces; lists issues which might benefit from a common approach
11	Haig to Linlithgow Letter	28	Appreciates that much preliminary consultation on Ministries need not take place until April; is not disturbed at having to wait until after meeting of A.I.C.C. before forming Ministry; agrees 12 April would be suitable date to summon legislature but will largely be guided by wishes of new Ministry
		Mar.	
12	Haig to Linlithgow Tel. (Unnumbered)	18	Explains his anxieties on Congress resolution on office acceptance and on line Linlithgow had suggested; feels it is not impossible that Congress will settle down in U.P. and work a radical policy;

			however considers this unlikely; is not sending for Pant until he hears further
13	Haig to Linlithgow Tel. 1-G	20	Is seeing Pant following Wednesday; considers he would have to press for immediate application of Section 93 if a break with Congress occurs
14	Haig to Linlithgow Tel. 3-G	24	Reports that discussion with Pant had reached complete deadlock over use of Governor's special powers; they decided to meet again but it is unlikely anything will come out of this
15	Haig to Linlithgow Tel. 4-G	25	Agrees he should aim at forming a ministry from minority elements, keeping it in office for some months
16	Haig to Linlithgow Tel. 5-G	29	At further meeting, Pant regretted he could not accept invitation to form Ministry; Haig is taking up immediately question of another Ministry
17	Haig to Linlithgow Letter	31	Reports discussions with Chhatari who had agreed to try to form Ministry; however at latest meeting he was in rather defeatist mood particularly in view of possible League attitude; Haig cannot be confident they can form Ministry
18	Haig to Linlithgow Letter	31	In interview Srivastava has expressed much more robust views on possibility of forming ministry; question of including Chintamani
		April	
19	Haig to Linlithgow Tel. 6-G	1	Chhatari reports that that day's discussions on forming a ministry have been very disappointing;

			League seems practically solid against joining; there is strong opposition among landlords; Chintamani and Maharaj Singh have refused to join
20	Haig to Linlithgow Letter	2	Chhatari has just submitted his list of ministers and ministry will take office following day; Haig had talked separately with possible ministers that morning

CHAPTER 2 : DOCUMENTS FOR 3 APRIL – 16 JULY 1937

		April	
21	Haig to Linlithgow Letter	4	Agrees with Linlithgow on line they should take with any resolution by legislature on behaviour of troops acting in aid of the civil power
22	Haig to Linlithgow Letter	5	Talk with Chhatari and Srivastava on courses open to new govt.; Haig feels they should not encourage ministry to engage in fight with Congress if Congress were shortly to express themselves ready to take office; Muslim League position
23	Haig to Linlithgow 1st Report	7	Following elections had been widespread apprehension at likelihood of Congress taking office; after Congress refusal, complete mental readjustment has occurred; Chhatari's negotiations to form ministry; new ministry inclined to take fairly vigorous line; sugar cane and food situation; summarises present political position
24	Haig to Linlithgow Letter	10	Govt. propaganda in the vernacular on breakdown of discussions with Congress

25	Haig to Linlithgow 2nd Report	23	Ministry decides to hold Coronation Durbars in every U.P. district and to retain govt. in Lucknow during hot weather; govt. publicity; action on food situation; ministry's main activity to be tenancy reform; proposal for hydro-electric grid; meeting of Congress M.L.As.; believes pressure on Congress to accept constitutional powers will become stronger; great activity in Muslim affairs; meeting of non-Congress M.L.As. and M.L.Cs.; attitude of Scheduled Castes; believes ministry has strengthened its position but that it is not popular
26	Haig to Linlithgow Letter	24	Agrees with Linlithgow's views on publicity and propaganda; ministry are hoping to obtain Rs. 40,000 quickly and are fairly hopeful of developing an effective party organisation
27	Haig to Linlithgow Letter	29	Refers to No. 26; explains the way he had intended to use a non-Congress party organisation; agrees Governor should depend essentially on his own machinery
		May	
28	Haig to Linlithgow 3rd Report	7	Uncertainty continues over Congress's intentions; conference of Commissioners; villages are quiet but Congress impression on them remains strong; Oudh taluqdars reject ministry's proposal to give tenants hereditary rights; publication of cabinet's programme; alternative favoured by ministry to creation of a party; Muslims are disintegrated and uncertain; Congress to hold meet-

			ing of M.L.As.; future prospects uncertain
29	Haig to Linlithgow Tel. 7-G	13	Has received resolutions passed by meeting of M.L.As.; wishes to reply somewhat fully and indicates what he would say; considers it would be necessary to suspend constitution and legislature in event of breakdown; discusses idea that ministry might resign before meeting legislature
30	Haig to Linlithgow Letter	16	Sends copy of his reply to resolutions of M.L.As.; asks Linlithgow to stress to Chhatari undesirability of ministry resigning before meeting legislature; asks him also to hearten Chhatari; Haig explains his objections to formation of another minority ministry
31	Haig to Linlithgow Letter	21	Future policy towards Congress; agrees Viceroy should take any possible steps to facilitate office acceptance
32	Haig to Linlithgow 4th Report	24	Resolutions of M.L.As.; indications of strong desire of local Congress to take office; standing of present government has not improved; reason for its inability to form an organisation; cabinet has considered its tactics when legislature is summoned; difficulties in including Scheduled Caste member in ministry; Muslim League situation; Sunni-Shia rioting in Lucknow; sugar cane situation in Gorakhpur; possible Congress agitation on resettlements and revisions of settlements

33	Haig to Linlithgow Letter	25	Explains why he is unsympathetic to Chhatari's suggestion that they should give Congress one more chance to take office before present ministry face legislature
34	Haig to Linlithgow Tel. 9-G	25	Refers to No. 31; has no further suggestions as to how they can get in closer touch with Congress
		June	
35	Haig to Linlithgow 5th Report	7	Believes feeling in Congress in favour of office acceptance has further strengthened; speculates on Gandhi's thinking; concern over situation in eastern U.P., particularly Gorakhpur; cabinet has been rather inactive although some ministers are meeting ministers in other provinces; main problem before cabinet will be budget; fears ministers may lower canal rates; other matters under consideration; feeling between Sunnis and Shias remains exceedingly bitter; Muslim feeling generally is hardening
36	Haig to Linlithgow Tel. 12-G	17	Ministers and he agree that 29 July would be suitable date for summoning legislature
37	Haig to Linlithgow Draft Tel. (not sent)	17	Agrees they should do all they can to encourage Congress to take office; suggests a way they might meet Congress
38	Haig to Linlithgow Letter	23	Reports discussion in cabinet on tactics if Congress decides to take office; ministers seemed anxious they should offer to make way for Congress before Working Committee's decision
39	Haig to Linlithgow 6th Report	23	Chhatari's and Drake-Brockman's talks with Pant; Pant's attitude to office acceptance; three members

			of present ministry feel Viceroy's statement is excellent; cabinet's views on probable reactions to Statement; Katju talks to Srivastava about Congress's long-term intentions; date for summoning legislature; Cabinet gives up idea of borrowing to finance new schemes; prosecutions for extremist speeches; demand for release of political prisoners; report on Madhe-Sahaba agitation at Lucknow; forthcoming bye-election in Bundelkhand; sugar conference at Naini Tal
40	Haig to Linlithgow Tel. 14-G	24	Reports that reactions in U.P. to Viceroy's statement have been extremely favourable
41	Haig to Linlithgow Tel. 16-G	25	Reports that Chhatari has written asking for Congress to be given another opportunity to take office; asks for Linlithgow's views on action to be taken including date when Chhatari's letter should be published
42	Haig to Linlithgow Letter	30	Pant's anxieties (expressed through intermediaries) about Haig making nominations at that time to Upper House
		July	
43	Haig to Linlithgow Tel. 17-G	1	Explains why he does not favour Bihar procedure of summoning Legislative Assembly in two stages
44	Donaldson to Laithwaite Letter 376-G.S.P.	5	Sends reports indicating that Congress activity in villages was increasing
45	Haig to Linlithgow 7th Report	7	Has made no attempt yet to contact Pant; has taken no action

			on Chhatari's letter mentioned in No. 41; Haig's nominations to Upper House; delay in appointment of Advocate-General; cabinet settles principles of budget and disposes of other matters; attitude of ministers in charge of law and order; Bundelkhand bye-election
46	Haig to Linlithgow Letter	9	Question of Governor presiding at cabinet meetings likely to be an issue with a Congress ministry; if this occurs, would not normally preside but would keep his right to do so in tact; asks whether Viceroy would object to this
47	Haig to Linlithgow Tel. 20-G	9	Is meeting ministry following day; believes they will wish to make way for Congress as early as possible
48	Haig to Linlithgow Tel. (Unnumbered)	10	Continues No. 47; ministry have tendered resignation; has asked Pant to see him
49	Haig to Linlithgow Tel. 22-G	12	Pant, whom he had seen that day, seemed genuinely hurt that Haig had made nominations to Legislative Council without consulting him; has issued statement on matter; Pant has accepted invitation to form Ministry
50	Haig to Linlithgow Tel. 23-G	15	Refers to No. 49; Pant reported to have been well pleased with their meeting; does not believe that Press tel. from Allahabad will affect their personal relations if Pant confirms his acceptance of office
51	Haig to Linlithgow Tel. 24-G	15	Agrees as to importance of not taking steps in one province which might have awkward

			relations in another; asks whether Viceroy has any general policy on release of political prisoners and if he wishes to be consulted before any action is taken
52	Haig to Linlithgow Tel. 25-G	16	Agrees it would be unwise to press disagreement with a Congress ministry over release of political prisoners to the point of a break; indicates how he would handle issue
53	Haig to Linlithgow Letter	16	Expresses regret if his statement in No. 49 involved possibility of embarrassment to other Governors; explains he agreed to issue statement in order to secure Pant's definite acceptance of office
54	Haig to Linlithgow Tel. 26-G	16	Pant has given him five names for his cabinet; Congress ministers will take oaths of office next day

CHAPTER 3 : DOCUMENTS FOR 17 JULY – 30 SEPTEMBER 1937

		July	
55	Haig to Linlithgow Tel. 27-G	17	Pant has remarked to Donaldson that Rules of Business (particularly on Governor's functions) could not be agreed to by self-respecting ministers; Haig feels difficulties may arise if he takes line indicated by Linlithgow
56	Haig to Linlithgow Tel. 28-G	17	Has not been possible to get hold of Sharma; only first four persons listed in No. 54 have taken office as Ministers
57	Haig to Linlithgow 8th Report	21	Chhatari ministry tenders its resignation; old cabinet disposes

No.	Document	Date	Summary
			of some unsettled issues; Chhatari ministry had handled their charges satisfactorily and period was one of comparative rest and tranquillity; Haig's first interview with Pant; Governor feels statement he issued was undoubtedly wise from provincial point of view; Pant evidently having difficulty making up his Cabinet; future prospects will depend very largely on relations Haig can establish with Pant; matters on which Pant has concentrated; Haig's remarks at swearing-in ceremony and Pant's address to departmental secretaries; talk with Pant on position of Governor; fears of a general strike in Cawnpore
58	Haig to Linlithgow Letter	22	Quite appreciates position about Governor presiding at cabinet meetings; Pant has taken this much better than anticipated
59	Haig to Linlithgow Tel. 29-G	22	Intends to tell Pant he would have to resist any proposal to fly Congress flag on public buildings
60	Haig to Linlithgow Tel. 33-G	30	Pant has said he could not accept Governor presiding at cabinet meetings; Haig could not attend that day's meeting and believes Pant would not hold out on the point by time of next meeting
		Aug.	
61	Haig to Linlithgow Tel. 37-G	5	Reports talk with Pant on release of political prisoners held in the Andamans and elsewhere; strong feeling in cabinet on issue
62	Haig to Linlithgow Tel. 38-G	5	Pant is very determined to balance budget; he appears reluctant to cut

			pay of services but thinks he may be driven to such a proposal
63	Haig to Linlithgow 9th Report	6	Remaining members of cabinet sworn-in; arrangements for Governor's interviews with ministers; remaining nominations made to Upper House; appointment of Advocate-General; hopes question of his presiding at cabinet meetings is now settled; release of political prisoners; Cawnpore situation continues to give anxiety; Congress demonstrations at opening session of legislature; election of Speaker of Assembly and President of Council; Pant's statement on Govt. policy; Assembly opposition crystallising into two parts; budget – understands Pant has given up idea of cut in services' pay; people in general somewhat uncertain and bewildered; enclosure: statement by Pant of govt. policy
64	Haig to Linlithgow Tel. 39-G	7	Pant has raised in cabinet question of release of some violent prisoners; Haig has asked for opinion of police but suspects there will be no case for refusing to accept ministry's advice
65	Haig to Linlithgow Letter	8	Cabinet has discussed issue of Governor presiding; Haig stated his position and said he must insist on it; apart from one threat, discussion proceeded in a most amicable and reasonable way
66	Haig to Linlithgow Tel. 40-G	9	Explains why Pant does not favour an assurance of good behaviour by released prisoners; Haig suggests,

			instead of this, that govt. should issue statement of policy
67	Haig to Linlithgow Tel. 41-G	12	Doubts if ministry would agree to any hunger-strikers being forcibly fed; Haig himself would order such feeding; asks if he would be supported by Linlithgow and Zetland
68	Haig to Linlithgow Tel. 42-G	13	Has considered cases of prisoners proposed for release by ministry and feels all could be released without grave menace to peace of U.P.
69	Haig to Linlithgow Tel. 46-G	16	Argues that ministers should not be allowed to appeal to service associations for voluntary pay cuts; does not anticipate any proposal by ministry for pay cuts
70	Haig to Linlithgow Tel. 47-G	16	Has heard ministers are considering reduction of travel allowances by 25 per cent; indicates how he would act
71	Haig to Linlithgow Letter	17	Ministry have issued executive orders staying proceedings for ejectment of tenants and realisation of arrears of rent pending legislation; Haig expresses his concerns and seeks advice on his powers and responsibilities
72	Haig to Linlithgow Tel. 48-G	18	Agrees as to importance of developing social contacts with ministers; problems if ministers did not attend Lucknow investiture or Governor's address to legislature
73	Haig to Linlithgow Tel. 50-G	20	Is taking action as agreed on release of five Kakori prisoners; Pant has agreed to make statement suggested in No. 66

74	Haig to Linlithgowx Tel. 51-G	20	Repeats his message to Anderson (Bengal) on release of prisoners
75	Haig to Linlithgow 10th Report	22-23	Haig's cabinet meetings with ministry; measures Governor is taking to keep in touch with developments; discussions on budget; appointment of twelve Parliamentary Secretaries; ministry deserve considerable credit for temporary settlement of Cawnpore general strike; Govt. Committee of Enquiry into Cawnpore disputes is to be set up; discussion with Pant on communists; Pant's statement on release of political prisoners; two men in custody threaten hunger-strikes; refers to No.71 – govt. has issued statement appealing to tenants to pay their current rents; Haig believes cabinet are anxious not to do anything which would seriously upset land revenue system; budget will be of very reasonable character; ministry intending to impose tax on agricultural incomes; they also propose moderate cut in travel allowances; they have not proposed cut in canal rates; Haig's concern at what is happening in districts – too early to judge how situation will develop; outlook of ministry reasonable but fears they may not be able to control followers in the country; Haig's talk with Pant on 23 Aug. 1937
76	Haig to Linlithgow Tel. 52-G	23	Refers to No. 72; has talked to Pant and feels that ministers and their followers would attend

No.	Document	Date	Summary
			Governor's address to legislature; Pant evidently thinks difficulty over social contacts may be gradually overcome
77	Haig to Linlithgow Tel. 53-G	24	Attitude govt. servants should adopt on saluting Congress flag and singing 'Vande Mataram'; best way to get their message to services would be by speaking to Commissioners
78	Haig to Linlithgow Tel. 54-G	25	Is concerned about receptions being organised for released Kakori prisoners; Pant has tried to prevent them but has failed; Haig feels they cannot agree to more releases
79	Haig to Linlithgow Letter	30	General situation in U.P. seems definitely to be deteriorating; remains to be seen whether govt. can keep control over province
		Sept.	
80	Haig to Linlithgow Letter	4	Reiterates his view that he cannot now agree to further releases of prisoners; doubts whether he can trust Pant's judgement that released prisoners will not re-offend
81	Haig to Linlithgow Report (Unnumbered)	6	Pant's illness; both houses of legislature are meeting; has had friendly interview with Tandon; considers they have now reached new phase in provincial affairs; Haig's concern over demonstrations following release of Kakori prisoners; his disappointment that Pant was unable to control Congress Left Wing; Haig's visit to Cawnpore – his anxieties over developments there; violent spirit of first Palestine

Day demonstrations in Cawnpore and Lucknow; activities of communists will need serious attention; zamindars are emphatic in protests against ministry; collection of agricultural rents at a standstill; hopes situation with services will right itself

82 Haig to Linlithgow Tel. 57-G | 10 | Reports talk with Pant who did not press for any further premature release of prisoners; Pant asked for cases of Dublis and Kar to be reconsidered but Haig thinks he will accept Governor's view

83 Haig to Linlithgow Letter | 12 | Refers to No. 71; ministry are introducing Bill providing authority for executive orders; real test whether ministry can control tenants and Congress workers will come with collection of *kharif* rents

84 Haig to Linlithgow Tel. 61-G | 14 | Refers to No. 82; cabinet have indicated that their political position would be weakened by suggested policy; Haig now proposes early release of Dublis and Kar on their giving clear undertakings about their future conduct; he would also agree to release (on similar terms) those political prisoners who are comparatively harmless but would require cabinet to firmly oppose release of dangerous prisoners

85 Haig to Linlithgow Report U.P-1. | 22 | Deteriorating situation in Cawnpore; meeting arranged in Lucknow between Owen (D.C., Cawnpore) and Haig, Pant and others; settlement plan worked out and agreed by parties concerned;

			not appropriate to take action against Cawnpore extremists at present; conflict of views between Pant and S.P., Gorakhpur on situation in district; Pant alleges trouble is entirely due to mishandling by local officers; Haig's discussion with Grant (Commissioner, Gorakhpur); Haig concerned about Pant's attitude to police reports; need to check original sources of police reports; appointment of Indian officer of the police to investigate more important complaints of corruption; idea of departmental enquiry into conditions in Gorakhpur; instructions to S.P. have not materialised; question of release of remaining Kakori and other political prisoners; Assembly session – strain of budget proceedings on ministry; Haig pleased with reception to his speech to Legislature; Bill passed to legalise 'Stay Orders' on certain cases before revenue courts; govt. position on agrarian matters is one of great difficulty; talk with Jahangirabad on Congress policy; dispute with Pant over a posting at Saharanpur; explanation for Pant's conduct; importance of Governor touring – Haig's future tour programme; Muhammad Ibrahim to face bye-election
86	Haig to Linlithgow Letter U.P.-3	24	Extracts from C.I.D. report published in *Bombay Chronicle* had been sent to Congress Committee; Pant has promised to

			take very special care with such reports in future; Haig considers it not improper for Pant to use party machinery to investigate complaints and this has been useful
87	Haig to Linlithgow Letter U.P.-4	25	Explains why he does not favour a visit to India in 1938 by King George VI or the holding of a Royal or Viceregal Darbar

CHAPTER 4 : DOCUMENTS FOR 1 OCTOBER – 31 DECEMBER 1937

		Oct.	
88	Haig to Linlithgow Letter U.P.-6	5	Gives his views on the suitability for release of a further 13 political prisoners
89	Donaldson to Laithwaite Letter 644-G.S.P.	6	Decision of U.P. Assembly that Speaker had the power to require or permit any member who was sufficiently acquainted with English to address it in Hindustani; Haig feels no action is advisable for the moment
90	Haig to Linlithgow Report U.P.-7	7	Nehru's statement to the mill-workers of Cawnpore has helped to calm situation; Katju to visit Gorakhpur and make unofficial enquiry into conditions; one of the Parliamentary Secretaries to make informal enquiry into conditions in Jhansi; Haig's idea that statement should be issued on relations between Congress and district authorities; student violence in Lucknow; case of Dublis causing some difficulty; reductions in travelling allowances; Assembly passes resolutions on use of *khaddar* for govt. uniforms,

No.	From/To	Date	Summary
			establishment of Constituent Assembly, and adoption of Hindustani (No. 89); dispute between ministry and council; obstructive attitude of some landlords on collection of rents; Pant's desire to settle govt's. tenancy policy as soon as possible; importance of landlords organising themselves; British policy on Palestine likely to affect U.P.; Muslim opinion uncertain and irritable; services seem in reasonably good heart
91	Haig to Linlithgow Letter U.P.-8	7	Explains that resolution on *khaddar* commits govt. to very little; student behaviour in Lucknow
92	Haig to Linlithgow Tel. 63-G	10	Refers to Press reports that U.P. is to release 10,000 prisoners; says actual proposal is for 2,500; has directed cabinet should consider matter
93	Haig to Linlithgow Tel. 65-G	13	Answers Linlithgow's questions on jail release (see No. 92); as there are precedents, does not see how he could now argue releases would be menace to province
94	Haig to Linlithgow Letter U.P.-9	15	Reports problems which have arisen over silver jubilee functions at Allahabad University; is concerned Congress flag may be flown when Governor attends and feels it might be better for him to break away from celebrations
95	Haig to Linlithgow Letter U.P.-10	15	Reports talk with Pant on release of political prisoners (see No. 88); Pant accepted that certain prisoners must remain in jail but wished others to be released on

			their giving assurances; Haig feels they must stand fast
96	Haig to Linlithgow Tel. 66-G	17	Refers to No. 93; source of information to press may have been a Parliamentary Secretary; has suggested Pant issues communiqué giving correct information
97	Haig to Linlithgow Tel. 70-G	20	Release of two Madras prisoners would weaken his general position but explains why it would be difficult for him to press Madras govt. on matter
98	Haig to Linlithgow Letter U.P.-11	24	Cabinet have discussed principles of general jail delivery; between 2,500 and 3,000 prisoners will be released
99	Haig to Linlithgow Letter U.P.-12	24	Reports further talk with Pant on release of remaining terrorist political prisoners; Pant asked for question to be placed before cabinet and indicated what might happen if Governor and ministry failed to agree; Pant also wished to take immediate steps for the freeing of the five prisoners whose release had been agreed; he raised issue of Bihar releases
100	Haig to Linlithgow Report U.P.-13	24	Release of prisoners; Allahabad University jubilee functions; situation in Gorakhpur, Jhansi and Cawnpore; official committee considers ministry's proposed tenancy reforms; decision not to retain Stampe; substitution of a civilian secretary in Irrigation Dept.; League meeting in Lucknow has removed Muslim sense of uncertainty
101	Donaldson to Laithwaite	31	Asks what authority can invalidate those rules drafted by the legis-

	Letter 716-G.S.P.		lative assembly which are plainly contrary to provisions of Govt. of India Act
		Nov.	
102	Haig to Linlithgow Report U.P.-16	8	Haig's tour of Bareilly and Meerut divisions; his impressions: (1) of depression and nervousness in the police as a result of Congress activities, (2) that relations between landlord and tenants were unsatisfactory and there would be difficulty collecting *kharif* rents, (3) that Hindu-Muslim relations were becoming markedly more strained; Ibrahim wins Bijnor bye-election; cabinet to discuss violent speeches in eastern U.P., attacks on police in Cawnpore, and police situation generally; enquiry reveals serious state of affairs in Jhansi; zamindars' conference in Lucknow; situation in Cawnpore rather obscure; proposed appointment of Paliwal as rural development officer; Haig feels he should not attend Allahabad University jubilee; Haig's speech at concluding ceremony for Ganges Canal hydro-electric scheme; hopes Congress will not press release of political prisoners to definite issue
103	Haig to Linlithgow Letter U.P.-17	9	Reports talk with Katju on Allahabad University jubilee functions; has re-stated his conditions for attending and agreed to wait a further week before taking a decision
104	Haig to Linlithgow Letter U.P.-18	10	Following Congress's Calcutta session, Pant says ministry must

			now actively oppose grant of titles; he has indicated they will formally ask for practice to be discontinued in U.P.; Haig imagines there is no question of this occurring; Governor seeks advice on his right to obtain recommendations
105	Haig to Hallett Tel. 71-G	11	Pant has only raised informally the issue of the release of political prisoners and Haig feels he was not intending to press matter to an issue
106	Haig to Linlithgow Letter U.P.-19	11	Has little information on Congress's Calcutta session but judges U.P. ministers have emerged with their position substantially unshaken; Nehru seems to be working in close cooperation with ministry on certain matters
107	Haig to Linlithgow Letter U.P.-21	17	Refers to Appendix 10; believes this discloses very misleading impression of his relations with his officers and the administration; certain solutions do not seem so simple to him as perhaps they do to Linlithgow; Lansdowne speeches
108	Haig to Linlithgow Letter U.P.-22	17	Refers to No. 102; explains that his remarks on police methods were not intended to refer to a case of handling a riot such as occurred recently in Bihar
109	Haig to Linlithgow Letter U.P.-24	18	Refers to No. 107, para. 3; both Commissioner and D.C. would like prosecution instituted for Lansdowne speeches; is taking matter up with Pant
110	Haig to Zetland Tel. 80-G	27	Sends figures of prisoners released from U.P. jails

111	Haig to Linlithgow Tel. 81-G	27	Cabinet were against prosecution of Parmanand without prior warning; however Haig said his special responsibilities were involved and they did not demur to issue of an order for prosecution (subject to necessary legal examination)
112	Haig to Linlithgow Report U.P-28	28	Recalls that he had said to Linlithgow that general aim of policy should be to give Congress every chance of working constitution subject to two conditions he specifies; cabinet discussion on Parmanand case and other cases involving violent speeches; cabinet agrees to revised rules on reporting of political speeches; Haig's speech to annual police parade aims at reassuring all ranks; Horton establishes promising relations with Pant; Pant's speech to police parade in Cawnpore; relations between district officers and local Congress; Gwynne's circular letter (Appendix 9); conditions in Jhansi and Agra; Gorakhpur position decidedly more reassuring; communal situation; parliamentary committee on tenancy questions is pursuing its enquiries steadily; Haig's talk with Katju on rural development scheme; annual convention of Agra University; Cawnpore labour enquiry committee
113	Haig to Linlithgow Tel. 82-G	29	Refers to No. 111; Pant has told him cabinet has referred prosecution of Parmanand to a com-

			mittee of the Congress Working Committee; Haig intends to proceed without awaiting outcome of consultation
114	Haig to Linlithgow Tel. 84-G [?83-G]	29	Muslim worker at Elgin Mills, Cawnpore has been murdered; he was prominent in bringing strikers back to work; indicates measures they have taken; Hindu-Muslim feeling in city is distinctly bad
		Dec.	
115	Haig to Linlithgow Letter U.P.-31	2	Cawnpore situation – agrees that he should stay in background as long as possible and explains why he acted as he did; believes it is fortunate that D.M. took the initiative on his own responsibility; Haig could not acquiesce in any attempt by ministry to modify D.M's. orders; line Haig intends taking with ministry
116	Haig to Linlithgow Tel. 84-G	5	Has discussed Cawnpore situation with Pant whose attitude seemed satisfactory; does not think Pant will propose over-ruling D.M.
117	Haig to Linlithgow Tel. 86-G	7	Pant has raised question of Parmanand's prosecution and feels latter's arrest in Delhi has introduced new complication; suggestion that if cabinet publicly accepted responsibility for having ordered prosecution, and if Parmanand received substantial sentence in Delhi, it might not be necessary to proceed with U.P. prosecution
118	Haig to Linlithgow Letter U.P.-34	7	Discusses two areas where the Ministry were considering using an ordinance in furtherance of

			their controls on sugar; asks whether Linlithgow would object to the issue of such an ordinance
119	Haig to Linlithgow Letter U.P.-35	7	Refers to No. 104; asks for early indication of his views on Pant's attitude towards grants of titles
120	Haig to Linlithgow Report U.P.-37	9	Pant is handling Cawnpore labour situation only in a very tentative and gradual way; Parmanand issue; Pant raises question of release of remaining political prisoners; Haig is hopeful that police situation will gradually improve; he fears there will be some difficulty collecting rent payments in eastern U.P.; Mrs Pandit has lunch with him; anti-tuberculosis appeal; cabinet consider proposals for start of prohibition; cabinet have practically decided to terminate functions of existing honorary magistrates and honorary assistant collectors
121	Haig to Linlithgow Letter U.P.-38	10	Repeats his views in No. 120 on anticipated problems with rent collections; mentions particularly Gorakhpur and Allahabad districts
122	Haig to Linlithgow Draft Tel. (Not Sent)	10	Pant appears to suggest that communiqué should be published stating that U.P. govt. had ordered prosecution of Parmanand but in view of Delhi prosecution, U.P. govt. would not proceed with theirs; govt. would make it clear that if offence were repeated, U.P. prosecution would take place; Haig feels advantages of this course of action are very great
123	Haig to Linlithgow Tel. 89-G	12	Summarises Pant's proposal on Parmanand case as in No. 122; has

No.	Document	Date	Summary
			told Pant only safe course is to proceed with U.P. prosecution; after consulting some members of Congress Working Committee, Pant says serious developments are likely to ensue if no way out of difficulty is found
124	Haig to Linlithgow Letter U.P.-40	13	Reports further conversation with Pant on Parmanand case; considers there is very definite possibility he will resign; Pant feels prosecution would weaken his position with his party in the future
125	Haig to Linlithgow Letter U.P.-41	14	Action in the event of ministry resigning
126	Haig to Linlithgow Tel. 92-G	15	Explains that U.P. security situation has markedly improved with the arrest of Parmanand and other ex-Kakori prisoners; also Pant's action on Cawnpore has impressed; if ministry were not prepared to resign, Haig could hold them to the U.P. prosecution of Parmanand; otherwise he could proceed on lines suggested in No. 122; seeks Viceroy's views
127	Haig to Linlithgow Tel. 94-G	17	Thanks Linlithgow for his approval of policy suggested in No. 126; doubts whether Parmanand would give assurance he would not repeat offence; considers he will have to go cautiously about this
128	Haig to Linlithgow Tel. 95-G	18	Refers to No. 127; has spoken to Pant; gives the lines of a statement the Premier would be prepared to put out; this is acceptable to Haig; Pant believes Parmanand would

			not give assurance; asks for early instructions
129	Haig to Linlithgow Letter U.P.-42	19	Reports Pant has shown some desire to entrust to Parliamentary Secretaries some delegations of ministerial authority; explains problems which have arisen with P.Ss.; hopes cabinet will agree to issue of instructions; enclosure: Note on P.Ss. in U.P.
130	Haig to Linlithgow Tel. 97-G	21	Will try to get Pant to make as strong a general statement as possible but does not believe Premier will give up his insistence on specific warnings to individual speakers before prosecutions; is not seriously disturbed about this at present
131	Haig to Linlithgow Tel. 99-G	23	Reports that, despite Parmanand's short sentence in Delhi, Pant is not prepared to proceed with U.P. prosecution; Haig explains why he feels they should agree to drop prosecution and issue agreed statement with such additional provisions as Pant will accept
132	Haig to Linlithgow Tel. 100-G	23	Refers to No. 131; sends text of passage Pant has agreed to add to statement
133	Haig to Linlithgow Report U.P.-44	24	Pant's general position and attitude arising from the Parmanand affair; Nehru's attitude; Congress prestige high; payment of rents is crucial issue for U.P.; ministry do realise need to improve Cawnpore labour situation but are less vigorous in action than Haig would wish; Haig's visit to Gorakhpur – its agrarian and administrative conditions are

worst in U.P.; Allahabad University jubilee celebrations go off well; cabinet discussion on prohibition policy; three Muslim bye-elections all go in favour of League; Haig wonders if Congress will re-consider its attitude towards League; Sunni-Shia dispute in Lucknow; forthcoming meeting of legislature

APPENDICES

		Date	
		1937	
		Mar.	
A1	Linlithgow to Zetland Letter	17	Explains his misgivings over Haig's performance as Governor of U.P.; fears it may not be possible to keep him for the remainder of his term
		April	
A2	Pant to Donaldson Letter	8	Presses for early meeting of U.P. Legislative Assembly
A3	Pant to Donaldson Letter	11	Says that delay in summoning Legislative Assembly is in contravention of the Govt. of India Act
A4	Statement issued by U.P. Cabinet	13	Rejoinder to Congress statements; reasons why they have formed a ministry
A5	Note by Ewart	19	Says there is uncertainty in Secretariat circles about practical working of new system of govt.; Ewart's anxieties about the U.P. situation
		Aug.	
A6	Note by Ewart	20	Working of the administration (both at the centre and in the districts) under the Congress ministry

		Sept.	
A7	Gwynne to Phillips and all U.P. District Magistrates Letter 534P/VIII	15	Speeches at ordinary political meetings should no longer be reported; outlines procedure to be followed in special cases where it was felt necessary to report speeches
		Nov.	
A8	Haig to Pant Note	3	Explains his serious concern at a number of developments which are weakening respect for authority; indicates measures they need to adopt; asks for note to be laid before early meeting of cabinet
A9	Gwynne to all U.P. District Magistrates Letter 712(I)/III	10	Importance of establishment of relations of mutual confidence between district authorities and leaders of Congress
A10	Linlithgow to Haig Letter	15	Refers to No. 102; explains his considerable unease at U.P. situation; seeks information on many points; asks Haig to go to Delhi for discussions with him
A11	Linlithgow to Zetland Letter, para. 10	19	His continued misgivings about Haig's suitability as Governor
A12	Linlithgow to Zetland Letter	25	Following their discussions in Delhi, doubts whether Haig will be able to hold U.P. together for a further two years; unless matters greatly improve feels they may have to persuade Haig to retire at the end of his leave in Sept. 1938
A13	Note by Ewart	28	Visit to Lucknow and Cawnpore
		Dec.	
A14	Communiqué issued by U.P. Govt.	-	Advice to tenants on payment of rent

A15	Linlithgow to Haig Tel. 467-GC	20	Conveys information from Ewart regarding attitudes of various senior members of Congress to the action of U.P. ministry
A16	Linlithgow to Haig Letter	24	Explains in detail his objections to circular in Appendix 9
A17	Communiqué issued by U.P. Govt.	27	U.P. govt. are not proceeding with case against Parmanand but issue general warning that violent speeches will not be tolerated
A18	Note by Ewart	29	Considers that ministry's public examples of a stiffening attitude may be expected to improve the situation very considerably; encloses two letters from Blunden (C.I.O., Lucknow)

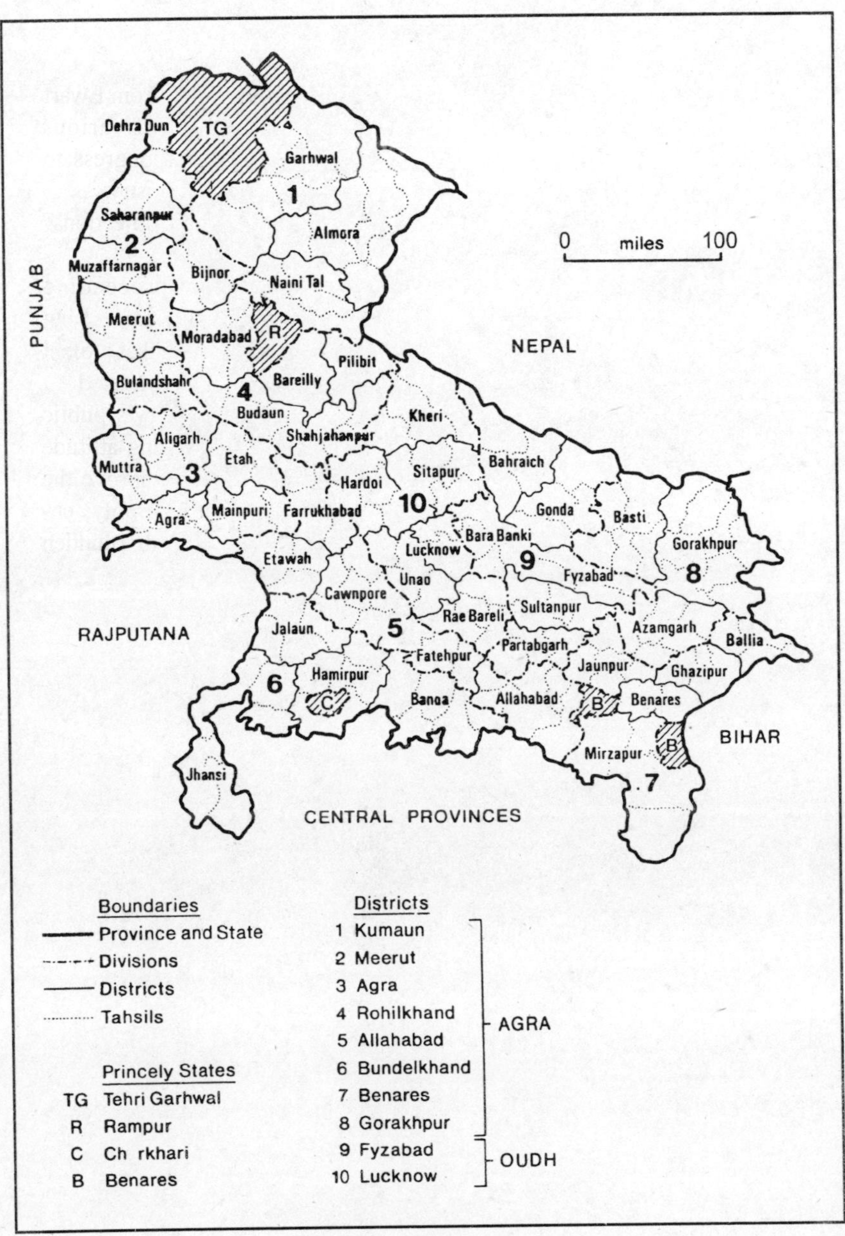

Map of the United Provinces

CHAPTER 1

Documents for 15 October 1936 – 2 April 1937

1

HAIG TO LINLITHGOW
R/3/1/1

Private and Personal Camp,
October 15th, 1936

My dear Lord Linlithgow,

I am writing with reference to Your Excellency's letter of the 11th October 1936[1] about information regarding provincial politics. I shall be very glad indeed to send Your Excellency once a month reports of the nature you indicate. I am just off for a short holiday in the hills and should propose to send the first report after I have got back to Lucknow, probably about the beginning of November. Our provincial politics are complicated by many different cross currents, and I think my first report will have to be of considerable length in order that Your Excellency may be able to understand fully the situation as I see it. Changes also in the strength of different currents are fairly frequent, and during this next fortnight activities will be in progress which may have some appreciable effect on the general situation, of which I shall not be able to judge until I get to Lucknow. But I will endeavour to send Your Excellency a full report at the beginning of November, and monthly reports thereafter.

Yours sincerely,
HARRY HAIG

2

HAIG TO LINLITHGOW
R/3/1/1

Secret and Personal

Camp,
October 29th, 1936

My dear Lord Linlithgow,

I am sending Your Excellency my first report on political conditions in the United Provinces. I have marked it "Secret and Personal" as I have written with considerable frankness about tendencies and personalities. I think I had better, in the first place, give you as a general background the position as it stood up to about the end of August last and subsequently explain the more recent changes.

2. The coming elections will be a struggle between the Congress and the non-Congress elements. I will deal first with the Congress. When I arrived in the Province in December 1934, it was clear that Congress influence was at a low ebb. This was not surprising. The Congress workers themselves were exhausted by the two civil disobedience struggles, and dejected by the complete failure of the second. The people generally had lost faith in Congress promises; and, as is always the case in India, were ready to support the more powerful party, which was quite clearly the government. It is true that the fall in prices had hit an agricultural Province like ours very hard, but the measures taken by Lord Hailey's government to remit rents on a liberal scale had removed any possibility of appreciable agrarian unrest. The new scale of rents could be paid by the tenants, not with any great margin, but at any rate without serious hardship. The landlords, though their income was diminished, realised the inevitability of this and made the best of it. In these conditions the Congress had little opportunity for functioning and, on the surface, appeared to count for very little. Appearances were confirmed by the result of the local boards' elections held at the end of 1935. Congress, though contesting a number of seats, had little success outside the towns.

3. The return of Jawaharlal Nehru, however, and the holding of the Congress session at Lucknow last April started a new phase. The Congress had found a leader with a name and personality that appealed to the masses, and possessing unusual initiative, determination and authority. The first reactions of his presidential speech were to alarm seriously all the vested interests, not only landlords, but businessmen and professional men, and

to intensify the resolution on the part of these powerful interests to oppose the Congress. But gradually his doctrines, by rather milder repetition, seemed to lose their first alarming quality, and to pass into the category of political phrases, which by long practice can be consumed innocuously on the largest scale. Meantime the Congress tried to concentrate attention more on their traditional appeal, representing the national revolt against foreign domination. While economic doctrines are still being preached, which are as repugnant to a large section of Congress as they are to the more conservative elements in the country, this does not seem to prevent the bourgeois Congressmen from working with enthusiasm for the Congress cause. There are the most profound differences amongst Congressmen as to future policy; but they appear for the moment to agree to leave those differences in the background while they unite to overthrow what they describe as the loyalist and reactionary forces, in other words those who support the government as it is.

4. But though the Congress was in this way steadily pulling itself together and strengthening its own forces, I think it is true to say that up to about the end of August they had made extremely little impression on the great mass of non-Congress opinion, and I was myself somewhat surprised during my monsoon tour to find so little evidence anywhere of public activities by the Congress.

5. The main non-Congress of [?or] conservative force in this Province is bound to be the great body of landlords – a privileged class which has always been in the closest and most friendly relations with the government and which regards its existence as dependent on the support of the government. It was evident that in the new constitution the struggle would be between the Congress and the landlords, and Lord Hailey had, for some time before he left, been impressing this fact on a body which by long tradition was lethargic, disunited and dependent on government to give it a lead. A short time before I came to the Province the landlords organised themselves, doubtless with the encouragement of Lord Hailey, into a "National Agriculturist Party" which, however, functioned independently in the two Provinces of Agra and Oudh. They secured a good deal of publicity, particularly at a time when the Congress were doing nothing, and before long came to be regarded as the nucleus for opposition to the Congress. At the same time their organisation hardly extended beyond the paper it was written on, and they had none of the characteristics of a life [?live] and vigorous political party. Many of the landlords frankly disbelieved in the necessity of organisation. Their view was that they could by their personal influence control the votes of their tenants and

that the ordinary methods of propaganda were superfluous, while their political horizon was limited to their own personal success at the election. Gradually, however, these ideas have been losing ground and the landlords on the whole have been coming to realise that if they are to compete with the methods of Congress, they must have something more effective behind them than mere tradition and threats, and that argument must be met by argument. But it is a long step from the theoretical recognition of this fact to any practical activities; and the idea of working for a party is still foreign to many of them. During the last year the Party has strengthened itself by opening its doors, though somewhat reluctantly, to the business community, by forming certain working committees, whose work is apt to be interrupted by illness, domestic engagements, &c., and by carrying on a fair amount of press propaganda. But they have had the utmost difficulty in raising funds and consequently in establishing district organisations or any effective system of widespread propaganda. Nevertheless, up to the end of August they seemed to be getting on reasonably well in their own not very effective way, and the general impression was that in the great majority of constituencies the National Agriculturists, if they could only prevent their supporters fighting each other on personal grounds, would be able to defeat the Congress.

6. The National Agriculturist Party, standing as it does for the existing economic order of things, particularly in the matter of land tenure, was naturally a non-communal body. The interests of the Hindu and Muslim landlords are identical and they can, in an election, give great help to each other through the influence the Muslim landlord has over his Hindu tenants and vice versa. But the communal question has been during the last six months obtruding very strongly into the affairs of the Party, and has become a source of appreciable embarrassment and weakness. Two factors in the main have produced this result. The first was Mr. Jinnah's launching of a new policy for the all-India Muslim League, which involved the formation of specifically Muslim parties to contest the elections in every Province. This was entirely contrary to the first principles of the National Agriculturist Party, and one might have supposed that the prominent Muslims who were leading the Agriculturist Party in the United Provinces, particularly the Nawab of Chhatari and Nawab Sir Muhammad Yusuf, would have repudiated Mr. Jinnah's ideas at once, especially as it was obvious that the all-India Muslim League was to be merely the means whereby Mr. Jinnah was to utilise the Muslim vote for the purpose of his own advanced nationalist policy. Actually, however, the two Nawabs did not at first like to break away from the Muslim League, the name of which stands for a good deal in this Province. They contemplated with reluctance an electoral

fight against the old Nationalist Muslims who would have the support of the Muslim League, and they hoped that it might be possible to avoid this unpleasant development by manoeuvre and compromise. Eventually, however, after a good deal of harm had been done by rousing the suspicions of the Hindus, they found that they could not maintain their precarious relations with Mr. Jinnah and at the same time remain leaders of the non-communal Agriculturist Party, and they finally broke openly with Mr. Jinnah and reconciled themselves to fighting the Muslim League.

7. But the very fact that their position among their own community was to some extent weakened by this necessary action, made them particularly nervous about the communal activities of the Hindus within the Agriculturist Party. They were naturally susceptible to accusations that they themselves had declined to fight under a communal banner and had allied themselves with a party professedly non-communal but actually dominated by Hindu communalists. Some colour was lent to these accusations by important developments in Hindu Mahasabha politics. Pandit Madan Mohan Malaviya, who might on the political stage be regarded as the Hindu counterpart of Mr. Jinnah, was working for the establishment of an all-India Hindu party which would in many respects be in close sympathy with the Congress, but at the same time would secure the very powerful support of Hindu communal feeling. A party of this kind would have cut clean across the National Agriculturist Organisation and would have attracted to itself a large number of Hindu landholders and might have secured very wide support from the mass of the Hindu electorate. Some of the Hindus in the Agriculturist Party were determined to fight this danger, and a long struggle has been in progress between what are in effect two different wings of the Provincial Hindu Sabha, each endeavouring to establish its supremacy. Malaviya has been definitely defeated in so far that he has been unable to secure control of the Mahasabha machinery, and in consequence the idea of a Hindu party has practically lapsed. But the non-Congress Hindu Sabhaites, in the course of their struggle against Malaviya, have naturally had to emphasise their own Hinduism, and as they include prominent members of the Agriculturist Party, this has roused great suspicion among the Muslims. I do not myself believe that they are inspired by intolerant Hindu feelings; but with an election approaching they cannot disregard the Hindu sentiments. They will not stand at the elections as members of the Hindu Sabha but as members of the Agriculturist Party. They will at the same time however derive such advantage as they can from being members of the Hindu Sabha. Sir Jwala Prasad Srivastava, though he is not an actual office-bearer in the Hindu Sabha, has been the most prominent force in organising this

opposition to Malaviya and preventing the capture of the Hindu Sabha by Congress sympathisers. He has thus become an object of considerable suspicion among Muslims, though in fact he is, I think, singularly free from communal feeling.

8. Another matter which has accentuated suspicion between the two communities within the Agriculturist Party is the question of the Chief Ministership. The three men who have been most prominent in the organisation of the Agriculturist Party are the Nawab of Chhatari, Nawab Sir Muhammad Yusuf and Sir Jwala Prasad Srivastava. The Nawab of Chhatari has an important position in United Provinces politics, having until recently been a member of the United Provinces government for many years and having acted as Governor on two different occasions. He is a prominent landlord and personally popular. He is clearly by record and position the most obvious choice for Chief Minister if that post is to go to a landlord. There is no Hindu landlord who occupies a comparable position. On the other hand, a good deal of Hindu feeling has been roused in opposition to any such idea. It is said that it would be monstrous for a Province with over 80 per cent. of Hindus to have a Muslim Chief Minister. The Hindu who is generally mentioned as an alternative to Chhatari for the Chief Ministership is Sir Jwala Prasad Srivastava, who undoubtedly has more ability, drive and political capacity than any other member of the Agriculturist Party. But he is not a landlord. There is no doubt that there is some rivalry between these two for the Chief Ministership, and that this has been having a disruptive effect on the Party and accentuating communal feeling within it. They both recognise the disadvantages of pressing any such issue at the present moment, but one cannot get away from the fact of this conflict of interest in the background, though on the surface they are on quite good terms.

9. The National Agriculturist Party of Oudh means in effect the Taluqdars. They ought to be able to control the elections in Oudh, for the Taluqdars have a much stronger position in their estates than the Zamindars of Agra. But they are apt to be swayed by foolish personal jealousies or (friendships), and there is always the danger that they may fritter away their power in unnecessary quarrels. There is no real leader among them. The Raja of Jahangirabad, who is President of the British India Association, is a prominent member of the Agriculturist Party. Nevertheless finding that he was going to be opposed by the Muslim League and that his seat would not be secure, he has publicly agreed not to stand as a member of the Agriculturist Party, but as an Independent, and in return for this the Muslim League have promised not to oppose him. This indicates well enough the state of political principle in Oudh. Raja Sir Rampal Singh, an

old man, who possibly has more personal influence among the Taluqdars than any other individual, is by temperament a wobbler, intellectually a Liberal, and above all, a very strong Hindu. He is President of the Agriculturist Party of Oudh, and at the same time President of the Provincial Hindu Sabha, and probably politically much more in sympathy with Chintamani than with those whom he is supposed to lead. The young Raja of Mahmudabad, who is the owner of one of the most important estates in Oudh, is completely under the influence of Mr. Jinnah and is one of the principal supports of the Muslim League. The man who has done more to organise the Agriculturist Party in Oudh than anyone else is Raja Maheshwar Dayal Seth, the Secretary of the Party. He is intelligent, active and consistent; but because he is not by position one of the most important of the Taluqdars, his activities have roused a good deal of jealousy among his fellows.

10. The Liberals are in numbers only a handful and they seem even more incapable than the Agriculturist Party of organising themselves as a political party. Their influence depends on their own personal capacity, and in particular on Mr. Chintamani. He came to the United Provinces from Madras as a young journalist and all his working life has been identified with the United Provinces. As editor of the *Leader* he exercises a very great influence. His criticisms are personal and trenchant, and his victims quiver. He is a strong Nationalist who has yet been firmly opposed to the direct methods of Congress. He is a typical representative of a great deal of intelligent opinion in the Province; but with it all, he has surprisingly little political support in terms of membership of the legislature. In the Legislative Council he is the chief critic of government, and from this point of view fully deserves his conventional title of "Leader of the Opposition". But those who formally acknowledge his party leadership are few. This only emphasises the fact, which I have mentioned before, that the real struggle for political power is between the Congress and the conservative or landlord elements. The Liberals are electorally a comparatively small middle party. It is an astonishing thing that a man like Chintamani had to depend for his seat in the present council on the friendship of a particular Taluqdar and, as is popularly believed, the improper influence of the Indian Deputy Commissioner of the time. He represents the district of Partabgarh in Oudh, a purely rural area, and it is generally said that he would be unable to address his constituents in their own language; at any rate he never makes any effort to do so.

11. Mr. Chintamani is an ambitious man. He was one of the two first ministers in the present Constitution. He would be very glad to be a minister in the new constitution. But he is difficult to work with. At present he

snaps and snarls at everyone. He is the most effective critic of the Congress in the Province. At the same time he is the most bitter critic of the Agriculturist Party. He has at present no constituency in sight, though he may get a seat through the friendship of some landlord. In point of ability he would strengthen any non-Congress government; but his temper is such that it is doubtful if in fact he would be anything but a source of weakness. His Liberal views would make him reluctant to support necessary measures for maintenance of order, and he is an extremely communal Hindu. Moreover, he and Sir Jwala Prasad Srivastava are long-standing and determined political enemies, and I do not think it is in the least likely that they could work together. I think therefore Mr. Chintamani will remain as the outside and trenchant critic of everything and everybody. The number of Liberals who will get into the new legislature will be, I think, trifling. I should imagine they would retain their individuality and not ally themselves with either party. They would sympathise with a good many Congress views, but would strongly oppose anything in the nature of economic upheaval or confiscation.

12. The foregoing gives what I am afraid is rather a discursive picture of the background of our United Provinces politics. In the last two months there have been considerable developments. The Congress have opened their electoral campaign and the success they have achieved is definitely beyond expectation. Jawaharlal Nehru's tour in the west of the Province was a resounding success. Similar tours will no doubt be repeated in other parts of the Province, and other important Congress leaders will also tour. These well-advertised activities have coincided with a period of almost complete stagnation on the part of the Agriculturist Party. They have been slow in getting their propaganda and organisation to work. While they could make something of a show when there was no opposition, their methods appear to be strikingly inadequate compared with the live work of the Congress. At the same time the communal jealousies which I have described above have been exercising a somewhat paralysing effect, and the Muslims have been frightened by the apparent progress of the Muslim League. This in my judgement is largely due to their own inactivity. There is a general feeling of depression and uneasiness in the non-Congress ranks. The Congress trumpets are sounding, and in many places the walls of Jericho seem only too ready to fall down. But I think these feelings will disappear if only the Agriculturist Party can get their work started more effectively. Their leaders are under no illusion as to the necessity for immediate and effective action; but there seems to be the greatest difficulty in getting anything done. I think, however, Sir Jwala Prasad Srivastava

will succeed in putting some real life into the working of the Party. He is trying hard.

13. Though the Congress have undoubtedly frightened their opponents recently, I have no doubt they have their own difficulties. Quarrels and personal rivalries are not confined to the Agriculturist Party, and the recent suggestion at a meeting of the Provincial Congress Committee that the Congress should not contest the elections was not, as I was inclined to suspect, a mere piece of propaganda in support of their assertion that government were working actively against them, but apparently represented a genuine feeling that they could not possibly get a majority in the Province, and that therefore it might be better to adopt the popular tactics of a walk-out. In spite of all the weaknesses and difficulties of the non-Congress men, which I have indicated above, the general opinion still is that they will secure a working majority over the Congress. But the size of that majority is put a good deal lower than it would have been two months ago.

14. Most of the foregoing was written while I was on tour and has required little alteration in the light of information received since I returned to Lucknow two days ago. The Agriculturist Party are continually threatened by suggested defections from their own supporters, not on the ground that they do not believe in the principles of the Agriculturist Party, but that in many cases they have been given to understand that they may not be opposed, or may not be opposed so vigorously, if they stand as Independents rather than as Agriculturist Party candidates. It is exactly the argument which was used with effect in the case of the Raja of Jahangirabad. The temptation is applied particularly to Muslim members, who think they have some chance of avoiding a contest with the Muslim League by taking this weak line. But some quite prominent Hindu landholders also are being approached in the same way, and are showing a tendency to wobble. I do not, however, myself think this will go far. There is also no doubt that Raja Sir Rampal Singh's recent utterances and activities within the Agriculturist Party of Oudh have rather upset the Muslim members. But this is only a further illustration of the feeling of suspicion which undoubtedly exists between the two communities at the present time. There is nothing in this which makes me change my general estimate of the position given above.

Yours sincerely,
HARRY HAIG

3

HAIG TO LINLITHGOW
R/3/1/1

Secret and Personal Camp,
December 2nd, 1936

My dear Lord Linlithgow,

I am sending my second monthly report on political conditions in the United Provinces in continuation of my letter of October 29th. During the last month the position has not altered fundamentally; but, on the whole, with the approach of the actual electoral contests, it is becoming rather clearer. The phase of depression in the Agriculturist Party, which I mentioned in my last letter and which was bred of inactivity, seems to be passing away, as I had anticipated. The most important event has been the selection of candidates by the Agriculturist Party of Agra, which in this respect had been behindhand as compared with the Oudh Party. Though their task is far from complete, they have at any rate made a beginning, and I imagine within the next week or two they will complete their selections. The selection of candidates is possibly the most important function that the Party can perform. There is hardly a constituency where there are not two or three non-Congress aspirants. The Party realises that three-cornered contests will play straight into the hands of the Congress. Persistent efforts are therefore being made to secure that only one non-Congress candidate stands. But I expect that in many cases the candidate who is eventually not selected by the Agriculturist Party may still stand as an Independent and force a three-cornered fight. Another feature which seems to be emerging is this. The Party recognise that the practical support they can give to candidates is not great, and they are beginning to feel that if they can get the right candidates to stand, this is the most important contribution they can make to their own success. Candidates will depend on their own individual merits. A natural corollary of this is that a certain number of candidates, who are in effect put up by the leaders of the Agriculturist Party but have to depend on their personal influence for success at the election, may prefer to stand as Independents rather than as party candidates. But this is likely to be merely electoral tactics and I think would not affect their political allegiance once they were elected.

The Muslim League is not functioning happily. The Raja of Salempur, who is a Taluqdar of good standing, is the Chairman and Mr.

Khaliquzzaman, an ex-Congressman and practically a present one too, and Chairman of the Municipal Board of Lucknow, is the Secretary. The relations between these two are hardly those of political colleagues. Salempur, who is an amiable person of no political capacity, is obsessed by a desire for political leadership, which has led him in the past into the Nationalist Muslim camp and induced him on this occasion to join Jinnah's party. Khaliquzzaman, on the other hand, is an extremely acute and ambitious man. He has no intention of allowing Salempur to secure any position of leadership from Muslim League activities, and the position really is that both desire that the other should be defeated at the elections. The young Raja of Mahmudabad is, I think, beginning rather to regret his association with the Muslim League and is not likely to take any very active part in the elections on its behalf.

Communal feelings within the Agriculturist Party are on the whole less acute. To some extent they have been eased by the resignation of Raja Sir Rampal Singh from the Presidentship of the Oudh Party. Rampal Singh is a sick man. In his letter of resignation he made some unpleasant remarks about the Party, in which he has really never had any belief. But they are in difficulties about finding a new President owing to the jealousy among the Taluqdars. Jahangirabad would be the obvious President, but as he has openly declared that he will not stand on the Agriculturist Party ticket, it is hardly possible to put him in.

The Liberals have been showing considerable activity during the month in the Agra division, where they have put forward a number of candidates. Chintamani is to stand in the Etah district in a constituency which should be safe for him through the influence of an important Zamindar, Rao Krishnapal Singh. The Raja of Tirwa who is Secretary of the Agra Agriculturist Party (and an amazingly incompetent one) is also believed to have been flirting with the Liberals and encouraging them to put up candidates in the Agra division. If he were to break away, it would be little loss to the Agriculturist Party. In character and outlook, though not in influence and ability, he rather closely resembles Raja Sir Rampal Singh.

There will be some important contests in the election. The Congress, unable to attack Sir Jwala Prasad Srivastava directly, as he will be securing a seat through the Upper India Chamber of Commerce, are concentrating against Lady Srivastava who is standing for the women's seat in the Cawnpore district. They are putting up against her Mrs. Pandit, the sister of Jawaharlal Nehru. Not only is she already working very actively, but it is said that Jawaharlal Nehru will come down to support her, and it is even rumoured that Gandhi will be brought to Cawnpore to lend his support.

The Srivastava family, however, are putting up a very strong fight and I think Lady Srivastava should be successful. She is already, day after day, going round the villages and holding election meetings. In Cawnpore city efforts are being made to put up a candidate to oppose the Congress. If a suitable candidate can be found, it is not impossible that Congress might be beaten even there. In Lucknow city there will be a vigorous fight in the Muslim seat between Khaliquzzaman and the Agriculturist Party candidate. Here again if a really good man is found, which seems a little doubtful at the moment, Khaliquzzaman would probably be beaten, but not otherwise.

On the whole, the position is that canvassing is really starting. The Congress are working very actively and are much more vocal than their opponents. Commissioners generally report Congress activities as far greater than those of the other side. On the other hand, the non-Congress candidates seem in the rural areas to be quite confident of success in most places, apart from three cornered contests, and one must remember that noise and press propaganda are not everything at an election. On the whole, the Agriculturist Party leaders are still very confident that the Congress will not get more than some 70 seats, to which of course would have to be added a certain number of Muslim Leaguers.

Yours sincerely,
HARRY HAIG

4

HAIG TO LINLITHGOW
R/3/1/1

Secret and Personal — Camp,
January 6th, 1937

My dear Lord Linlithgow,

I am writing my third report on political conditions in the United Provinces in continuation of my letter of December 2nd. During the Christmas holidays I had been rather out of touch with political developments; and even now, as I am in Allahabad, I have not seen the members of my government recently. But since I have been here, I have had interesting talks with Sapru and Chintamani. I find they both estimate the probable number of Congressmen in the new Assembly at round about 80. The estimate slowly increases, but still no one seems to anticipate an actual majority for Congress.

During December there were indications that the Hindu-Muslim feeling in the National Agriculturist Party, which I have mentioned before, was becoming more acute, and that it remained very undesirably identified with the reputed rivalry of the Nawab of Chhatari and Sir Jwala Prasad Srivastava for the Chief Ministership. These feelings seem to have been accentuated by the process of selecting party candidates. A belief seemed to prevail rather widely that candidates were being supported because of their general adherence to one or other of the chiefs of the party rather than on their personal merits. Certainly some unfortunate decisions were taken in the selection of candidates, though this was probably inevitable in view of the processes by which they were selected. Now that that very difficult phase is over, it may be hoped these feelings will tend to subside, and that there will be more evidence of a general desire to support the party candidates against political opponents who make no concealment of their intention to destroy the landlord position and influence, if not to confiscate their property.

The nominations took place just before Christmas, and within the short period allowed for withdrawals, a large number of withdrawals took place, so that in many constituencies there is now a straight fight between the Congress and non-Congress candidates. There is still, however, in many constituencies a superfluity of candidates which may or may not be reduced before the actual polling. Returning officers had to decide with promptitude a large number of objections to nominations. A few of the decisions have been a little surprising but it cannot be alleged that on balance the advantage has gone to one side or the other. There is no appeal against the decisions of returning officers, though I notice that some of those aggrieved by the decisions are threatening subsequent election petitions. The unopposed returns include both the Nawab of Chhatari and Sir Jwala Prasad Srivastava, and, as the result of the rejected nomination of a Congress candidate, Raja Maheshwar Dayal Seth, Secretary of the Oudh Party. I do not think any prominent Congressman has been returned unopposed.

I get the impression, though I repeat that I am a little out of touch at the moment, that the Muslims are just now rather happier about conditions than the Hindus. The Muslim League is going through a bad time. Jinnah's patchwork was never likely to stand much strain, and with the approaching elections the rents are appearing in many places. However the Muslims may label themselves for the purposes of the election, whether National Agriculturists, or Independents, or even Muslim Leaguers, I have a feeling that at the end they will form a fairly compact body (save for personal rivalries which will tend to divide them), and that the numbers of those prepared to go in with the Congress will be very small.

On the Hindu side, I think the National Agriculturists of Oudh seem fairly confident. In the Province of Agra, however, where the number of large landlords is smaller, there seems to be a good deal more uncertainty, and it is in the rural constituencies in certain parts of the Agra Province that the Congress might secure successes on a scale not at present anticipated.

On the whole the Zamindars have been rather slow in getting to work with their canvassing. I was told that as soon as nominations were over they would start work intensively. Their methods, however, in general differ considerably from those of the Congress. They rely much more on the personal canvassing of those who are supposed to be able to command or influence votes rather than on mass appeals direct to the voters. In some constituencies caste influences form a very important cross current. There are great numbers of the rural electorate who would be inclined to give their votes to a fellow casteman, no matter whether he were Congress or non-Congress, and among the non-Congress in many cases the insistence of two or three candidates on standing has its basis in caste feelings.

As the election campaign intensifies we begin to hear more about the difficulties of the position of government servants. There is no doubt that the Congress have been utilising the debates in the Legislative Assembly in order to intimidate government servants, and create the impression that a government servant who does anything to displease the Congress is likely to get into trouble. It has also been alleged that a good many subordinate government servants were quietly giving help to Congress candidates, and we have felt it advisable to issue a circular making it plain that there is not one rule for the Congress and another for everyone else. The main difficulty, however, that seems to be felt in some government quarters is one which we have recognised for a long time past and tried to deal with by general instructions which we sent out as long ago as last July. The Congress are more and more making their campaign one of attacking and vilifying the present government. Provided they do not proceed to extreme lengths, government servants have to stand by and do nothing. This produces, so it is said, a general impression on the public mind that the Government are afraid of the Congress; otherwise they would take steps, by the methods which are so easily open to them, to discourage this type of Congress propaganda. I fear the circumstances in the present election put the Congress in this respect in a very strong tactical position, which they are exploiting to the full. There is nothing in our instructions that we can properly change, and though there may be a certain amount of misunderstanding of our position, particularly among the lower ranks of the police, I do not think on the whole there is any general impression that the Government are unduly favourable to a body which is preaching independence and the destruction of the coming Constitution.

When the elections are over the Congress will have their own difficulties, and these will be, in my opinion, serious, for it does not seem to me that at that stage they can any longer maintain the present superficial appearance of unity, concealing the most fundamental differences of outlook and policy. As for prospects, I would again repeat what I said in my last letter, that noise and press propaganda are not everything at an election. It is part of the election tactics of the Congress to profess an overwhelming optimism. But even where they really feel it, it would seem that they are sometimes disappointed. I have just been reading a letter from the Commissioner of Meerut[2] about the municipal elections that have recently taken place in Hapur. There was extensive betting on the result and a certain Congress candidate was being backed at 5 to 1 on. He was beaten by an opponent with odds of 4 to 1 against, and it is said that considerable sums of money changed hands. On the other hand, if, as seems probable, the Congress are in a minority, but have 70 to 80 seats and perhaps another 15 sympathisers, it may be a matter of considerable difficulty to secure a government with sufficient cohesion and ability to function effectively in the face of a strong and enterprising opposition.

Yours sincerely,
HARRY HAIG

5

HAIG TO LINLITHGOW
R/3/1/1

Secret and Personal

Camp,
January 26th, 1937

My dear Lord Linlithgow,

I should like to explain to Your Excellency precisely what our attitude has been in regard to the question of banning the Congress "Independence" resolution,[3] as certain aspects will not be apparent from the official correspondence. When the Government of India telegram suggesting action reached us, I discussed the matter with my Executive Council, both Ministers unfortunately being away. The view expressed was that action of this kind would on the whole have a harmful effect on the prospects of non-Congress candidates. At the same time it did not seem necessary on general grounds to take strong action against the Congress, and we felt that if possible it was better to avoid exceptional measures just before the polling, in view of our long continued policy of non-interference with the Congress campaign. We were, it is true, receiving a great deal of information to the effect that the Congress propaganda was vigorous and was making an impression. But it did not seem to be achieving results greater than one had always expected, and there was little to suggest that an impression was being created which might be seriously dangerous to the peace of the Province. Those were the conditions in which we decided not to take action against the "Independence" declaration.

On Sunday evening we had a reply from the Government of India pointing out that the action already taken by several Local Governments had the effect of making the "Independence" declaration liable to seizure throughout British India. This, and the publicity which had been given to the whole matter by the action taken by other local governments, created a new situation. We felt that it was impossible for us not to seize documents that had been declared forfeited to government, and that if we took action we must do so effectively and comprehensively, and in that case, it was better that we should issue our own notification, so that there could be no misunderstanding about our attitude or ground for suggesting that we were half-hearted in the matter.

But while this action was, I think, inevitable in order to conform to that taken by other local governments, I want to make it plain that during the discussion we had on Monday morning to decide our policy, I personally had my view altered, and became convinced that the action was definitely required in the interests of this Province. Sir J.P. Srivastava was able to attend our meeting. He had just returned from a tour round the constituencies, and his judgment of the situation was somewhat alarming. He said that he found everywhere a feeling that government were afraid of the Congress and that this was having a deplorable effect on the non-Congress candidates. Apart from the actual electoral results of the atmosphere that is being created, I myself felt that there is some reason to fear that we may be coming within reach of serious unrest in some parts of the Province. I saw yesterday a prominent landholder from a very unpolitical district of eastern Oudh, who a month ago had regarded his return to the Council as an absolute certainty. Now he was almost in a state of despair. He had himself been moving about in the villages and he was immensely impressed by the influence that the Congress propaganda was having. He gave me instances of the kind of things that are being done. He declares that the Congress are preaching everywhere that in two months the British government will disappear and that it is to be replaced by Congress raj. This, I fear, is how the ideas of democracy are presented to the ordinary voter. Volunteers are going about with note-books and asking tenants what their present rent is. The tenant says perhaps Rs. 2 a *bigha*. The Congress volunteer says: "That's all right. If you vote for the Congress, that will be put down to 4 annas." He writes it down in his note-book and the unfortunate villager is duly impressed. I am inclined to think that candidates are at the moment in closer touch with what is going on in the villages and certainly in the minds of the villagers than our district officers are, and I feel that things may have gone rather further than we officially realise. All this has convinced me that it is decidedly a good thing that we have taken this action against the Congress. And I think we may have to consider stiffening up the attitude of the administration in regard to Congress attacks on Government during the next two weeks, and possibly taking a pretty firm line also immediately after the elections, if the situation seems to demand it.

As to electoral prospects, I can really add little to what I said in my letter of January 6th. I think Congress prospects are steadily improving and though a Congress majority is not anticipated, the margin against them and their sympathisers may be so narrow as to cause a good deal of embarrassment.

Yours sincerely,
HARRY HAIG

6

HAIG TO LINLITHGOW
R/3/1/1

Secret and Personal

Camp,
February 4th, 1937

My dear Lord Linlithgow,

In continuation of my letter of January 26th, I think it may interest Your Excellency to know that I have had the opportunity in the last few days of talking with a good number of our District Officers and Commissioners who have come in to Lucknow in force for the three days' leave we have given as usual for the Civil Service Week. On the whole, the views they express are very similar. The Congress propaganda, particularly in the last fortnight, has been extremely intensive and effective, and there is no doubt that it has produced a very considerable impression on the electorate. For the most part the propaganda seems to take the form of holding out attractive promises to the tenants as to what will be done for them if the Congress are returned, and direct attacks on the present government are not so much emphasised. All those with whom I have talked agree that on the surface at any rate the people are still perfectly friendly to government officers, and it would thus seem as if all this propaganda were being taken, as it ought to be, mainly as electioneering. At the same time of course one cannot ignore the possibility that seeds are being sown widely which may germinate later. For the present, however, it would seem that no dangerous conditions are being created.

With regard to the result of all this on election prospects, no one really knows. Those who a few weeks ago would have been prepared to offer fairly confident predictions are now doubtful what the results may be. It is indeed impossible to estimate how far the effect of the Congress campaign will be reflected in the election results. In many cases of course where the Zamindar candidates are beaten, the verdict will be one of suicide, for they persist in fighting each other when the result is the certainty of handing over the seat to the Congress. This, however, is merely a symptom of the fundamental weakness of the Zamindars, namely, their inability to subordinate their own petty and personal interests to a larger policy. That weakness, I fear, will in any case show itself in other ways later on.

As to the result of the election it is really idle to speculate. We must simply wait and see. But there is no doubt that one of the possibilities one may have to contemplate is a situation of practical stalemate.

Yours sincerely,
HARRY HAIG

7

HAIG TO LINLITHGOW
R/3/1/1

Secret and Personal — Camp,
February 13th, 1937

My dear Lord Linlithgow,

In continuation of my letter of February 4th, I can now give Your Excellency a fairly clear picture of the results of the elections to the Lower House, even though a number of the results are not yet out officially. There is no doubt that the Congress have had remarkable and wholesale successes. I do not think anyone would put their numbers at less than 120 in a house of 228, and the number might well run up to 130 or 135. In any case it is plain that they will definitely have a clear majority. In addition, they will presumably have some understanding with the Left Wing of the Muslim League, from which no doubt they will take two Muslim ministers, and they might have in this way some 15 Muslim supporters. This would give them a substantial and assured majority, particularly as the opposition will be lacking in organization and probably slack in attendance. The opposition, so far as I can judge at present, will consist of about 50 Muslims, some of them returned as National Agriculturist candidates, some as Independents, some as Muslim League, but I think likely to coalesce into a definite Muslim party, very vigilant about Muslim interests. In addition, there will be perhaps 20 Hindus, five or six Scheduled Castes, and about six Indian Christians, Europeans and Anglo-Indians.[4]

2. It is generally assumed here that the local leaders of the Congress will desire to take office, and unless there is some unexpected decision at the Congress meeting at Delhi, this may I think be taken as fairly certain. Everybody assures me that Mr. Govind Ballabh Pant is believed to favour this course.

3. The question of the spirit in which a Congress government will take office is one on which I cannot yet form an opinion. I was talking today, for the first time since the elections, to my two ministers, separately. Sir Jwala Prasad Srivastava, who had a very bitter contest on behalf of his wife in the Cawnpore district, takes a gloomy view of the future. He maintains that the Congress have stirred up bad feeling in the villages, that they intend to keep in this respect the ground they have won, and that they will use their power in the government to prepare the way for conditions which will break down the present Constitution and the ability of the British government to maintain itself. Sir Muhammad Yusuf, on the other hand, though he is generally reputed to be extremely old-fashioned in his political outlook, does not take nearly so gloomy a view. He believes that the Congress will make an endeavour to work the government constitutionally, and that though they will no doubt go out for spectacular tenancy reforms and concessions, in fact they will not be able to get very far, because quite a considerable number of those who have been returned on the Congress ticket do not believe in extreme measures or wish to run the risk of revolution. Moreover, the Second Chamber, which is certain to be a conservative body, will act as a check

on any hasty action.[5] The general opinion, so far as I can gauge it, is closer to that of Sir Muhammad Yusuf than to Sir Jwala Prasad's anticipations. I think Sir Jwala Prasad may have had his views unduly coloured by the experiences he has encountered in this quite exceptional election at Cawnpore, during which the Congress exceeded all bounds of decency and seem to have succeeded to a large extent by mob methods and mob feeling. I shall of course give every chance to a Congress government to work constitutionally, and I hope this is in fact what will happen; but if I find that their object is not really to work the Constitution but to undermine the whole position in preparation for a revolutionary mass movement, then I think it would be better to break fairly soon; and when one does break, to have no half measures but to use all the powers under Section 93 of the Government of India Act to their fullest extent.

4. As to the causes of the overwhelming Congress successes it is a little difficult yet to write with confidence. There is no doubt that the Congress propaganda was astonishingly intense and effective, particularly in the last fortnight. The weight of it was in the direction of holding out alluring prospects to the villager of what would happen if he voted for the Congress, and on the whole I should judge that the villager felt it was at any rate worth while seeing how much there was in these promises. So far there is little to corroborate Sir Jwala Prasad's Cawnpore experience that any serious anti-government feeling has been aroused in most places.

5. Apart from this, the Zamindars themselves have contributed to their own downfall. They had their own petty personal feuds. In many cases I think they were over-confident and believed that their authority would secure votes and that it was not necessary to canvass the individual voters. A great deal of harm was done by the unfortunate rivalry between Sir Jwala Prasad Srivastava and the Nawab of Chhatari for the Chief Ministership, which has eluded both of them. That led to unsuitable candidates being put up because they were thought likely to support one or other of the aspirants, and to their receiving on that account lukewarm support. But whatever the causes, the results have been quite astonishing. In Oudh some of the most important Taluqdars with reasonably administered estates have been defeated, and in the Gorakhpur division, where there are a number of very large Zamindars believed to have an exceptionally strong hold on their tenants, they have practically without exception been defeated. These are the two main surprises. In the west of the Province Congress successes on a pretty large scale were anticipated. But Oudh and the east of the Province have been a great surprise to everyone. It is clear that under present conditions the big landlord cannot

in general stand up to Congress in an election. An interesting feature of the results is that there will be few Hindu landlords in the Assembly (apart from special representatives through the landholders' constituencies). On the other hand, most of the important Muslim landlords will be in. This will give added weight to the Muslims in the opposition.

Yours sincerely,
HARRY HAIG

8

HAIG TO LINLITHGOW
MSS.EUR.F. 115/16

Secret and Personal *February 13th, 1937*

I was very glad to get Your Excellency's secret and personal letter of 10th February[6] about consultation on various matters of procedure in connection with the formation of ministries. The general situation which is likely to confront us in a number of provinces seems to me likely to be similar, and I am fully in agreement that some degree of uniformity is desirable.

2. With regard to para. 2 of Your Excellency's letter, I am generally in agreement with the proposals as to the form of the announcements. There is, however, one point not touched on by Your Excellency, which seems to me of importance and to require some measure of uniformity, and that is the approximate date at which Governors in provinces where there is a Congress majority should announce that they have invited the Congress leader to assist in forming a council of ministers. The circumstances are peculiar. Ordinarily, as soon as the situation arising from the election was clear, the Governor would approach one of the leaders and would expect to receive an answer practically at once as to his willingness to endeavour to form a Government. In the case of the Congress, however, it has been announced that the matter is to be dealt with on an all-India basis, and that a decision is not likely to be reached until a meeting has taken place in Delhi in the 3rd week of March. I think it would place a Governor in a derogatory position if he announced publicly, say at the end of February, that he had invited the Congress leader to help him form a ministry and the Congress leader kept him waiting three weeks for an answer. It does not seem to me that that is a position [in] which the Governor should place himself. On the other hand, I do not think it desirable that the Congress should be left for any long period in any practical doubt about the willingness of the Governor to take the normal constitutional course,

and invite the Congress leader to help him form a government. What, therefore, I feel very strongly inclined to do, if Your Excellency does not think that it would be embarrassing to others, is to send for Mr. Govind Ballabh Pant, the Congress leader, and have a talk with him about the 25th February, merely saying that I wish to have a preliminary conversation with reference to conditions arising out of the result of the elections. At that interview I would make it plain to him that I was aware that he was not in a position to give me an answer at once, and that I would, therefore, not make any formal request to him. But I would endeavour to sound him generally and I would explain to him the practical disadvantages of putting off a decision on this matter till late in March, and would indicate an approximate date at which I might make a formal offer to him. This might be about a week before the Congress meeting in Delhi. I would put no announcement into the press about this preliminary interview. If there is a probability of the Congress accepting office, I attach considerable importance to getting in touch with the Congress leader fairly soon, otherwise misunderstandings may arise. But I do not wish to issue any formal announcement until near the time of the Congress meeting. It would, I think, be inconvenient if the Governors in provinces where there is a clear Congress majority issued their formal invitations at widely different dates.

3. Another matter in which I think it is desirable to have a uniform policy settled beforehand is in regard to the action to be taken in the event – I hope unlikely – of Congress refusing to accept office where they are in a clear majority. In this province I should no doubt send for one of the opposition leaders and invite him to form a government; but I think one must assume that the answer would clearly be that the task was impossible. At that stage, I think that there should be no delay and no half measures. Another election would be futile. If the majority party deliberately refuse to accept the responsibilities which the constitution throws upon them, the constitution has broken down, and I consider that the Governor should immediately assume all the executive and legislative powers under the Government of India Act and suspend the legislature. I think I could administer the affairs of the province with the assistance of two members of council, and I should probably propose to retain my two existing members if they were prepared to remain.

9

HAIG TO LINLITHGOW
R/3/1/1

Secret and Personal

Camp,
February 17th, 1937

My dear Lord Linlithgow,

In continuation of my letter of February 13th, one can now begin to gauge the first effects of the elections on the big landlords. They are in varying degrees bewildered, frightened and angry. They put great efforts into the electoral campaign and spent money freely. The result is a complete reversal of all their anticipations. They are very apprehensive of what the Congress may do to them. There is also a good deal of resentment against the attitude of government. One cannot help understanding their feelings. Their argument runs as follows. We have for generations been loyal to the government and the government have supported and encouraged us. In this election we have been fighting not only our own battle but the battle of the government, for the Congress have throughout made it clear that they are attacking the whole system of government and the British connection. But the government have stood by indifferent and allowed us to be beaten. In many cases even government servants have definitely worked against us. (This is a very common allegation, but I doubt if there is much substance in it, save for the lower paid government servants.) As I mentioned to Your Excellency in Lucknow, there is always a certain tendency among this class, if they are beaten, to lie down, and there are not wanting those who think that their best chance of saving anything out of the wreck is to hasten to tender their submission to the Congress. This would in fact, in my opinion, ensure their downfall, for the Congress after using them and reducing them to practical impotence would then finish them off. I think the more sensible realise this clearly enough, and it seems to me probable that they will try to pull themselves together and organise resistance. There are even those who say that while they have been beaten at the polls the next fight will be with other weapons. But this is in the main bravado.

2. The Muslim situation is still obscure. There are rumours that the Congress will make considerable efforts to win over at least the whole of the Muslim League group, realising that if they do this and thus split the Muslims seriously, they will render the whole opposition ineffective. I

think they are fully alive to the danger of having an active and united Muslim opposition. Nevertheless, it seems doubtful whether for the ministry they will pass over the handful of genuine Congress Muslims in favour of those who are clearly not in real sympathy with the Congress aims; and even if, to begin with, they attach a fair number of Muslims to themselves, I doubt whether this attachment will last. But both the Muslims and the landlords may be affected by what happens in other provinces, and there are rumours from Bihar that the Congress are making some impression on these classes there.

3. Sir J.P. Srivastava is in the mood to continue the fight, and he could do a great deal to give weight to the opposition. He realises that in view of the figures I gave to Your Excellency in my last letter, the leader of the Opposition must be a Muslim. I have seen the Nawab of Chhatari recently. He talks very sensibly about the whole position, but he is not a natural fighter and I am inclined to doubt whether he would take on the position of leader of the Opposition. It is not impossible that this would fall on Sir Muhammad Yusuf, who has considerable skill in what one might call the unseen working of the political machine.

4. Much will depend on the Upper House. Here, again, I fear that the landlords have been caught napping. They were so confident of success in the Lower House that comparatively few men of ability and position are standing for the Upper House, and the demoralization caused by the Congress victory will to some extent be reflected even in the elections for the Upper House. It is understood that Congress or Congress sympathisers may amount to as many as 20 out of 52 elected members. My nominations will be of considerable importance.

5. Everyone assumes that the Congress intends to take office, and I do not think they will require any kind of encouragement from me. In view of the situation that is now developing, the uncertainty of the attitude of the Muslims and the landlords and the soreness among the latter, I have come to the conclusion that it would be unwise for me to go out of my way to see the Congress leader at any early date. I think this would merely depress the opposition elements and increase this probability that they would lie down and allow themselves to be trampled on. My present idea, therefore, would be not to send for Mr. Govind Ballabh Pant until just before the Delhi meeting, or even perhaps not till after it. There is I think a good deal to be said for the latter course.

6. The Congress have presumably two lines of policy which they will pursue: (1) To make spectacular concessions to the tenants and establish their influence with them. (2) To pursue more vigorously the whole

programme of attack on the Constitution and the British connection. The second line has been the undercurrent all through the present election, and I think we may expect it to be stressed more strongly once the Congress are in office. The Commissioner of Meerut[7] has just sent to government some extracts from speeches delivered by Jawaharlal Nehru in his recent visit to the Meerut district and they illustrate so clearly what is I am afraid being said on a very wide scale that I attach them to this letter for Your Excellency's information. The line of approach both to the Muslims and to the landlords would certainly be – Our primary quarrel is with the British government, join us in condemning and attacking it and we will be prepared to make certain terms with you. It is difficult to judge what is the impression created by the election in the villages. On the whole I think the impression so far is very wide but not yet deep. It remains to be seen whether the Congress try to continue their work in the villages without intermission. It is possible of course that the Congress in office will tone down, but on the whole I am very much disposed to doubt it. There is a fairly general idea that they will wish to remain in office for a year or 18 months and then at some moment that suits them break.

7. When the Congress government take office, a great number of points will arise on which the Governor will have to take a definite line either of acquiescence or of opposition. The Congress governments will be working to a large extent to one single policy indicated to them by the All India Congress Committee. If the Governors deal with these matters on different lines, their position will be greatly weakened. I have no doubt Your Excellency has already been considering the importance of settling an all-India line for Governors to take on these matters. I do not know whether Your Excellency has considered, or would think it desirable, to have a conference at Delhi of all the Governors of the provinces in which there will be Congress governments. Speaking for myself, I think this would be of the greatest value. We could then act with much more assurance. In any case, at a later stage, I should greatly value the opportunity of coming into Delhi for a day and discussing with Your Excellency a number of points which I think are likely to arise in this province.[8]

Yours sincerely,
HARRY HAIG

ENCLOSURE TO NO. 9

COPY OF EXTRACT FROM A DEMI-OFFICIAL LETTER FROM THE COMMISSIONER, MEERUT DIVISION

At Mowana he (Jawaharlal Nehru) said:

"That Government rule by despotism and sheer force passing laws whether people liked them or not. That trade of the Government is flourishing at the cost of our industries. Nothing can be done unless the Government is changed. The English Government can never do anything for us. I think this Government cannot continue any longer. The real fight or swaraj will begin after the elections."

At Meerut he said:

"The force of the population is now up and against the Government. The Viceroy announced that no public servant will take any part in the elections, but secretly he encourages them to oppose the Congress. The District Magistrate and other officers are interfering in these elections and are oppressing people in many ways. There have been Emperors who have been set aside; the Viceroy is nothing in this comparison. I may tell you that I see no longer life for the British rule now."

At Rasna he said:

"Your money which you pay in revenue, rent and taxes goes to the British Government. That money goes to England and we are running into debt. Our country looks almost deserted and there are only a few schools of the District Board. It is all like this because the Government is in the hands of a few who carry it on in their own interest. The Government is foreign and so there are no hospitals and the little arrangement that there is at once corrupt and insufficient. Now others make law for us and we have to obey them under the pressure of the army. The officers are not appointed by your consultation, they may be good or bad and so often they are bad. So in every village there must be committees and panchayats of the Congress."

10

HAIG TO LINLITHGOW
MSS.EUR.F. 115/16

Private and Confidential *February 23rd, 1937*

I am most grateful for Your Excellency's personal and confidential letter of 20th February 1937,[9] and I shall be much interested to see the correspondence with Hyde Gowan.[10] While I think it may be convenient that there should be some degree of uniformity in regard to details of procedure, I had really in my mind a different set of ideas, which I am afraid I did not make quite clear in my last letter. There are likely to be a number of questions of policy which will arise in an identical form in the provinces with Congress governments. Indeed, it is not improbable that they may be deliberately raised in every one of these provinces as a result of directions from the All India Congress Committee, who may quite possibly couple their agreement to acceptance of office with instructions that certain conditions must be fulfilled. If different Governors take a different line in regard to these questions, it appears to me the position may become exceedingly difficult. Let us assume that Governors A, B and C meet the Congress over one of these points of controversy, and that Governor D declines to do so. The ministers of Governor D may well be encouraged to push their claim to the point of declaring that unless it is conceded they will resign, well knowing that Governor D would be on weak ground in breaking with his ministry on a point which had already been conceded in other provinces. At the same time if he submits to this pressure and is forced to change his attitude, he weakens his own position greatly. If on the other hand we are firm and united on certain points, it is very unlikely that we shall really be challenged on them, unless Congress are prepared for a general break. A further consideration is that these points of controversy, if they arise, are bound to form the subject of discussion in parliament, and the Secretary of State will have to take a line on them. From this point of view too, I venture to think it would be convenient to have a general understanding as to what the line should be. I do not suggest for a moment that in the handling of political situations, which may differ a good deal in different provinces, or in dealing with special provincial problems, such as for instance my own land revenue and tenancy questions, Governors should have their discretion fettered. But it does seem to me that if at the beginning one could have a few fixed points instead of a blank sheet of paper, we might in the end be able to present a more satisfactory picture of a Congress government in operation.

As to the method by which agreement could most conveniently be reached on these points, Your Excellency is in the best position to judge. I was merely expressing my own feeling that personal discussion might be the shortest way to agreement. It would also, I think, be valuable to discuss with others who will have to handle somewhat similar situations the many problems that are likely to arise even where we are not aiming at definite conclusions. I understand from Donaldson that Your Excellency feels there might be objections to anything like a formal conference. I might, however, have opportunities of meeting neighbouring Governors, for instance Hallett, and I should greatly value later on the opportunity of visiting Your Excellency and getting a general idea both of any fixed points and of the line that other Governors are inclined to take on other matters.

Perhaps I might indicate very briefly the kind of points on which some uniformity might be desirable. In the first place, there are things in the nature of demonstrations, such as a proposal to hoist the Congress flag on government buildings, or to put the Police into *khaddar*. These seem to me inadmissible in principle and dangerous in their probable effects. I should imagine everyone would refuse to accept such proposals, but it might be well to make sure. Under the general category of law and order a number of particular problems will no doubt arise which will have to be handled by Governors in accordance with their judgement of the merits of the particular situation in the province. But there may be some general points, such as a demand for amnesty to political prisoners, on which a clear and general decision can be taken. Then there may be a number of points of importance in connection with the treatment of the Services; for instance, the extent to which it may be reasonable to allow reduction of pay for existing incumbents, or the attitude towards anything like a general attack on government servants for alleged action in elections, such as a proposal to set up a general inquiry. In these matters again I think it would strengthen the hands of all of us, if we worked on similar lines. Another question which I think might require uniformity of treatment is the precise action to be taken in the event of it being necessary for the Governor to exercise his powers under Section 93. Also a discussion on the tactics of trying to put a minority party into power if the majority party refused office, or subsequently resigned, in preference to using at once the powers contained in Section 93 would be valuable, though here I do not suggest that there need be any kind of uniformity, as it is probably essentially a matter for judgement in accordance with the local situation.

11

HAIG TO LINLITHGOW
MSS.EUR.F. 115/16

Private and Confidential *February 28th, 1937*

I am writing in answer to Your Excellency's personal and confidential letter of the 22nd February 1937,[11] with which you enclosed an extract from your letter of 19th February to Gowan. I fully appreciate the point that a great deal of the preliminary informal consultation, which we had previously contemplated taking place in March, is not really necessary, and that we can, and probably must, postpone it till after the 1st April. I had been looking into this matter, and I do not think I shall be faced on this account with any serious practical difficulty. I certainly should not be disposed to try and rush my new Government on this account.

Nor am I disturbed at the necessity of waiting till after the meeting of the A.I.C.C. before extending a formal invitation to the Congress leader to help me in forming a government. There is really no alternative government possible in this province, so I am bound to wait; and if I wait, I may as well do it with a good grace. It would no doubt be a serious complication if the government were not formed by the 1st April; but I can hardly believe that the Congress party, if they have made up their mind to accept office, will not be able to arrange about the constitution of a ministry in the ten days or so that would be available, and if they proved in this matter dilatory they would put themselves clearly in the wrong.

With regard to the summoning of the new legislature, we had contemplated a brief formal session early in April. As summonses could not go out before the 1st April, I am disposed to agree that a suitable date would be about the 12th April. But I do not quite appreciate the advisability of any uniform date for this purpose. It appears to me essentially a matter that should be settled in accordance with provincial conditions, and I should contemplate consulting my ministers and being guided very largely by their wishes. Indeed, if they do not wish to have a meeting of the Assembly at all in April, I do not know that I should press it on them strongly. Again, as to the nature of the business, our idea certainly was to confine it to the formal necessities, but that again would be a matter on which I should consult my ministers and give full weight to their wishes.[12]

12

HAIG TO LINLITHGOW
Telegram
MSS.EUR.F. 115/14

Private and Personal *March 18th, 1937*
(Unnumbered)

Your telegram No. 164-S, dated March 18, 1937.[13] I note that Congress resolution[14] represents victory for Right Wing and I am fully conscious of advantages on a broad view of Congress taking office. At the same time I feel somewhat uneasy as to line suggested for Governor.

2. As Your Excellency says we must take the resolution as it stands. The last words appear to me, and I assume also to Your Excellency, to imply practically complete surrender of Governor's special powers. The special powers are intended, as I understand them, for use in connection with action taken within the constitution. A reduction of the pay of government servants by 50 per cent would be entirely constitutional; so would inequitable action against minorities; so would refusal to take action against some subversive movement. Indeed I find it difficult to understand what action outside the constitution would be in the case of ministers, unless they were openly to defy the Governor, which is hardly conceivable. The words therefore must I think be taken to mean that the Governor will not interfere with anything Congress govt. choose to do. In other words they amount to a complete negation of the important constitutional responsibilities placed upon Governor by the Act.

3. The crux of the matter to my mind consists in the words "and is able to state publicly". This must mean that the Congress leader will make a public statement that he is satisfied that the Governor will not use his special powers, etc. Such a statement if made would be untrue. I emphasise the point that it would be a statement and not merely as suggested in para. 4 of Your Excellency's telegram an inference. If the Governor allows the statement to stand it must be presumed by the public to represent accurately the trend of conversation and so far as the public is concerned Congress will have secured what in fact the Governor in his conversation with the leader has denied them. I regard this as a typical example of Gandhi's tactics. The effect of such a statement on non-Congress opinion in this province would I think be deplorable and I should have supposed reaction in England might be not inconsiderable. The position of the Governor would it seems to me to be seriously compromised. On the

other hand if Governor publicly denies statement of leader then all question of office acceptance is at an end. My inclination would be to put some of these considerations plainly to the leader and make it clear that I could not acquiesce in a statement that does not represent the facts.

4. I am also disposed to think it dangerous to say anything to Congress leader which might be interpreted as identifying Governor with Congress policy. In this province policy is likely to be sooner or later extreme. I should not attempt to interfere except in case of real necessity, and probably greater part of policy could be pursued without my having opportunity to interfere even if I wished to. But that is quite a different matter to my pledging myself to assist in a policy with a great deal of which I may be in the strongest disagreement. I venture to think the only sound line is to take the point emphasised by Your Excellency that the Governor stands outside the party, that he will follow strictly constitutional line in regard to policy that may be adopted by ministers, recognising that almost invariably the responsibility is theirs, not his, and that he will not attempt to offer any kind of indirect obstruction to them in the carrying out of their policy. But he cannot pledge himself not to fulfil the responsibilities laid upon him by the Constitution if such a situation should arise. While I should not wish to be too blunt I feel that the only sound basis of working with a Congress government is one of sincerity, and that ambiguous phrases in the long run make for misunderstanding and friction.

5. As regards the general policy of inducing the Congress to accept office I fully recognise that the working of a Congress government may have important results. It is not impossible, though I think in this province unlikely, that they will settle down and work what I may call a genuine though radical policy. Moreover, their actions will undoubtedly give rise to opposition which may have a sobering effect. On the other hand if they take office mainly with a view to embarking on a mass movement after six months or a year, which is the general view here, the trouble when it comes will be much more intense and critical, than if we were to face it at once, which I feel confident we could do now without undue risk. On balance I should prefer Congress to take office, though the risks of the situation developing dangerously are grave. But I do not feel it would be right to purchase this result at the expense of compromising the position of the Governor and shaking the confidence reposed in him by non-Congress and service opinion. Never have the safeguards been more important than now, and in my opinion we must not even appear to be abandoning them.

6. Meantime I propose not to send for Pant until I hear again from Your Excellency.

13

HAIG TO LINLITHGOW
Telegram
MSS.EUR.F. 115/14

Clear the Line *March 20th, 1937*
Private and Personal
No. 1-G

I am very grateful for your telegram No. 176-S of 19 March[15] which makes the position quite clear. I accept Your Excellency's views throughout and shall use my best endeavours to secure the result at which we are aiming. I am asking Pant to see me on Wednesday morning.

2. Should a break unfortunately occur my view based on my observation of the situation in this province as it is developing is that conditions would be too dangerous to permit of an ineffective minority government functioning for some months. Situation would require immediate remedial legislative measures for tenants (which I could take while minority government could only talk about its intentions) and probably vigorous executive action and assumption of powers in regard to law and order from which a minority government might shrink. Moreover though I would have to offer government to minority I do not think it at all likely from what I have heard that they would be prepared to accept. If therefore a break with Congress should occur I should have to press for immediate application of section 93.[16]

14

HAIG TO LINLITHGOW
Telegram
MSS.EUR.F. 115/14

Clear the Line *March 24th, 1937*
Private and Personal
No. 3-G

I have just had a long conversation with Pant, conducted in an atmosphere of personal friendliness on both sides, but very disappointing in its results. When I said that I wished to consult him about the formation of a ministry he referred me at once to the Congress resolution. He explained that he was the representative of an organisation and that he was bound by its mandate. In the course of discussion he went on to explain that he was personally in agreement with the position taken by Congress which he could not in any way vary. He made it clear that the resolution meant precisely what it said, that the words "in regard to their constitutional activities" might be regarded as superfluous, and that the demand was that the Governor would not use his special powers of interference or set aside the advice of his ministers in any circumstances. He suggested that it would be a sufficient safeguard, if things were going badly, that the Governor had the power to dismiss his ministers. He explained his general attitude as being that he did not feel equal to assuming the responsibility for the administration unless he was certain that he could pursue the whole of his policy unhampered. We had a perfectly friendly discussion about the limits on the practical exercise of the special powers, but it was clear that his objection was to the whole principle. He said that there were certain parts of the Government of India Act which, though he disliked them greatly, he was prepared to accept because they were mandatory, such as the pay and control over all-India services, but he could not reconcile himself to possible interference by the Governor of the discretionary kind contemplated by the provisions about special responsibilities, individual judgement, etc. I assured him of my desire that the Congress should form a ministry, of my readiness to work with him in relations of perfect confidence, of my help and support, of my realisation of the spirit of the constitution and of my desire not to use special powers lightly or in-advisedly. He received these assurances in a most friendly spirit and did not question them but returned always to the point of principle. It was quite clear that he was not prepared to make any statement of a general character, such as suggested in para. 2(*c*) of your telegram no. 189-S of 22nd March.[17] I got the impression that he was bound down strictly by instructions though he himself agreed with those instructions and that he could not even if he wished to depart from them. I also think that he was genuinely disappointed at my attitude when I had to explain to him that constitutionally it was not possible for me to agree to any such demand. Congress seem to have persuaded themselves that Governors would make no difficulty about their demand.

2. Though we had reached a complete deadlock at the end of our conversation I suggested to him that as similar conversations were taking place in the next day or two in five other provinces and as it was clear that the matter would have to be handled on similar lines by all it would be desirable not to put out any statement to the effect that we had reached a

deadlock. I am therefore with his approval issuing a statement to the effect that our discussions have been postponed and that we have decided that it would be desirable to meet again at a later date which we have tentatively fixed as March 29th. I did this with the idea that he might consult his people further. He did not say that this would be useless, but I do not think anything will come of it. I told him I would communicate the result of our conversation to you, but so far as we are concerned it seems to me clear that we cannot budge at all.

15

HAIG TO LINLITHGOW
Telegram
MSS.EUR.F. 115/14

Private and Personal *March 25th, 1937*
No. 4-G

Many thanks for Your Excellency's telegram No. 188-S of 22nd March.[18] In view of situation as it now appears likely to develop, with moderate Congress men probably rather bewildered and uncertain as to their goal, I agree that I should aim at forming a ministry from minority elements and keeping it in office for some months. If this plan proves feasible and safe I should consider carefully in consultation with the ministers and in the light of Your Excellency's observations the two alternatives suggested in para. 3 of your telegram.

16

HAIG TO LINLITHGOW
Telegram
MSS.EUR.F. 115/14

Clear the Line *March 29th, 1937*
Private and Personal
No. 5-G

I met Pant again this morning. After restatement of our respective positions he said he regretted he could not accept my invitation to form a ministry. I am issuing communiqué, and am taking up immediately the question of another ministry.

17

HAIG TO LINLITHGOW
MSS.EUR.F. 115/18

Private and Personal *March 31st, 1937*

I saw the Nawab of Chhatari on the evening of the 29th and he agreed to try and form a ministry. The following figures may be of interest. The number of those in the Legislative Assembly not elected on the Congress ticket is 95. Of these 66 are Muslims, 27 belonging to the Muslim League and the remaining 39 having a general allegiance to Chhatari. The 29 non-Muslims consist of Hindu Zamindars, Scheduled Castes, special interests and minor minorities – a heterogeneous collection who could probably be controlled for the most part by Sir J.P. Srivastava.

2. When I saw Chhatari on the evening of the 29th, he was in quite good heart and we discussed the possibility, in view of the Congress refusal of office, that a certain number of those returned on the Congress ticket might in the course of four months possibly be won over. I had already ascertained that Srivastava would be willing to work with Chhatari.

3. Chhatari came to see me again yesterday evening, the 30th. He was in rather a defeatist mood. Srivastava had promised his support, but Chhatari's primary task naturally was to try and secure the adhesion of the Muslim League whose leader is Khaliquzzaman, a man very anxious for office and who has been in close negotiation recently with the Congress, from whose views he is not very far apart. Khaliq refused to join Chhatari, his reason being that the new ministry could not last more than four months and that any one who joined it would be politically discredited. Khaliq's own position, however, in the Muslim League is precarious, for there are at least two other aspirants to its leadership. There is to be a meeting of the League on the 4th April. I fear it is impossible to bring it on earlier. It has been agreed that the question of joining a government should be discussed with the League on that date. They may as a body refuse, or they may split, in which case Chhatari would have no difficulty in securing a minister from among them. Chhatari, however, indicated that if the Muslim League refused as a body to have anything to do with the ministry, he might find it impossible to go on. Meantime, Chhatari is meeting a number of his own followers on the 1st April.

4. I think Chhatari has been rather shaken by the views expressed by Khaliq. He put to me very definitely two points:

(*a*) That it is really futile to take office merely for four months, that they can do no good to the country, and that they would merely damage their own personal reputations.

(*b*) That it is likely that the Congress will start an agitation which will require strong repressive measures, and that a ministry in such a position will not be able to take such measures. (This is a valid point, though I have been very careful not to suggest any such thing to Chhatari. Your Excellency will remember that I mentioned the point in para. 2 of my telegram No. 1-G of March 20th, 1937.)

5. Chhatari has also, at my suggestion, communicated with Chintamani with a view to seeing whether his support could be secured. But he thinks that Chintamani would refuse to join such a government and would be opposed to the principle of forming one. He believes that Sapru is opposed on principle to a minority government being formed. Certainly Sapru when I saw him a fortnight ago expressed that view to me. It appears that he has expressed it also to others.

6. If Chhatari finally abandons the task of forming a ministry, it might still be possible to get someone else to take it on; but I feel it is important not to have a ministry which would be regarded as a mockery and would in fact be a source of weakness.

7. Chhatari hinted that his own attitude might be affected by the question of arrangements in the event of my having to take over the administration after the defeat of the temporary government. He seemed to suggest that if the leaders of this government could look to some provision as advisers under my administration, they might be prepared as it were to cut their throats politically by accepting office under these circumstances. But if at the end of four months they were merely to retire into private life, the prospect would be less attractive.

8. I think in any case it would be desirable now to explore the arrangements that would be suitable if it is necessary to act under Section 93. I still hope that it will be possible to form a ministry, but I cannot be confident about it. I fear in any case that the present unsatisfactory state of suspense will have to continue till after the Muslim League meeting on April 4th. I shall see Srivastava today and possibly get some more definite views from him, and I shall keep Your Excellency fully informed of developments.

9. Chhatari in his present mood seems to have given up all hope of securing accretions of strength during a ministry of four months, though my own feeling is that there will be so much disappointment among

Congressmen at not taking office that the situation is not without possibilities. But as he at present views the position, I think he would probably wish to avoid meeting the legislature and therefore the conclusion indicated in Your Excellency's telegram No. 269-S,[19] dated the 30th March, may be of value.

18

HAIG TO LINLITHGOW
MSS.EUR.F. 115/18

Private and Personal *March 31st, 1937*

Since writing my letter to Your Excellency this morning, I have seen Sir J.P. Srivastava, as indicated in para. 8 of my letter. He expressed much more robust views and is I think, with a little backing, prepared to try and make the government, if formed, a positive and effective body, and is not without hope that, as suggested in para. 9 of my letter, they might win over a certain amount of support from the other side. He thinks that Khaliq will not come into the ministry, and that Khaliq is merely pursuing dilatory tactics in refusing to call a meeting of the Muslim League before the 4th April. On the other hand Salempur, who is Khaliq's main rival in the Muslim League, would probably, if approached in the right way, be very ready to come in. This might involve a breach in the League, and no doubt there would be a good deal of reluctance that this position should develop. But if it did come to a break, Srivastava does not think Khaliq would have a following of more than 6 or 7 out of 27. On the whole the prospects of forming not only a government, but a reputable government, seem to me distinctly better than when I wrote this morning, reporting my interview with Chhatari. Chhatari has gone off to Delhi for the day, but I understand will be back here tomorrow morning.

2. Srivastava is definitely keen on getting Chintamani to join the ministry, and seems to think that he might possibly consent. A question of principle might arise in that event on which I should be glad if Your Excellency could give me your views. Chintamani could of course be appointed a minister without being a member of the legislature. On the other hand it would be possible to nominate him as a member of the Upper House. I had been given to understand, at a time when we were expecting Congress to take office, that Chintamani would not be averse to being nominated to the Upper House, but I felt considerable difficulty in principle in making such a nomination in view of the terms of paragraph XIX of the Instrument

of Instructions.[20] Chintamani would be most appropriate as an elder statesman, but that does not appear to be contemplated by paragraph XIX, and I do not quite know what interest he could be held to represent, as one cannot I think interpret those words as including a political party, such as the Liberals. Chintamani also stood for election to the Assembly and was beaten; but I think it will be inevitable for several of my nominations to the Upper House to be made from persons who were beaten for the Assembly.[21]

19

HAIG TO LINLITHGOW
Telegram
MSS.EUR.F. 115/18

Private and Personal *April 1st, 1937*
No. 6-G

Chhatari who returned from Delhi this morning in fairly good heart has reported this evening result of today's discussions which are very disappointing. He approached Salempur who, while expressing personal readiness to join cabinet, said he would have to resign from Muslim League and has little expectation of bringing any appreciable following. It seems likely that Muslim League will be practically solid against taking office.

2. Chhatari also had a meeting with his own followers. Opinion was divided but there was strong opposition in many quarters to taking office. Zamindars feel that there would be no reality about it, and that they would merely be used as a temporary convenience by government. The Madras expression "Interim government" has made a bad impression on them, and this is much reinforced by Gandhi's statement[22] which they think foreshadows possible accommodation with Congress before long. Moreover, they believe that situation will soon develop in which government will have to use repressive measures and frankly they want the Governor to do this and are not prepared to attempt it themselves. Nor it seems do they believe in the policy of making any immediate concessions to tenants or pursuing a really liberal line. They would therefore have nothing to show for their four months' office.

3. Apart from this there is a general feeling, the result doubtless of Congress propaganda, that a minority government is constitutionally improper and that it will have no moral backing. Chintamani has definitely refused to join cabinet on this point of principle. It is understood that

Sapru is very strongly opposed to it. Maharaj Singh has refused. Liaquat Ali Khan made a strong speech in the meeting today against it. It seems pretty clear that opinion generally is definitely against forming a government.

4. Chhatari gave me to understand that if I pressed him strongly he might agree, as a matter of loyalty but not conviction, to form a government which would probably be confined to four members. But I understood him to say that in that case he would wish to meet the Legislators at once and if beaten there resign.

5. I will have conversations tomorrow with others so as to check up the general accuracy of these views and after reflecting on situation will communicate my own views. I report this meantime for information.

20

HAIG TO LINLITHGOW
MSS.EUR.F. 115/18

Private and Personal *April 2nd, 1937*

I am glad to say I have just secured from Chhatari his list of ministers, and we shall have a ministry in office tomorrow. After sending last night my telegram of 1st April, I thought over the situation very carefully. The position was that after three days Chhatari was more uncertain than he had been when I first asked him about forming a ministry. I had felt bound, after asking him, to leave him to handle the situation in his own way; but I saw the situation was getting steadily worse and I began to have considerable doubts whether the general attitude of irresolution was not largely due to Chhatari's own frame of mind. I therefore this morning sent for all those whom Chhatari had mentioned as possible ministers and talked to them separately very much on the lines of Your Excellency's letter of 1st April[23] (though that only reached me this evening). I found they were all quite prepared to come into a ministry, and appreciated the points I made. I then saw Chhatari and put my views to him very strongly. He did not conceal his own belief that it was a mistake to take office; but eventually he said that he would do as I wished, and I asked him to bring me his definite answer this evening with his list of ministers. This he has just done. It will not be at all a bad ministry, and I think now that the plunge has been taken, they will function quite well and I believe attract a reasonable amount of support. The atmosphere in Lucknow was getting steadily worse, and that was why I felt this morning that I must push things to a decision immediately. There was a mischievous leading article in this morning's *Pioneer* which still further encouraged Chhatari's hesitations.

I was very glad to get Your Excellency's letter of 1st April this evening and to know your views, with which I am in full agreement.

NOTES

1. In this letter Lord Linlithgow asked Sir Harry Haig to send, at possibly monthly intervals, a confidential appreciation of developments in the local political situation in the U.P. The Viceroy wished this appreciation to be of a more personal character than the existing fortnightly reports sent by the Chief Secretary. MSS.EUR.F. 115/16.
2. Mr Percy Marsh.
3. In January 1930 the Congress Working Committee passed a resolution calling on the country to celebrate 26 January each year as 'Purna Swaraj Day'. In January 1935 the Working Committee further asked members to hold public meetings on 'Purna Swaraj Day' (or household meetings where public meetings were prohibited). At these meetings a lengthy resolution (worded in Hindustani or the local languages) was to be passed. This resolution began: 'We remind ourselves on this, the solemn national day, that Complete Independence is our birthright and we shall not rest till we have achieved it....'
4. The actual results of the 1937 elections to the U.P. Legislative Assembly were: Congress 133; Independents 41; Muslim League 28; National Agriculturist Party 25; Liberals 1.
5. Lord Linlithgow minuted: 'These Second Chambers will have to go easy for a bit and give ground where no vital principles are involved, or there will be serious friction between the houses.'
6. MSS.EUR.F. 115/16.
7. Mr Percy Marsh.
8. Lord Linlithgow replied in a letter dated 20 February 1937. He said that he would be delighted to see both Sir Harry and Lady Haig in Delhi a little later on. He would consider the idea of a Governors' Conference but felt it inadvisable to lay plans too soon. There was a real advantage in Governors handling uniformly certain of the problems they would have to face. R/3/1/1.
9. See note above.
10. Sir Hyde Gowan was Governor of the Central Provinces and Berar at this date.
11. MSS.EUR.F. 115/16.
12. Lord Linlithgow's reply, dated 4 March 1937 is on MSS.EUR.F. 115/16. It is evident from Linlithgow's reply that arrangements had been made for Sir

Harry Haig to visit the Viceroy on 8 March. While in New Delhi he would have the opportunity of talking with Sir Maurice Hallett who would also be there. See also Appendix 1.

13. In his telegram 164-S of 18 March 1937 to Sir Harry Haig, Lord Linlithgow drew attention to the Congress resolution on acceptance of office in the provinces (see next note). The Viceroy felt that while there could be no question of an assurance by Governors on the use of their special powers, they would be ill-advised to turn away from the Congress resolution. In discussions with Pandit Pant, Linlithgow suggested that Haig should say that while he was bound to operate within the Act and his Instrument of Instructions, he could informally assure Congress ministers of his full help, sympathy and co-operation. MSS.EUR.F. 115/14.

14. The resolution adopted by the All-India Congress Committee at its meeting in Delhi on 17 and 18 March 1947 was based on a Working Committee draft. The relevant part of the resolution read:

    'The All-India Congress Committee authorises and permits the acceptance of offices in provinces where the Congress commands a majority in the legislature, provided the ministerships shall not be accepted unless the leader of the Congress party in the legislature is satisfied and is able to state publicly that the Governor will not use his special powers of interference or set aside the advice of ministers in regard to constitutional activities.'

15. This telegram replied to No. 12. In it Lord Linlithgow said that there could be 'no question of compromising in any way the position of a Governor in regard to safeguards. But once that is out of the way you will agree with me, I am sure, that we must so steer our course as to give the maximum of assistance to those elements in Congress which are prepared to accept office.' MSS.EUR.F. 115/14.

16. Lord Linlithgow replied in telegram 186-S of 21 March 1937. Part of this telegram reads:

    'I realise your difficulties but I am sure that it is most important to exhaust all alternatives before falling back on Sec. 93 and it will in my view be most desirable that in the circumstances which you envisage you should do what you can to persuade minorities or coalition to accept office even if they are to be defeated within a day or two. If they have been so defeated and Congress on a second invitation refuse to decline [accept] office your path is clear for introduction of Sec. 93. But it is of great importance that we should fall back on that section only after leaving no stone unturned.' Ibid.

17. MSS.EUR.F. 115/14.

18. In this telegram Lord Linlithgow conveyed Lord Zetland's view that the formation of Ministries should be delayed by no more than a day or two. In paragraph 3, the Viceroy outlined two expedients for dealing with the situation

where the majority party refused office and where it was important to postpone resort to Section 93. These expedients were: (*a*) that while the opening session of the legislature should not be deferred ministers should not resign on a vote of no-confidence; (*b*) that the first session should be delayed as long as possible. MSS.EUR.F. 115/14.

19. In telegram 269-S of 30 March 1947, Lord Linlithgow said he had discussed with Lord Zetland the date when the Provincial legislatures should first be summoned. Zetland recognised 'it is for Governors to decide in the light of their local circumstances after consulting their ministers on which date legislature can be convened and agrees that should they decide to postpone the meeting to July or August they would entirely be within their rights in doing so.' MSS.EUR.F. 115/18.

20. Paragraph XIX of the *Instrument of Instructions* to Governors read:

    'It is Our will and pleasure that the seats in the Legislative Council to be filled by the nomination of Our Governor shall be so apportioned as in general to redress, so far as may be, inequalities of representation which may have resulted from election, and in particular to secure representation for women and the Scheduled Castes in that Chamber.' *Parl. Papers*, H. of C. paper No. 1, vol. XX, 1936-7, pp. 1031-8.

21. Lord Linlithgow replied to Nos. 17 and 18 in a letter dated 1 April 1937. The Viceroy said he attached the utmost importance to the formation of a ministry in the U.P. and he hoped Sir Harry Haig would 'lend all the persuasion and employ all the personal pressure in your power to bring about its formation'. It was vital that the U.P. was not the only province in which it proved impossible to find a team to carry on. A very heavy responsibility rested on the landlords to constitute, or lend support to, a body of men who could try to work the government within the scheme of the 1935 Act. 'What we have to encourage in these Taluqdars', the Viceroy continued, 'is a little more fighting spirit.' As regards Mr Chintamani, Linlithgow advised Haig to appoint him as a Minister and then arrange a bye-election in due course. MSS.EUR.F. 115/18.

22. In a statement which appeared in the Indian press on 30 March 1937, Mahatma Gandhi said: 'I am the sole author of the office-acceptance clause of the Congress resolution.' He added: 'There was no intention whatsoever to lay down a condition whose acceptance would mean any the slightest abrogation of the Constitution.' Their object of transferring power to the people 'could not be secured unless there was a gentlemanly understanding between the Governors and their Congress ministers that they would not exercise their special powers of interference as long as the ministers acted within the Constitution. Not to do so would be to court an almost immediate deadlock after entering upon office.'

23. See note 21 above.

CHAPTER 2

Documents for 3 April – 16 July 1937

21

HAIG TO LINLITHGOW
MSS.EUR.F. 125/126

Camp,
April 4th, 1937

My dear Lord Linlithgow,

I have considered carefully Your Excellency's secret letter dated 25th March 1937 regarding discussion or action by the Provincial Legislature in respect of the behaviour of troops when acting in aid of the civil power. I agree with Your Excellency that discussion will have to be faced if necessary, but that any resolution to set up a committee of enquiry can be dealt with as proposed in Your Excellency's letter,[1] with which I am in full agreement.

Yours sincerely,
HARRY HAIG

22

HAIG TO LINLITHGOW
MSS.EUR.F. 115/18

Private and Confidential *April 5th, 1937*

Many thanks for Your Excellency's letter of 4th April.[2] I think it is important that you should know how things look like developing here. I saw Chhatari this morning. He has been having conversations with the new cabinet, and his attitude was in marked contrast to that of the days when he was wondering about forming a government. He seems now to be determined to try and make a good job of it. He asked me to send for Sir J.P. Srivastava, who had certain ideas which he thought it was desirable should be discussed jointly. Sir J.P. joined us and said that in his opinion there were really two courses open to the government, and that they must make up their mind very soon as between them. The one was merely to mark time, occupy their posts, and try to keep things reasonably quiet until they were inevitably pushed out in July or August. The other was to adopt a vigorous and militant policy, to attack the Congress, to consolidate their own ranks, to use every effort to convert the minority into a majority, and to push on with a definite permanent policy of their own on the assumption that they had at least a fighting chance of maintaining themselves through the budget session. He said that this was a choice that required most careful consideration. The worst thing of all would be to start on a vigorous policy, which would cause a great deal of ill-feeling in the Congress ranks (one of the first things he would contemplate would be a large number of election petitions, for which he maintains there is ample material), and then for any reason draw back and not carry it through. I gather that at the moment the cabinet on the whole would be disposed to pursue a vigorous policy. They will discuss this matter among themselves in the course of the next two or three days and come to a decision.

2. The reason I am troubling Your Excellency with this at the moment is that since this conversation I have seen a leading article in the *Statesman* of today which urges very definitely a policy of further exploring the position with the Congress on an all-India basis, and seeing whether it is not possible still to induce them to take office. I see suggestions of the same type also in today's *Hindustan Times*. Now it may well be that, taking a broad view, it would be desirable that the Congress, even now, should take office, and there is of course always the possibility that in August, if they throw out the present government, they may be prepared to take office. But it seems to me that it would hardly be right for us to bring pressure on the landlords, as I have done, to take office and to let them engage themselves in a fight with the Congress with the gloves off, which would certainly enrage the Congress, if there were any possibility that the situation might suddenly be transformed and before they have been able to do much more than irritate the Congress, the Congress as the result of an all-India settlement were to express themselves ready to take office. My own feeling is very much in agreement with what Your Excellency said in para. 1 of your letter of the 1st April.[3] The landlords must exert themselves now, if they hope to survive; and if they wish to adopt a fighting policy, I do not feel that I should discourage them. But

though I think in any case they would be wise to use their present opportunity to close their ranks and organise, it might not be wise for them to go all out against the Congress, if there is any considerable probability that Congress may change their policy as the result of some kind of settlement.[4]

3. In regard to details of the present position, the Muslim League situation is of special importance. The Muslim League meeting yesterday, as was anticipated, condemned Salempur for joining the government, but not very vigorously, and it is evident that he has a definite following. The Muslim League are at present being buoyed up with the hope that the Congress will take office and with the assurance that, if so, it will make an alliance with them. It is interesting to observe that up to the time when Pant first saw me, i.e. the period when the Congress themselves seemed to contemplate office, they appeared to be taking a very stiff attitude towards the Muslim League and refused to make any kind of agreement with them. Immediately after Pant's first interview with me, when he must have known that office acceptance was out of the question, the Congress made overtures to the Muslim League and practically offered them two posts in the cabinet. These negotiations have, I understand, since been continued and the assurances reiterated. It is possible to suppose that the Congress are pursuing a deliberately dishonest policy, and having no intention to take office, are holding out hopes to the Muslim League in order to prevent them joining the alternative government. Otherwise we must suppose that Congress have suddenly changed their previous policy of aloofness. If my present government begin to make good, they seem to be fairly confident that a considerable number of the Muslim Leaguers will gradually drift over to them; and that seems to me likely.

23

HAIG TO LINLITHGOW
R/3/1/2

Private and Confidential

Camp,
April 7th, 1937

My dear Lord Linlithgow,

I am sending my first report of political conditions in the United Provinces under the new Constitution. There is so much going on at present and the situation is so fluid that I propose, to begin with, to send these reports fortnightly. I shall send copies of these reports direct to the Secretary of State in accordance with the instructions contained in his Despatch Reforms, No. 1, dated the 17th March 1937.[5]

2. The latter half of March was a time when events moved in a surprising way, and opinion fluctuated widely in sympathy with events. It had been assumed for some time in this Province that the Congress would certainly take office. Though there were not lacking those who realised that the true test of the new Constitution would come only through the nationalist elements taking office, there was on the whole a widespread apprehension as to the practical results. Even the Liberals, who might have been expected to be the first to welcome such a development in accordance with their own principles, were seriously alarmed at a position in which the more moderate Congressmen would be directing the machinery of government, while the Extremists under the leadership of Jawaharlal Nehru would be organising revolution almost unhampered outside. It was generally assumed that, however, excellent the intentions of the more moderate Congressmen might be, they would be unable in fact to oppose the policy of Jawaharlal Nehru in this Province. The landlords naturally were full of apprehension, and realised that their very existence was threatened. There were traces of uneasiness in the Services, and among the common people there was a feeling sedulously fostered by successful Congress candidates and other Congress workers, that Congress *raj* was coming, which they were apt to interpret as being inconsistent with British *raj*. It was a period of uneasy expectancy, nobody quite knowing what was likely to emerge. The non-Congress elements in the Legislative Assembly were sufficiently alarmed to try to sink their differences and get together, and a movement was started for forming a united opposition which would be advised from the background by Sir Tej Bahadur Sapru. This move however had not proceeded beyond discussion.

3. In these conditions the decision of the Congress not to take office involved everyone in a complete mental readjustment. Congressmen as a whole were, I think, very genuinely disappointed. They had pictured in bright colours the rewards of victory, the authority they would exercise, their power over their enemies and over the Services, and it was a bitter disappointment when these pictures suddenly vanished. In the villages I should imagine, though I have not yet had any very definite reports, that the immediate effect is likely to have been a considerable diminution in the prestige of Congress. Moderate Nationalist opinion seemed to forget its former apprehensions about the results of a Congress ministry and to realise very clearly the disadvantages of breaking away from constitutional

procedure. There seemed to be a feeling that the Congress had made a mistake not only from their own point of view but from the point of view of the country. It was presumably under the influence of feelings of this kind that the Liberals, without exception, refused to take office in the minority government. Not only did they refuse to co-operate, but the *Leader* has been pouring its contempt on the new government as freely as it pours its wrath on the Congress.

4. When Mr. Pant finally declined on the 29th March to form a government, I asked the Nawab of Chhatari the same evening to undertake this task. He was the only person to whom I could turn. The number of those in the Legislative Assembly not elected on the Congress ticket is 95. Of these 66 are Muslims; some 28 belonging to the Muslim League and the remaining 38 having a general allegiance to Chhatari. The 29 non-Congressmen consist of Hindu Zamindars, Scheduled Castes, special interests and minor minorities. It was evident that the new ministry must be led by a Muslim and that Chhatari had the greatest following among Muslims, particularly as a certain number of the Muslim Leaguers are not really in sympathy with the rather extreme policy of Khaliquzzaman, their leader, and are in fact naturally closer to Chhatari's views. Chhatari, however, found great difficulty in forming a ministry. Khaliq immediately declined to have anything to do with it and worked actively against its formation. The Liberals, whom Chhatari was anxious to include, unanimously declined. He tried Mr. Chintamani, Sir Maharaj Singh and Sir Sita Ram without success. He was thus thrown back practically on the landlord and conservative interest. He himself was in some difficulty, as he did not wish to be accused of disrupting the Muslims which, owing to the attitude of Khaliq, was bound to be the result of his forming a ministry. After some hesitation, however, he agreed to form a ministry, the members of which were in fact quite pleased to take office. It consisted, besides Chhatari, of my two ex-ministers, Sir Muhammad Yusuf and Sir J.P. Srivastava, the Raja of Salempur, who represents the right wing of the Muslim League, Raja Maheshwar Dayal Seth, one of the younger Taluqdars and an intelligent and liberal-minded landlord who had done a great deal of work in organising the Agriculturist Party in Oudh, and two other landlords without much experience of public affairs – the Maharajkumar of Vizianagram and the Raja of Tirwa. The communal composition is three Muslims and four Hindus. Under normal circumstances it had been assumed that the Cabinet would consist of two Muslims and four Hindus; but in view of the nature of the support to this ministry, the addition of another Muslim was inevitable.

5. The Muslim League position is obscure and uncertain. When the Congress appeared to be contemplating taking office, they had adopted a very rigid attitude with regard to the Muslims and it was understood that they would not take in any Muslim who did not sign the Congress pledge. The Muslim League, under the leadership of Khaliq, were exceedingly ready to come to a settlement with them, but the Congress showed no signs of accepting this position. On the other hand, as soon as Mr. Pant had seen me on March 24th and office acceptance appeared to be impossible, overtures were immediately made by the Congress to the Muslim League and I am told they were offered two seats in the cabinet. These negotiations have since continued and there is no doubt that the Muslim League are looking forward to an alliance with the Congress and taking office. What the intentions of the Congress may be in this manoeuvre it is difficult to understand.[6] At present it looks as if the new government will gradually attract to itself a fair number of the Muslim Leaguers, who are certainly not for the most part in sympathy with the Congress, and may be naturally inclined to support a government which is led by a Muslim.

6. The new Cabinet has possibilities. It is too early of course yet to say how it will shape; but it shows some signs of an inclination to take a fairly vigorous line and to try to evolve a policy of its own, not merely accepting as inevitable its extinction in three or four months and preparing for its own demise. There is even some talk of trying to secure a majority in August, though I confess I do not myself see how that could be possible. But Srivastava is essentially a fighter and fertile in expedients. The Chief Minister is keen on an idea, which he has had in his mind for many years, of solving the tenancy problem by a scheme of land purchase, and he intends to have the possibilities of this carefully examined in the Secretariat. One of the attractions to him of this idea is that it is one which has never been put before the electorate by the Congress,[7] for there is a general feeling that anything that may be done or attempted by the present ministry on the normal lines of tenancy reform would be regarded as indirectly the result of the Congress agitation and would merely send up the credit of the Congress.

7. Generally speaking, the conditions are not favourable for widespread agitation in the villages, for on the whole the harvest that is now being reaped is a good one and the prices of wheat and the other *rabi* crops have risen lately in a most satisfactory manner. There are, however, two unfortunate features. The sugar cane situation is giving rise to serious anxiety. The area under sugar cane this year is very much higher than it has ever been before and the supply of cane is undoubtedly a good deal

more than the market can properly absorb. This would have given rise to difficulty in any case, but the difficulty has been accentuated by the enhancement of the sugar excise duty. This has not been passed on to the consumer by a rise in the price of sugar and consequently the whole burden has fallen on the industry. There were threats, which though they may have contained an element of bluff, contained also an undoubted element of reality, that large numbers of sugar factories would close down on the 1st April. This would have been a major disaster for our sugar cane crop, for in the areas of chief production it was estimated that one-third of the crop was standing unsold on that date. To meet this situation, we reduced the minimum price of sugar cane by three pies a maund from the 1st April and that undoubtedly eased the situation. The factories are still working, but it will almost certainly be necessary to reduce the minimum price by another three pies from the 15th April, and probably by a further three pies from the 1st May. If this is done, it may be anticipated that the factories will for the most part work the full period and the cultivators although getting a reduced price will not be faced with a dead loss.[8] I may add that the figures we have got about sugar cane sowings for next year are reassuring, and do not think we shall have a recurrence of these conditions.

8. The other unfortunate feature was the very heavy hail-storm that struck a considerable area of the Province towards the end of February. The damage in certain areas was exceedingly severe, so much so that as a precaution famine test works have been opened in one or two places, though at present they are not attracting labourers. But when the harvest is reaped, we may find that certain small famine works have to be undertaken in particular localities, and a good deal of more general relief is being given. It still remains to be seen how rents will come in. There are no signs of any definite refusal to pay rent, but as a result of the Congress promises of wholesale reduction of rents there was in many places a marked reluctance to pay. I think that with the present government in office it may be anticipated that rents will come in fairly normally.

9. The present position is that the landlords have been considerably heartened by the new turn of events. The villagers seem at the moment to be settling down and waiting to see what will happen. There is no noticeable development of anti-British or anti-government feeling. On the other hand, the Congress have not yet shown their hand, and it is not clear what policy Jawaharlal Nehru will pursue. The new ministry are convinced that it would weaken their position fatally if they were to meet the legislature in April, and I am entirely in agreement with them. I do not therefore propose to summon the legislature until July or August. The Congress will be very

indignant at this decision, and may try to stage some spectacular demonstration.

Yours sincerely,
HARRY HAIG

24

HAIG TO LINLITHGOW
MSS.EUR.F 115/18

Private and Personal *April 10th, 1937*

With reference to Your Excellency's telegram No. 302-S, dated April 7, 1937,[9] about giving publicity in the vernacular to my communiqué announcing the breakdown of discussions with the Congress, I had been considering the general question how any effective publicity could be spread in the villages. My feeling was that my communiqué would be too technical in its language to be easily appreciated in the villages, and that even if it were shortened and simplified, Congress would be likely to represent in reply that they had been only too anxious to take office in order to carry out their promises to the tenants, but that when they asked for the assurances which alone would have enabled them to carry out those promises, they were refused by the Governor. My communiqué might even make propaganda of this type look plausible in the villages. I have since heard that the Congress have in fact already started propaganda on these lines and have issued a leaflet in the villages making this statement.

I have given a good deal of thought to this question as a whole, and my view at present is that publicity of the restrained and balanced type, which alone a Governor could under present circumstances use, would be ineffective as against Congress publicity which is restrained by no canons of truth or fair play. Propaganda in the villages against the Congress to be effective must be vigorous and must attack them strongly on their weak points, and accuse them of having misled the electorate and having shirked their opportunities of trying to make good their promises. This can only be put out by a party organisation. My ministers are considering at the moment the organisation of party propaganda on a large scale. I cannot yet say whether they will in fact embark on this, though they are I believe very favourably disposed to the idea. Unless they do take this up, I fear there is not much that can be done by ordinary publicity statements in the villages; but I will continue to consider the matter closely, for I realise its importance.

25

HAIG TO LINLITHGOW
R/3/1/2

Private and Confidential

Camp,
April 23rd, 1937

My dear Lord Linlithgow,

I am sending my second fortnightly report on political conditions in the United Provinces under the new Constitution. The new ministry has settled down to its work most vigorously and effectively, and I am more than pleased with the spirit in which it is tackling its difficult task. At the beginning they were naturally uncertain about their future. The stream of propaganda from the English edited press in India, particularly the *Statesman*, in favour of negotiations with the Congress, and the prominence given to the constant statements of Lord Lothian,[10] produced an impression that His Majesty's government were contemplating some compromise which would install the Congress in power and send the new ministries in discredit out of their offices almost as soon as they had assumed them. A complete change came over the situation, however, with the speech of the Secretary of State,[11] which was felt to indicate quite plainly that the British government stood firmly by the position which it had already taken up, and made it pretty clear that the new government could depend on remaining in office at any rate until about August when it would have to meet the Legislature. A small matter at the very beginning gave an indication of the spirit of the ministry. When considering the coronation celebrations, they felt it desirable to go rather beyond the suggestions made by the Government of India, and decided to hold durbars in every district, as they felt that this would really be appreciated by loyal people and be an encouragement to them. One of their first actions which has caused considerable consternation in the secretariat was to decide against moving the headquarters of government this year to Naini Tal. This was more than a mere popular gesture. The ministers felt strongly that in the peculiar conditions now prevailing, they must themselves remain throughout the hot weather in the plains in the closest touch with men and affairs, and they were also anxious to show that Rajas and Nawabs were as capable of facing the discomforts of a hot weather as any Congress patriot. The retention of the secretariat in Lucknow was really incidental to this main principle. Actually the conditions for the Secretaries will not be so bad as they had at first anticipated. They will probably all be allowed to go up to Naini Tal for about six weeks during the worst part of the hot weather, though the ministers intend to stay down almost continuously. I myself am moving up on the 10th May so as to hold the coronation celebrations in Naini Tal, and I propose to remain there till about the 15th July, when I shall come down again for six weeks or two months.

2. The ministry has also put up a very vigorous answer[12] to the attacks made upon them by the Congress, justifying their assumption of office and carrying the war into the enemy's country by accusing the Congress of running away from their responsibilities and dishonouring their promises to the villagers. It is interesting to observe that though Pant and other Congressmen have replied to this statement with a good deal of personal abuse, they have said nothing on the main point brought against the Congress, which confirms the impression that there is really no effective answer to this line of argument. The ministry have taken steps to have their statement circulated very widely throughout the Province, in villages as well as towns, and I think its effect should be good. The whole question of publicity, however, is engaging their close attention. They realise that the feature of the next few months is likely to be the propaganda campaign on both sides. They have no party organisation at present, which can do propaganda for them, and they appreciate clearly the limitations, both constitutional and practical, on propaganda through government agency. They are still discussing intensively methods and principles, but the present idea is to use the government agency to the fullest extent that would constitutionally be reasonable, and at the same time to develop as rapidly as possible their own party organisation. For this purpose funds are essential. They hope that the nucleus will be provided by the landlord associations, and they are fairly sanguine of getting some Rs. 40,000 quickly. With this sum they ought to be able to work up a fairly effective organisation throughout the Province.

3. They are also paying great attention to the personal side of publicity. For instance, in dealing with the difficult problems of fixing the minimum price of sugar cane, which I referred to in my last letter, they decided that the minister concerned should, in the first place, go to Meerut, hold a conference with the factory owners, the cultivators and the local officials and then announce on the spot a decision which had already been taken by the cabinet. The minister also paid a similar visit to Gorakhpur. Again, the Chief Minister and the Revenue Minister paid a visit to the Cawnpore district in order to announce personally in a number of villages the remissions that are being given on account of the hail-storm. This appears

to have had an excellent effect locally, particularly as it had been suggested that as the Congress had refused to take office, it was not known what remissions, if any, would be granted. The same two ministers intend to pay a similar visit to a number of villages very badly affected in the Rae Bareli district. The effect of all this is to show, at any rate in these districts, that the action that is being taken is not being taken by the Congress, but in spite of the Congress.

4. With regard to policy generally, I am glad to find that the ministry are not really anxious to go in for pretentious promises, which every one would know they could not possibly carry out and which would merely present an unconvincing imitation of the Congress programme. For a moment some of them were somewhat attracted by this idea, after the publication of the Bombay programme, but they soon realised that this would do them no good, and that it was wiser to continue on their own lines and to devote themselves to a programme which could be reduced to practical measures that could be laid before the Legislature when it meets. The main item will be tenancy reform. They are intending to set up a committee very shortly to recommend immediate action. The main item, which I hope they will accept, will be the grant of occupancy rights to all tenants in chief. But this will probably be supplemented by a number of measures directed to removing the many grievances in small matters and the petty tyrannies from which the tenants suffer. The provisions for ejectment for non-payment of rent might also be made less stringent with general advantage. If the present arbitrary powers of landlords in matters which closely concern the tenants, such as the grant of land for building houses or the right to plant trees and so on, are removed, the opportunities for the landlords' servants to bully the tenants will be greatly reduced. With regard to the pitch of rents and stability of rent, this matter is already being tackled by the comprehensive re-settlement and revision programme that we are carrying on, and the new ministry intend to continue with this. The position therefore, if this policy works out as I hope it may, would be that tenants would have real stability of tenure and fair rents, while our finances would not be affected by any reductions in land revenue or lowering of canal rates which would involve the Province in bankruptcy unless new measures of taxation falling inevitably on landlords were introduced.

5. Another measure which the ministry are likely to take up energetically though of course the actual construction of the scheme would take time, is the proposal for a hydro-electric grid in the east of the Province which appears to be a very attractive proposition and financially sound. They

will also apply themselves to such measures as may be possible in relief of educated employment. The old government went into this matter in some detail and various measures which they had approved have not yet been introduced. The new government will be able to take credit for these.

6. The Congress M.L.As. held a meeting at Lucknow to consider their policy on the 11th April. A day or two before I received a letter from Pant[13] in which he asked me to inform him before the meeting what was my intention about summoning the Legislature. I replied, after consultation with the cabinet, that I had no immediate intention of summoning the Legislature, and that I proposed to do so when my ministers were in a position to place their budget proposals and programme before it. This decision was criticised on the lines anticipated, and the Congress have now called a meeting at Lucknow early in May, to which they have invited all M.L.As. and at which they talk about formulating a programme for the Assembly, in order to give effect to the will of the people. Whether they will go so far as some of their more extreme members suggest and pretend to function as if they were the Legislature seems to me a little doubtful, particularly as the number of non-Congress M.L.As. who may attend this meeting is likely to be small. The agitation for calling the Legislature in so far as it is based on the rights and responsibilities of the legislators is very hollow, inasmuch as the avowed intention of the Congress, if the Legislature were summoned, would be to create a situation in which the Governor would have to take over the administration, the Legislature would be suspended and the legislators would therefore be at once deprived of their rights and responsibilities.

7. My impression is that the more Congress look at the situation, the more unsatisfactory it appears to be from their point of view, and particularly in the eyes of the rank and file. They will see the ministry doing and proposing things that they would naturally have done themselves and for which they might have expected to get the credit. They have no real answer to the charge that they have deceived the electorate; and if they spread propaganda in the villages to the effect that they have been prevented by the Governor from carrying out their promises to the tenants, in very many cases the reaction of the villages will not be resentment against the Governor, because promises which always seemed a little too good to be true have not been fulfilled, but a feeling that the Congress were promising what they could not perform and that the Governor is a stronger power than the Congress. It seems clear that the Congress have no intention at present of embarking on revolutionary agitation, and if that is their temper, the pressure to accept the constitutional powers that await

them seems likely to become steadily stronger. Even if that does not produce a change in the official policy of the Congress, there is perhaps a growing likelihood that many of those who have entered the Legislature on the Congress ticket, without being very convinced Congressmen, will not indefinitely allow themselves to be deprived of the power and privileges to which they have been looking forward as members of the Assembly; and therefore even if the Constitution has to be suspended for a time, it seems to me possible that before long some combination might be found with a view to forming a Government which would be in a position to command a majority.

8. There is great activity in connection with Muslim affairs and it is difficult to keep track of all developments. Broadly speaking, what has happened is this. Khaliq, who is at the moment President of the Muslim League Parliamentary Board, has begun almost openly to identify himself with the Congress. He had an interview with Jawaharlal Nehru with a view to settling the terms on which the Muslims could join the Congress, and as Chairman of the Municipal Board, Lucknow, he invited Govind Ballabh Pant to perform with due ceremonial the hoisting of the Congress flag over the Municipal office. These activities, combined with the avowed policy of the Congress to capture the Muslim masses, have seriously alarmed the non-Congress Muslims. Jinnah has made clear his strong opposition to the Muslims joining the Congress. Shaukat Ali has been enlisted on the same side, and at a meeting of the Muslim League Parliamentary Board which is to be held on the 25th of April it looks as if battle will be joined. If so, Khaliq is likely to be defeated and might be driven out of the League into the Congress, which the more moderate Muslims would regard as a very satisfactory solution. They do not think he would carry with him more than ten M.L.A. followers. On the other hand, Khaliq, who is nothing if not adroit, may not wish to burn his boats in this manner, and if he finds himself in danger of defeat may try to remain in the Muslim League by accepting some kind of compromise. But on the whole the non-Congress Muslims are very much alive to the dangers of the situation and are very active. They are contemplating themselves approaching the masses through the Maulvis whose popular talents appear to be available to both sides for a consideration. This however requires the raising of money, which is always a difficulty.

9. The meeting of the non-Congress M.L.As. and M.L.Cs. called by Chhatari on the 18th April in Lucknow was not a success, mainly because Sir Maharaj Singh made a very strong speech attacking the formation of the ministry and the failure to summon the Legislature. There is no doubt

that this speech, coming from one who only a few weeks ago was occupying the position of Home Member to this government, had a very disintegrating effect on the supporters of the ministry. The ministers resented it greatly, as it appeared to be unnecessary for him to express these damaging views or to attend the meeting at all if he did not agree with them. There is a general belief that Sir Maharaj Singh has close natural affinities with the right wing of the Congress. The attitude of the Europeans and Anglo-Indians also was somewhat disappointing to the ministry, as they refused to commit themselves to anything without consulting their constituents. It may be that the minor minorities are somewhat apprehensive of antagonizing the Congress unnecessarily, realising that at any moment the Congress might take the power that is within their grasp.

10. On the other hand, the depressed classes, or some of them, are agitating continuously for the inclusion of a Scheduled Caste minister in the present government, and it is believed that some of the Scheduled Caste representatives elected on the Congress ticket might be won over. I fear, however, this resolves itself mainly into a matter of personal interest. The Scheduled Castes representatives are mostly at loggerheads with each other, and each potential leader is looking to his own advantage.

11. On the whole, I think that the ministry have definitely strengthened their position in the last fortnight and are working well together and working hard. They are certainly not popular. They are denounced as reactionaries and government men. There are still many dissensions and jealousies among those who ought to be supporting them, and the effect of Sir Maharaj Singh's speech shows how very precarious their hold is even on their professed followers. Nevertheless power attracts respect, and at present they are using their power wisely. In the Province as a whole I think the estimate given in my last report holds good. Congress have lost ground by not taking office, and vigorous propaganda against them might have considerable effect on the now doubtful and slightly sceptical villager. I shall however be in a better position to form a judgement on this matter after the 1st May, when we are holding a Commissioners' conference which I hope will be of value from many points of view, both in giving us first-hand information of what is going on throughout the Province and in bringing Commissioners in touch with the ministers and their policy.

Yours sincerely,

HARRY HAIG

26

HAIG TO LINLITHGOW
MSS.EUR.F 125/126

Private and Confidential

Camp,
April 24th, 1937

My dear Lord Linlithgow,

Your Excellency's letter of April 10th, 1937,[14] regarding publicity and propaganda deals with a subject that had been causing me a good deal of thought, and lays down principles of great value in the present difficult and unusual conditions. I have found it of great use, and am generally in complete agreement with Your Excellency's views.

2. I agree that present conditions probably justify some degree of propaganda through government agency beyond what would normally be permissible. There is of course the danger of creating a bad precedent which would be followed by future governments, and this is a limiting consideration which should certainly be borne in mind. At the same time, as some of my ministers are inclined to argue, if the Congress come into office they will probably endeavour to do what suits them, whether there is or is not a precedent, while on the other hand their propaganda machinery is so well organised that there might be little temptation for them to use Government agency in an unreasonable way.

3. This question of publicity and propaganda is recognised by my ministry to be an issue of the first importance at the present moment, and we have had already two discussions about it at our cabinet meetings. A sub-committee of the cabinet is going to examine the matter further, and we shall also discuss it at the Commissioners' conference which is to be held on the 1st of May. The necessity of publicity through government agency on the one hand and of propaganda through a party organisation on the other is generally accepted. The difficulty lies in fixing the dividing line between these two, and also in the fact that the party organisation does not at the moment exist, while the need for action is urgent.

4. While there is a general recognition of the constitutional limitations on the use of government agency, there is some difference of opinion as to the practical value of trying to put out propaganda in this way. It is urged that propaganda coming openly from government sources is always suspected, and that in the matter of distribution (e.g. of leaflets) the government agency which consists largely of patwaris is unreliable, as

the elections have shown plainly that a great majority of the Patwaris are definite supporters of the Congress. Moreover, it is recognised that the mere written word does not go very far. It requires to be supplemented by the spoken word; and this can hardly be done in a systematic manner by government servants, nor can government servants under present conditions organise public meetings. On the other hand, it is recognised that while propaganda carried on through a party organisation may be in many ways much more effective, it requires in the first place funds and in the second place it takes time to organise So far as funds are concerned, the Ministry hope to get some Rs. 40,000 quickly, in the main from the British India Association and a few of the larger landlords. Once they have the money, they are fairly hopeful that they would be able to develop an effective organisation pretty soon; but at present the idea is that in the starting of such an organisation some unobtrusive assistance from district officers will be required. When once the party organisation is properly started, it will work in very closely with the government publicity organisation.

5. With reference to publicity by the Governor himself through statements or speeches, I appreciate that in certain circumstances this may be necessary. But in present conditions it seems to me better, as far as possible, to leave publicity of this kind to the ministry. For instance, I myself suggested to my ministers a good many of the points which they included in their statement justifying their position, which also contained a vigorous attack on the Congress position and a reply to many of the arguments that Pandit Govind Ballabh Pant had used in writing to my Secretary about summoning the Legislature. I could not myself have made nearly such an effective rejoinder, as it is not desirable that I should be drawn into a personal controversy with the Congress leader. But, as I have said above, I fully recognise that on special occasions a carefully phrased statement of the position may be required from the Governor.

6. I am also very fully in agreement about the necessity of the position being made plain to government servants. This idea has been elaborated in Your Excellency's letter of April 16th,[15] and before I received that I had already been thinking on precisely these lines. One of our Commissioners had written in suggesting that government servants generally were somewhat bewildered and unable to follow the political situation, and when I went off for a few days' shooting I took the opportunity of drafting out a pretty full statement of the main points at issue and some indication of possible developments in the future which I had decided to send to all Commissioners, District Officers and Superintendents of Police with

instructions to use the material contained in it freely in conversation with their own subordinates, with officers of other departments of government and with non-officials. Just as I had completed it I received Your Excellency's letter of April 16th and was very glad to find that our views were so completely in accord. I enclose for your information a copy of this letter[16] which is being issued by the Chief Secretary and which will, I hope, help our officers generally to understand the position more clearly. I think it may be desirable to follow this up from time to time by further letters or bulletins as suggested by Your Excellency. I am inclined to think, however, that it would not be wise to communicate anything direct to the lower grades of officers. I think it is better to give a fully argued statement of the case to superior officers and let them pass it on in their own way to their subordinates. I should like to repeat how very fully I am in agreement with Your Excellency's general estimate of the position as given in your letter of April 16th.

7. I also agree fully that if the Governor has to assume power under Section 93 of the Act, he will have to undertake vigorous propaganda through government agencies throughout the Province. A great deal was done on these lines during the civil disobedience movement and much experience was gained. We are now reviewing the position, and if the situation arises, we shall I hope be ready with suitable machinery. It should also be possible to work in with the party organisation which by that time we may hope will have been established.

8. As to methods, the press and leaflets are undoubtedly important; but these require to be supplemented by a more personal approach by word of mouth. That is where the Congress have their great advantage at present. They have their sympathisers and workers in almost every village. Something can undoubtedly be done by government servants, but more perhaps indirectly than directly, and it is certainty important that they should be kept fully and regularly informed of the situation and lines of arguments. Meetings too have their value; but these and the more personal side of propaganda can best he carried out by a party organisation. I think one must also remember that actions speak as loudly as words, and that the general attitude of the countryside, if the Governor has to take over the administration, will be largely determined by the vigour and resolution of government policy, which will very quickly be reflected in the attitude of government servants.

Yours sincerely,
HARRY HAIG

27

HAIG TO LINLITHGOW
MSS.EUR.F. 125/126

Personal and Confidential

Camp,
April 29th, 1937

My dear Lord Linlithgow,

Many thanks for Your Excellency's letter of 27th April 1937 about publicity and propaganda.[17] With reference to what I said in paragraph 7 of my letter of April 24th about working in with a non-Congress party organisation, all I had in mind was that, broadly speaking, the way in which people in this Province always look at these questions at present is that the Congress are on one side and "government" on the other. This view would be accentuated if, owing to the action of the Congress, the Governor had to take over the administration. The Governor must keep as many people and as much public opinion as possible on his side, and those whom he would find in general supporting him, would be precisely those who would be supporting any non-Congress party that may have been formed. Broadly speaking, therefore, the activities of the Governor on the main issues of policy would be likely to be supported by, or at any rate not in conflict with, the main objectives of the non-Congress party; and if it was a question of countering revolutionary activities, as it well might be, the Governor might get valuable support from such a party. I did not mean that I should place too much reliance on any such organisation,[18] for one cannot be very sure that it will have been called into existence, or that it would be functioning with any vigour. All I had in mind was that a great deal of the government propaganda might be adopted and disseminated by such an organisation if it were in existence. But I quite agree that the Governor should depend essentially on his own machinery.

Yours sincerely,
HARRY HAIG

28

HAIG TO LINLITHGOW
R/3/1/2

Private and Confidential

Camp,
May 7th, 1937

My dear Lord Linlithgow,

I am sending my third fortnightly report on political conditions in the United Provinces under the new constitution. The state of uncertainty regarding Congress intentions continues unchanged, even after the Allahabad discussions, and this uncertainty produces a paralysing effect on all the minor interests whose first concern is to avoid being crushed by the impact of more powerful forces, and on the large army of temporizers and self-seekers who do not know which way to turn.

2. I might begin by giving the general impression conveyed to me by the Commissioners whom we had summoned for a conference on the 1st May. We discussed among other things the existing conditions in their divisions. I think there is no doubt that the rather dangerous elation among Congress supporters of which there were indications in March has died down. The villages are outwardly quiet, and there is no reason to think that the material there is at present in an inflammable state. There are no acute grievances. There are no doubt many things which the villagers would like to obtain and which they are hoping to get through Congress agency, but the pitch of rents with the large remissions granted at the time of the slump still in force is not unreasonable, and on the whole the *rabi* harvest has been a good one. The grievances therefore are the normal grievances to which the tenants have been long accustomed. There is nothing outstanding on which agitation can be founded. The Congress impression created in the villages by the election still remains very strong. The only propaganda which the villager hears is Congress propaganda. In some areas Congress influence is being kept alive continuously by active work. In others work seems to be in abeyance, possibly owing to some shortage of funds. But in many places the Congress organizations are functioning actively, collecting grievances and trying to take the credit for any remedial action taken by Government. It would seem that at present the villagers in general are still expecting that Congress will grant them the promised benefits. No idea has yet become prevalent that owing to the Congress refusal of office these benefits may not be received. It is being preached

sedulously that any benefits that may come from the government will be extorted by the Congress. This of course is entirely in accordance with the general mentality of the villager. He still looks upon the government as the authority and Congress as the agitating force whereby government may be moved to act. The conception of Congress themselves being the government and able to act on their own responsibility has probably not penetrated very far into village minds, and at the moment I imagine it is not an idea that Congressmen are concerned to spread. There is some tendency, particularly in the east of the Province, for tenants to be backward in paying rent, and there is some talk of their paying only what they can afford. But there are no signs of any concerted or deliberate refusal to pay rent. The tone of some speeches, particularly in the east of the Province, is unsatisfactory, and it would seem that action may be needed for checking them. This matter will have to come before the cabinet shortly. On the other hand, there are no signs of Congress as a whole desiring to embark at present on any direct action movement. The rank and file of the Congress workers would seem to have their minds still turned towards the taking of office, and what could be achieved by taking office.

3. The main problem that has been confronting the cabinet during the fortnight is the preparation of its programme, and in particular its attitude towards tenancy reform. The Revenue Minister, Raja Maheshwar Dayal Seth, is a firm believer in pursuing a liberal policy towards the tenants, and he placed before the cabinet proposals for setting up a committee at once with a view to preparing Bills to amend the Agra and Oudh Tenancy Acts which could be placed before the Legislature in August. The proposed terms of reference to the committee which were detailed covered a number of general grievances of the tenants, but the main item was the grant of hereditary rights to statutory tenants. In the Agra Province, where occupancy rights are already very largely enjoyed, this would affect about 25 per cent. of the tenants but in Oudh, where occupancy rights are practically unknown, it would probably affect some 75 per cent. These proposals were approved by the cabinet who believed that representatives of the landlords would be prepared to serve on the proposed committee. They decided, however, before proceeding further, to have informal discussions with the British Indian Association of Oudh and the Agra Zamindars' Association. These discussions took place at the beginning of the week and were more formal and larger than had originally been contemplated. The British Indian Association representatives expressed themselves as absolutely opposed to any action of the sort at the moment; the Agra Zamindars' Association by a majority agreed to the cabinet

proposals. The objections of the Oudh Taluqdars represented in part that element of backwoodsmen who, while in a state of panic two months ago, now consider that no concessions at all should be made to the tenants. But though the grant of hereditary rights to statutory tenants would be generally disliked by the Taluqdars, a great many of them realise that it is bound to come before long, and appreciate the probability that if I have to take over the administration, a measure of this kind might be carried out by me. The principal objection of men of this mode of thinking is one of tactics. They think that, particularly at the present moment so soon after the elections, any concessions given to the tenants would be generally believed to be the result of Congress action; and it cannot be denied that at present that is the general feeling in the villages. But besides that they are most reluctant to give away anything for nothing. Their argument is that the present ministry cannot in fact carry through any proposals for tenancy reform, and therefore it is merely a matter of saying what they propose to do; and to say in advance that they are prepared to give hereditary rights seems to them unwise. When the time comes they will be prepared to give way, but they clearly hope that they will be able to strike some bargain and get some compensation. Even if they have to face the Congress, they feel that their position will be stronger in resisting more sweeping proposals if they have not already voluntarily surrendered the principle of hereditary rights. They are in fact concerned over the tactics of bargaining. The cabinet felt the disadvantage of not being able to put forward any definite proposals in connection with tenancy reform; but they considered, and in my opinion rightly, that it was out of the question to make proposals which would antagonize the greater part of their supporters. They therefore gave up the idea of appointing any kind of committee, and put a somewhat colourless sentence into their programming which kept alive an examination into the possibility of reform of the Tenancy Acts.

4. The cabinet's programme, of which I enclose a copy,[19] was published yesterday. I think it is a good document, and I am told first reactions are favourable. It is of course very highly coloured in the sense that it is suggested that all the ideas and schemes are well on their way to introduction, whereas many of them have only just been thought of and hardly examined. But as a programme for the next five years or so it has considerable merits, and they have endeavoured not to propose measures which would be likely to be beyond the financial resources of the Province or outside practical politics. They have made a great point of the relief of debt in the villages, which they contend, and I think rightly, is a more pressing problem for the villager than the reduction of rent. This is a relief

that could be given at the expense of the moneylender instead of the landlord, and as the Bania is invariably a supporter of Congress, this is not only economically sound but good politics. Much may be made of this point later.

5. I wish I could see clearer signs of any development of a party to support the government or oppose the Congress, or any prospects of party organisation. As a government I think the cabinet is continuing to work excellently, but they are not gathering to themselves that political support which one had hoped they would be able to command. The idea that they would form a solid nucleus to which other elements would as time went on attach themselves does not seem likely to be fulfilled. The old jealousies, personal and communal, are not far below the surface; and in any case the landlords have no sense of discipline or unity, except in defence of what they claim to be their rights. The latest idea, which perhaps contains an element of soundness, is that instead of trying to start a new party, which means an elaborate paper organisation on the top and a good deal of quarrelling about offices and positions, they should try to start practical work in each district by developing an organisation which would not primarily be a political party, but would be devoted to the promotion of good relations between landlords and tenants. They think of calling it the "Desh Sevak" (service of the country), and the idea would be that each of the seven ministers would in the next month or so take seven districts and get local people (not necessarily the wealthy and high placed) who really would be prepared to work, to start such an organisation. This would give them what they badly need, and that is some machinery for putting out their propaganda; and it might also do what is equally required, and that is encourage the landlords to maintain better relations and closer touch with their tenants.

6. The Muslims are at the moment disintegrated and completely uncertain of their policy. This situation has been created partly by the strong bid that the Congress are making for attracting the Muslim masses and partly by the personal ambitions and adroit manoeuvrings of Chaudhri Khaliquzzaman, who is the leader of the Muslim League Parliamentary Board. The Muslims are frankly alarmed at the Congress attempt on the Muslim masses and fear it may be successful. In the absence of a strong and united Muslim policy some are inclined to wonder whether it is wise to oppose such a powerful body as the Congress. On the other hand, the majority, I believe, are determined to oppose the Congress, and are only waiting for a lead. This they seem likely to get from Jinnah. As for Khaliq's manoeuvres, I shall not attempt any prophecy as to what will be the

outcome. His main object is to secure a minister's post for himself. He has endeavoured to do this by joining the Congress, but I gather his personal reception by Jawaharlal Nehru was not very cordial. He is working at present for a close understanding between the Muslim League and Congress, with the idea that if the Congress come into power, they will have to take a Muslim minister from the Muslim League. But he has gone so far in the direction of negotiating with the Congress that large numbers of Muslims, including Mr. Jinnah, are seriously disturbed and an important meeting is taking place today in which there will be a trial of strength between Jinnah and Khaliq. This may clear the atmosphere. But the confusion in the Muslim ranks is a definite source of weakness to the government.

7. The Congress members of the Assembly are holding a meeting on the 9th and 10th May, and have invited all other members of the Assembly. On the whole the non-Congress members seem to intend to keep away, but a certain number have announced their intention of going, professedly in order to argue with the Congress and persuade them to take office.

8. The prospects for the future are wholly uncertain. There is still a fairly widespread belief that the Congress may take office, and that seems to be the definite desire of a great many non-Congress people. The approaching meeting may afford an opportunity for this body of opinion to bring itself to bear on the Congress members. But the Congress will be bound by their all-India policy. Meantime, the depressed classes continue to agitate their claim for a post of minister, and the cabinet will be considering shortly whether it might be wise to concede their claim.

Yours sincerely,
HARRY HAIG

P.S.: I am sending a copy of this letter direct to the Secretary of State.

29

HAIG TO LINLITHGOW
Telegram
MSS.EUR.F. 115/18

Private and Personal *May 13th, 1937*
No. 7-G

I have received copies of two resolutions passed by the meeting of M.L.As. at Lucknow on 9th May: the one declaring non-confidence in present ministers; the other calling upon Governor to convene the Assembly forthwith.

2. I feel it is desirable for me to reply somewhat fully. The actions of the Governor have been rather widely criticised; there is a perfectly good answer and silence suggests that my action cannot be justified. From my point of view therefore I consider an argued statement of an essentially constitutional kind, but avoiding the controversies as to causes of Congress refusing office, is desirable. I believe also it may be of value in this Province to bring the rank and file of the Congress at an early stage up against the consequences of the present policy and give them plenty of time to think over their course of action. For this purpose it is essential for me to indicate my assumption that if, when the Legislature is summoned, the Congress decline to form a ministry and decline to allow any other ministry to function the Constitution and presumably the Legislature itself will be suspended. If I can put this point clearly I can then end, as I wish to, by saying that when the Legislature is summoned the responsibility for deciding on the future constitutional development of this province will lie in its hands.

3. As Your Excellency knows my view is definitely that if a breakdown comes it will be necessary to suspend the whole Constitution including the Legislature. But though I am very anxious to indicate this view, I am not sure whether it would be embarrassing to Your Excellency's policy or not in accordance with your present views. My own belief is that administratively there are very strong arguments for this course and that politically nothing is so likely to bring a change in the attitude of a considerable number of members of the Assembly as its suspension. At present I gather that many Congressmen have a vague idea either that a breakdown will be followed by another election, or that the Legislature will be allowed to continue in operation enjoying the privilege of irresponsible criticism like the Assembly at the Centre. That of course would be an arrangement that would exactly suit the Congress M.L.As.

4. I am discussing with my cabinet tomorrow the question of the issue of some such statement. One possible difficulty has emerged in conversation with Chhatari. He seems to contemplate the possibility suggested to him by Raghavendra Rao[20] of the Central Provinces that the ministry would resign before meeting the Legislature. If that were their intention I should find it difficult to justify not summoning the Legislature at an early date, for one of the main grounds in my opinion for not summoning is that the ministry should have a chance of meeting the

Legislature and placing its detailed measures before it. I doubt if the cabinet as a whole would support Chhatari's views, which seem to me to indicate timidity.

5. There is however another point which, as it also came from Raghavendra Rao, is possibly also connected with this idea. That is that the ministry after resigning and being provided with finance by the Governor's powers should again take office and function still in a minority. I have always felt that this would be constitutionally unjustifiable and I do not believe that my ministers would be prepared to hold office on such humiliating terms. I mention this because another point I wished to make in my statement was that I had no intention of endeavouring to maintain indefinitely in office a ministry which does not command the support of the Legislature. I think it is most desirable to make that plain to the public.

30

HAIG TO LINLITHGOW
MSS.EUR.F. 115/18

Private and Personal *May 16th, 1937*

I have despatched this morning my answer to Babu Purshottam Das Tandon and enclose a copy for Your Excellency's information.[21] I think what I have said is, from the point of view of this Province, worth while, and as I mentioned in the telegram I have just sent to Your Excellency[22] I hope it will not be in any way embarrassing to your policy. Your telegram of the 14th May[23] has been of very great value to me.

2. With regard to Chhatari, I should be grateful if Your Excellency could stress the undesirability of the ministry resigning before meeting the Legislature. Chhatari is greatly attracted by this idea; but most of the remainder of the cabinet are at present I think convinced that they ought to meet the Legislature. But if Chhatari continues to press on them the more timid view, their morale may be weakened. If Your Excellency could also endeavour to hearten Chhatari generally it would certainly be useful. I am afraid he really has little belief in what he is doing and little heart in it, and this attitude is not encouraging to the cabinet.

2. [3.] With regard to the possibility of another minority ministry taking office after a breakdown, though, as I have said, I do not think this could be regarded as a practical possibility in this province (because I do not think we could find people to face such a position) I should like to make

clear to Your Excellency what I meant when I said that I felt this would be constitutionally unjustifiable. The ministers have, under the constitution, very wide powers as against the Governor. The justification for their exercising those powers is that they are responsible to the Legislature. If in fact they are not responsible to the Legislature, we are installing in power a body of men who are really responsible to no one – neither to their own Legislature nor to the British Parliament. As a temporary measure that situation, which is not likely to give rise to practical difficulty, can well be faced, as it is being faced now; but I do feel that it would be difficult to justify carrying it on over any prolonged period. I have felt this for a long time, but I have seen recently that Rajagopalachariar[24] has raised the same point. Apart from this constitutional aspect, I do not myself understand how ministers could face the situation. It will either be necessary to avoid summoning the Legislature for a long period, or the ministry would find themselves, when the Legislature was sitting, subjected to daily humiliations; and I should have supposed that they would have been utterly discredited in a very short time. I am conscious that satisfactory arrangements for administration under Section 93 are not easy to devise. I hope to write to Your Excellency after a little time on this subject; but it seems to me that the Governor will have to be himself responsible, his responsibility being to Parliament.

31

HAIG TO LINLITHGOW
L/PO/6/100: FF. 20-9

Secret and Personal

Governor's Camp,
May 21st, 1937

[Dear Lord Linlithgow,]

I am writing at once in answer to Your Excellency's secret and personal letter of May 18th, 1937.[25] I feel I can do so, because I have given a good deal of thought recently to the problems discussed in your letter, and I find myself practically throughout in agreement with Your Excellency's views and conclusions.

2. In the first place, I may deal generally with the considerations stated in para. 21 of your letter. I should like you to understand that I not only acquiesce in these views, but believe in them. In March last the situation in this province appeared to me to be very menacing. Every one with whom I discussed it, and by no means merely the die-hard element, was

agreed that Congress would take office with the intention of preparing the way, after a short time, for a revolutionary movement, and the mischief that could be done by a Congress government in six months under these conditions would obviously be very great. Nevertheless, I accepted the inevitability of the views expressed by Your Excellency, particularly in your telegram No. 176-S, dated the 19th March, 1937,[26] and having made up my mind to a Congress government I was genuinely disappointed when it became clear on the 24th March that the Congress would not take office. Since that time, the situation in this Province has changed very greatly. As I have explained to Your Excellency in my various reports, the dangerous spirit of elation among the Congress supporters has disappeared and there has been to my mind an increasingly plain development of constitutional ideas among the Congress and indications that a great many of them desire to work the Constitution genuinely. As we shall not get any real solution of our difficulties in this Province until the advanced elements have undertaken responsibility and tried their hand at administration, and as the practical dangers of that course have to my mind greatly diminished in the last two months, I am fully in agreement that we should do everything we reasonably can to encourage the Congress now to take office.

3. I am therefore fully in agreement with Your Excellency's intentions, as expressed in paras. 2 and 3 of your letter, to take any steps that may be possible, within the terms of the Act and of the policy hitherto adopted, to facilitate office acceptance. I am afraid, however, I have not been able to think of any definite step that can be taken other than further assurances on the same lines as those already given. An assurance by Your Excellency would certainly be valuable and in my opinion is very desirable; but it has its limitations, for it will be necessary to be careful (and I realise that it is Your Excellency's intention to be careful) not to compromise the fundamental position we have hitherto taken, namely, standing strictly on the basis of the Act, though administering that Act in the most liberal spirit. I say this in particular, because, though the minorities have not been very vocal, I am convinced from a number of conversations, that the minority communities generally, and not merely the Muslims, are profoundly grateful for the line which His Majesty's government have taken. As to the Muslims, anything which suggests a weakening in the safeguard in section 52 of the Act in regard to minorities would create a situation the outcome of which it would be difficult to foresee; but it might so weaken the position of those who are at present in control of the bulk of Muslim opinion that we might find the Muslims going over as a whole to the Congress. That danger I know is fully before Your Excellency, and

there is nothing in your letter which suggests any kind of intention of taking action which might produce such a result. I merely mention the point because it seems to me that if we are not going to move from our fundamental position, there really is not much that can be done on the lines discussed in paras. 2 and 3 of your letter. I am proposing myself to make a speech on Wednesday next the 26th, as mentioned in para. 2 of my telegram No. G-8 dated May 16th.[27] I hope this will fit in with Your Excellency's general plans.

4. I might at this point say a word about the issue of dismissal versus resignation discussed in para. 20 of your letter. The question has always presented itself to me in the light of an attack on the principle of para. 8 of the Instrument of Instructions.[28] Under that paragraph the Governor, if he finds it necessary to disagree with the advice of his ministers, takes action in accordance with his own views. It is then left to the ministers, if they find themselves unable to acquiesce in the action taken by the Governor, to resign. The Congress demand, as I understand it, is that instead of that procedure the Governor, if he differed from his ministers, should have no power to act inconsistently with their advice, but would be bound, if he felt it necessary to insist on his view, to dismiss his ministers. This was in fact, as Your Excellency will see from my telegram No. 3-G dated the 24th March,[29] one of the suggestions made to me by Pant in our first interview. It would be equivalent to abandoning the principle laid down in the Instrument of Instructions, and would of course most gravely weaken the power of the Governor to fulfil his special responsibilities. I understand from Your Excellency's letter that there is no question of trying to meet the Congress on this point. I am sure that the Muslims would feel that it would be equivalent to abolishing their safeguards.

5. With regard to the possibility of an early summoning of the Legislature, I have already expressed my views publicly in the letter sent to Purshottam Das Tandon.[30] The arguments I have there used in favour of delay are not merely debating points. I do in fact believe that time is on our side in this matter, and that the longer (within reason) the Congress have to reflect on their position, the more likely they are to come in. There is also some reason to suppose that moderate Congressmen are really in agreement with this view. That is merely a personal impression, and it may well be wrong. But I imagine your Excellency will agree that once the Legislature meets, the question is put to the issue and a definite decision one way or the other will have to be taken by the Congress with little delay. Those therefore, like some of the Europeans, who are beginning now to clamour for an immediate summoning of the Legislatures are really demanding that the question should be put to the issue at once. I doubt whether the

Congress would be prepared to reach a decision with Nehru out of India. On the other hand, I recognise that if once the situation is judged to have settled itself one way or the other, it is not desirable to prolong the state of uncertainty uselessly. Naturally if the Congress gave clear indications that they would take office, we would summon the Legislature at once; and if it became perfectly clear that they would not take office, then again the Legislature should be summoned without undue delay. But in that case I am inclined to think we should give the present ministry a fair chance of completing their budget and their programme. Our budget can hardly be ready for presentation before the 26th July. That is the date to which my Finance Minister is working, and I understand from him that the Finance Ministers in Bombay and Madras are also working to the same date. I should certainly prefer to delay the summoning of the Legislature till then, subject to any considerations of general policy.

6. I come now to the measures that will have to be taken if the Congress persist in their refusal to take office. I am, as Your Excellency knows, entirely in agreement with you that in this Province we shall have to assume complete power under Section 93 and suspend the Legislature; also that dissolution would be constitutionally unnecessary and from the practical point of view a fatal error in our provincial conditions. I quite agree that it would be desirable gradually to let it be known informally that there is no chance of a dissolution.

7. With reference to the question of resignation by the ministry before meeting the Legislature, I am very strongly in agreement with Your Excellency's views. As to the possibility of passing straight into Section 93 without facing the Legislature, it had not occurred to me that such a course could even be contemplated.

8. With reference to para. 18 of your letter, I fully agree about not committing oneself to ministers in regard to the future, particularly as to their part, if any, in the picture. I have been careful not to discuss with any of my ministers the details of future arrangements, though I have made it plain to them that, in my opinion, if Congress refuse to take office, it would be necessary for me to take over the administration under Section 93. I fear that they are all looking to be provided for under these arrangements; but that is evidently out of the question. I am not quite clear whom I should want to take as advisers, and I am entirely uncommitted to any one.

9. With reference to para. 19, the question of contact with Congress has been in my mind a good deal in the last week or so. Pant is in Naini Tal, and seems to be in a mood for contact. He rang up Sir Jwala Prasad Srivastava a few days ago and discussed with him for twenty minutes on the telephone the sugar cane situation, and suggested that it might be met

on non-party lines. The next day another of my ministers, the Raja of Tirwa, who used to know Pant in the old days, went to his house and had an hour's conversation with him about the general position. I understood from Tirwa that Pant naturally did not depart from the general position of Congress in demanding that ministers should, if necessary, be dismissed, but the fact that he had this long conversation seems to me to indicate a possible inclination towards settlement. Another rather surprising development I have seen in a press telegram this morning, and that is a statement by the publicity committee of the Congress party in the U.P. Legislature explaining in detail what the Congress propose to do if conditions permit them to form the provincial ministry. The whole statement seems to be drafted on the assumption that Congress will take office. There is some impression here that Pant is not only keen to take office, but hopeful that he will be able to. I shall certainly do what I can to keep in touch with these developments, though I do not think it likely that I could see Pant myself. He is not a free agent. But I will keep my eyes open.

10. That is the position during this period while we are waiting for a decision. But if the Congress decide against office acceptance, the position will be completely changed, and though I agree with Your Excellency that after assumption of the administration under Section 93 it will be necessary continually to be on the look-out for an opportunity of getting out of a position which by its nature cannot be permanent (vide your para. 12) we must at the same time guard against the danger of weakening our position by appearing to parley with what would then, I assume, be an enemy. I feel that if action is taken under Section 93, we shall inevitably have to take a firm line with Congress propaganda and Congress action, and I should myself be very much surprised if before long Congress did not embark on a movement of direct action. We must be very careful in those circumstances not to throw away the strength of our position. If it is necessary to fight, we shall have to fight the Congress with both hands, and not fight them with one hand and make conciliatory gestures with the other. We have had experience in the past of what happens when the trumpet sounds with an uncertain voice. But I know that Your Excellency appreciates this point entirely.

11. With reference to any definite suggestions of how we could at the moment get in closer touch with Congress, I will, as requested in para. 19 of your letter, send a telegram after considering the matter a little more carefully. At the moment I have no clear ideas as to methods.

Yours sincerely,
HARRY HAIG

32

HAIG TO LINLITHGOW
R/3/1/2

Strictly Confidential

Camp,
May 24th, 1937

My dear Lord Linlithgow,

I am sending my fourth fortnightly report on political conditions in the United Provinces under the new Constitution. Just after I wrote my last report, the meeting of M.L.As. convened by the Congress was held in Lucknow. Not many non-Congress M.L.As. attended, and several of those who did attend went as critics. The proceedings were temperate and the speeches not as strong as might perhaps have been expected. Two main resolutions were passed: one declaring no-confidence in the present ministry; the other calling upon the Governor to summon the Legislature forthwith. Copies of these resolutions were forwarded to me by Babu Purshottam Das Tandon, who had been elected as Chairman of the meeting. I felt it was desirable to give a reasoned reply, both as a matter of courtesy and in order to strengthen my own position. There had been a good deal of criticism of my action in not summoning the Legislature, and this had not been confined to Congress quarters. Accordingly I sent a reply to Babu Purshottam Das Tandon, of which a copy is enclosed.[31] The effect of this, I think, has been satisfactory. Babu Purshottam Das Tandon sent a reply to my Secretary's letter, which, except for one passage, was not unreasonable in tone and kept the discussion on the plane to which I had directed it. The *Leader* published a leading article on the whole supporting the line I had taken, and the *Hindustan Times* made a not unfriendly reference to it as giving an indication that the authorities desired to keep the door open.

2. I am increasingly impressed by the indications of a strong desire on the part of the Congress in this Province to take office, and also by the apparent disposition to moderate the extreme programme which Congressmen were talking of in the first flush of victory. I enclose a copy of a statement[32] issued by the publicity committee of the Congress party in the United Provinces Legislature explaining in detail what the Congress propose to do if conditions permit them to form the provincial ministry. The whole statement seems to be drafted on the assumption that Congress will take office. I think they have undoubtedly been influenced by the programme put out by the present ministry, and the realisation that if

they do not take office, others may be in a position to pursue a liberal and popular policy. Pandit Govind Ballabh Pant, the leader of the Congress party in this Province, is staying in Naini Tal which is his hot weather home, and there is an impression that he is not only anxious to take office, but hopeful that he will be able to. I am endeavouring, as far as possible, to keep in touch with Congress opinion. The decision, however, does not lie with our local Congress M.L.As., but with Mr. Gandhi and Pandit Jawaharlal Nehru.

3. The position of the government has not improved during the last fortnight. There are no signs of their winning for themselves the convinced support of the non-Congress elements. This, I am afraid, must be attributed mainly to their own failure up to date to organise or even to attempt organisation. The result of this lack of organisation is a tendency to regard them as seven individuals fortunate enough to be filling positions of authority and profit, and not as representatives of those who are opposed to Congress policy.

4. The causes of the inaction of the government in this direction have become apparent recently. They have not been agreed as to the nature of the organisation. The Muslim members intend to give their primary allegiance to the Muslim League, and are determined not to come into a non-communal party. On the other hand, the Hindus have been urging the necessity of forming a non-communal party if any effective results are to be achieved. It is clear now that the decision of the Muslims on this point is definite, and that no new or revived non-communal party embracing all the non-Congress elements can at present materialise. The non-Congress Hindus are left by this decision in a difficult position and without any organisation of their own. I sincerely trust that they will not succumb to the temptation of arraying themselves under their communal organisation, namely, the Hindu Mahasabha, for that would make co-operation between non-Congress Muslims and Hindus impossible. I think it is more likely that the Hindus, if they can form any organisation at all, will form a non-communal organisation of their own, something on the lines of the Liberal Party, which could be joined by all communities, but presumably would not be joined by the Muslims. There is still talk of organising work on non-party lines for the promotion of good relations between landlords and tenants in the districts, and this is neutral ground on which the Muslims and Hindus could with advantage meet. The cabinet are holding a meeting in Lucknow in a few days' time at which they will finally decide whether they will take up the active work of organisation in the next two months or not. They recognise that if they are to do anything, they can no longer

delay. Various individual members of the government are keen to try to start organisation work in the districts, but I am not sure what the decision of the cabinet as a whole will be.

5. The cabinet have also been considering their tactics when the Legislature is summoned. The Premier (as the Chief Minister is now called by request of the Council of Ministers) was attracted by the idea of resigning before meeting the Legislature, as he was greatly impressed by the difficulties of their position when the Legislature should meet. I do not think this represents the view of the cabinet as a whole, or is likely to be their decision, for they recognise how deeply they might be discredited if they held office for four mouths on the plea of preparing a programme to be submitted to the judgment of the Legislature and then finally resigned on the eve of meeting the Legislature without ever putting their programme forward.

6. There has been further talk about the desirability of including a Scheduled Caste member in the ministry. There are, however, considerable practical difficulties. Financially provision is not available for another minister, and he could only receive the salary to which he is entitled by a voluntary surrender of part of their salaries by the other ministers. Moreover, the difficulty of finding a reliable man and one who would bring any kind of strength to the cabinet is considerable, and I do not think that the proposal is likely to go much further.

7. There have been important developments in the Muslim situation as the result of the meetings of the Muslim League Parliamentary Board at Lucknow a fortnight ago. Mr. Jinnah attended the meetings and his influence was decisive. It was made quite plain that the League would not stand for any policy of merging the Muslims in the Congress or allowing the Muslim League to become a mere appendage of the Congress. They decided also that the Muslim League would not as a party attend the meeting of M.L.As. convened by the Congress.

Chaudhri Khaliquzzaman's policy was completely defeated, but he professed to accept the policy laid down by the League under Mr. Jinnah's influence. There is to be a meeting, I understand, of the League itself towards the end of August and by that time it is expected that the more conservative Muslims will have re-established their control over the League and that Chaudhri Khaliquzzaman will be unable to maintain the office he at present holds. The principal consideration, apart from Mr. Jinnah's personality, in bringing about these results is the alarm that has been caused among the Muslims generally by the Congress attempts to capture the Muslim masses. Those who have hitherto represented the community feel very strongly that if the community is to retain its individuality, no efforts must be spared in resisting the attempts of the Congress to absorb them. I fancy for this purpose considerable sums of money must be forthcoming, and that we may see before long a big campaign among the Muslims emphasising their communal and religious interests and attacking the Congress. The danger of course is that communal feeling will be worked up undesirably. But this seems to me to be the inevitable reaction to the Congress move.

8. Meantime a very unfortunate outbreak of rioting has just been reported from Lucknow between the Sunnis and Shias. Extremely strained relations have existed for over a year owing to the claim of the Sunnis to be allowed to recite the praises of the four companions of the Prophet and the counterclaim of the Shias that if so, they should be allowed to utter the curse upon them. The Sunni agitation of last year, which had assumed the form of passive resistance to the orders of the local authorities, was attracting a great deal of attention and threatened to become an all-India question. Feeling was allayed by my receiving deputations both of the Sunnis and the Shias in Lucknow during last cold weather, and the movement of passive resistance was abandoned by the Sunnis on my assurance that if we could not secure agreement between the two sects I would appoint a committee to look into the whole matter. After long conversations the two parties proved irreconcilable, and towards the end of March I appointed a committee of two (the President being a High Court Judge) who took evidence in April and are at present writing their report. But as the time for decision was approaching, the feeling on both sides has been getting more acute, and it has now broken out in this unfortunate form.

9. The celebration of the coronation throughout the Province went off very well, and there seems to have been a great deal of spontaneous loyal feeling. General conditions in the province remain, as far as I can judge, as I described them in my last letter. A good deal of publicity has been given to the sugar-cane situation in Gorakhpur owing to a recent visit of Pandit Govind Ballabh Pant to that area. I explained the sugar cane situation in paragraph 7 of my letter of April 7th, and the present position is referred to in the fortnightly demi-official letter of May 19th of which a copy is enclosed. The government have throughout been in the closest touch with the Gorakhpur situation, and I doubt if anything more can be done at this late stage. The amount of cane still standing has been reduced considerably in the last fortnight, but it is obvious that a fairly substantial amount is bound to remain unsold in two tahsils. Elsewhere in the Province I think

we can congratulate ourselves on having got the cane crop disposed of entirely in spite of the very difficult conditions.

10. There is one important matter of policy on which the Congress might possibly try to raise an agitation among the tenants, and that is the question of resettlements and revisions of settlements which are in progress at present in a number of districts. This was a policy which we started something over a year ago after prolonged consideration, as the only effective means or getting out of the present unsatisfactory and dangerous position of having remissions of revenue amounting to over one crore and remissions of rent amounting to nearly four crores annually, resting on no legal basis, but depending merely on executive orders which, though intended to be purely temporary, have had to be continued now for over five years. We started the resettlement and revision operations last year, and I had anticipated that during the elections the Congress might make a considerable point of them in the districts in which the operations were in progress. But surprisingly little attention was directed to this matter. I think the fact is that though on the whole the rents as they stand at present with the executive remissions will be somewhat increased, it is realised that they will only be fixed at rates fully justifiable after careful enquiry by the settlement and revising officers, and that these rates so fixed will be legally valid and cannot be enhanced for ten years, whereas the present remissions could be removed at any moment by executive order. The new rates of rent will in any case be well below the existing legal rents, and this also must carry weight with the tenants. Moreover, prices have now risen considerably above the rate prevalent when the remissions were first given. The Congress, however, have now declared in a recent resolution that they are opposed to the continuance of these resettlement and revision operations, but so far there is no indication that they intend to try to raise an agitation against them. The rehabilitation of the Provincial Finances is dependent on the continuance of these operations, for without them there seems little prospect of recovering any substantial part of the 112 lakhs of land revenue that has been surrendered.

Yours sincerely,
HARRY HAIG

33

HAIG TO LINLITHGOW
MSS.EUR.F. 115/13

Private and Personal *May 25th, 1937*

Many thanks for Your Excellency's private and personal letter of 22nd May, describing your conversation with Chhatari.[33] I am grateful for what Your Excellency has done. I have not seen him since his return, and may not see him again till early June when he will be coming up here. But I had a letter from him, in which he refers, without developing the point, to the proposal as a matter of tactics to give the Congress one more chance of refusal before they face them on the floor of the House. He is evidently referring to the suggestion described in para. 4 of Your Excellency's letter.[34] I quite agree with Your Excellency that to tender their resignation after the Legislature had been summoned would be to invite from Pant the reply you have suggested. On the other hand I am inclined to think that to go through this procedure at an earlier date would not be helpful to the solution we both have in mind, namely, acceptance of office by Congress. It would force Pant into what would be virtually a second refusal at a time when, if my view of the situation is correct, he could do nothing but refuse; and I think this would merely make the general situation more difficult and an ultimate acceptance less probable. Even from the point of view of my present ministry, I do not myself attach to this manoeuvre the importance which Chhatari does. I do not really believe it would strengthen their position at all. Consequently I am inclined to be unsympathetic to the whole idea.

2. With reference to para. 6 of Your Excellency's letter,[35] I think there is something to be said for a more or less similar course of action by the minority ministries if they can agree among themselves. I think they are keeping in touch a good deal, and I expect many other things, besides finance, will be discussed at Bombay early in June when the Finance Ministers meet.

3. I shall be very glad to know Your Excellency's views about arrangements for administering under Section 93 – a matter on which I find considerable difficulty in arriving at satisfactory conclusions.

34

HAIG TO LINLITHGOW
Telegram
MSS.EUR.F. 115/18

Secret and Personal *May 25th, 1937*
No. 9-G

Reference para. 11 of my secret and personal letter of May 21st. I fear after reflection I can suggest nothing more. The real obstacle to office acceptance is not the attitude of the moderate Congressmen, who already believe in it, but the policy of the all India leaders. I am still inclined to think that the best help we can give to the moderate men is to give them time so as to try and overcome the opposition of the leaders. I do not know whether Your Excellency has definite information that the office acceptance men really want the Legislatures summoned as early as end of June. Such scraps of information as I get, admittedly inconclusive, suggest that in this province they may in reality not be dissatisfied at idea of Legislature meeting middle or end July.

35

HAIG TO LINLITHGOW
R/3/1/2

Strictly Confidential Camp,
June 7th, 1937

My dear Lord Linlithgow,

I am sending my fifth fortnightly report on political conditions in the United Provinces under the new constitution. The feeling in favour of acceptance of office, which I mentioned in my last report, has, I think, further strengthened during this fortnight. As Your Excellency is aware, I took occasion to make a speech on the 26th May in which I tried to elucidate the constitutional position of the Governor as I understood it, and to explain the spirit in which the constitution would be worked. This speech, of which I enclose a copy,[36] has been, I think, very well received, judging by press comments both in the Province and outside it. Three of our Congress leaders in the Province made short statements about it, copies of which are attached,[37] and Dr. Katju later issued a more elaborate statement. Pant's statement was somewhat rigid and disappointing, and practically confined itself to a complaint that I had not dealt with issue of dismissal versus resignation, which he maintained was now the outstanding question. I interpret his attitude as meaning that he is in no position to contribute to any further accommodation, and publicly he can only mark time. As I mentioned in my last letter, the decision rests with Gandhi and Nehru, and it would seem, from what Your Excellency has told me, that the channel of personal approach, which will probably be necessary if we are to reach a satisfactory settlement, is to be through Madras by means of the projected interview between Rajagopalachariar and Erskine.[38] Pant is not cast for any part in the negotiations and is presumably afraid of saying anything which might not be in accordance with Gandhi's tactics. I got the same impression as the result of certain tentative overtures which I launched for opening communication with Pant if necessary. The reply in effect was that he had nothing that he wished to communicate, that the Congress had placed all their cards on the table, and that the only point at issue was dismissal versus resignation.

2. On the other hand, Mohan Lal Saksena made a statement on my speech, which I think is probably more representative of the real opinion of the rank and file of the Congress towards office acceptance, and suggests that so far as they are concerned they are satisfied with what has been said and would be very glad to come in.

3. Gandhi's recent statement[39] is regarded here as indicating quite a new tone on his part, and it is assumed that he really does now wish that Congress should take office. I hope myself that this may lead to a settlement. It seems to me possible that Gandhi finds the office acceptance mentality among Congressmen so strong that he realises that if he keeps them out of office they will not be prepared to support any movement of direct action. But unless direct action were to follow rejection of office, the policy would be one of futility, and he may therefore have made up his mind that there is really no alternative from the Congress point of view to acceptance of office. I think there is little doubt that in this Province at any rate the majority of Congressmen are not prepared to go in for civil disobedience, unless there is a very remarkable change of feeling.

4. Further reports about the Coronation celebrations emphasize their enthusiasm and spontaneity. It seems to me distinctly significant that there should be such genuine feelings of loyalty to the Crown. As I have mentioned before, it would seem that there is in the Province no general hostility to the British connection or to government officers. The feeling in favour of the Congress is based partly on the very natural nationalist

desire to govern themselves and partly on the vague but widespread hope that the Congress may be able to remove all the grievances and difficulties that at present exist. The Congress are continuing their work in the villages, but I do not think they are at the most doing more than trying to maintain the position which they won at the time of the elections; and I fancy in many places feeling must have cooled down a great deal. The only part of the Province which seems to give cause for future anxiety is the east, particularly the Gorakhpur division. This is a very densely populated and consequently poor area. Last year it was considered by the landlords to be an area where Congress influence was almost negligible, and where the numerous big landlords would be able without difficulty to control the elections. The results completely falsified these expectations and I think in no other part of the Province has Congress influence, worked up during the elections, maintained itself so effectively. Collections of rent and revenue in this part of the Province are very backward, and there is a clear reluctance on the part of tenants to pay their rents, based on expectation that Congress will still give them considerable relief. The eastern parts of Oudh too will require careful watching.

5. The cabinet has been somewhat inactive during the last fortnight. The ministers have been in the plains, while the Secretaries for the most part have been in Naini Tal. A cabinet meeting was held towards the end of May in Lucknow, the first at which I did not preside. They discussed the question of party organisation; but, as I had anticipated, no practical conclusions emerged. The difficulty, which I explained in paragraph 4 of my letter of May 24th, seems be insuperable and the Hindus do not see their way to any effective organisation. At present they seem inclined to try and keep alive the National Agriculturist Party; but this was greatly discredited as a result of the elections and has always been regarded with hostility by the Liberals. Not much therefore can be expected from this as a nucleus. As a result of this paralysis the ministers are doing none of that practical organising work in the districts which was the main reason for their deciding to remain in the plains, and they could really have been more usefully occupied recently had they been up in Naini Tal instead of enduring the hot weather, as they have been doing lately, in their own homes. But they will be here for the King's Birthday on the 9th June, and I hope they will stay on at least for a fortnight and get through some necessary consultation with each other, for there are many problems which they have to face. In the meantime it has probably been useful that certain of the ministers have been getting in touch with ministers in other Provinces. Our Revenue Minister, for instance, attended the Cattle

Conference at Simla and has returned not only impressed by the Conference and the possibilities of doing something for the improvement of cattle, but pleased at the opportunity of being able to discuss political tactics with ministers in the other minority governments. The Premier has been paying a visit to the Premier of Bihar.[40] I have not seen him since his return, but I understand he too has been discussing tactics. The Finance Minister has just left for Bombay to attend the meeting of Finance Ministers there, and he too is looking forward to the discussion of tactics with ministers from other Provinces.

6. The main problem now before the cabinet will be the Budget. The Finance Minister has been applying himself with the greatest energy and initiative to eliminating the deficit of 40 lakhs shown in my financial provision for the first six months of the year. Every department has been set to work to try and produce further economies. In certain respects revenue prospects are decidedly more favourable than they were when we made our estimates last March, and already I believe the Finance Minister sees his way to reducing the deficit from 40 lakhs to 20 lakhs, and he is not without hope that he may even practically eliminate it without recourse to any drastic action, such as cutting the pay of the services or introducing fresh taxation. Having got the normal budget to as favourable a position as possible, he then intends to put up before the cabinet the various proposals that have come forward for fresh expenditure, and to suggest that if any of them are approved, proposals should also be made for fresh taxation to cover them. Suggestions will, however, no doubt be made that new schemes should be to some extent financed by borrowing; but the Finance Minister at any rate, and I think the other members of the cabinet too, understand the grave dangers of such a course. Meantime, the Finance Minister will take the opportunity of his visit to Bombay to discuss terms for a loan to cover capital expenditure to which we are already committed and which may amount to something like a crore, mainly in connection with our hydro-electric and tube well schemes.

7. On the whole, I hope that the financial outlook of the cabinet will be sober and responsible. There is, however, one point of danger. This is a proposal that canal rates should be lowered. This is a measure which can be carried out by the government by executive order, and herein lies its main attraction. The ministry realise that their programme is only a paper programme, and that nothing can really be done without the approval of the Legislature. They are likely therefore to go out of office without having in fact achieved anything.[41] There has been for some time an agitation for reduction in canal rates, which till recently were high on wheat and barley

in relation to prices. The recent rise in wheat and barley prices has destroyed a great deal of the practical justification for reduction in the canal rates on these crops. Nevertheless, there is a good deal of support in the cabinet for the proposal that in order to secure some political credit and popularity for themselves the rates on wheat and barley should be reduced. This would cost the Province, on the smallest possible reduction, 6 lakhs a year recurring, and if the rates were reduced by Re. 1 per acre, would cost over 12 lakhs. If this were done, it would seriously embarrass our future finances and would be particularly inconvenient to me if I had to take over the administration of the Province in August. I shall put this point plainly to the cabinet when we next discuss the matter. They held their first discussion in Lucknow during my absence and were unable to reach any conclusion.

8. Other ideas which are under active consideration are:

(*a*) The setting up of debt conciliation boards for village debtors on the lines of those that have been working with some success in other Provinces. I hope myself that they will push on with this, for I think the scheme is well worth trying. Our very elaborate debt legislation of 1934 has really done little or nothing to relieve the village debtor.

(*b*) There is a very ambitious scheme for accompanying debt reduction in the villages by a completely new system of agricultural finance through a new bank. The proposals (or ideas, for they have really hardly reached the stage of proposals) are based on the Agricultural Bank of Egypt. I am myself inclined to be very sceptical whether such an ambitious scheme could really be brought into practical working, or could be a success, though it is attractive enough on paper; and I am somewhat apprehensive of trying in effect to displace the existing system of agricultural finance through the village moneylender which, with all its defects and abuses, does at any rate work and fulfil its main object of providing village finance. It seems pretty clear, however, that the present government cannot get beyond the stage of talk and discussion in this matter.

(*c*) The Revenue Minister tells me that he hopes to take up again the question of tenancy reform which was dropped as a result of the discussions with the landlords described in paragraph 3 of my letter of May 7th. He tells me that some of the principal opponents among the Oudh Taluqdars to the proposals then put forward have now modified their views and might be prepared to agree to the setting up of a committee. I have not had any recent conversation with any other ministers or with any of the big landholders on this subject, and it may be that the Revenue Minister is too sanguine; but he proposes to bring this matter up for further discussion at the next cabinet meeting which will be held about the middle of the month.

9. The Lucknow riots referred to in my last letter were brought under control after a few days by the effective and vigorous measures taken by the local authorities. Feeling, however, between the Sunnis and Shias remains exceedingly bitter, and we shall be faced with a very difficult problem when we have to decide on the action to be taken on the report of the committee. There is a general impression that these riots were really provoked by the Shias, who believed that the committee's conclusions were likely to be against them and wished to show the authorities that if there was to be any change in past practice, it would be resisted by the Shias by all possible means. The Sunnis on their part have shown also a most uncompromising spirit, and Chaudhri Khaliquzzaman in particular has exercised a pernicious influence, taking pains to stiffen Sunni opinion merely in order to promote his own personal political interests. It will obviously be long before reasonable feelings can be expected to prevail.

10. I have heard nothing definite in the last fortnight about the progress of Muslim organisation as against the Congress, but I think there is no doubt that Muslim feeling generally is hardening and I fear we may be approaching a time of more pronounced Hindu-Muslim tension.

Yours sincerely,
HARRY HAIG

36

HAIG TO LINLITHGOW
Telegram
MSS.EUR.F. 115/20

No. 12-G *June 17th, 1937*

I discussed today with my ministers date for summoning Legislature. We are all agreed that July 29th would be suitable. It will be impossible to have budget ready before then. Will this date fit in with Your Excellency's general policy, and has Your Excellency any views about the date when an announcement should be made?[42]

37

HAIG TO LINLITHGOW
Draft Telegram (Not Sent)
MSS.EUR.F. 115/18

June 17th, 1937

I am grateful for information contained in Your Excellency's telegram 558-S dated June 16th.[43] In view of Congress feeling described in your telegram and attitude of Gandhi I fully agree that we should do everything we reasonably can to encourage Congress to take office. When I first read Gandhi's latest statement it occurred to me that in so far as Congress position rested on genuine uneasiness and did not represent either attempt to nullify safeguards or to put themselves in strong tactical position in event of breakdown it might be met to some extent by saying that in the event of breakdown Governor would issue public statement explaining nature of disagreement which led to resignation of Ministers. This would at any rate meet the point the Governor should not disguise publicly his share of responsibility for breakdown.

2. The difficulty about a Governor dismissing his ministers or calling upon them to resign is that Governor is put in a false position for he would presumably not be anxious to lose his ministers and would much prefer that they should continue in office accepting the decision which he had felt bound to take. If we were looking for some compromise that would save Gandhi's face it might perhaps be found in combining the two positions. If a serious disagreement arose and it became clear that Governor and ministers must part company Governor might perhaps put out a statement explaining the nature of the disagreement and that neither side felt they could give way. He might say that he had no desire merely on account of this disagreement to part with his ministers, and that he would have preferred that in spite of it the ministers should continue in office. This had unfortunately proved not to be possible, and Governor regretfully recognised the position, and as ministers were not prepared to remain in office in these circumstances he had asked them to submit their resignations which he accepted with regret.

3. This is admittedly a rather absurd way of stating a position which is clear enough.[44] But ideas of this sort may possibly be explored if Congress response to Your Excellency's statement is favourable.

38

HAIG TO LINLITHGOW
MSS.EUR.F. 115/13

Private and Personal *June 23rd, 1937*

In continuation of my letter of June 17th, 1937, with which I forwarded a draft letter from Chhatari,[45] I had a very interesting discussion with the cabinet today regarding their tactics if the Congress do decide to take office. One view put forward was that even if Congress gave an unequivocal statement of their readiness to take office, the present ministry might continue till they met the Legislature at the end of July. I gather that Katju had rather suggested this idea to Srivastava, and indicated that the change over might then be effected in a friendly atmosphere and with goodwill on both sides. This would mean that the budget would be introduced by the present ministry. Naturally this idea makes some appeal to the Finance Minister who has put in a great deal of work on the budget. The general feeling, however, was against this. Most of the ministers were not prepared to credit the Congress with brotherly feelings, and they felt that from their own point of view it would be better that the Congress should frame their own budget rather than take over the budget from the present ministry and be able to put down any failure to implement promises in the next six months to the fact that they were bound by the present ministry's budget. Moreover, the Premier has made it clear more than once that the ministry will be only too ready to resign their posts as soon as Congress indicate that they are prepared to take office, and I myself feel that it would be very difficult not to make the change of government as soon as the Congress indicated their readiness to assume responsibility.

2. If, therefore, the Working Committee, either unequivocally or subject to further conversations, accept the principle of Congress taking office, I should contemplate a formal conversation with Pant almost immediately after the Working Committee's decision has been published. The ministers, however, seem anxious that a formal offer from them to me to make way for the Congress should precede the Working Committee's decision, and Chhatari has prepared another draft letter on much the same lines as the one I sent with my letter of June 17th. The idea of the ministers is that I should send a copy of this letter to Pant and ask him whether he is prepared to meet me and discuss the position. He would no doubt reply that he would prefer to say nothing until after the Working Committee's decision.

The ministers are inclined to think it would strengthen the dignity and grace of their withdrawal if their readiness to withdraw were formally indicated before the Working Committee had announced their decision. Hitherto I have felt it desirable to postpone action in this matter because I was reluctant to place Pant in the position of having to give me a second formal refusal. Now, however, we have definitely reached the last Act. A final decision has got to be taken by the Working Committee, and it would seem to me a possible course that I should communicate such a letter to Pant formally about the end of the month. I am still not sure, however, that that might not be to cause him unnecessary embarrassment, which I am naturally anxious to avoid. I shall be discussing the matter further with Chhatari in a day or two.

3. Since writing the above I have received Your Excellency's letter of 21st June regarding Chhatari's draft.[46] I shall of course do nothing until I know what Your Excellency's general ideas are.

39

HAIG TO LINLITHGOW
R/3/1/2

Strictly Confidential *June 23rd, 1937*

My dear Lord Linlithgow,

I am sending my sixth fortnightly report on political conditions in the United Provinces under the new constitution. Until the issue of Your Excellency's statement there has been little that is new to record about Congress opinion towards office acceptance. The Premier paid a visit to Pandit Govind Ballabh Pant about a fortnight ago, and had a long and friendly conversation with him. His impression was that the Pandit, though willing and indeed anxious to accept office, was clearly not a free agent, and was reluctant to get down to a practical discussion of difficulties. He was inclined to insist very much on Mr. Gandhi's demand that if there were a serious disagreement, ministers should be dismissed. The Premier got the general impression at that time that Congress would not take office.

2. Subsequently the Pandit paid a long visit to Sir Digby Drake-Brockman, Chairman of the Public Service Commission, who is an old friend of his and who had previously called on the Pandit. The conversation lasted an hour and a half, and Drake-Brockman told me subsequently in strict confidence that he and Pant discussed matters with considerable

frankness, and that he got the impression not only that Pant and the majority of the United Provinces Congressmen were exceedingly anxious to take office, but that they might even be prepared to break away and take a line of their own. I cannot believe that this is a correct impression, and Drake-Brockman admitted to me that Pant's expressions were decidedly ambiguous. But Drake-Brockman at any rate formed the clear view (*a*) that Pant is very anxious to take office; (*b*) that he still has a certain diffidence as to how a Congress government would be treated by the Governor, based on what Drake-Brockman describes as an inferiority complex; and (*c*) that given encouragement he would be likely to come out strongly in favour of office acceptance.

3. Drake-Brockman stressed so much the desirability of further personal reassurances to Pant that I thought it advisable that he should write a letter to Pant, saying that after reflecting over their conversation, he felt it might be a good thing if Pant were to see me; and that if Pant felt that this would be of any advantage, he was sure there would be no difficulty in arranging an interview. This letter was written a few days ago and there has at present been no answer to it. If any interview were to take place, I contemplated that it would be strictly private and that it should be kept out of the Press. It would suit neither Pant nor myself that an interview should take place publicly at this stage. He would probably get into trouble with his own people, and I might also find that my ministers would not altogether appreciate my action. The new situation, however, created by Your Excellency's statement makes me feel that it would be definitely a mistake for me to see Pant now under those conditions. As I shall explain separately, it seems to me likely enough that I shall be seeing him formally before long.

4. Your Excellency's statement was published yesterday morning.[47] I sent a copy to Pant. I discussed the statement with three of my ministers who came to see me yesterday. They all independently took the same line. They consider that it is an excellent statement, that it puts the whole position clearly and unmistakably, and that while it is most conciliatory to Congress and should reassure them in respect of any genuine doubts they may entertain, at the same time it makes it clear that the safeguards are not going to be abandoned and that the Governors will be expected to exercise their powers if real necessity arises. This is entirely in accordance with their own views of the line that should be taken, and they approve highly of the statement. They could offer no opinion as to the probable reactions of Congress.

5. We had a cabinet meeting today, and at the end of it I had a long talk with my ministers about the probable reactions of Congress. Sir J.P.

Srivastava had met Dr. Katju yesterday and had a long conversation with him. Katju spoke with great frankness. He said that he was entirely satisfied with Your Excellency's statement, and he was confident that Congress would now take office. He said they had really secured what they wanted. There had been a fourth reading of the Bill in India, and this had gone in accordance with the wishes of the Congress. They were impressed by the sincerity of Your Excellency's statement and felt they had secured what they really wanted, namely, a change of heart on the part of the British government. Moreover, it is fairly clear that Congressmen are feeling that if they continue to make difficulties about accepting office, they are likely to lose ground in the country. They are keeping the electorate quiet with explanations and misrepresentations, but the electorate cannot be fed indefinitely on words, and they are afraid that it will soon be getting impatient. My ministers think that M.N. Roy's draft resolution, a copy of which I attach,[48] is very significant, and shows that on a realistic view even Congressmen of a pronounced left wing tendency are beginning to realise that they must take office. I can offer no opinion as to what Nehru's reaction will be, or what would be the effect of strong opposition by him, but I have no doubt from what I have heard that the general opinion of Congressmen in this Province will be very strongly in favour of office acceptance.

6. Dr. Katju in his conversation with Sir J.P. Srivastava did not conceal the fact that the Congress leaders, and he himself, did not contemplate the Congress allowing themselves to be tamed by office acceptance. Their intention is to do what they can to improve the condition of the tenants and carry out other beneficial measures for the next eighteen months or two years. But as soon as they feel that the first impetus of these popular measures is exhausting itself, and as they begin to suffer from the fissiparous tendencies that office may engender, their intention will be to force a break on an issue which will not be economic, but will definitely be Indian versus British, and in this way create a situation which will lead either to further constitutional changes or to a mass movement, for which by that time they might be prepared. They realise that at present they are not ready for a mass movement. It is I think as well that our satisfaction with the issue of the present phase, if it turns out now as we all hope it may, should be tempered by a realisation of what the Congress leaders have at the back of their minds. Our hope must be that in the course of the next 18 months or two years we may, by the working of the constitution and by contact between the Congress and the administration, produce such a change of feeling that the policy of the Congress leaders could not be carried into effect. But optimism in this matter must be cautious.[49]

7. I had a very interesting discussion with the cabinet regarding the tactics for the change of government if the Congress do decide to take office, and on this I am addressing Your Excellency separately.[50]

8. The ministers have all been in Naini Tal since my last report, and they will remain here till the end of the month, by which time we hope to have got through a number of important discussions, particularly on the budget. They will then go down to Lucknow at the beginning of July, and I shall probably follow about the 10th July. As I have told Your Excellency separately, the ministers and I myself are all in agreement that the most convenient date for summoning the Legislature in this Province would be the 29th July. We contemplate that no serious business would be done during the remainder of that week, and the budget would then be ready (but not before then) for presentation at the beginning of the next week on the 2nd August. As the whole political situation is very fluid at the moment, I am in no hurry to make any announcement about the date for summoning the Legislature. All this of course is the programme framed on the assumption that Congress do not indicate early in July their readiness to accept office, which would create a totally different situation.

9. The visit of the Finance Minister to Bombay has been of very definite value in regard to the question of financing new schemes by borrowing. He has returned firmly convinced both of the unsoundness of such a policy and of the practical impossibility of carrying it out even if it were attempted. He had some useful conversation with Sir James Taylor[51] and was able to explain to the cabinet the likely reactions of the market to any proposal for unsound borrowing. The cabinet were entirely convinced and have quite given up all idea of financing new schemes by borrowing. Their intention is to come as near as possible to balancing the budget on the existing basis, and then to lay before the Legislature a certain limited number of new schemes which would have a definite attraction, and at the same time to indicate how they could be financed by new taxation. But I do not think that anyone anticipates that the Legislature will be prepared to do anything in the way of financing new schemes by new taxation proposed by the present ministry, and I understand that the ministers do not propose to do much more than indicate possibilities. They have had no further discussion on the question of canal rates. It is clear that the Finance Department at any rate will strongly oppose any proposals for reduction of canal rates, and I am trying to get the ministers to realise that it would really be a solid achievement and one of which no one could deprive them of the credit if they were able to present a

practically balanced budget in August, which would evidently be out of the question if they threw away revenue by reduction in canal rates.

10. I judge from reports that Congress activity in the villages has been increasing lately and the tone of speeches is certainly deteriorating. We have already authorised District Magistrates to proceed under Section 108 of the Criminal Procedure Code against speakers who in their judgement require to be restrained. We have also recently authorised several prosecutions under Section 124-A of the Indian Penal Code. These are I think in all cases against left wing or communist Congressmen. Among these is Sajjad Zaheer, the young communist son of Sir Wazir Hasan, late Chief Judge of the Chief Court of Oudh. He has been, ever since his return from England a year or two ago, a very active communist worker. His prosecution for a seditious speech was sanctioned last cold weather, but at the urgent entreaty of his father, who gave a guarantee that the son would refrain in future from seditious speaking, the prosecution was withdrawn. The young man immediately repudiated the father's assurance and there can be no ground now for further leniency. Incidentally, Sir Wazir Hasan has now openly espoused the Congress cause. We have refrained from instituting a prosecution against Dr. Lohia, the Secretary of the Foreign Department of the All-India Congress Committee, in respect of two or three very bad speeches, because we felt that at the present time this would unnecessarily antagonise the Congress organisation. But if the Congress do not accept office, it will, I am convinced, before long be necessary to proceed against persons of the type of Dr. Lohia.

11. We still have in our jails a certain number of revolutionary prisoners, mostly those who were convicted some ten years ago in the Kakori case,[52] which disclosed a considerable organisation for revolutionary dacoity. We have had from time to time hunger strikes by some of these Kakori prisoners, and one of them has now gone on hunger strike (not for the first time) in order to support his demand that all political prisoners throughout India should be released. The government are taking a firm line, both about the demand and about the hunger striker, and the probabilities are that the hunger strike will go on for a considerable time without danger to the life of the prisoner. But the ministers have felt themselves somewhat embarrassed, in pursuit of this policy, when they found that simultaneously the young man who attempted to murder Sir John Anderson was being released and sent to England for training, apparently at government expense, and also that the revolutionary prisoners in Burma are being released as a gesture of conciliation.

12. The report of the committee consisting of Mr. Justice Allsop of the

Allahabad High Court and Mr. Ross, Collector of Jhansi holding charge of the division, on the Madhe-Sahaba question in Lucknow has been received. It is being kept very strictly confidential at present. The report seems to me an admirable document, and will give the government a clear line, which I think they will certainly accept. But naturally its conclusions will not be satisfactory to both sides. I had a preliminary talk yesterday with the Premier, the Chief Secretary, and the Commissioner[53] and Deputy Commissioner[54] of Lucknow who both happen to be in Naini Tal, and it was provisionally decided that the report should be accepted and that it should be published simultaneously with the government orders upon it, probably about the 20th July, after all precautions have been taken locally against a renewal of disturbances. This policy of course will have to be endorsed by the cabinet. It will probably not be put up to them until about the 10th July. I do not myself anticipate that there will be renewed rioting, but it is likely that a troublesome agitation may be revived and continued for some time. The fact, however, that all the claims on both sides will have been examined in this very impartial and authoritative manner and that government will come to definite conclusions on the new points raised since the orders of Sir John Hewett[55] were passed will, I hope, in the end lead to a gradual cessation of the trouble.

13. A Muslim bye-election in Bundelkhand, polling for which takes place about the middle of July, will be treated as a trial of strength between the Congress and the Muslim League. I do not think the Muslim League have done a great deal at present, but I fancy they will put a good deal of effort into it from now onwards. Jinnah is interested himself in the election. If the Congress were to be successful, it would undoubtedly be a serious blow to the Muslim League.

14. A very representative conference on sugar has just been held in Naini Tal. It consisted not only of officers of the local government, who are closely connected with various aspects of the sugar industry, but representatives of the cane growers, the sugar manufacturers and the sugar merchants. The Bihar government also sent representatives, and the conference was a practical body which was in a position to express authoritative opinions on the various problems with which the industry is confronted. I attach a copy of the press note.[56] We received a letter recently from the Government of India, Finance Department, criticising our policy in inducing the factories to continue crushing sugar cane as long as possible, and suggesting that the measures we took by this action and by lowering the minimum price of cane, so as to enable the factories to continue working, were not in the real interest of the industry. I think

possibly the Finance Department hardly appreciated the situation with which we were faced or the fact that by our action we averted what would have been, in my judgment, a most serious agrarian crisis in certain parts of the Province. Apart from that, it is interesting to find that this conference, thoroughly representative of all those interests practically engaged in the industry, has endorsed the action we took. The following is an extract from the proceedings: "It is generally felt that the reduction made in the minimum price of cane had naturally resulted in some loss to cane growers, but that the action taken had saved the situation and averted a serious crisis. The representatives of sugar manufacturers agreed that the action taken by the government was right and proper, those of sugar merchants admitted that in the circumstances there was no other way out of the difficulty, and those of cane growers held that the action was beneficial to the growers." Another point of interest which has emerged from this conference is that "sugar manufacturers were inclined to hold that the fall in the sugar market was not due to the over-production of sugar, but to a general feeling of nervousness in the market. This tendency had been aggravated by the increase in the sugar excise duty and the market had become disorganised. They pointed out that the stocks of sugar held by dealers were abnormally low at present and that was responsible for the large stocks at factories." This view of course is in direct conflict with that of the government of India, Finance Department, who appear to hold that the entire crisis was due to overproduction, and had nothing to do with the excise – a view which I must confess appears to me untenable. I hope they may re-examine their view in the light of the facts of the situation as disclosed at the sugar conference. The outlook for the future appears to be more promising than I had ventured to anticipate, though much practical work has to be done in order to meet the difficult and complicated conditions.

Yours sincerely,
H.G. HAIG

P.S. : With reference to paragraph 3 above Pant has now written to Drake-Brockman saying that in view of Your Excellency's statement and the fact that the Working Committee is going to consider it on 5th July, he is not sure if any useful purpose would be served by our meeting at this stage. As this is also my own view, the matter is being dropped.[57]

40

HAIG TO LINLITHGOW
Telegram
MSS.EUR.F. 115/18

No. 14-G *June 24th, 1937*

Your telegram 604-G dated June 22.[58] Reactions in this province to Your Excellency's message and broadcast have been so far extremely favourable. Typical views from Congress and non-Congress circles in Naini Tal which I believe represent general provincial opinion are given in paras. 4 and 5 of my fortnightly report despatched today. I understand that Pant's view is identical with that of Katju given in my para. 5. The *Leader* comments very favourably.

2. I have no doubt that office acceptors throughout Province are very satisfied with the statement but the reactions of the irreconcilable element, Nehru and his followers and of the Congress socialists and their probable course of action have not been disclosed. General opinion is that the rank and file are bringing pressure on the leaders and that these feel that further refusal may lose them support among the masses.

41

HAIG TO LINLITHGOW
Telegram
MSS.EUR.F. 115/13

Clear the Line *June 25th, 1937*
Private and Personal
No. 16-G

My private and personal letter of 23 June. Chhatari has actually sent me a letter which concludes by saying that he hopes I will now give the Congress another opportunity of taking office, and that in doing so I will assure them that present cabinet will make way for a majority party ministry as soon as the latter is willing to function.

2. I discussed the situation with Chhatari this morning. Though from point of view of his party he has been anxious to write this letter he would be prepared to cancel it if we thought it would be embarrassing to us. I should not however like to suggest this to him unless it were most clearly necessary, and I see myself no necessity for making such a request.

3. Chhatari has made it clear that he does not press for early publication of his letter. He has no desire that it should be published before meeting of Working Committee, though he attaches great importance to it having been written before then and indeed as early as possible after Your Excellency's statement. It is in fact dated June 23rd. It will serve his purpose if it is published when I send for Pant if Congress decide to take office, or at any time before meeting of Legislature if Congress do not take office.

4. In these circumstances I think it would be reasonable that perhaps about end of month I should communicate letter formally to Pant and ask him whether on basis of it he is prepared to meet me and discuss question of taking office. I should publish neither Chhatari's letter, nor my letter, nor Pant's reply until after meeting of Working Committee, unless Pant was agreeable. The correspondence however would have to be published as soon as Working Committee's meeting was over.

5. I see from D.I.B.'s report of 19th June that Rajagopalachariar is reported to want Governors to invite Congress to accept office before the meeting of the Working Committee. If this is so, action suggested would at any rate not be likely to embarrass those in favour of office acceptance, and they might actually like the facts to be published.

6. I should be grateful if Your Excellency could give me your views about the situation and advise me whether you see objection to my acting as suggested above.[59]

42

HAIG TO LINLITHGOW
MSS.EUR.F. 115/13

Personal and Confidential *June 30th, 1937*

Many thanks for Your Excellency's personal and confidential letter of 29th June regarding Chhatari's letter and our general attitude towards the Congress at the present moment.[60] So far as Chhatari is concerned, I told him, after receiving your telegram of the 27th June, that I proposed to take no action on his letter for the present. I fully appreciate the advantages of the line suggested by Your Excellency, of leaving the Congress alone for the present, and indeed my own inclination has always been a little in that direction.

2. In this connection I think Your Excellency will be interested to hear of a recent interchange with Pant. On the 24th June I received a letter

from Sir J.P. Srivastava saying that Pant had sent him a message through Katju in regard to the Upper House nominations which he had heard I proposed making very shortly. He wished me to be informed that if these nominations were made at this juncture, that would give a fresh cause for misunderstanding in Congress circles and make it difficult for those who were in favour of office acceptance. The position was that I had been turning over the question of these nominations in my mind for some time, and had indeed intended to make them about a fortnight before. But a decision was held up owing to the necessity of making certain inquiries about one or two persons I had in mind. I wrote at once to Sir Jawala Prasad Srivastava and said that I should be most reluctant to embarrass the Congress in any way owing to the time at which my nominations were announced, and I quite appreciated that their announcement at the present juncture might be inconvenient. At the same time I was definitely committed to three out of the six nominations I was proposing to make, and I had also made up my mind about the other three. I pointed out that if I postponed the announcement until the Congress had taken office (if that should be their decision) there might be embarrassment to myself if my new government made representations to me to which I could not accede and which they might choose to make a ground of complaint against me. I asked Sir J.P. to convey these views to Pant and say that I should be quite prepared to withhold my nominations if he felt that my making them now would weaken his position, but that I hoped that if so, he would not cause me embarrassment when I had to make the nominations. Sir J.P. went round to see Pant and showed him my letter, and the next day wrote to me a full account of his conversation. Pant took the line which was perhaps to be expected. In the first place, he was evidently perturbed at my having been told that he had sent a message or request to me, as he was not in a position to approach me either directly or indirectly about any matter. He merely desired to apprise Sir J.P. of his views, so that Sir J.P. could advise me if he thought proper. It must not be assumed that he was in favour of office. Until the Working Committee had made a decision, he was out of the picture. All this he emphasised repeatedly and even rang up Sir J.P. afterwards to impress it on him again. At the same time he explained that the nominations if announced at this stage would be interpreted as an unfriendly act to the Congress and might impair the chances of an honourable settlement, but it was entirely for me to decide what action I should take. He also made it quite clear that if the nominations remained unmade, he would bring pressure to bear on me to modify them in accordance with his wishes.

3. I decided not to make the nominations for the present, but made no further communication to Pant. The incident merely illustrates:

(*a*) that one cannot expect anything in the nature of a gentleman's agreement with a Congressman;

(*b*) that in spite of all his talk in Naini Tal about office acceptance, Pant is, as many people had assured me, essentially frightened of Nehru and most unwilling to do anything to displease him. This I fear may have some bearing on the probable policy of Congress in this province should they finally accept office.

43

HAIG TO LINLITHGOW
Telegram
MSS.EUR.F. 125/126

Clear the Line — Naini Tal,
No. 17-G — *July 1st, 1937*

Your telegram No. 654-G dated 1st July.[61] I am opposed to Bihar procedure in the United Provinces. From practical point of view it would be extravagant, for it would mean paying travelling allowances twice. Moreover procedure seems to me hesitant and difficult to justify. When Legislature is summoned after all this delay, it should be allowed to function and not be sent away again to go through formalities.

2. I have always been in favour of giving Congress plenty of time. But I think my programme gives them all the time they require. I propose that Legislature meets on Thursday, July 29th, and that remainder of that week will be spent in preliminary formalities. Real business would not start till Monday, August 2nd. This appears to me to place vital decision sufficiently late, while giving members time to settle down. If Congress have still not made up their mind, there is no need at all for them to force issue at very beginning of session.

3. I agree that if intention had been to summon Legislature in middle of July, arguments in Your Excellency's telegram would have force. But I definitely do not want to summon Legislature before July 29th, and to do so would in my opinion merely complicate situation.

4. I was about to announce intention of summoning Legislature on July 29th in accordance with your telegram No. 640-G of June 28th. I should like to make announcement before Working Committee meets.

44

DONALDSON TO LAITHWAITE
R/3/1/2

Confidential | Camp,
D.O. No. 376-G.S.P. | *July 5th, 1937*

My dear Laithwaite,

In His Excellency the Viceroy's personal and confidential letter of 30th June 1937 to Sir Harry Haig, paragraph 6, he says: "I would be grateful if you could refer me to the reports mentioned in paragraph 10 of your letter[62] in so far as these may have come to the Government of India." This refers to a statement in Sir Harry Haig's letter that, from reports, Congress activity in the villages had been increasing and the tone of speeches getting worse. In reply I am asked to refer you to paragraphs 7 and 8 of Gwynne's fortnightly D.-O. to Thorne, No. 6/1-C.X. of June 20th, of which I attach a copy for ready reference. Also to paragraph 303 of the Secret Police Abstract of Intelligence for the United Provinces, dated June 19th, 1937, and to paragraph 316 of the same Abstract, dated June 26th, 1937.[63] These secret Abstracts are no doubt available in the Central Intelligence Bureau and with them, very probably, further reports to the same effect from the Provincial D.I.G., C.I.D.,[64] and from the Central Intelligence Officer in this Province. It may be noted that the Commissioners' fortnightly reports just received, which are being embodied in the current fortnightly D.O., indicate some slackening of these activities, due to the excessive hot weather just before the rains, and to the coming of the rains when villagers are occupied in cultivation.

Yours sincerely,
J.C. DONALDSON

ENCLOSURE TO NO. 44

GWYNNE TO THORNE[65]

Confidential | Civil Secretariat, United Provinces, Naini Tal,
D.O. No. 6/1-C.X. | *June 20th, 1937*

7. Outwardly political activity has again been slight, though Congress activity in the villages is increasing. Important features have been (1) the large number of kisan conferences, at which speakers have indulged in

intemperate speeches, the worst of which are being examined; (2) the establishment of village Congress committees or panchayats in the various divisions of the Province. This is in accordance with the deliberate policy of Congress at present not to attempt the establishment of parallel institutions, but to set up ultimately in every village a Congress committee to establish mass contact and to undertake subterranean propaganda in order to undermine the present administration and to demonstrate the power of Congress; (3) vigorous attempts at establishing contact with the Muslims. In this respect they are said to be gaining some success with the Muslim educated unemployed. The Muslim League, however, remains firm. In Aligarh the local Ahrars are realising that opposition to Mr. Jinnah's programme is not likely to meet with success. They are therefore now representing that they are not really opposed to it and are in fact not urging Muslims to join Congress, but Congress to join the Ahrar party.

8. Government have issued orders sanctioning prosecution under Section 124-A, Indian Penal Code, in several cases, the proceedings in which will shortly be started. The most important person whose prosecution has been ordered is Sajjad Zaheer, son of Sir Wazir Hasan and a bigoted Communist. His prosecution was directed last autumn, but was withdrawn on the assurance given by his father that he would abstain from seditious speeches. This assurance he immediately repudiated. Dr. Lohia of the All India Congress Committee, Allahabad, made three very objectionable speeches, all of which were seditious and actionable. Had he merely been a Communist leader or held no important position in the Congress organisation, this government would have sanctioned his prosecution. In view, however, of the fact that he is Secretary of the Foreign Department of the Congress, and working in close touch with Pandit Jawaharlal Nehru, and a prosecution if instituted now may create difficulties in the settlement of the present impasse, the United Provinces government, who are anxious to decrease rather than to widen the breach between the Congress and the government, decided that it would be inopportune and inexpedient to sanction prosecution at the moment.

45

HAIG TO LINLITHGOW
R/3/1/2

Strictly Confidential

Camp,
July 7th, 1937

My dear Lord Linlithgow,

I am sending my seventh fortnightly report on political conditions in the United Provinces under the new constitution. So far as constitutional developments are concerned, the last fortnight has been a period of waiting. The Congress leaders have refrained from public pronouncements, and in accordance with the general attitude agreed upon with Your Excellency in separate correspondence I have made no attempt to make contact with Pant. I heard today from Sir J.P. Srivastava that Pant sent for him urgently to come and see him just before Pant himself went to Wardha a few days ago. Sir Jwala Prasad got the impression that Pant wanted some reassuring statements for the purpose of putting them before the Working Committee. It looked as if Pant was afraid of criticisms by Nehru about conditions in the United Provinces, and Pant wanted to fortify himself. He certainly asked rather elementary questions about the official attitude to which he must have known the answers.

2. I have taken no action on Chhatari's letter to me saying that he hoped I would now give the Congress another opportunity of taking office, and that in doing so I would assure them that the present cabinet would make way for a majority party ministry as soon as the latter is willing to function. I have explained the position to Chhatari and he does not press for any action to be taken at present. Several of the ministers seem to be more than doubtful about the wisdom of this letter. Meantime the situation is defining itself more clearly, and I have announced my intention of summoning both houses of the Legislature on the 29th July. The budget will be ready for presentation on Monday, the 2nd August.

3. As I mentioned to Your Excellency in a separate letter, I may find myself somewhat embarrassed in regard to the nominations to the Upper House. I had intended to make them about a month ago, but the necessity of making certain enquiries delayed the matter; and when I was ready to make my announcement, I received a message from Pant that an announcement at this stage, before the Working Committee had reached their decision, might be an embarrassment to those who wished to accept office. I have postponed the announcement; but now that the Legislature

is definitely being summoned during this month, it is clear that the nominations must be made soon and my present idea is to announce them soon after the Working Committee's decision is known. I suspect from Pant's attitude that he is anxious to get me into a position in which he could bring pressure to bear on me to make nominations in accordance with his wishes, and therefore to delay the matter as long as possible. While I think it would have been unwise to announce my nominations contrary to Pant's desire just before the meeting of the Working Committee, I cannot believe that a matter like this would have any appreciable effect on the big question of office acceptance. Pant is undoubtedly nervous of the attitude of Nehru, but I am not sure that to some extent he is not combining this with putting up a bluff on me. My nominations will be non-political, and I have no intention of nominating people because they are Congressmen any more than because they are supporters of the Agriculturist Party. The Congress party in this Province have, I think, from the beginning been disposed to attach what I regard as unreasonable importance to these nominations on the ground that they may affect the balance of parties if it comes to a joint session. Numbers are, it is true, fairly evenly balanced in the event of a joint session. I myself, however, attach little importance to this, for if the opposition had a majority in a joint session and used it to reject a major proposal of the government, this would enable the government to demand a general election – a demand which I could hardly resist – and I am sure that would be the last thing the opposition would desire.[66] I do not therefore think that in the last resort the opposition would reject a major proposal in a joint session.

4. Another appointment which has been delayed, but deliberately, is that of the Advocate-General. Owing to the two recent appointments from the Bar to the Allahabad High Court, there really is no one, outside the ranks of Congress sympathisers, who could fill the position with more than moderate adequacy. The ministers too have been divided among themselves, and there is no one whom they are unitedly anxious to appoint. As the post is one the need of which we do not feel in this Province apart from its parliamentary duties, I have delayed making the appointment, thinking that if the Congress were to take office before the Legislature met, I might allow them to make their own selection. It seems evident that anyone appointed on the advice of the present ministry would find it difficult to retain his post under a Congress government. If, however, it seems that the Congress will take office, but not until after the Legislature has met, then it will be necessary to appoint an Advocate-General within the next ten days or so.[67]

5. The cabinet had three long meetings on successive days at the end of last month in order to settle the principles of the budget and dispose of other important questions as a preliminary to the ministers returning to the plains. The budget deficit, largely owing to a somewhat fuller estimating of revenue, has been reduced from 40 lakhs to about 15 lakhs, but to this must be added certain new money totalling about 4 lakhs which the cabinet decided they must put in in order to show that they were making a beginning with part of their constructive programme. The objects for which money is provided are all sound. The budget may therefore show a deficit of something like 20 lakhs instead of 40. The question of reduction in canal rates, which would cost 6 to 8 lakhs at least, was discussed and on the whole the cabinet was opposed to it and the matter was dropped. But the Premier and the Revenue Minister were both keen about it and intend to raise it again in Lucknow on the 10th July. If the Congress are going to take office, they feel that it would bring them some credit to anticipate the Congress in taking this step. Personally I disagree and several members of the cabinet also disagree. The final decision may turn on the attitude of the Finance Minister. The cabinet have decided to draft a Bill, based largely on the principles of the Central Provinces Act, for debt conciliation, and this I think is very sound. On the whole I am inclined to think that where villagers are seriously impoverished the cause is usually debt rather than high rents.

6. Your Excellency mentioned that the Secretary of State and you yourself would be glad to know something of the attitude of ministers in charge of Law and Order. Chhatari, the Premier, holds the Home portfolio, and the Maharajkumar of Vizianagram that of Law and Justice, which includes jails and consequently the release of prisoners. Chhatari, as Your Excellency knows, is somewhat acutely sensitive to criticism, particularly press criticism, and his natural inclination is to meet his critics half way. At the same time he has had long experience, as Home Member under the old Constitution, of the practical aspects of administration and appreciates the official point of view. So far as concerns the ordinary running of the administration, Chhatari handles it very sensibly and without friction. He has been confronted with two major problems of policy – prosecution for seditious speeches and release of political prisoners. In both cases his attitude has been what might have been expected. He was personally somewhat reluctant to institute prosecutions for sedition, but the matter was put before the cabinet who showed a more decisive attitude and laid down a satisfactory policy which Chhatari has accepted. In my opinion, the prosecutions for sedition now being undertaken are quite adequate. In

regard to release of political prisoners and the further complication of the hunger strike by one of the Kakori prisoners, Chhatari has constantly been calling attention to the matter, which is in the Maharajkumar's portfolio, and would evidently like to do something to gain what he would regard as political credit. But he has made no definite proposals, and in fact it is difficult to do anything practical at the moment short of a general release, which he is not prepared to face. He is bringing the matter up for discussion at the next cabinet meeting in Lucknow on the 10th July. The outlook of the Maharajkumar of Vizianagram is quite different. He thinks out what he considers to be the right course and is guided by that and not by considerations of possible political advantage. At the same time he realises his own inexperience as compared with Chhatari. He has throughout been definitely opposed to any release of political prisoners.

7. The Muslim bye-election in Bundelkhand, which I mentioned in my last letter, is attracting a good deal of attention and the Congress are putting real effort into it. Indeed, it is said that Jawaharlal Nehru himself will visit the area. The Muslim League leaders, however, appear so far to be extremely apathetic. The Premier himself, for instance, has I believe given a little money, but has otherwise shown no outward interest in the election at all. Indeed, his attitude towards it seems to me more like that of a Governor than of a party leader. Possibly the Muslim Leaguers will bestir themselves a little more; but not much time now remains, and at present all the indications are that the Congress, largely through the inertia of their opponents, will win this rather crucial election. The publication of the Palestine report at this juncture may destroy such chances as the Muslim League may still possess, for I imagine the Congress will use it to stir up Muslim feeling against "British Imperialism".

Yours sincerely,
HARRY HAIG

46

HAIG TO LINLITHGOW
MSS.EUR.F 115/13

Private and Confidential *July 9th, 1937*

I am inclined to think that the question of the Governor presiding at cabinet meetings may become an issue of some importance with a Congress ministry. I discussed the matter twice with Your Excellency before the new Constitution came in. My original intention was not to force my presence on a ministry that was reluctant to have me presiding, and to preside only on occasions when there really was some special reason for me to put my views before the cabinet. Your Excellency felt, for reasons which I quite appreciated, that it would be better to establish a normal practice of presiding.

2. With my present ministry there has been no difficulty at all. The Premier made it clear to me at the very outset that he hoped I would preside, and I have therefore presided at every cabinet meeting held, except one when I was absent. There is no doubt that this has been advantageous to the disposal of business, and I think all the ministers have felt that there would have been difficulty in getting through the work if I had not been presiding. It has also been of great advantage to me to know precisely what are the views and currents of opinion of the cabinet as a whole and of individual members.

3. I gather from press reports that Governors have been presiding, if not invariably at any rate usually, in all the Provinces, and not merely in those with minority ministries. The practice, however, has been giving rise to a good deal of comment in the press, and in this province in particular it has been commented on repeatedly in an adverse manner by the *Leader*, which seems to regard the practice as inconsistent with the true spirit of the Constitution.

4. In these circumstances it seems to me almost certain that a Congress ministry will raise definite objection to the Governor presiding normally at cabinet meetings. They could hardly take a less independent line than a liberal paper like the *Leader*. They will be very much on their dignity to begin with, and talking a great deal about "no interference in day to day administration", and I am disposed to think that it would be a mistake to fall into a quarrel with my ministers at the very outset on a point like this. I feel that for me to preside over an unwilling and sullen cabinet would be of no use to anyone.

5. At the same time I am impressed by the fact that Indians, whose judgment is entitled to consideration, with whom I have from time to time discussed this matter in general terms, have nearly always taken the view that it is better to leave a cabinet of the Congress type to itself and not to force one's presence on it. They feel that ministers are much more likely to seek one's assistance if it is not thrust upon them. Psychologically I think they are right.

6. My own disposition therefore is, while maintaining in tact my right to preside, to inform the Chief Minister, if he makes a point of my not presiding, that I have no wish to cause him any embarrassment or to

antagonise the cabinet, and that while there may be certain occasions on which I may wish to be present at their deliberations and to express for their consideration my own views, I shall not preside unless there is some special reason for which it seems to me desirable that I should.

7. I should be glad to know whether Your Excellency feels there is any general objection to my taking this line. I feel myself rather strongly that this is not a matter on which to quarrel with one's ministers.[68]

47

HAIG TO LINLITHGOW
Telegram
MSS.EUR.F. 125/126

[No. 20-G] *July 9th, 1937*

Your telegram No. 694-G of July 8th.[69] I shall meet my government in Lucknow tomorrow and will telegraph after discussion with them. My belief is that they will wish to make way for Congress as early as possible and not wait for Legislature to meet. That is certainly my own view of what should be done.

48

HAIG TO LINLITHGOW
Telegram
MSS.EUR.F. 125/126

Unnumbered *July 10th, 1937*

In continuation of my telegram No. 20-G of July 9th. Ministry have tendered their resignation today. I have asked them to continue in office until new government is formed. I have telegraphed to Pant who is somewhere in Bundelkhand asking him to see me on Monday with a view to formation of a government.

49

HAIG TO LINLITHGOW
Telegram
MSS.EUR.F. 125/126

Clear the Line *July 12th, 1937*
No. 22-G

I saw Pant today. He seemed genuinely hurt at my having made nominations to Upper House without consulting him in spite of circumstances in which postponement of announcement was made. He said it had given rise to comment and made his position difficult and that were it not for disturbance that would be caused in whole of India, he would hesitate to take office. At the same time he made it clear that it had been his intention to press me to make all nominations in interests of Congress, which I could not possibly have agreed to. After a long and quite friendly conversation we eventually agreed that following statement should be made:

"Pant raised question of recent nominations made by Governor to Upper House. His Excellency assured Pant that in making nominations he had no intention of hampering Congress party in any way in pursuit of its activities. On the contrary it was his firm determination to do all he could to give them his full and genuine co-operation. He was intending to make the two remaining nominations and also the appointment of Advocate-General in consultation with new government."

Pant has accepted my invitation to form a ministry and will submit his list of ministers on July 16th when new government will take charge. We parted amicably. It was always my intention to keep two nominations in reserve for possible use in connection with Congress, and proposal was my own.

50

HAIG TO LINLITHGOW
Telegram
MSS.EUR.F. 125/126

Clear the Line *July 15th, 1937*
No. 23-G

With reference to my telegram No. 22, July 12th. I subsequently heard independently from Chhatari and Srivastava, both of whom Pant had visited on evening of 12th July, that he was very well pleased with result of our interview and feeling happy. I have no information as to what is behind this morning's Associated Press telegram from Allahabad which represents a modified version of a most uncompromising telegram issued yesterday afternoon. One may assume Nehru has insisted on a strong protest, but I have no idea what line Pant will take.[70] It is out of the question for me to cancel nominations and he must know this. On the other hand, he personally and Congressmen generally in the United Provinces are so far committed to forming a ministry that it is difficult to suppose that they could really refuse on this issue. The issue in effect would be the old claim that Governor should under no circumstances use powers given to him by Constitution, for their claim is as explained in my telegram of 12th July that all nominations should be made in the interest of Congress. It is an attempt to compromise position of Governor. It also perhaps represents first trial of strength between Nehru and Pant. If Pant tomorrow confirms his agreement to take office, I do not think this incident will affect our personal relations about which after our talk on Monday I am disposed to feel hopeful.

51

HAIG TO LINLITHGOW
Telegram
MSS.EUR.F. 125/126

Clear the Line *July 15th, 1937*
No. 24-G

With reference to paragraph 2 of Your Excellency's letter of July 13th to which I shall send a reply. I agree as to importance of not taking steps in one Province which may have awkward reactions in another. One of issues with which I am likely to be confronted is release of political prisoners, and I should be glad to know whether Your Excellency proposes to lay down any general policy, or would like to be consulted before any action is taken here.

52

HAIG TO LINLITHGOW
Telegram
MSS.EUR.F. 125/126

No. 25-G — Lucknow,
July 16th, 1937

Your telegram No. 731-G of July 15th.[71] Release of political prisoners. As to general attitude I agree with statement of position at beginning of paragraph No. 3, particularly in view of fact that Governor's special responsibility is limited to prevention of any grave menace.

2. In the United Provinces the position is as follows:

(*a*) Five Kakori prisoners serving long sentences, mostly transportation for life. They have all done about ten years already. This was an important revolutionary dacoity conspiracy. Two of these prisoners have within the last year or so been on prolonged hunger strike, one of whom is Bakshi who has ceased his strike.

(*b*) Eighteen persons convicted at various times of miscellaneous offences of revolutionary violence or possession of bombs or arms. They are mostly serving considerably shorter sentences than Kakori prisoners.

(*c*) Certain number of persons convicted under Section 124-A or 153-A in respect of communist or seditious speeches. There are 10 of these except those who have been convicted recently.

(*d*) There will be certain number who are under prosecution for sedition or communistic speeches. Most important is Sajjad Zaheer.

3. My general feeling is in agreement with Your Excellency that it would be unwise to press disagreement with ministry about any of these to point of break. The Province is at the moment reasonably quiet, and it would be difficult to hold that release of these men particularly under proper conditions would be a grave menace to its peace. At the same time I should propose to try and secure (*a*) that each case should come under individual consideration and that ministers should understand what these men have been convicted for and should hear the views of the police about effect of release; (*b*) that in the case of those convicted of violence if possible they should not be released without giving assurances of good behaviour; (*c*) that if possible they should be released at different times on the basis of their individual cases; and (*d*) again if possible that some

of those who have been convicted of miscellaneous crimes of violence should not be prematurely released at all. I would contemplate discussing with my Ministers on these lines and emphasising their responsibility.

4. So far as speeches are concerned, it seems to me inevitable that they will insist on releasing those who are guilty of seditious speech and withdrawing pending prosecutions and that it would not be wise to take attitude of strong opposition to this. At the same time it would be reasonable to put up to minister [?ministry] that these speeches are being made, that they presumably agree that they are very undesirable and though they may not like previous methods of dealing with such speakers, they ought to address themselves to curing the evil in some other way. They might perhaps distinguish between seditious and communist speech and take firmer line about latter.

5. My conclusion on the whole therefore is that probably it will be necessary to release practically all political prisoners as described above in this Province, but that if releases are carried out as I suggest, effect is not likely to be dangerous.

6. I am particularly anxious that Kakori prisoners should not start another hunger strike. Ministry might find it difficult to hold out against this while to give in to it would produce deplorable effect.

53

HAIG TO LINLITHGOW
MSS.EUR.F. 125/126

Private and Confidential *July 16th, 1937*

My dear Lord Linlithgow,

Many thanks for Your Excellency's letter of 13th July, which reached me yesterday afternoon.[72] I was particularly glad to get it, as it made your position about the principle of nominations so clear. I had been under some misapprehension on this point owing to Your Excellency's reference in paragraph 3 of your letter of the 9th July to "Pant's not unnatural anxiety to have some control himself over the making of your nominations". I had mistakenly got the impression that I was taking a somewhat more rigid view on principle than Your Excellency favoured. Your letter showed me that the position was quite the reverse.

2. I am sorry that my action in putting out the statement involved the

possibility of embarrassment to other Governors, a thing which I am most anxious to avoid. I had been looking upon the difficulty as solely my own, as I was under the impression that the nominations in other Provinces had been made. I have been very conscious from the moment Pant raised the question in June that it was a mistake to have left the nominations so late. I ought certainly to have foreseen the possibility of trouble. The fact is I rather dropped the matter, after some correspondence with Your Excellency, which suggested to my mind that there was no immediate hurry about getting on with it. But I quite realise that it would have been wiser to take it up again earlier than I did.

3. I also appreciate Your Excellency's views about what I said in my statement regarding the making of nominations though the matter had not at the time struck me. The fact is I felt that it was desirable to clinch matters with Pant straight away. At the end of one and a half hours' talk, he was still rather hesitating in his mind whether he should not go off and consult Nehru before definitely committing himself to forming a ministry. I put it to him that if our interview ended in this inconclusive way, it would be likely to create difficulties for both of us, and he fully appreciated this. He then suggested that I should make a statement more or less on the lines agreed upon, and I felt it was worth doing in order to secure his definite assent to the formation of a ministry. It would not have been possible to refer the matter to Your Excellency, even if it had at the moment struck me that it might be desirable, for delay and uncertainty were precisely what had in my opinion to be avoided. I therefore took the responsibility of acting. If it has proved embarrassing to Your Excellency or to the other Governors, I can only express my sincere regret.

4. Actually, in spite of the alarmist press telegram of yesterday, my agreement with Pant was effective. He is coming round at 3 o'clock this afternoon to give me his list of ministers (not, I understand, quite complete), and he has made it clear that he is not going to raise any further questions about nominations.

5. I am very fully conscious of the extreme difficulties we shall have to face in the next few months, which in my opinion will be far greater than anything with which we have been confronted hitherto. I shall endeavour to keep Your Excellency in the fullest touch with what I am proposing to do in all matters of importance.

Yours sincerely,
H.G. HAIG

54

HAIG TO LINLITHGOW
Telegram
MSS.EUR.F. 125/126

Clear the Line
No. 26-G

Lucknow,
July 16th, 1937

Pant saw me this afternoon. He raised no question of nominations. He gave me five names for his Cabinet:

Himself;
Kidwai;
Katju;
Mrs. Pandit; and
Piyare Lal Sharma.

He said that he had not yet received formal agreement of two latter, though he was confident of acceptance. He promised to telephone to me this evening on receiving confirmation, and meanwhile it was agreed that formal announcement should be withheld. He is not ready with remainder of cabinet and is evidently having trouble about suitable Moslems. He will either add one Moslem to five names already given, or two Moslems and one Hindu, making 8. He was anxious to start work with his nucleus of five and to this I have agreed. Ministers will take oath of office tomorrow.

NOTES

1. Lord Linlithgow had argued that a resolution by a provincial legislature recommending the establishment of a committee of enquiry on the behaviour of troops would in fact relate to a federal matter which was outside its executive authority. The Governor would have no option but to reject such a recommendation. MSS.EUR.F. 125/126.
2. In his letter of 4 April 1937 Lord Linlithgow thanked Sir Harry Haig for No. 20. The Viceroy entirely agreed with Haig's decision to push matters in respect of ministry formation. MSS.EUR.F. 115/18.
3. See No. 18, note 21.
4. Lord Linlithgow replied to Sir Harry Haig's question in a letter dated 7 April 1937. The Viceroy felt that Haig could 'go ahead on your strong suit with all confidence, though naturally it is impossible to give any guarantee against

a complete climbing down by Congress.' Linlithgow judged that within Congress 'such feelings of regret [at not accepting office] as there may be will be intensified as Congress see minority ministries actually functioning. Psychologically, I should have thought that the right course is to adopt as actively a policy as possible consistently of course with avoiding trailing one's coat.' MSS.EUR.F. 115/18.

5. L/P&J/9/287.
6. Lord Linlithgow minuted: 'But is it!'
7. Lord Linlithgow minuted: 'Also ownership makes conservatives!'
8. Lord Linlithgow minuted: 'A point for P.J. G[rigg], but don't rub in!' Sir James Grigg was Finance Member of the Government of India at this date.
9. In his telegram 302-S of 7 April 1937 Lord Linlithgow reported that the Governor of Bihar (Sir Maurice Hallett) was taking steps to give special publicity in the vernacular to his communiqué announcing the breakdown of discussions with Congress. MSS.EUR.F. 115/18.
10. Lord Lothian had been Parliamentary Under-Secretary at the India Office, 1931-2. In a lengthy letter to *The Times* published on 6 April 1937, Lothian stressed the importance of the introduction of democracy in India. He felt that in the Dominions 'the Governor, when responsible government exists, has usually decided to act on its advice – which is why the system has hitherto always led gradually but inexorably to complete self-government'. He spoke in a similar manner in the House of Lords on 8 April.
11. On 8 April 1937 following the speech of Lord Lothian. See *Parl. Debs.,* 5th series, House of Lords, vol. 104, cols. 875-85. Lord Zetland concluded his speech: '[T]he reserve powers are an integral part of the constitution . . . [but] there is no reason why the reserve powers of the Governors should come into play. Whether they do or not must, of course, depend upon the policy and proceedings of the Ministries themselves.'
12. See Appendix 4.
13. See Appendix 2.
14. In his letter to Governors of 10 April 1937, Lord Linlithgow said that he was anxious that there should be a proper and adequate presentation of the case of the government and the Governors. He added that 'during the first stage, when the Governor is dealing with a minority ministry, it may, as I see it, be difficult to avoid a certain amount of propaganda through the permanent machinery and at the cost of Government'. However Linlithgow stressed: 'it must continue to be our policy and object to get Congress into office wherever they have a majority, and anti-Congress propaganda will inevitably embitter the situation, and incidentally provide Congress, when they do take office, with a thoroughly bad example which they would be quick to follow'. MSS.EUR.F. 125/126.
15. Ibid.
16. Not printed.

17. In his letter of 27 April 1937, Lord Linlithgow had expressed concern at Sir Harry Haig's views as to the possible use of non-Congress organisations to publicise the Governor's policies. (See No. 26.) Linlithgow felt that during a Section 93 regime, a Governor would be concerned as far as might be practicable to stand aside from any party organisation. MSS.EUR.F. 125/126.
18. Lord Linlithgow minuted: 'Or *any* for the *act* of propaganda.'
19. Not printed.
20. Mr Raghavendra Rao was Premier of the Central Provinces and Berar between April and July 1937.
21. Babu Purshottam Das Tandon had forwarded the two resolutions passed by the M.L.As. at their meeting on 9 May 1937. (See No. 29.) In his lengthy reply (sent by Mr Donaldson), Sir Harry Haig said that the present situation had arisen because of the refusal of Congress to take office. Haig felt it was only fair to the present ministry 'that they should be given full opportunity of placing their measures before the Legislature'. He also felt that it was only fair to the members of the Legislature 'that they should not reach a decision on the grave constitutional decisions that have arisen until they have had ample time to consider them from all aspects and without haste. But when these conditions have been fulfilled, His Excellency will not delay the summoning of the Legislature.' MSS.EUR.F. 115/18.
22. Telegram G-8 of 16 May 1937. Ibid.
23. Telegram 429-S of 14 May 1937. Ibid.
24. Mr C. Rajagopalachariar was Congress leader in Madras at this date.
25. Lord Linlithgow's letter of 18 May 1937 to Governors discussed future action towards Congress. In paragraph 2 the Viceroy said he felt there was little sign of a split in Congress and that they might be in for a long fight. However he thought they had now reached a stage at which they should actively consider their immediate constructive policy and whether any step could be taken. In paragraph 3 Linlithgow said he had in mind that he should issue something like a message or public statement 'emphasizing the nature of the assurances and explanations which have been given by the Secretary of State and by Governors; indicating my entire agreement with Zetland's view of the attitude which a Governor would adopt in the matter of his special responsibilities; and expressing the hope that, now that the situation has been clarified, earlier doubts or misgivings will no longer persist or impede the normal working of the constitution.' In paragraph 18 Linlithgow warned Governors of discussing in too great detail with existing ministers certain of the alternative courses of action open to them. Governors should carefully avoid being identified with a particular party or give the impression that a minority ministry could have a share in government in a Section 93 situation. In paragraph 20 Linlithgow discussed the desire of Congress that its ministries should be dismissed by Governors in the event of a disagreement rather than themselves resign. In

paragraph 21 Linlithgow urged Governors to adopt the long view whatever the difficulties. 'So long as the present Act is in operation, and so long as Congress represent the largest party in the Legislatures, it must inevitably be our object to secure the help of Congress in carrying on the administration.' I.O.R. Brabourne Papers (MSS.EUR.F. 97).

26. See No. 13, note 15.
27. MSS.EUR.F. 115/18.
28. The relevant portion of paragraph VIII of the *Instrument of Instructions* to Governors read:

    'In all matters within the scope of the executive authority of the Province, save in relation to functions which he is required by or under the Act to exercise in his discretion, Our Governor shall in the exercise of the powers conferred upon him be guided by the advice of his Ministers, unless in his opinion so to be guided would be inconsistent with the fulfilment of any of the special responsibilities which are by the Act committed to him … [in which case] Our Governor shall, notwithstanding his Ministers' advice, act in exercise of the powers by or under the Act conferred upon him in such manner as to his individual judgment seems requisite.' Parl. Papers, H. of C. paper No. 1, vol. XX, 1936–7, pp. 1031–8.
29. No. 14.
30. See note 21 above.
31. See No. 30, note 21.
32. Not printed.
33. Lord Linlithgow had seen the Nawab of Chhatari within the previous week. He reported that Chhatari had given him a positive assurance that in no circumstances would he leave Sir Harry Haig without a ministry with which to face the legislature. MSS.EUR.F. 115/13.
34. Lord Linlithgow said that during the interview the Nawab of Chhatari had suggested that the U.P. minority ministry would, once the Legislature had been convened but three or four days before it was due to meet, place their resignations in the hands of the Governor. Haig would refuse to accept the resignations and with the full knowledge of the minority ministry would send for the Congress leader. Haig would intimate to Pandit Pant that his present ministers were well aware that they were only a minority in the Legislature and had no desire if the majority party were prepared to take office to stand in their way. The Governor would enquire whether Congress were now prepared to take office.

    After consideration, Linlithgow caused Chhatari to be informed that he felt that it would be better if the proposed tendering of resignations took place before the Legislature had been convened. Otherwise it would not be difficult for the Congress leader when summoned to reply that he was not prepared to commit himself at that stage and that he desired to await the verdict of the Legislature. Ibid.

35. In paragraph 6 of his letter, Lord Linlithgow reported that the Nawab of Chhatari had suggested there was a good deal to be said for the following of a common course of action by all the minority Ministries. The Viceroy was not sure about this idea and feared it would lead to the suggestion that there was an undue degree of coordination. Ibid.
36. Not printed.
37. Not included in R/3/1/2.
38. Mr C. Rajagopalachariar was the Congress leader in Madras at this date and Lord Erskine was the Governor.
39. In a statement issued on 2 June 1937, Mahatma Gandhi said that he would be satisfied if, instead of dismissing Congress ministries in the event of a difference of opinion, Provincial Governors asked for their resignation. 'I am very anxious,' he added, 'that Congress men should take office but only if Government show willingness to conciliate them. All conciliation moves so far have come from Congress. Do Government really want Congress in office or do they not? If they do it is time they made a friendly gesture.'
40. Mr Muhammad Yunus was the Premier of Bihar at this date.
41. Lord Linlithgow minuted: 'Better, if possible, let Congress take the first step, lest they take a second when they succeed.'
42. In his telegram 579-S of 18 June 1937 Lord Linlithgow said he wished to postpone his reply to the present telegram until his Statement had appeared and they could see reactions to it. MSS.EUR.F. 115/20.
43. In telegram 558-S of 16 June 1937, Lord Linlithgow gave an account of the recent interview between Lord Erskine and Mr Rajagopalachariar. The Viceroy felt that the pressure on Congress to accept office was becoming increasingly strong. He had worded his statement (see note 47 below) in the most conciliatory manner possible. He was sure Sir Harry Haig would 'agree that it is most important that we should continue if anything to err on the side of over-emphasising our anxiety for the co-operation of Congress'. The Viceroy was most anxious to avoid a breakdown and they could consider their general policy further in the light of the response to his statement. MSS.EUR.F. 115/18.
44. Sir Harry Haig here deleted a sentence in the draft which had read: 'But there is of course something in the point made by Pant in his recent statement that Ministers can be expected to resign only when they have lost the support of the Legislature and not merely when they cannot get their way with the Governor.'
45. In his draft letter sent on 16 June 1937, the Nawab of Chhatari invited Sir Harry Haig to enter into further discussions with the Congress party with a view to their taking office. Haig told Lord Linlithgow that Chhatari's proposal had not been discussed with the cabinet and it could not be taken for granted that they would accept it. MSS.EUR.F. 115/13.
46. In his letter of 21 June 1937, Lord Linlithgow said he entirely agreed with Sir Harry Haig that the right course was to wait and let the situation develop

in the light of reactions to his Statement. They must, he thought, keep an entirely free hand as regards tactics. Ibid.

47. In his statement of 21 June 1937 Lord Linlithgow dealt with the question of the Governors' special powers. He said they related to strictly limited and clearly defined areas and a Governor was not 'free, or is entitled, or would have the power, to interfere with the day-to-day administration of a Province' outside his special responsibilities. Before taking a decision against the wishes of Ministers, Governors would spare no pains in making clear the reasons which had weighed upon them. Given goodwill on both sides, conflicts need not in a normal situation be anticipated.
48. Not included in R/3/1/2.
49. A minute by Lord Linlithgow indicates that the information in this paragraph was to be sent to Lord Zetland.
50. See No. 38.
51. Sir James Taylor was Governor of the Reserve Bank of India at this date.
52. The so-called 'Kakori case' came out of action taken by a group called the 'Hindusthan Republican Association' which had for its object the establishment of a Federal Republic of the United States of India by organised and armed revolution. Four dacoities were committed by the group in 1924 and 1925 in three of which it murdered people. The last dacoity took place on a railway train at Kakori on the main Lucknow-Dehra Dun line. Twenty-two persons stood trial for the dacoities and twenty were convicted. Four received death sentences, five were sentenced to transportation for life and the remainder received terms of rigorous imprisonment. L/P&J/7/1261: f. 251.
53. Mr G.M. Harper.
54. Mr H.J. Frampton.
55. Sir John Hewett was Governor of the U.P. between 1907 and 1912.
56. Not included in R/3/1/2.
57. Lord Linlithgow minuted: 'How is this to be reconciled with his latest telegram re Ministry's offer to resign being sent to Pant.' See No. 38.
58. In telegram 604-G of 22 June 1937 Lord Linlithgow asked for a brief telegraphic report of local reactions to his broadcast and Statement. MSS.EUR.F. 115/18.
59. Lord Linlithgow replied in telegram 638-S of 27 June 1937. The Viceroy noted that:

> 'Chhatari has actually made announcement to Associated Press more or less on the lines taken by him in his letter and I should have thought this had made his position and that of your Ministry vis-à-vis Congress sufficiently clear. I do not think that there is anything to be gained by the publication of his letter before Working Committee meets, and my own suggestion to you would be that if published at all (I do not suggest that it should be cancelled) it could best be published immediately before meeting of Legislature.'

Linlithgow was inclined to mark time until they knew the disposition of the Congress Working Committee. MSS.EUR.F. 115/13.

60. Lord Linlithgow's letter of 29 June 1937 referred to his telegram 638-G of 27 June (see note above) and elaborated the views therein. The Viceroy felt: 'we shall do best to let matters take their course for the time being, await the summoning of the Legislatures, and not for the moment perturb ourselves about making contact with Congress leaders'. Ibid.
61. In telegram 654-G of 1 July 1937, Lord Linlithgow asked certain Governors for their views on the desirability of adopting the Bihar procedure of summoning the Legislature for a meeting solely to take oaths and elect officers. The Legislature would then adjourn and meet again in early August 1937 for the transaction of ordinary business. Linlithgow felt this would give Congress time to think things over. MSS.EUR.F. 125/126.
62. i.e. No. 39.
63. The texts of the paragraphs mentioned in this sentence are not included in R/3/1/2.
64. Mr B.G.P. Thomas.
65. Mr J.A. Thorne was Joint Secretary to the Government of India, Home Department at this date.
66. Lord Linlithgow minuted: 'An important point.'
67. Lord Linlithgow minuted: 'Even so, it might in effect be a Congress nomination.'
68. In response to this letter Lord Linlithgow sent a circular telegram to all Governors. (No. 721-G of 13 July 1937.) The Viceroy felt it was important that the principle of Governors presiding at cabinet meetings should be maintained. However, he accepted there might be advantage in greater elasticity as follows: (*a*) by Governors absenting themselves at say every fifth or sixth meeting; (*b*) by Governors using their discretion to leave a meeting at a certain point so it could discuss items having a special party complexion or importance. Linlithgow asked Governors for information on their practice since April 1937 with regard to cabinet meetings. MSS.EUR. F. 115/13.
69. This telegram is not included in MSS.EUR.F. 125/126. However on 7 July 1937, the Congress Working Committee, meeting at Wardha, had decided on office acceptance and no doubt Lord Linlithgow had asked Sir Harry Haig how he intended to respond to this development.

    In its resolution the Working Committee noted the Statements of Lord Zetland, Lord Stanley (Under Secretary of State for India) and Lord Linlithgow and stated that 'though they exhibit a desire to make an approach to the Congress demand they fall short of the assurances demanded'. However, the Committee felt 'the situation created as the result of the circumstances and events that have since occurred, warrants the belief that it will not be easy for the Governors to use their special powers'. The Committee desired to make it clear that office was to be accepted and utilised for the purpose of working along the lines laid down in the Congress election manifesto. This was to further in every possible way the Congress policy of combating the new Act and of prosecuting the constructive programme.

70. Pandit Pant had left Lucknow on the afternoon of 13 July 1937 to acquaint Pandit Nehru (as President of Congress) with what had transpired in his talk with Sir Harry Haig. The Associated Press messages referred to by Haig may refer to a statement which Maulana Azad made to the A.P. on 13 July. Azad said that nothing had yet been decided on the formation of the U.P. ministry and the matter would be discussed at Allahabad. With regard to Muslim League participation in the Ministry, Azad said 'if any party wanted to join the Congress it must give up its separate identity and identify itself with the Congress.' *Leader*, 15 July 1937, p. 11.

71. In paragraph 3 of his telegram 731-G to Governors on the question of the release of political prisoners, Lord Linlithgow stressed the desirability of avoiding an immediate breach with the Congress ministries. For 'with a Ministry responsible for law and order it would be difficult to take too firm a line merely because of one's own anticipations of danger if they after full discussion are prepared to accept responsibility for any breach of peace and tranquillity which may result from release'. MSS.EUR.F. 125/126.

72. In his letter of 13 July 1937 to Sir Harry Haig, the Viceroy said he did not feel altogether easy at the terms of the communiqué which the Governor had issued. He considered it 'unfortunate that any *public* undertaking as regards prior consultation over nominations should have been given, for it may well place other Governors in a very difficult position'. Linlithgow was not suggesting a rigid or inflexible attitude towards Congress and they should endeavour to meet Congress's suggestions so far as practicable. However, it was 'essential that Congress should not think that because they have on our terms accepted office, they have got us on the run'. Ibid.

CHAPTER 3

Documents for 17 July – 30 September 1937

55

HAIG TO LINLITHGOW
Telegram
MSS.EUR.F. 115/13

Clear the Line *July 17th, 1937*
No. 27-G

Reference Your Excellency's telegram No. 721-G dated 13th July.[1] Pant has not himself on any occasion said anything to me about the Governor presiding over cabinet meetings. But today he remarked to Donaldson that the Rules of Business which he had been looking at were not such as self-respecting ministers could agree to. He referred in particular to the Governor approving the agenda of cabinet meetings and to the Governor presiding. I am at the moment doing nothing, but I think it is clear, as anticipated in my letter of July 9th, that question of Governor presiding will be pressed as an important issue. I think it should be possible to convince him about the agenda.

2. I do not yet know Pant sufficiently to be confident of my judgement about him, but he seems to me a person greatly swayed by his feelings and perhaps likely to take an extreme view over a point like this which he may regard as a crucial test of his position and our intentions. It is difficult at present to form an opinion of his real attitude towards the position of the Governor. Speaking to me on Monday he was exceedingly emphatic about the necessity of my assistance and explained that he would be quite unable to carry on the administration unless he felt that I was able to help and even, I understood, advise him continually. I formed the opinion that he was perfectly genuine in what he said. There was no trace of any feeling

of wishing to keep the Governor at a distance. The impression he conveyed was quite the contrary. But it is possible that while picturing me as playing an important part he also pictures that part as being played very much in background.

3. I report the situation in the meantime as difficulties may arise at any moment if I am to take the line indicated in your telegram of 13th July, and if there is serious trouble on this point, non-Congress opinion in this province will, I feel, be definitely with Pant.

56

HAIG TO LINLITHGOW
Telegram
MSS.EUR.F. 125/126

No. 28-G *July 17th, 1937*

My telegram No. 26-G, July 16th. It was not possible to get hold of Sharma last night as he was travelling to Meerut. Communiqué therefore issued without mentioning him and today Pant seems to have different opinion and wishes to leave him over for consideration with second detachment to which I have no objection. Ministry therefore have taken office consisting only of the first four names.

57

HAIG TO LINLITHGOW
R/3/1/2

Strictly Confidential *July 21st, 1937*

My dear Lord Linlithgow,

I am sending my eighth fortnightly report on political conditions in the United Provinces under the new Constitution. During the last fortnight things have moved very fast, and on a number of important issues I have had separate correspondence with Your Excellency which I need not repeat.

2. I arrived in Lucknow on the morning of July 10th. I saw Chhatari at once, and we agreed that the ministry should tender its resignation without delay. They had a half-hour meeting by themselves before I arrived for the cabinet meeting, and decided to submit their resignations. We then

had a long cabinet meeting trying to dispose of a number of unsettled issues. After considerable discussion they decided, to my relief, not to reduce canal rates. They also decided not to discuss the question of the release of political prisoners. They spent some time on the principles of a Debt Conciliation Bill, which they decided, I think wisely, to publish for eliciting public opinion even though they could not get any further.

3. At my request they agreed to continue in office until the new government was settled, and I did not accept their resignations formally until the afternoon of the 16th. During that time we had one rather difficult discussion about Muslim educational policy, a matter which had been under consideration for a long time and was practically ready for a pronouncement. The discussion, as was inevitable, took a somewhat communal turn, but eventually an agreement was reached which was reasonably satisfactory to both sides, and a communiqué on the subject was issued.

4. It has occurred to me from something Your Excellency said in your letter of 9th July that you may have derived from my letters a somewhat misleading impression of the general working of the Chhatari cabinet. I have naturally mentioned the various points of difficulty that have arisen, and though they all required careful consideration and some handling, I should like you to understand that the ministry both individually and as a whole have been extremely pleasant, considerate and generally speaking easy to deal with, certainly as compared with the standards that must be expected in the future. Chhatari's administrative experience, and his qualities of good temper and tact were a genuine asset. Sir J.P. Srivastava put in some really valuable constructive work, and the new ministers handled their charges satisfactorily. They would have found difficulty in holding together without my assistance, but they were always ready to listen to what I had to say, and so reasonable in discussion when taken the right way that it lightened my task immensely. In spite of a good many difficult general problems that confronted us during the last three and a half months, I look upon that period as one of comparative rest and tranquillity. Even though we may, I hope, come through the approaching period with success (and I realise that we are playing for high stakes), in many respects it is going to be a vastly more difficult business.

5. I have already told Your Excellency about my interview with Pant when he came to see me for the first time on July 12th. He was a good deal upset about my having made my nominations to the Upper House, and complained that they would have the effect of weakening the position of Congress. I had always had it in mind that if the Congress took office, I

might consult them about a suitable representative of Labour, who would obviously be in sympathy with the Congress, and in the course of conversation I volunteered that I would also consult him about the remaining nomination. I also mentioned the fact that the Advocate-General's post still remained to be filled.[2] These things made a considerable impression on his mind, but he was still genuinely hesitating whether he should not consult Nehru before committing himself to accepting my invitation to form a ministry. I felt that if he went away and consulted Nehru, we might have very serious complications, and it seemed to me of the first importance to clinch the matter there and then and put out a statement. He asked me to include in the statement some reference to the nominations, about which I have since had correspondence with Your Excellency, and to this I agreed. I think from the point of view of our provincial situation what I did was undoubtedly wise. He had to go to Allahabad the day after his interview with me in order to consult about the *personnel* of his cabinet. At Allahabad there was a good deal of talk about the nominations, and it is clear both from press statements and from what he himself has told me since that he was pressed very strongly on the subject. But he took the line that he had given me his word and that he could not go back on it; and in fact when he returned, as promised, on the 16th to give me the proposed names of his cabinet he made no further reference to the nominations.

6. Pant is evidently having considerable difficulty in making up his cabinet. When he came to me on the afternoon of the 16th he gave me five names: himself, Mr. Kidwai, Dr. Katju, Mrs. Pandit and Mr. Piyare Lal Sharma, the latter being a Vakil of no very great note from Meerut. He said he had not had the formal assent of the two latter, but he hoped to obtain this by the evening and it was agreed that the communiqué should go out that evening, giving the names of those who by that time had given their assent. Later he found it impossible to communicate with Mr. Sharma, who was travelling back to Meerut. The communiqué therefore included only the first four names, and the next day he told me that though he had had the assent of Mr. Sharma, he wished now to leave this matter over and announce the remainder of his cabinet at one time. It looks to me as if Mr. Sharma may possibly not find a place in the end. I have no real information as to the precise difficulties that are confronting Pant. He is uncommunicative and I have not questioned him. The main difficulty, however, is that of securing one or two additional Muslims. He told me he contemplated a cabinet of either six with two Muslims, or eight with three Muslims. He was evidently counting on a Congress success in the Jhansi

bye-election, where a competent Muslim – Sherwani – was standing, but it has been clear for a day or two that the Muslim League candidate has won the election and this result has now been announced officially. This leaves the Congress with practically no Congress Muslim other than Kidwai to put in, and talk seems to be proceeding as to the possibility of an agreement with the Muslim League whereby they would have two members in the cabinet. It is hardly worth while speculating as to how the situation will develop. Pant told me yesterday that it would still be two or three days before he could let me have his final list. So far the composition of the cabinet is less extreme than might have been expected, but if the Muslim League conversations[3] fall through, I anticipate that the cabinet will assume a more extreme complexion.

7. The prospects of the new administration working out on reasonably satisfactory lines depend, I think, very largely on the relations I am able to establish with Pant. He represents the more moderate element in the cabinet, and will I anticipate have his own difficulties continually with the extremer element both inside the cabinet and outside, particularly with Jawaharlal Nehru. At the same time Pant has a rather curious combination of characteristics, though I do not yet feel that I know him sufficiently well to be able to estimate the comparative importance of the various characteristics in shaping his general outlook and conduct. He is a sincere enthusiast for the public good, as he sees it, and is particularly determined to ameliorate the lot of the peasants. He is much under the influence of democratic principles and theories, which he holds with conviction and tenacity. He is easily swayed by his feelings, and has what I might call a genuine sentimental outlook on affairs. At the same time he has an unusually acute dialectical brain and, I should judge, a keen sense of the advantages of a tactical position. But while I think that from this point of view one has to be very wide awake in dealing with him, I believe that according to his own principles he attaches great importance to frank discussion and to observing an agreement once it has been reached. In practical matters, so far as I can form an opinion at present, he does not seem to me quite so clear-headed as one would have expected from his dialectical powers and his sense of tactics. Finally, he has some rather attractive personal characteristics, not the least among which is a sense of humour. Those are the elements, so far as I have been able to observe them at present, in the character of a man on whose relations with myself a great deal will depend.

8. I shall not go at any length into the questions of release of political prisoners and the Governor presiding at cabinet meetings, which have

formed the subject of detailed correspondence between us. With regard to political prisoners and allied subjects, though Pant has very definitely forced the issue and indeed, through some misunderstanding, put a statement into the press to only part of which at the time I had agreed, I cannot complain that his practical outlook has been unreasonable or that he has tried to push forward proposals which represent more than the minimum which he is bound by the general policy of Congress to try and secure at the outset.[4] The points on which he has concentrated are:

(*a*) cancelling security demanded from newspapers and presses other than on communal grounds, but he has abstained from raising the question of refunding securities that have been forfeited;

(*b*) cancelling orders proclaiming certain associations to be unlawful. After a full discussion with the Inspector-General of Police[5] I am satisfied that there is no real practical danger involved in this. The notifications have been in force for over five years, and the associations have really ceased to function. Where they have wanted to continue their activities, they have started under a new name[6] and are functioning now, for instance, the Yuvak Sangh instead of the Youth League, and the Mazdur Sabha, Cawnpore, instead of the Workers and Peasants Party, Cawnpore; and really the withdrawal of these notifications is not much more I hope than cutting away dead wood. There is perhaps a danger that the withdrawal of the notifications may lead to a movement for the revival of the organisations, but in any case it is always possible for organisations of this type to be started up again, as I have already explained, if there is any real demand for them.

To these two points I agreed on Sunday. The other immediate items in his programme were:

(*c*) the withdrawal of pending prosecutions for sedition;
(*d*) the cancellation of securities taken under Section 108;
(*e*) the release of prisoners convicted under Section 124-A.

These were the matters about which a semi-official statement was made before I had given my assent, though I had had some general talk with him on the subject. I have since looked into the details of these, and agreed. There is not much in them, only four releases, for instance, under Section 124-A, and two of these with sentences practically expired. In regard to persons convicted for offences connected with violence, which is a much more important matter, he proposes to examine the cases individually and I hope we shall be able to arrive at reasonable conclusions.

9. When my present four ministers were sworn in on Saturday, I addressed a few words of welcome to them, and in particular stressed the point that behind all their far-reaching projects and policies there was an immensely important background. For a considerable time past Congress and the government had been regarded as antagonistic forces. Now Congress are the government. I pointed out that that fact demanded perhaps a good deal of mental adjustment. The great public services of the Province would now be engaged in carrying out the policy of a Congress government. I said I was confident that their desire would be to perform their duties loyally towards those to whom their duty is now owing, and I added I was sure that the ministers on their part would recognise that the services are the services of the Province, not of a party, and that so long as they carry out their duties to the government loyally and efficiently, they should be able to feel that they will be treated on their merits. After the swearing-in the ministers went down to the Secretariat and there Pant assembled the Secretaries and addressed them for about an hour. I attach a report[7] of what he said, which has been published in the papers. So far as I have heard the Secretaries felt that his attitude was sincere and not unfriendly, and on the whole I think the address did good.

10. I was somewhat disturbed yesterday on finding that the press statement about political prisoners, to which I have referred above, had anticipated my assent, and I felt it necessary to have this matter out plainly with Pant. He came to see me yesterday afternoon, and we had the most satisfactory talk that has yet taken place between us. He explained that what he had done was due to a genuine misapprehension about my intentions, and I fully accepted what he said. I then took the opportunity to have a general talk with him about the position of the Governor under the Constitution. He raised immediately, though in a tone of moderation, the question whether I would preside at cabinet meetings. I told him that normally that would be the procedure. We discussed the matter for a time, both from the point of view of general principle and practical advantage, and he said he would like to raise it again when the cabinet was complete. But he took it more quietly than I had anticipated. I also took the occasion to explain to him my general position under the Rules of Business and the Secretariat Instructions and the necessity for me to keep myself fully informed of what goes on. Here again he was perfectly reasonable, though he said that when the full cabinet was formed, there might be certain matters in connection with the Rules that he might want to raise. Altogether

I was very well satisfied with this talk, which was both frank and perfectly friendly.

11. There is some apprehension of serious industrial trouble in Cawnpore. For the last six months or so there have been occasional short-lived strikes in particular mills, and only at the beginning of the month there was one such strike at the New Victoria Mills, in which Sir Jwala Prasad Srivastava has a controlling interest, which lasted for a week or two, but was settled satisfactorily. Now the workers of the important group of Kamlapat Mills have come out, and some threats are being made that this may develop into a general industrial strike in Cawnpore. The District Magistrate[8] has asked the Premier to go over to Cawnpore and use his influence to prevent such a development. The Premier has been in touch with the principal Labour leader in Cawnpore, and I understand he is likely to go over there today. I think there are reasonable prospects that he will be able to prevent any further developments. Labour was probably stirred up a good deal during the general election, and it is not unnatural that the assumption of office by the Congress should lead them to think that the time may be propitious for securing concessions. On the other hand, if this matter does not go too far, it will not be a bad thing that the Congress ministers should at the very outset have some practical experience of the possible dangers of the labour situation in Cawnpore.[9]

Yours sincerely,
H.G. HAIG

58

HAIG TO LINLITHGOW
MSS.EUR.F. 115/13

Private and Confidential *July 22nd, 1937*

Many thanks for Your Excellency's personal and confidential letter of 19th July.[10] I quite appreciate the position about presiding over cabinet meetings, and as you will have seen from my letter of yesterday, I have already told Pant that that is my intention, and he took it much better than I had anticipated. I am not sure that my private opinion in regard to this problem as relating to a Congress ministry does not remain as before, in spite of the number and weight of authority against it.[11] But I fully appreciate the importance of uniformity in this matter, and as soon as I heard from Laithwaite over the telephone on Sunday what the policy was I was entirely prepared to conform. It is indeed far easier to take this line when it is being taken in all other provinces.

59

HAIG TO LINLITHGOW
Telegram
MSS.EUR.F. 125/126

Clear the Line *July 22nd, 1937*
No. 29-G

I see in today's papers that Premier has hoisted Congress flag at his residence and that it is stressed that this is government building. Heard nothing about this until I read it in papers. My first inclination was to regard it as a rather unimportant demonstration perhaps intended to lead me into a remonstrance which would seem unreasonable. The fact however that so much stress has been laid in press paragraph on this being a government building makes me suspect that it may be first in a policy intended to lead to a claim to fly Congress flag on public buildings used for public purposes. I am therefore proposing to see Pant and, while making a light reference to his flying the flag on his house and saying that naturally ministers can do what they like in their own houses, I should have to resist definitely any kind of proposal to fly Congress flag on public buildings used for public purposes. I feel I must give him this warning. I should be grateful to know whether Your Excellency has any comments. The main point is that I propose to take no objection to what he has already done. My view is that a minister can do as he pleases with his own house even if it be one rented from government or even allotted to him free, as this may eventually be part of his personal remuneration.[12]

60

HAIG TO LINLITHGOW
Telegram
MSS.EUR.F. 115/13

Express *July 30th, 1937*
No. 33-G

I had a rather disturbing interview with Pant yesterday evening regarding Governor presiding at cabinet meetings. When I first informed him some days ago of my intention normally to preside, while he expressed his plain disagreement in principle, he left me with the impression as reported in para. 10 of my letter of July 21st, that he would acquiesce under protest.

2. Question came up yesterday as it is essential for cabinet to hold meeting today. I told him I agreed to their holding meeting and that it was impossible for me to be present as I was still confined to bed, but that he would understand that the principle which I had explained to him at our last interview remained in tact. He then said that he had been thinking the matter over very carefully since our last conversation and that he definitely could not bring himself to accept this position. It was a matter of principle with him. His conception was that of a Council of Ministers working as a Council and discussing their policy and tendering their advice to the Governor. It was wholly foreign to his conception of the Constitution that the Governor who had his own definite functions to perform should also take part in the deliberations of his Council. I understood him to say that if there were some definite matter which the Governor wished to discuss with his Council or on which he wished to communicate his views to them, then he would naturally come and preside, and this was what he contemplated as the intention of the words used in the Act. Apart from the objection of principle, he said that the individual members of the cabinet would find it difficult to express with perfect frankness their views in the presence of the Governor, that on matters in which they might differ considerably among themselves they might feel it necessary to preserve a united front before the Governor, and that in this way deprived of the opportunity of really frank discussion among themselves they might not arrive at sound conclusions. He spoke with great politeness and even I think conviction regarding the assistance that the Governor might be able to give them during their deliberations, and he stressed more than once that his objection was not in the least of a personal character, that he did not anticipate any unpleasantness, but that it was a matter of principle to which he attached the highest importance.

3. Question arises how this deadlock is to be resolved. At an early stage of the conversation he suggested that he could not take part in cabinet meetings if held under the presidency of the Governor. Later he said more than once that this was a matter on which he felt so strongly that he would be prepared if necessity arose to resign. I do not think he has really thought out what his course of action would be, and if he is given time for reflexion and sees that the system is adopted in all other provinces I think he may eventually come round. But I think Your Excellency should know that he did use to me definitely language indicating the possibility of resignation.

I told him, apart from the stock arguments, that this was really an all India question, that so far as I knew this policy was being adopted in all provinces, but that I would communicate the purport of our conversation to Your Excellency, though I held out no hope that there would be any change in policy.

4. The matter is most unfortunate. Pant has lately been extremely helpful and anxious to make things easy. The question of the nominations which might have given rise to some disagreement was settled to my satisfaction. He selected as Advocate-General a man whom the late government would probably have appointed and who was in my opinion the best man available. This was a surprising decision and has got Pant into trouble with his own people. But he shows a good deal of courage in these matters. When I saw him yesterday I think he was a little sore and battered after two days of Nehru, who I fancy was trying to bully them all. It would be a thousand pities to come to a break with Pant over this issue. I do not think myself that given time he will press his objection to the point of resignation. But he is a somewhat incalculable person and stands very firmly on principles.

5. Meantime my illness provides perhaps a convenient breathing space. It was obvious I could not preside today. The Civil Surgeon has pressed me strongly to go up to Naini Tal for a fortnight as soon as possible to give myself a chance of picking up quickly and I am proposing to leave on Saturday, August 7th. Between then and now I think we could avoid the necessity of another cabinet meeting. By the time I came down from Naini Tal, Pant would have had plenty of time to consider his position; and if in fact this system has been adopted in other provinces I do not think he would hold out. Does Your Excellency agree with these suggestions for handling the matter?[13]

61

HAIG TO LINLITHGOW
Telegram
MSS.EUR.F. 125/126

No. 37-G *August 5th, 1937*

Your telegram No. 290-G.C. of August 4th regarding Andaman prisoners.[14] Before receipt of your telegram I had had some talk with Pant yesterday on question of clemency to prisoners convicted of offences in connection with violence in the United Provinces and the course of discussion was in fact on the lines suggested by Your Excellency in paragraph 4 of your telegram. Pant told me he had been looking into some of individual cases and he was inclined to think that those who had served half their sentences might be released. I suggested that instead of adopting any general rule of this kind it was desirable that an attempt should be made to assert [?ascertain] the circumstances of each individual case and in particular that it was necessary to know what views of Police were about various prisoners. He took line that in case of men like Kakori prisoners who had been in jail for ten years the police could not know their present mentality or probability of their resuming dangerous activities, that in any case they had got to be released some time at expiration of their sentences, and that there was nothing to suggest it would be more dangerous to release them now than two or three years hence. I said that when men were released at the end of their sentence, it involved no responsibility on Executive government, but if government released them prematurely, it took upon itself a very definite responsibility for consequences, and if it was taking a risk it must know what that risk was. I said it would be necessary in any case for me to know what the police view about individual prisoners was both in regard to their activities before arrest, the present nature of movement in Province with which they had been connected and consequently the probability of movement receiving any impetus from their release. I put it to him strongly that both from point of view of his responsibilities and of reassuring police who were working under him, it was very desirable that he himself should call for views of police and not leave it to me to do so. I think what I said made an impression on him and he said he would think it over further.

2. We had some discussion as to why political opinion should be sympathetic towards people who had committed crimes of this kind. He said it was impossible to ignore motive. His main position is that if these men are treated to some generosity, they will not resume their old courses. But I pointed out to him the danger that they might think they were being released owing to popular sympathy with objects underlying activities. In effect it is a question of political pressure on government. He told me he was already being accused of acting in a reactionary way in not having released these prisoners.

3. Our discussion was quite friendly and did not directly raise the issue of Governors' responsibility. At the same time I made it clear that these matters would have to be considered in some detail and I do not think he will expect any immediate decision. He will however be very anxious to come to some conclusions before Assembly next meets about August 25th. I have not myself yet looked into any of the details of these cases, as it

seems to me that it will not be my function to do this until matters come to me formally. I have no doubt that point I indicated in paragraph 6 of my telegram No. 25-G of July 16th about the possibility of another hunger-strike by Kakori prisoners is present to Pant's mind, though we neither of us mentioned the matter.

4. Since writing above I have seen a draft of a letter to the Government of India about the Andamans hunger-strike which appears to have been prepared in accordance with views of cabinet as a whole and before my conversation with Pant. While the main object is to acquaint the Government of India with strong feeling aroused in the United Provinces by this hunger-strike and to ask for the return of United Provinces political prisoners in the Andamans, it makes very sweeping statements in support of the claims of hunger-strikers and giving way to hunger-strikes. I am endeavouring to secure a considerable toning down of this letter, but it shows I fear that feeling in cabinet regarding release of our own "violent" prisoners will be good deal stronger than I had gathered from my conversation with Pant and it indicates very plainly what would be the attitude of cabinet if one of the Kakori prisoners started a hunger-strike.

62

HAIG TO LINLITHGOW
Telegram
MSS.EUR.F. 125/126

No. 38-G *August 5th, 1937*

Your Excellency's telegrams Nos. 288 and 289 of August 4th.[15] Before receipt of these telegrams I had general talk about Budget yesterday with Pant. He is very determined that Budget should be balanced, but he is not prepared to impose fresh taxation for the present, his position being proceeds of fresh taxation should be devoted to new schemes and that Budget should be balanced by retrenchment of some kind which would not harm nation-building activities. According to his latest estimates which are less sanguine than those of late Finance Minister, the Budget will disclose a deficit of 28 lakhs. It seems quite evident to me that cannot possibly be covered by normal retrenchment. He appears definitely reluctant to reduce the pay of Services, but seems to think he may be driven to make such proposal. I do not think he would be prepared to cut pay of provincial and subordinate services while leaving that of all-India

Services untouched, and he realises that there would be no chance of Secretary of State agreeing to reduction in pay of all-India Services. He did not mention to me the possibility of making an appeal to members of all-India Services. But he said that if he could not get money by reducing the pay, he would have to see whether he could not get it by reducing travelling allowances or special allowances. I did not argue the point with him at the moment. I imagine he could not get very much by reducing travelling allowances, while to do so on any appreciable scale would be inadmissible as being an indirect attack on pay sanctioned by Secretary of State.

2. Really he is attempting the impossible and before long I think he will realise that he must have a deficit in Budget unless he is prepared to impose fresh taxation or to cut pay of Services which are within his power, while leaving all-India Services untouched. I appreciate fact that if he does propose to cut pay of Services within his power, the question of my special responsibility would arise, and that matter would require to be discussed with Secretary of State.

63

HAIG TO LINLITHGOW
R/3/1/2

Strictly Confidential

Camp,
August 6th, 1937

My dear Lord Linlithgow,

I am sending my ninth fortnightly report on political conditions in the United Provinces under the new Constitution. I have myself been a good deal handicapped during this fortnight as I went down on the 23rd July with a bad septic throat which kept me in bed for over a week and has left me still feeling not very strong. The Civil Surgeon has urged me to get away to Naini Tal for a fortnight, as he thinks this will enable me to pick up quickly, and consequently, though it is not convenient, I am leaving on the night of August 7th for Naini Tal and propose to be back in Lucknow again on the morning of the 20th.

2. Negotiations with the Muslim League, which in the end led to nothing,[16] caused considerable delay in the completion of the cabinet, but eventually Pant informed me on the 28th that he wished to complete the cabinet by the appointment of Pandit Piyare Lal Sharma and Hafiz Muhammad Ibrahim, the latter being a Muslim who had secured election

as an Independent, but had subsequently gone over to the Congress. I had these two up the same day, and they took the oath of office before me while I was still in bed. The complete cabinet, which consists only of six members, is on the whole of a comparatively moderate character. The real extremists have all been omitted, with the possible exception of Mr. Rafi Ahmad Kidwai. The two most important and most able members are the Premier himself and Dr. Katju, the latter at the time of his appointment being the leading lawyer at the Allahabad High Court bar, and they are both on the whole men of reasonable views. Mrs. Pandit, sister of Jawaharlal Nehru, has charming manners, is full of intelligence and discusses administrative problems in a most practical and reasonable way. Owing to my illness it is only within the last day or two that I have established contact with the individual members of the cabinet, though I have seen Pant frequently. Before I saw the other members, I was anxious to ascertain his general views about procedure. I asked him whether it would be convenient to them that I should see them regularly once a week as I used to see the members of my late government. He said they had not contemplated any such regular interviews, but they would always be ready to see me at any time that I might send for them. On the whole Pant's idea evidently is that the main questions of policy should be put before me by him. I think this is a perfectly satisfactory arrangement on which to start work. I have no doubt that as time goes on I shall see quite as much as I want to of the other ministers. Meantime, I am arranging to see each one of them individually before I leave for Naini Tal. The ministers have settled down very well with the Secretaries and speak in terms of high appreciation of them.

3. I had to settle my last two nominations for the Upper House while I was still in bed, but they gave much less trouble than I had anticipated. I wanted to nominate a real representative of labour, and I selected, Pandit Harihar Nath Shastri, the President of the Mazdur Sabha of Cawnpore, who, though he has given a good deal of trouble in the past, showed signs of being helpful and anxious to work in with the government in connection with the present strike situation. Unfortunately, as so often happens, as soon as a Labour leader shows signs of being reasonable he is thrown over by his followers, and that I am afraid is what is happening now. For the other nomination I wanted a Muslim lady, and decided on Lady Wazir Hasan, who, while she was in Lucknow, took a good deal of interest in women's work.

4. Another problem that had to be settled at the same time was the appointment of the Advocate-General. I had had some talk with the Premier

and found he was fully in agreement with me that our primary requirement was a sound lawyer of sufficient standing in his profession. I was very glad when he put up to me the name of Dr. Narayan Prasad Asthana, who was on the whole, in my opinion, the best man available and would probably have been selected by the late cabinet. He is a Liberal in politics, and the appointment brought down on the cabinet very outspoken criticism from their own followers. But they stood up to it well, and the appointment has set, I think, a very sound precedent.

5. I have had a good deal of correspondence with Your Excellency about the question of my presiding normally at cabinet meetings, and I have placed you fully in possession of the strong objections that the Premier raised to this principle, objections which at one time he suggested he might have to push very far. I had another long conversation with him on the subject a few days ago, and while he did not in any way abate his objection in principle, he seemed to be coming round to a realisation of the fact that he would have to acquiesce. He said that before giving me a final answer he would like to consult the members of the cabinet. Yesterday, however, a matter came up which obviously required a very early cabinet meeting. I wrote to him about this and said that while I did not at all wish to press the issue at the moment, it did seem very desirable to have a meeting of the cabinet before I left on Saturday evening, and that if the cabinet meeting were held before I left, I should feel bound to attend. He wrote back very reasonably, agreed that a cabinet meeting should be held before I left, and raised no further objection. I hope that this will settle this troublesome question, but the decision is certainly decidedly distasteful to the Premier. He has told me that he would like to discuss at this cabinet meeting the question of the Rules of Business. I gather that they wish to raise certain points for my consideration, and I have agreed that we should discuss them.

6. The problem which now seems to me likely to give the most serious trouble in the near future is that of the release of the political or revolutionary prisoners who have been convicted of offences connected with violence. I have communicated the present situation in some detail to Your Excellency in my telegram No. 37-G., dated 5th August. The political pressure on the cabinet to do something substantial in the way of releasing these men, particularly the Kakori prisoners, will obviously be very strong, and the cabinet themselves will be emphatically in favour of taking this course and will want to pass orders before the Assembly meets about the 25th August. The question whether I could justifiably regard the release of these men as constituting a grave menace to the peace and tranquillity

of the Province is very doubtful, though I have not yet looked into the cases in detail. If, owing to pressure by me on the cabinet, there were appreciable delay about passing orders, there is to my mind a likelihood that one or more of the Kakori prisoners will start another hunger-strike, particularly in view of what the Andamans prisoners appear to have secured. That would create a situation which would be as difficult as could be conceived, since it would be doubtful whether on merits I should be justified in refusing to release them. The cabinet would clearly not be prepared in any way to resist such a hunger-strike and would demand instant release. To release them under these circumstances would have a deplorable effect, far worse than if they were released previously without the coercion of a hunger strike. Though I recognise the complications that have been introduced by the hunger-strike in the Andamans, I am still disposed to think that if we are to avoid a situation which would place the cabinet and the Governor and the administration in the most deplorable position, the conclusions stated in my telegram No. 25-G of July 16th, and in particular in paragraph 5 of that telegram, should be acted upon.

7. The labour situation in Cawnpore continues to give cause for anxiety. As I have indicated above, those labour leaders who have shown an inclination to moderation are finding that they cannot carry their followers with them. The Premier's attempt at settling the strike failed, as the agreement was repudiated by the labour organisations. Dr. Katju, the Minister for Industries, visited Cawnpore yesterday and his efforts also appear to have been unsuccessful. The communist element are not prepared to consider the convenience of a Congress government, and indeed evidently feel that with a Congress government in office, they have an excellent opportunity of pushing their extreme claims. The police report that the situation has been aggravated by the release, on which the cabinet insisted, of five labour leaders in Cawnpore who had been dealt with under Section 108 of the Criminal Procedure Code. The Premier was not prepared to believe in the danger of these communist agitators. Now, I think, he is beginning to realise his mistake.[17] There is, I understand, no immediate apprehension of any serious breach of the peace, though the local authorities are taking all necessary precautions; but it looks as if the strike, which has now extended to several mills, would continue for some time and may spread further.

8. The opening of the first session of the new Legislature on the 29th July was made the occasion for very striking Congress demonstrations outside the Council House. The Congress flag was hoisted, there were organised processions of villagers, and a good deal of public-speaking,

Nehru himself being one of the speakers. The demonstrations undoubtedly impressed people in Lucknow with the strength of the Congress, and the landlords were considerably alarmed at the general tone.

9. The election of Speaker of the Assembly and President of the Council took place on the 31st July. Babu Purshottam Das Tandon was elected without opposition as Speaker, but he caused a great deal of comment and criticism by announcing that he did not believe in the British practice of the Speaker cutting himself off entirely from politics, and that while he would conduct the business of the Assembly with complete impartiality, he intended to remain an active member of the Congress party. This was probably part of the understanding in accordance with which Babu Purshottam Das Tandon was put up as Speaker instead of being included in the Cabinet. He was in fact at one time regarded as a possible rival to Pant for the Premiership, and doubtless he was not prepared to accept the Speakership if it meant abandoning his position in the party. The election of the President of the Council was contested but Sir Sita Ram, who had been for many years President of the old Legislative Council and had been nominated by me to the present Council, was elected by a substantial majority over the Congress nominee. I think this is a satisfactory result, for Sir Sita Ram will, from his experience, make an excellent President and he has a high reputation for impartiality. It seems me particularly satisfactory that he has been elected as President of the Upper House in view of Babu Purshottam Das Tandon with his unorthodox views having become Speaker of the Assembly. The Congress were very anxious to secure for one of their men the Presidentship of the Council, but they seem to have reconciled themselves now to the situation.

10. The Premier made a general statement of the policy of the government, a copy of which I enclose. Apart from the affirmation of the goal of Independence and the rest of the extreme theoretical position of the Congress, the practical programme was on the whole on fairly moderate lines. It is particularly interesting to see that on the big questions of reform of the tenancy law and debt relief the government intend to consult all shades of opinion and to include representatives of all parties in the committees which are to be set up to consider these difficult matters. Both in the Assembly and in the Council notices were given of motions for the adjournment of the House to consider the action of His Majesty's government with regard to the Palestine Report. In both cases I disallowed the motion, as I considered it was a bad precedent to allow discussion of foreign affairs in the provincial Legislature. There was very little criticism of my action.

11. The Opposition in the Assembly appears to be crystallising into two parts. There is first the Muslim League Parliamentary Board under the leadership of Khaliquzzaman, which includes those Muslims who approach most closely to the Congress policy and were conducting the negotiations about joining the Congress government which eventually proved abortive. The other part is a so-called independent party under the leadership of the Nawab of Chhatari, which consists of the remainder of the Muslims and a handful of Hindus. They claim to number 32 which must be something in excess of the Muslim League Parliamentary Board section. I think the landlords will argue their case very fully when the actual proposals of the government come forward.

12. The Legislature sat for only five days and have now adjourned. They will meet again about the 25th August, and it is anticipated that the session will last a month. The budget will be introduced on the 1st September. The cabinet will have great difficulty with the budget. The Premier, who has taken the Finance portfolio in addition to that of Home, is not prepared to accept the more sanguine anticipations of his predecessor, and estimates that, as the budget stands at present it will show a deficit of 28 lakhs. He is very anxious to wipe out this deficit without recourse to fresh taxation. He has been turning over in his mind the possibility of covering the deficit by making a cut in the pay of the Services, but he is definitely reluctant to do this, and the latest information I have is that he has given up the idea, though I cannot be positive yet about this. I cannot myself understand how, if he does not touch the pay of the Services, he can possibly cover this deficit of 28 lakhs by retrenchment. I am sorry that I shall be away from Lucknow while he is considering his main budget proposals, but I hope to be kept in close touch with what is going on and to be here again in time for the final discussion on the budget.

13. I am naturally concerned mainly at present with the very numerous points of difficulty and delicacy which arise at headquarters in connection with the launching of the Congress government. But behind all this one has to consider what is the effect on the minds of the people of the Province and the members of the services. It is too early for me yet to form any judgement about this, and indeed the situation in these respects is still, I think, very fluid. People in general are somewhat uncertain and bewildered, and it will be some time before they settle down to a new attitude.[18]

Yours sincerely,
HARRY HAIG

ENCLOSURE TO NO. 63

STATEMENT BY PANT OF GOVERNMENT POLICY

Lucknow,
August 2nd, 1937

With your permission I shall now make the statement I had promised on Saturday. Before placing an outline of our immediate programme I think I should say a few words about the basic policy of the Congress.

The attitude of the Congress towards the new Constitution is well known. It has been clearly defined in its resolutions and in the election manifesto on which we sought the suffrage of the people. The Congress stands for complete independence and for a constitution framed by the people of India through a constituent assembly. The present constitution had been condemned by all communities and political organisations in this country and the Congress had made it clear before as well as after the elections that it had sought entry into the Legislatures not to co-operate with the new Constitution but to combat the Government of India Act and the policy underlying it. The Congress has accepted office in deference to the widespread desire expressed in India as well as in England and it shall be our endeavour throughout to implement the programme placed before the country by the Congress and to build the strength of the nation in order to accelerate its progress towards the cherished goal.

On this occasion I think it would be appropriate to state that in carrying out that programme we shall always keep before us, as directed by the Congress, the declaration of fundamental rights adopted at its Karachi session. That declaration guarantees to every citizen of India of every caste and creed the right of free expression of opinion, free association and combination, freedom of conscience and the right freely to profess and practise his religion, subject to public order and morality. It also guarantees the protection of the culture, language and script of the minorities and affirms that all citizens are equal before law, irrespective of religion, caste, creed or sex and that no disability would attach to any citizen, by reason of his or her religion, caste, creed or sex in regard to public employment, office of power or honour and in the exercise of any trade or calling.

The promotion of unity between all communities, castes and creeds shall be our constant aim and every effort will be made by us to maintain and advance such unity, and I have no doubt that the government will receive the co-operation of every honourable member of the House in this direction. The government will be bound to discourage and resist all attempts by whomsoever made to foment discord or ill-will between various communities.

The House may like to know the measures that we have adopted during the short time that we have been in office. Orders have been issued for the release of all prisoners convicted under Section 124-A of the Indian Penal Code, pending prosecutions under that Section have been withdrawn, bail bonds taken under Section 108 of the Criminal Procedure Code have been cancelled and all proceedings pending under that Section have been similarly withdrawn. The ban of illegality from association has been lifted. We have taken measures to restore full freedom to the press. Securities taken from presses and newspapers have been refunded, and the government recognising the principle of the freedom of press and in pursuance of their policy of observing strict impartiality in this matter, have given instructions that there should be no discrimination against any press or newspaper on account of the political opinions or affinities of its editor or manager, and that all questions of press advertisements, court notices and printing work should be treated impartially on a strictly business basis. We are reviewing a number of other cases of persons convicted for offences other than sedition with a view to releasing as many as we can. We have issued orders that nobody should be considered to be disqualified from any public office or for any class of service on the ground of his caste, creed, opinions, etc. We are trying to devise measures to deal effectively with the evil of corruption and are determined to eradicate it from the public services.

At the very outset the government were faced with a difficult labour situation in Cawnpore. As to our general policy towards industrial labour there is no room for any misapprehension. It has been clearly laid down by the Congress and it shall be our constant endeavour to work for the amelioration of the conditions of labour and for securing a decent standard of living for them. But at the moment we are anxious to find a solution of the present difficulties without any delay and to create a proper atmosphere for considering the whole question in a fruitful manner. A labour welfare officer has been appointed to look after the interests of labour, to secure immediate relief wherever possible and to promote good relations between the employers and the employed. Necessary legislation is under consideration and will be introduced without any avoidable delay. The hon'ble minister in charge of the department intends to keep himself in personal touch with all parties and the government earnestly hope that means will soon be found with the co-operation of labour leaders and employers to resolve the existing deadlock.

A thorough overhaul of the system of prison administration in these provinces is in the government's opinion necessary, and immediate steps will be taken to consider the problem from every point of view and to introduce necessary measures for reforming the administration and improving the conditions in the prisons. Government is aware that much popular discontent exists in regard to the manner in which honorary magistrates and collectors are appointed and the proceedings in their courts are conducted. Necessary inquiries are being made and proper measures will soon be taken to meet the public demand.

Government is of the opinion that local self-government in these provinces is capable of much improvement and to effect necessary changes the United Provinces Municipalities and District Boards Acts will carefully be examined and necessary amending legislation introduced at an early date. In the meantime all general elections to local bodies will have to be postponed.

As the House is aware the Congress has asked us to repeal repressive laws and we are examining the question with a view to initiating necessary measures without delay and the Congress party has appointed a Committee for this purpose.

The present Excise policy calls for drastic changes and the government will take necessary steps to remodel it, placing before itself the Congress goal of prohibition.

Several other subjects such as separation of judicial and executive functions, rural and industrial development, education and unemployment are also engaging our attention and we hope to make a definite declaration in this regard after the Budget Session.

I had indicated on Saturday certain steps which we intend to take forthwith in order to tackle the agrarian problem. I need not remind honourable members of the pitiable economic plight of the agricultural masses, their appalling poverty and the burdens of debts which so heavily press upon them. The need for the amelioration of their condition is urgent and calls for immediate action. The government have naturally been giving thought to this subject and are convinced that it cannot brook any delay. We have accordingly decided to appoint two committees, to work on which we intend to invite members from all sections of the Legislature. We wish that the reports of these committees would be made available to the House by January 1st next. It is our desire that the recommendations made by these committees may be laid before this House for consideration before the government takes a final decision and initiates the necessary legislation. It will thus be seen that we are anxious from the outset to seek in these vital matters the assistance of the entire Legislature and we wish to have the benefit of their co-operation even in these formative stages, as [?so] that the results attained may be as sound as possible. The House will of course have ample opportunities of discussing the Bill in its various stages after its introduction.

One of these committees will be appointed for the purpose of examining the existing laws relating to land revenue and tenancy, with a view to revising them in order to put an end to the distress amongst the peasantry. In the meantime steps will be taken to stay proceedings for ejectment of tenants, for enhancement of rent, for the realisation of rents due for periods prior to and including *kharif* 1344 *fasli* generally and, in the case of areas damaged by hail or other calamity in recent months, for *rabi* 1344 *fasli* as well, as also proceedings for the resumption of rent-free holdings and of groves. There is no more important or urgent problem than the readjustment of the relations between the government, the landlord and the tenant on a basis which will make the relief of the suffering peasantry and the promotion of their prosperity the first and foremost consideration. We consider that measures of real and substantial relief to them have been postponed too long and that such measures as have hitherto been taken have hardly touched the root of the problem of rural poverty.

I do not wish to anticipate the line which the committee may take; but I think the House will agree that the measures to be taken must include stability of tenure for all tenants, and also relief from the heavy burden of arrears of rent. I am confident too that, when concrete proposals are framed by the Legislature, they would be anxious that they should have retrospective effect in the case of proceedings of the nature described which are at present pending before the Revenue Courts, or which may be instituted in the course of the coming months. If I am right in thus anticipating the attitude of the Legislature, then it will serve no useful purpose, but can only result in needless trouble to the courts and to parties in such proceedings, if the proceedings are allowed to continue, only to be subsequently revised. The government therefore contemplate asking the Board of Revenue to issue orders to the Revenue Courts to stay proceedings of the kind indicated by me pending the enactment of legislation. There are precedents for this. In 1919, when the amendment of the Oudh Rent Act seeking to confer statutory rights upon tenants was in view, and again in 1924, when similar amendment of the Agra Tenancy Act was in contemplation, the Board of Revenue issued orders to the Revenue Courts which prevented tenancies from being terminated under the then existing laws. In the legislation subsequently passed, sections were embodied in both these Acts preventing ejectment of tenants under proceedings pending from a date well preceding the Act, so that such tenants might enjoy the benefits conferred by the amending legislation. The government, therefore, consider it to be a matter of elementary justice to safeguard the position of all tenants who are at present in possession of their holdings against ejectment on termination of their tenures under the existing laws, and from ejectment for arrears of rent, and also to protect other tenants who are liable for arrears of rent, as already detailed from the passing of execution of decrees and orders rendering them liable to pay these arrears, until such time as the Legislature have put into force steps for their relief.

Another committee will be appointed to consider the steps necessary to remove the burden of rural indebtedness and to propose measures of relief. Pending such legislation, government intends introducing a Bill to stay proceedings for the recovery of the debts of the peasantry through orders and processes issued under the existing law. It is our conviction that the measures taken since the slump in prices fall far short of the real relief which the masses so badly require. Some of the Acts which came into force in 1935 – the Temporary Regulation of Execution Act, the Regulation of Sales Act, and the Encumbered Estates Act – have passed beyond the date when debtors may still resort to them. There remain, as continuing measures, the Agriculturists' Relief Act and the Usurious Loans Act, neither of which, in the opinion of government, gives to the indebted peasantry the simple, immediate and direct relief which they need. Over and above that, we are faced with problems arising from the wording and the requirements of the Encumbered Estates Act and the Agriculturists' Relief Act, and the interpretations which the courts have placed upon these where the intention of the Legislature was not clear, or else was badly expressed. Again, our predecessors contemplated action for the reduction of tenants' debts by conciliation. Whether in fact such a method can really give effective relief, or whether the House, with the guidance of the Committee whose appointment is contemplated, can frame measures which have direct appeal and will result in direct benefit to the peasantry, is a matter for serious, even anxious, consideration. But I earnestly hope that the House will succeed in evolving suitable measures such as will benefit, not any particular class, but the many millions who live a hand-to-mouth existence under a crushing perennial burden of debt, and whom we have the honour to represent and to serve.

This is an object fully deserving of the sympathy of every honourable member of this House and we are entitled to their support in this respect not only on patriotic but also on humanitarian grounds. Let me now conclude with the expression of an earnest hope that all sections of this House will rise above petty considerations and will make a joint endeavour to ameliorate the pitiable lot of millions of our starving fellow countrymen.

64

HAIG TO LINLITHGOW
Telegram
MSS.EUR.F. 125/126

No. 39-G *August 7th, 1937*

Your telegram No. 840-G, August 7th.[19] Communication to Government of India about Andaman Prisoners will be official and confidential and cabinet have agreed to eliminate those portions which referred to demands of hunger-strikers and policy which should be pursued. It will be confined to a statement of feeling aroused in United Provinces and a request for return of our prisoners.

2. In cabinet meeting this afternoon Pant raised question of release of some of our own violent prisoners. He said he had been considering individual cases and had come to conclusions about ten which include all six Kakori prisoners. He wishes to release all these and to have orders passed at beginning of next week. I asked him whether he had got opinion of Police and he said he had not, as Inspector-General of Police was away. I said it was essential for me to see opinion of police and it was finally agreed that Pant's note together with opinion of police, which will be obtained immediately, should be sent to me at Naini Tal where I shall probably receive them on Monday. Pant says the six Kakori prisoners would normally have only two or three years more to serve having already served more than ten years. I gather the other four prisoners recommended for release have got only a few months of their sentences to serve.

3. I gather from unofficial enquiries from C.I.D. here they are not likely to have any serious objection to release of Kakori prisoners, and it looks to me extremely probable that constitutionally there would be no case for me to refuse to accept advice of my ministry, while politically I think it would be a serious mistake to oppose them. I would invite attention to paragraph 6 my report of August 6th. I fully recognise that release of these prisoners may be of some embarrassment to Bengal, but I am bound in

exercise both of my powers and my judgment to have regard primarily to conditions of my own Province.

4. The cabinet are not prepared to agree to demand assurances of good behaviour. There will be a number of other cases coming up for consideration a little later. They are all being examined on merits, but this batch which includes Kakori prisoners would be far the most important and would really settle our main anxiety here. I repeat that I have not yet seen details of these cases and must not be taken as having expressed a final view on their merits. What I have said is based on what I have heard from Pant and gathered unofficially from C.I.D.

65

HAIG TO LINLITHGOW
MSS.EUR.F. 115/13

Private and Personal *August 8th, 1937*

The question of my presiding at cabinet meetings did not after all pass over so easily as I had anticipated in para. 5 of my fortnightly report, dated 6th August. On Friday afternoon I received from Pant a note of the points he wished to raise about the Rules of Business, and found that he had included a re-draft of one of the Rules of Business, stating that the Premier would normally preside – the Governor would only preside when he thought it necessary to do so. Strictly speaking of course this issue could not be raised on the Rules of Business, as it would be quite inadmissible for the Governor to define or limit his discretion under section 50(2) of the Government of India Act by any kind of rule under section 59(3). But as the cabinet obviously wished to have the matter out and to get their view on record, I thought it advisable to face the issue plainly and let them say what they wished to say. The cabinet meeting took place on Saturday afternoon, and a few minutes before I went to it I was glad to receive Your Excellency's telegram No. 834-G, dated the 7th August,[20] though in fact this merely re-emphasized the decision already agreed upon between us. At the cabinet meeting Pant put his case as he has already put it to me several times before, and said that not only he but the whole cabinet felt very strongly on this point. As a matter of fact, apart from a few rather formal and technical arguments by Katju, no one else, except Pant, took part in the discussion. I started by making the point mentioned above about the impossibility of defining the discretion of the Governor by rules under section 59(3), and then went on to state my intention of normally presiding at cabinet meetings whenever I was at headquarters. I made full allowance for their feelings and explained that the decision was in no sense a reflection on their capacity to conduct their discussions, but was, so far as I was concerned, based mainly on the great desirability of maintaining close administrative contact. I pointed out how valuable it was both to myself and to them that we should know and know at the earliest stage how each was thinking, and I said that I thought that from this point of view it was most desirable that we should meet and discuss a variety of problems at cabinet meetings. At an early stage Pant stated that while of course I could make such rules or follow such practice as I thought fit, it was impossible for me to ensure that the ministers would accept the spirit of these rules, and he indicated plainly the possibility that they might proceed to discuss matters among themselves and reach conclusions and endeavour to reduce the cabinet meetings to a mere formality. I am inclined to think that this was merely a demonstration, the result of a feeling of wounded pride, for undoubtedly Pant feels very strongly that this system is injurious to his dignity. But the subsequent course of discussion at the cabinet meeting leads me to think that in practice they will not adopt such tactics. Apart from this one threat the discussion proceeded in a most amicable and reasonable way. Pant also stressed strongly his objection to the rule in the Rules of Business which makes me responsible for the agenda. But I told him that I thought this followed necessarily from the general position which I contemplated the Governor filling, and he finally, after having made his protest, dropped this. The other matters in regard to the Rules of Business which he had mentioned were connected with the functions of Secretaries, and he was perfectly reasonable about these and did not really press for any change in our existing system. On the whole I was very well satisfied with this discussion, for we have now had the thing out in the open at a cabinet meeting. I have explained that though I fully appreciate their feelings I cannot accept their proposals and have told them precisely what my intentions are. As I have said, with Pant I think it is a question of dignity, and possibly he feels more strongly on the subject than the other members of the cabinet. I noticed in the course of discussion that he talked of himself as Prime Minister, and these were the words that he had put into his suggested amendment of the Rules of Business. I paid no attention to this and continued to refer to him as Premier. But it is possible that in order to assert his position he may press to be styled Prime Minister. I fully recognise the objections to this, as indicated in Your Excellency's telegram on the subject, and will try, if possible, to ride him off.

The cabinet meeting, which lasted altogether two and a half hours, was in my view decidedly a success. We discussed a variety of important questions. On matters in which the responsibility was plainly that of the cabinet Pant was obviously a little prickly, and I was very careful not to give him any occasion for offence. But we also discussed a number of other things in which I was clearly interested, such as the Cawnpore strike, release of political prisoners, etc., and the discussions proceeded on a very satisfactory basis and with perfect good feeling. I do feel myself that it has been a great advantage to have met the cabinet and, as I hope, established reasonable working relations with them; and it is a very good thing that this has been done before I left for Naini Tal. There is no doubt that the two members of the cabinet who really count are Pant and Katju.

I have just arrived in Naini Tal and it is an exceedingly pleasant change after Lucknow.[21]

66

HAIG TO LINLITHGOW
Telegram
MSS.EUR.F. 125/126

No. 40-G Naini Tal,
August 9th, 1937

With reference to paragraph 3 of your telegram No. 845-G of August 8th.[22] Points taken by Pant were (*a*) that an assurance is of little practical value, what matters is mental attitude on those concerned; (*b*) that it takes away grace of act. This I think is real point to which they attach importance. From point of view of cabinet this is a political gesture and they do not wish it to be accompanied by an indication of distrust.

2. I did not think it convenient to argue out the matter at cabinet meeting, but it may be stressed by the police when their views are obtained, and I might press it further on cabinet, though I think they are likely to be very stiff over it.

3. I have been turning over in my mind possibility of securing object by a different method of approach. Real danger to my mind is that an impression will be created that government are not out of sympathy with policy of political violence on which these men had embarked or at any rate that they are not prepared to combat it. What I think that we want to secure is a statement of policy by government. They might say that these men were convicted of crimes which were based on belief in policy of

political violence. This is a policy which is not only contrary to interests of a country, but must be strongly opposed by whatever government is in power. The government are confident that these prisoners no longer believe in this policy and have no intention of pursuing it further. It is in that confidence that they feel justified in releasing these men who have already served long terms of imprisonment.

4. I am thinking of pressing this on cabinet as an alternative to an assurance of good behaviour. Does Your Excellency agree in this view?

67

HAIG TO LINLITHGOW
Telegram
MSS.EUR.F. 125/126

No. 41-G *August 12th, 1937*

I have today received details about the violent prisoners whom Pant wishes to release and hope to reach conclusions, which I will telegraph Your Excellency and will await reply before communicating my views to Pant.

2. Meanwhile, however, recent information and particularly your telegram No. 874 August 11th[23] suggest we are perhaps faced with a situation essentially different from that which I have hitherto been contemplating. My view has been that while regretting possible embarrassment to Bengal, so long as question is merely one of embarrassment, it is doubtful whether it is justifiable to let outweigh [*sic*] policy which on merits may seem to be required for the United Provinces. Also from constitutional point of view I have been doubtful how far a Governor can hold that embarrassment to another Province justifies him in taking action which he is only by the Act authorised to take in order to prevent [menace to] peace of his own Province.

3. I gather however from your telegram of August 11th that Your Excellency and Secretary of State are inclined to hold that Andaman hunger-strike may be a serious menace to jail discipline throughout [?India], and that from that point of view it is essential that nothing should be done in any Province which could in any way be regarded as an encouragement to hunger-strikers. You have already decided not to return prisoners from Andamans to any Province so long as strike continues. I am not sure whether Your Excellency proposes to go further and consider in the light of all circumstances as known to you, whether it should also be laid down as

a matter of All-India policy binding all Provinces that no violent revolutionary prisoners should be released prematurely while strike continues.

4. If such a conclusion were reached action would presumably have to be taken under powers of Governor acting on instructions from the Governor-General, and constitutional justification would be as indicated above, that Andaman strike may affect peace of all provinces. I am not quite clear as to circumstances in which Governor-General can exercise directly his powers under section 12(1)(*a*).

5. If this line is taken, we must face squarely the possible consequences that may ensue in United Provinces. We have some 14 revolutionary prisoners in Allahabad Central Jail including two Kakori prisoners who have already within the last 18 months been on prolonged hunger-strikes and it is not improbable that some or even all of these in the present atmosphere would start hunger-strike. In that case I should clearly have to refuse any proposal of my ministry that any of these men should be let out as a direct consequence of hunger-strike, the issue really being same as that in Andamans. There would however be a further complication. I doubt if ministry would agree to such prisoners being artificially fed. On the other hand, I should regard it as essential that they should be. If they are artificially fed, the chances of fatal termination are greatly reduced. We must take no avoidable risks of death, for a death as a result of hunger-strike under these circumstances would create a wave of feeling which might make it impossible for my ministry to continue in office. I should have to take the responsibility myself of ordering artificial feeding and ministry would probably make it clear that they differed. It will be necessary to consider this situation beforehand, and I would enquire whether, in the event of such a situation arising, I should have the full support of yourself and Secretary of State in ordering artificial feeding.

6. Apart from general question of policy, that is whether any violent prisoners should be released at present time, a further complication may arise in regard to certain of Kakori prisoners. Some of them have a bad revolutionary record in Bengal and though I might hold that their release would not involve any grave menace to peace of United Provinces, the Bengal government might possibly hold that it would involve menace in present circumstances to Bengal. If on that account the view prevailed that these prisoners should not be released, would such action be taken under my powers or those of Governor-General? Pant would not be slow to exploit the logical strength of his position if action were to be taken under my powers. Of course it would always be possible to avoid

communicating to Pant the full considerations and merely to inform him that I held that release of these men would be a grave menace to this Province.[24]

68

HAIG TO LINLITHGOW
Telegram
MSS.EUR.F. 125/126

No. 42-G *August 13th, 1937*

With reference to my telegram No. 41, August 12th. I have now considered details of ten prisoners proposed by Pant for release and have discussed with a C.I.D. officer sent from Lucknow for the purpose.

2. General situation in Province in regard to terrorism is that while there is a certain amount of talk going on and it would seem that efforts are still being made to collect arms there has been in last few years comparatively little in way of overt acts and such actions as there have been have been directed mainly to collecting money. There appears to be no formidable nucleus of conspiracy and here as elsewhere there is a tendency to turn from terrorism to communism.

3. Out of ten prisoners proposed for release six were convicted in Kakori case, and this is really the crucial issue. The case was very serious one: four were hanged, seven have been released after serving their full sentence and seven remain in jail, namely, these six and Govind Chandra Kar who is suffering from leprosy and has possibly not been mentioned by Pant because he is in a Bengal jail. All these men have already served over ten years and after allowing for remissions it is reported normal period of their sentence remaining to be served varies from two years eleven months to one year nine months. Three, namely, M.N. Gupta, Mukandi Lal and S.N. Bakshi, are not considered by C.I.D. to be of any very great importance. A fourth, namely, Dublis, was sentenced only to ten years in Kakori case which sentence he has completed; but he took part in serious jail riot involving murder in 1928 in Allahabad for which he was sentenced to transportation for life which was afterwards commuted to five years. This sentence he is at present serving in Andamans, but I understand he is not in cellular jail.

4. The two remaining prisoners, J.C. Chatterjee and S.N. Sanyal have a long record of serious revolutionary activity, and Chatterjee's activities have mainly been in Bengal. They are both potential organisers of some

importance. Sanyal has for some time been professing repentance, and I gather the C.I.D. would not be seriously disturbed at his release. Chatterjee would presumably return to Bengal.

5. Taking all these facts into consideration I am of opinion that looking at conditions of this Province there is not sufficient justification for me to hold that my special responsibilities would be attracted by their release particularly if it is made clear either by assurance of good behaviour or by a statement by government that releases imply no weakness in attitude of Government towards political violence.

6. The case of Govind Chandra Kar has not been put up. I think this is due to inadvertence and his case is bound to be raised shortly. He is a Bengali. Last year when he developed leprosy we were considering his release, as from our point of view he is not dangerous. When we consulted Bengal, they objected and said that if he were released, they would probably find it necessary to order his detention under Bengal C.I.D. We suggested that under the circumstances Bengal might care to keep him in one of their jails and they accepted this proposal. He is in Midnapore Jail.

7. The remaining four prisoners have been proposed for release on the ground that very little of their sentence remains to be served. They are (1) Kashi Rama – he was a dangerous character, one of accused in Delhi conspiracy case. He and his companions resisted arrest by firing on police and wounding two. For this offence he was sentenced to seven years. He is, however, due for release on October 10th. (2) Gokul Das is regarded as a dangerous revolutionary. It was not possible to prosecute him in a conspiracy case, though he was believed to be a leader. But he was convicted of possession of a pistol and sentenced to two years. He is due for release on September 3rd. (3) Roy was convicted of possession of explosives and sentenced to seven years. He is due for release on February 26th, 1938. The C.I.D. seems to have nothing very special against him. (4) Shib Singh is a somewhat dangerous communist agent. He was sentenced to one year under Criminal Law Amendment Act and Press Act and has less than four months to serve.

8. In the case of Kashi Rama and Gokul Das their record does not entitle them to consideration, but it cannot be held to be a matter of any real importance whether they are released now or one or two months hence. I think there is no objection to release of S.K. Roy. With regard to Shib Singh I should propose to point out to Premier nature of his activities which he may not altogether appreciate and would try to persuade him to withdraw his proposal. But if he pressed it I could hardly refuse to permit it.

9. Apart therefore from situation arising from Andamans hunger-strike, I am definitely of opinion that all these men could be released without involving grave menace to peace of this Province, particularly if assurance or statement of policy referred to in paragraph 5 is obtained. I recognise that Bengal are entitled to be consulted about Chatterjee, but I should regard it as very unfortunate if Chatterjee alone of prisoners were not released, and it would be difficult to justify from point of view of this Province. Chatterjee indulged in prolonged hunger-strike last year.

69

HAIG TO LINLITHGOW
Telegram
MSS.EUR.F. 125/126

No. 46-G *August 16th, 1937*

Your telegram No. 906-G of August 15th.[25] In your telegram No. 899-G of August 14th it is laid down as a general principle, with which I find myself in fullest agreement, that minister[s] should not be allowed to issue an appeal to Services for voluntary cut in pay. I cannot myself see any effective difference between an appeal to individual members of Services and an appeal to Service Associations. If a Services Association agrees by majority to such appeal, the minority are put in an even more unfair position than they would if appeal had been made individually. On the other hand, if majority decline to fall in with the appeal, the Service as a whole is subjected to odium of disregarding this appeal. I would therefore definitely urge that appeal to Service Associations should be treated on exactly the same principle as appeal to individual members of Services.

2. Moreover with the exception of All-India and Provincial Services I do not think there are in United Provinces many really effective or representative Service Associations and large numbers of government servants could not be approached in this way.

3. I consider if any cut in pay were to be made, it should be made by order of government, but that such order should not be passed unless Governor in consultation with Governor-General and Secretary of State is satisfied that it is in the circumstances a reasonable and justifiable order. I understand that is intention of Your Excellency's telegram No. 899-G of August 14th, and that it is not intended to rule out all consideration of a

cut in pay, but only principle of attempting to secure this by voluntary appeal to Services.

4. I may add that I do not at present anticipate any proposal for a definite cut in pay from my minister[s], and that if I do receive such a proposal, I fully recognise that there are important considerations against agreeing, but I assume that it will be necessary to consider such proposal on merits.

70

HAIG TO LINLITHGOW
Telegram
MSS.EUR.F. 125/126

No. 47-G *August 16th, 1937*

With reference to concluding passage of Your Excellency's telegram No. 838-G of August 7th.[26] I have just heard that my ministers are considering in connection with budget a proposal to reduce rates of travelling allowance by 25 per cent. My view is that ministers are fully entitled to reduce rates of travelling allowance provided they do not reduce them to such an extent that allowances do not cover the obligatory expenditure of officers and consequently the reduction amounts indirectly to a reduction in pay. If it did amount to an indirect reduction of pay, then the matter would have to be considered on same lines as a proposal for a cut in pay. Admittedly it may be difficult in practice to decide at what point the line should be drawn. But I should be glad to know Your Excellency accepts principle I have suggested and agree[s] there is no objection to my acquiescing to reduce travelling allowance rates provided this does not in my opinion over-step the line indicated above.[27]

71

HAIG TO LINLITHGOW
MSS.EUR.F. 125/126

Personal and Confidential

Camp,
August 17th, 1937

My dear Lord Linlithgow,

There is an important question of policy which though it perhaps does not raise any general issue which would affect other Provinces, is nevertheless one which is causing me some anxiety, and on which I should greatly value Your Excellency's advice. When the Premier stated to the Assembly the programme of the ministry, he said that it was the intention, pending legislation, to issue executive orders staying proceedings for ejectment of tenants and for realisation of arrears of rent, and that they intended to introduce a Bill to stay proceedings for the recovery of debts of small agriculturists. This statement came in for some criticism at the hands of the Opposition, but they did not make a great deal of it.[28] When on August 7th the first cabinet meeting was held which I attended, the Premier requested that a draft letter issuing orders to revenue courts staying proceedings should be laid before the cabinet, and though the papers only came to me in the morning, I felt it was impossible to refuse to include the matter in the agenda, particularly as I should not have another opportunity of holding a cabinet meeting for another fortnight. The letter confined itself to the action of revenue courts, and there was no mention of similar action being taken in regard to civil courts dealing with recovery of debts of small agriculturists. When the matter came up I called attention to this difference and was told that the issue of such orders to the civil courts would raise certain difficulties and that they probably intended as indicated in the Premier's statement, to put a short Bill before the legislature in September authorising postponement of proceedings in civil suits. In regard to the suits in revenue courts, they made a strong point that precisely similar action in regard to postponement of ejectments was taken by the United Provinces government in 1921 and again in 1924, when the Oudh Rent Act and the Agra Tenancy Act were coming under revision. The way in which they have put their case is that it may be taken for granted that legislation will be passed before long granting hereditary rights to tenants, restricting ejectment for non-payment of rent, and restricting recovery of arrears of rent, that this legislation will be given retrospective effect, and that to continue proceedings in suits which will *ex-hypothesi* be ineffective is undesirable from every point of view. I felt that even if I had any power to object to the issue of these orders – a point with which I deal later – it would be unwise without further full consideration to attempt to challenge the cabinet on one of the central points of their economic policy. It was quite evident that they were in no mood for argument, and I confined myself to suggesting certain difficulties to which they gave replies, and the cabinet then decided to issue these orders immediately. The orders have gone out.

2. Since I have been in Naini Tal, I have been reflecting on this position, and the more I reflect the more unsatisfactory it appears to me to be; so much so that on the 14th August I wrote a letter to Pant putting before

him in some detail the grounds of my uneasiness. In the first place, I raised the question of the legality of these orders, and suggested that the Executive government had really no more power to issue such orders to revenue courts than to civil courts. I suggested that the opinion of the Advocate-General should be obtained on this point. The ministry rely, I think, in the main on the precedents, and contend that they are merely doing what their predecessors had done without question. In the second place, I put before him the probable effect of the postponement of collection of arrears of rent on the minds of the tenants and the likelihood that they would apply the same principle to payment of the current rent with results that would be very serious on our revenue collections. Since I wrote to him, I have seen the fortnightly reports of Commissioners and a large number of them refer to the statement of policy which was made in the Assembly, stating that there are already signs that revenue collections may be appreciably affected in the future by such a policy. Finally, I put to him the apparent iniquity of refusing to allow landlords to collect rents for a period for which they had already paid to the government the land revenue. I suggested that when I returned to Lucknow we might discuss the whole situation carefully.

3. The politics of the matter, so far as I understand it, is as follows. There is little difference of opinion about the grant of hereditary rights to tenants, and therefore I doubt whether anyone would seriously object to executive orders staying proceedings in ejectment cases. But the landlords are likely to object very strongly to being deprived of their arrears of rent, and if an emergency Bill authorising postponement of proceedings for the realisation of arrears of rent were introduced in September, it is probable that the Upper House would refuse to pass it. The government would therefore be unable to proceed with this, which they regard as one of the central features in their programme.

4. At the same time it seems to me wrong in principle that they should pass executive orders which are not justified by law to secure a result which they cannot obtain from the legislature. Their own case no doubt is that they are merely anticipating the decision of the Legislature, and I have it in mind that I might in any case press them on this point and urge that if and when there is any serious doubt about the Legislature accepting their policy, there can be no justification for continuing action by Executive orders. This situation, however, would probably only arise in February after the committee has reported, when they will introduce their considered Legislative proposals. This would still leave the proceedings for recovery of arrears of rent suspended from now say to February.

5. Two issues really arise in the main for me:

(*a*) Whether I have any power to interfere with these proceedings.
(*b*) Whether if I have such power it would be wise to use it.

In regard to the first point, I am not clear whether a Governor has a general power to object to the issue of executive orders which are not justified by the law. I am inclined to think that he must be held to have such a power. There is also the question whether Section 300(1) of the Government of India Act would apply to such a case. I am myself inclined to think that this Section is intended to apply to the rights of landlords generally, provided the system of settlement or the particular grants under which they hold such rights date from before 1870; and if so that these rights include a right to collect rent, and that therefore any postponement of that right would bring Section 300(1) into operation. At the same time those with whom I have hitherto had an opportunity of discussing this point do not agree with me, and appear to hold that Section 300(1) is intended to have a much more restricted application. That is a legal point on which I should be very grateful to receive guidance from Your Excellency.

6. Assuming that either on the ground of general principle or in virtue of Section 300(1) I have the power to object to the continuance of executive orders on these matters, the vital question arises – what is the right policy to adopt? There is no doubt that the Congress ministry have taken office assuming that though in matters of law and order, protection of service, minorities and so on, they may find the Governor objecting to certain policies which they wish to follow, they will in the main be able without interference from the Governor to carry out their economic policy. So far as concerns the merits of their intention to cancel arrears of rent, I am entitled to, and intend to, point out to them the practical dangers of this policy. I conceive that I can do no more than that. But if in fact I have the power to object to their taking a short cut to their end, the question arises whether it would be wise to challenge them on this point and to provoke what might be a very serious crisis. Pant has already taken the line that he is committed to this action by his statement of policy before the Assembly, and I think if I were to attempt direct interference now, he might hold that this was so damaging to his position that he could not continue in office.

7. At the same time there are opportunities for reconsideration. The cabinet are not perhaps openly committed to not introducing an emergency measure in September authorising the postponement of proceedings in revenue courts, though they have in their letter to the Board of Revenue

expressed their intention of not following this course. They would, however, be very definitely opposed to introducing such legislation on account of the likelihood that the Upper House would not pass that portion of the measure which relates to postponement of proceedings for recovery of arrears of rent. I think it likely that they would feel so strongly the objections to this, that they might decline absolutely to take such action, and that if I were to insist that executive orders should not further be continued after they had had an opportunity of referring the matter to the Legislature in September, there would be a break. The other opportunity for reconsideration would arise, as I have already suggested, when their considered legislative measures are introduced. As their case is that they are merely taking this executive action in order to anticipate the decision of the Legislature, which they profess to be confident about, it might be possible to get from them a definite undertaking that if the Upper House in February does not accept any part of their proposals, the executive orders in respect of that part should at once be cancelled. They could still of course argue that in the end the Legislature would accept their proposals. But the action of the Upper House would impose such a delay that it would hardly seem reasonable to continue executive orders over such a long period. That however would still mean that these executive orders would have been in force and would have had their very far-reaching effects for some six months.

8. There is always the possibility that some compromise may be arrived at between the cabinet and the landlords, but it is impossible to foresee at present the development of the political situation. On this account my inclination would be to press for the second alternative mentioned in paragraph 7. But I should in any case be very grateful if Your Excellency could let me know what in your opinion are my powers and responsibilities in this matter.[29]

Yours sincerely,
HARRY HAIG

72

HAIG TO LINLITHGOW
Telegram
MSS.EUR.F. 125/126

No. 48-G *August 18th, 1937*

Your telegram No. 910-G, August 16th.[30] I agree as to importance of developing social contacts and have this matter very much in mind. It can only be secured gradually and it might do more harm than good to try and hasten the process unduly. With regard to ministers attending functions at which Governor is present, it has been the practice in this Province that on important formal occasions with which minister is concerned he would normally be present and I should certainly try to encourage this practice.

2. A difficult case will arise in connection with provincial investitures which are functions of marked formality. I hold two such functions in cold weather, one at Lucknow the other at Allahabad. If ministers did not attend Lucknow investiture it would be a matter of serious comment.

The distribution of Coronation Medals was on a different plane. It was a much less formal function and no one was invited who was not receiving a Medal, whereas all important officials and non-officials are invited to investiture which is treated like a Durbar. I should propose putting the general considerations to ministers, but in view of their objection in principle to honours and apparently to functions which emphasise the importance of Governor's position, I doubt whether they would attend.

3. With regard to attendance of ministers when Governor addresses Legislature, I [groups omitted] fully in deplorable situation would be created if ministers did not attend and that if necessary strong pressure should be brought to bear on them. At the same time I agree that it would be undesirable if any reluctance is anticipated to [?raise] the issue immediately though it clearly would not be possible to evade it for more than a limited period. My own feeling is that no great harm would be done if I did not address Legislature in coming September session but that I could hardly omit to do so in cold weather session. One of the difficulties no doubt will be in regard to behaviour of rank and file. If they absented themselves it would make it correspondingly difficult for ministers to be present. I hope ministers may take a reasonable line about this. But I have had no conversation with Pant on the subject and have no knowledge of how his mind is working. I will try to sound him and if there is anything further to report will telegraph again.

73

HAIG TO LINLITHGOW
Telegram
MSS.EUR.F. 125/126

No. 50-G *August 20th, 1937*

Many thanks for your telegram No. 936-G, August 19th.[31] I am taking action accordingly and repeat for your information my telegram to Anderson.[32]

2. Pant agreed to make statement on the lines suggested in paragraph 3 of my telegram No. 40-G of August 9th and I think that this will be definitely useful.

3. There will be I understand ten or twelve cases coming up for consideration. When I get proposals I shall communicate with Your Excellency, but on the whole I do not think that they will raise problems of great difficulty.

74

HAIG TO LINLITHGOW
Telegram
MSS.EUR.F. 125/126

No. 51-G *August 20th, 1937*

Following is text of my telegram No. 49-G, August 20th to Anderson: *Begins.* Many thanks your telegram No. 80, August 17th.[33] I am agreeing to release of five Kakori prisoners. Dublis, in accordance with suggestion made by Governor-General, will not be released until he reaches United Provinces, and it is proposed that he should leave Andamans by boat, September 23rd. Question of Kar has not come up yet.

2. I am very sorry that in the case of Chatterji and Sanyal this may cause you embarrassment, but I am doing all I can to see that Bengal prisoners do not take part in any formal celebrations of their release in Bengal. *Ends.*

75

HAIG TO LINLITHGOW
R/3/1/2

Strictly Confidential Camp,
August 22nd, 1937

My dear Lord Linlithgow,

I am sending my tenth fortnightly report on political conditions in the United Provinces under the new Constitution. I left Lucknow for Naini Tal on the evening of the 7th August, having presided over my first cabinet meeting that afternoon. I returned to Lucknow on the morning of the 20th, and that afternoon presided over my second cabinet meeting. Though from the point of view of work it was awkward having to be away from Lucknow at this time, my 12 days in Naini Tal were of the greatest value and set me up again and I am now feeling perfectly fit and normal. It is, however, a little unfortunate that while I was in Naini Tal the ministers were all in Lucknow working very hard, and now that I have returned and the budget is settled, naturally most of them are going off for short tours or holidays before meeting the Assembly which is being summoned for the 1st September. However, during the brief period available for discussion, I have had a long cabinet meeting on Friday afternoon and a talk with Pant that morning. I am having a long talk with him tomorrow to discuss a number of important problems, and I had a talk lasting one and a half hours yesterday with Katju on various problems that affect his departments. I think with our present system I shall be able to keep in quite sufficiently close touch with the ministers. Their importance, as I have indicated before, varies considerably. Pant and Katju are not only much the ablest, but they are administering the most important portfolios, Pant having Home and Finance, while Katju is Minister for Justice and Development, in addition to being in charge of Industries and, therefore, primarily responsible for handling the Cawnpore labour disputes. The two Muslim ministers do not seem to me very bright. Kidwai is in charge of Revenue, but it is clear that it is not he who thinks out and decides on the big issues of revenue policy. As for Secretaries, ever since the new Constitution came in, I have not given them regular weekly interviews, with the exception of the Chief Secretary; but I send for them whenever I feel I want to see them and retain an entirely free hand about this, and I feel that so far as the system is concerned I am in quite sufficiently close touch with them. The system worked satisfactorily during the period of the minority ministry, and there is nothing to suggest it will not work well now. In addition to this, I have provided by my Rules of Business that I see a very large number of files, perhaps more than may eventually be necessary but I felt it desirable in the beginning to err if anything on the side of seeing too much rather than too little. I am fully in agreement with Your Excellency as to the importance of the Governor keeping in close touch with the administration and with the ministers. I am not apprehensive that I am getting out of touch. The necessary difficulties attendant on the taking of office by the Congress and their having to meet the Legislature within a very short time, and my own illness which came most inconveniently, combined to create certain difficulties; but I hope now to settle down to quite a satisfactory routine.

2. The cabinet meeting on the 20th August, which was mainly concerned

with the budget, went off quite happily. So far as the budget is concerned, there had been a number of prolonged discussions by ministers among themselves in consultation with the Finance Secretary.[34] These were not cabinet meetings, and in the special circumstances that existed, they were in fact of great value in enabling the budget proposals to be put up at the cabinet meeting on the 20th in a clear and balanced way. While it was evident that the cabinet had on most points reached their conclusions already, they did not show any signs of being reluctant to discuss matters on which I wanted information or had suggestions to make.

3. Twelve Parliamentary Secretaries have been appointed. The number may appear excessive, but it is evident that this is one of the methods by which the ministry maintain control over their party and provide some rewards for the ambitious. Pant told me, in justification of the number of 12, that it had been their original intention to have a cabinet of nine, and nine Parliamentary Secretaries, and that when the cabinet was reduced to six, they did not wish to reduce the total number of members of the Legislature who should hold some official position. They kept it therefore at 18 – six ministers and 12 parliamentary Secretaries. So far the work of the Parliamentary Secretaries seems to have gone on without friction. We have made it clear by an office order that the Parliamentary Secretaries will not be in charge of departments or parts of departments and will not be interposed between the secretary and the minister. They have no responsibility for decisions. At present they are not noting on files at all, and I shall endeavour to maintain this practice. I dare say from time to time difficulties may arise, but I think the general understanding as to their functions and position is satisfactory. Since writing the above I have received your letter of August 20th[35] about the position of Parliamentary Secretaries, and I think you will agree that at present [?this] is satisfactory. I am fully alive to the dangers of development on different lines.

4. Since my last fortnightly report was written, the Cawnpore strike situation became very much more menacing, and then, after some anxious days, was settled for the time being by the men going back to work. For this result the ministry deserve considerable credit, particularly the Premier, whose final intervention was decisive, and Katju who had done useful work throughout. The position gave rise to a good deal of anxiety in regard to the preservation of order. At the end the strike was general, there were as many as 40,000 labourers out, and there were clear signs that the temper was getting worse. The local authorities were also very apprehensive that if rioting did break out, it would before long take a communal turn. Cawnpore is the most turbulent city in the Province, and

the communal riots which took place there in 1931 were the most terrible outbreak that the Province has experienced during my time in India. I was satisfied, however, that the ministers were taking a sound line about the necessity for preserving order and were in the closest touch with Owen, the District Magistrate, who throughout handled the situation admirably and had the confidence of the ministers. Large bodies of additional police were drafted into Cawnpore and all necessary precautions taken. Nevertheless, it was a great relief when a situation which might easily have resulted in a most serious outbreak was settled peacefully.

5. With regard to the policy as between the employers and the workmen, I was convinced that the best chance of achieving success was to leave the Ministers to handle the situation in their own way, and this judgement was I think borne out by the result. Their endeavour was to support the comparatively moderate labour element. Admittedly the word "comparatively" has to be emphasized strongly, for the Mazdur Sabha has in the past existed mainly by seeking occasions for stirring up trouble and the employers are profoundly distrustful of it and dislike having to recognise it or enter into any sort of agreement with it. Still the Mazdur Sabha was, under the influence of the ministers, throwing its weight in favour of a temporary settlement and a return to work as against the communist element which was simply out for mischief; and in the end an agreement was reached and the men went back to work. The employers showed, I thought, a rather unwise attitude of peevishness after the settlement had been reached, and complained that it had been forced on them and that they had no confidence in the Mazdur Sabha. To this the Premier issued a rejoinder which, from the point of view of temper, had the advantage over the employers. I enclose copies of these two statements.[36] Today I see in the paper a report, which I trust is not true, of a most dangerous and provocative circular issued by the Mazdur Sabha. There is no doubt the situation is still unstable, but I hope there will be no further trouble pending the setting up of the committee by government to enquire into the claims of both sides. I had a long talk yesterday with Katju about this committee. It is intended to have one representative of the employers and one of the Mazdur Sabha and to have three members nominated by government. I have impressed upon Katju the great importance of the government nominees being persons who would be regarded by both sides as impartial, as otherwise their findings were not likely to be accepted. He said that the cabinet fully recognised this and they were thinking of sounding both the employers and the Mazdur Sabha in regard to the persons they were proposing to nominate. I am not myself

clear whether the workers have any serious grievances, or whether they have merely been stirred up by general agitation and a belief that with the advent of the Congress government they will secure whatever they want. Improved housing would probably have some considerable effect on their contentment, and I think it likely that a special effort may be made in that direction.

6. I have had some discussion with the Premier, as regards his general attitude towards communists and the necessity of restraining them under the law. I emphasized my view that they might prove a serious menace to this Province, and that if the idea gets about that they are likely to receive lenient treatment here, we may have a considerable influx of communists from the Punjab where, I understand, they are treated in a much more vigorous manner. He recognised the dangers, but is still strongly influenced by his general principles in accordance with which the way to deal with communism is by argument and not by restraint. But I think he is beginning to appreciate also the other point of view.

7. While I was in Naini Tal I had considerable correspondence with Your Excellency about the question of releasing certain prisoners in this Province who had been convicted of crimes of violence committed in connection with political movements. When I arrived here on the 20th I communicated to the Premier the conclusions that had been reached, and orders are being issued today. The Premier is also putting out a statement, which I think will be of value, emphasizing the opposition of the government, and in particular of the Congress, to any movement involving violence, and explaining that it is in the confidence that these men have realised the futility of this policy and have no intention of pursuing it further that the government have felt themselves justified in remitting the remaining portion of their sentences. The prisoners dealt with are in the main the Kakori prisoners who have already served more than ten years of their sentences and are the most important of the so-called political prisoners now in custody. There will be a certain number of other prisoners also to be considered, but I do not think their cases are likely to give much trouble.

8. Two young men, who had apparently been arrested recently for distributing communist propaganda and are in custody awaiting trial, have announced their intention of going on hunger-strike unless the Andamans prisoners' demands are conceded. I am going to discuss with the Premier tomorrow how this is to be handled. I fancy the young men really are in search of notoriety.

9. I wrote to Your Excellency in some detail a few days ago about the

agrarian situation, and in particular the issue of executive orders by the government staying certain proceedings in revenue courts. I will not deal here with the legal position which I put to you in that letter, but there is no doubt that from the practical point of view the orders of the government are producing rather strong and immediate reactions. The chief practical danger which I pointed out to the Premier in a letter which I wrote to him from Naini Tal was that the orders for stay of proceedings in connection with suits for recovery of arrears of rent would produce an impression among the tenants that rents were no longer to be paid. Soon after I had written to the Premier on this subject, reports from Commissioners began to come in, indicating that these results were in fact beginning to show themselves. There were also complaints in growing volume in the press from zamindars reflecting a very real uneasiness or even consternation. In consequence of these various factors the government issued a communiqué a copy of which I enclose,[37] making it quite clear that while they thought it necessary to suspend proceedings for recovery of arrears of rent, it was an essential part of their policy that current rents should be paid, and appealing to tenants to pay their current rents willingly. It is the case of the cabinet that in fact arrears of rent are hardly recoverable and that all that happens is, when a tenant has got into arrears, that he pays approximately the full annual rent, of which part is credited to the current year and part to arrears, and that in this way he is kept indefinitely in arrear with his rent. This is the situation which they wish to escape from. But there is a very serious danger that the orders will make it extremely difficult to collect current rents. Much depends on what the ordinary Congressmen in the villages are doing, and this is a point which I have been impressing on the ministers since I came to Lucknow. If they want current rents to be paid, they must see that their people in the villages make this clear. I propose to discuss this further with Pant tomorrow. I have no doubt whatever about his intentions, but I am not sure how far he can control the Congress workers in the villages.

10. My general impression is that the cabinet are not anxious to do anything that would seriously upset the present land revenue system. They appreciate the fact that it is the foundation of our whole financial position, and while they are determined to do something for the tenants, they do not wish to make the position of the Zamindars too difficult. They are in fact I think definitely hoping for some sort of agreement with the Zamindars in regard to tenancy legislation. Katju said to me yesterday that in their tenancy legislation they would much rather get 12 *annas* by agreement than 16 *annas* by force, and this I am inclined to think represents their

genuine approach to this problem. They realise of course that if the Zamindars are driven too far, there may not only be disorder, but that changes may be held up for a considerable time by the Upper House. I think it is quite possible that this difficult problem will be settled by the normal processes of public discussion.

11. The budget as settled at our meeting on the 20th will be of a very reasonable character. By means of certain retrenchments (mostly lump cuts) they have brought the deficit down to only a few lakhs, but they are putting some 12 lakhs of new expenditure into the budget apart from 3 or 4 lakhs which the minority ministry had already put in. The main item will be a non-recurring provision of 10 lakhs for rural development, mainly improved communications, water-supply, cottage industries, &c. This will leave a deficit of about 17 lakhs. They intend to propose an entertainment and betting tax which they hope may bring them about 3 lakhs this year, and they will leave the rest of the deficit uncovered. Their ultimate scheme for providing the much-needed additional resources is to impose a tax on agricultural incomes. Their idea is to impose it at income-tax and super-tax rates on payers of land revenue of Rs. 5,000 and over, and for the purpose of simplicity to take the agricultural income as being equivalent to the land revenue paid. In practice of course the landlord's income is appreciably larger than the land revenue he pays. They estimate that a tax of this kind would bring in some 30 lakhs a year. They are evidently, however, doubtful about bringing forward a measure of this kind as part of their Budget proposals, and I have advised them that it would be wiser to wait a bit, make some detailed enquiries and prepare the way gradually. I think, if they introduce a measure of this kind simultaneously with what they are doing about arrears of rent, that the landlords might be driven too far and any possibility of an agreement with them might disappear. At present their intention is not to put forward proposals for taxing agricultural incomes until they have been able to survey the general position rather more carefully, and I think this would certainly be wise.

12. As I had indicated in my last letter, they have very wisely given up the idea of proposing a cut in pay. Their retrenchment proposals include a sum of 6 lakhs reduction in travelling allowance grants. This represents roughly a reduction of one-eighth, as the total travelling allowance bill for the Province is at present 47 lakhs. Actually the reductions in travelling allowance rates which they are considering are on a moderate scale. I have persuaded them that the actual rates require some further consideration and no final conclusion has yet been reached about them. But they have fully accepted the principle that the rates should not be reduced so as to

cause any loss to officers. The actual reduction in rates to my mind will clearly not give anything like an economy of 6 lakhs, and indeed they are hoping to secure economy to a considerable extent by closer administrative supervision of journeys. There is no harm in their taking credit for an economy of 6 lakhs under this head, but I am doubtful whether it will be realised in full, and so far as I can judge at present the actual reduction in travelling allowance rates will not be unreasonable or put officers to actual loss.

13. I was very glad to find there was no proposal for reduction of canal rates. My efforts to prevent the previous government throwing away in this manner 8 or 10 lakhs of income have turned out to be valuable. The previous government argued that the Congress were bound to take this step as soon as they came into power. Their anticipations were wrong.

14. In paragraph 13 of my last letter I indicated that apart from the various problems at headquarters, it is very necessary to watch what is going on in the districts and how these changes are affecting the minds of the people and the members of the Services. Point has been given to these remarks by the latest fortnightly reports from Commissioners. They all report incidents and tendencies which are undoubtedly unpleasant and which, if they were to continue or develop, might affect the administrative machine seriously. The attitude of the ministry towards these manifestations is indicated by a passage in the fortnightly report to the government of India, dated August 17th. "Commissioners according to their temperament see in this either signs of increasing lawlessness or little more than a temporary effervescence of spirit. The latter is probably the correct diagnosis, and it is hoped that too much will not be made of minor incidents during this transitional period. The Congress party leaders are not in favour of lawlessness or of hostility to government servants as such or of victimisation in any form." I think this does represent the genuine feeling of the ministry and that they are using their influence to try and restrain the exuberance of their followers. I am very ready to hope they may be successful and I certainly do not wish to press them unreasonably at this early stage on such points. But I still think it is too early to form an opinion as to how the situation is really going to develop. The Commissioner of Agra,[38] for instance, who is an experienced and well-balanced officer, gives a number of instances of lawlessness and attempted interference with the administration and says: "It is to be hoped that this spirit of lawlessness will soon subside. Some officers apprehend that if it does not, the authority of permanent officials in the district will be undermined and demoralisation set in amongst the rank and file. I view with particular

anxiety the situation in the Muttra district. Here the District Magistrate[39] complains that propagandists are moving about the rural areas inciting villagers against the police and other officials. Police reporters endeavouring to obtain reports of meetings are harassed and obstructed. This is reported from other districts also."

15. In general I consider that the outlook of the ministry is reasonable, and their policy sane. They have shown so far no signs of taking up unpractical ideas like prohibition or a vast expansion of education. They will really be pursuing, though by more radical methods, the objects which previous governments have been aiming at. The danger is that they may not be able to control their followers, not so much in the Assembly, as in the country. In Cawnpore Congressmen seem to have rallied to the government in pursuit of a moderate policy, and this is a hopeful sign. In the districts generally it remains to be seen whether Congressmen will give loyal support to the policy of the ministry. At present I think the prestige of the ministry stands high, and the omens are reasonably hopeful.

Yours sincerely,
HARRY HAIG

August 23rd, 1937

P.S. : I have had a very satisfactory talk with Pant this morning. He tells me the whole resources of the Congress organisation are being employed to make it clear in the villages that current rents must be paid. The Provincial Congress Committee is behind this and he believes they will be successful. In the same way it is clear that he has been doing everything he can through the Congress organisation to restrain the exuberance of Congress activities referred to in paragraph 14. His attitude towards the Zamindars also appears to be very reasonable, and he quite agrees as to the wisdom of postponing for the present proposals to impose a tax on agricultural incomes.[40]

76

HAIG TO LINLITHGOW
Telegram
MSS.EUR.F. 125/126

No. 52-G *August 23rd, 1937*

With reference to concluding sentence of my telegram No. 48-G of August 18th. I saw Pant today. We touched on the question of the Governor addressing the Legislature and I think it is quite clear not only that ministers would attend but that their followers would. He seemed to welcome the idea of my addressing the Legislature provided I dealt with ministry's programme. I said that that was a point I should have to consider with some care and I had not yet really thought out what I might wish to say if I did address the Legislature in September, but that I would have a further talk with him on the subject later.

2. I also touched on the question of social contacts. He made it clear that they were bound by a decision of Working Committee which they [?could not] disregard. At the same time he spoke in a most friendly way and evidently thinks (group corrupt) if we leave matter alone for the present, the difficulty may gradually be overcome. I gathered that if it were not for this prohibition, he would have no objection at all to accepting Government House hospitality.

77

HAIG TO LINLITHGOW
Telegram
MSS.EUR.F. 125/126

No. 53-G Lucknow,
August 24th, 1937

Your Excellency's telegram No. 911-G of August 17th.[41] With regard to Congress flag, I think we must start from position that flag is a party emblem and not a national flag. We do not want to show it any disrespect, but it is not consistent with impartial position of government servants to take part in any ceremony of saluting it. A government servant should normally not be present at any gathering where Congress flag is flown in a formal manner and audience are expected to stand in its honour. If he were to find himself unfortunately in that position, I agree that, in order to avoid creating an incident, it would be wise for him to stand, though under no circumstances salute flag. But conclusion is that a government servant should not place himself in a position of such embarrassment and therefore it seems to me that he should not attend any ceremony at which he knows that Congress flag is going to be saluted, and that if he himself is going to preside at any public function, he should satisfy himself beforehand that nothing of sort will be included in the programme.

2. Similar principles apply a good deal to "Vande Mataram". The song is not really understood in this Province and its singing is primarily a

nationalist demonstration. Though at first meeting of our Assembly I understand all members stood up, I very much doubt whether Mussalmans really appreciated doing this or whether they would be prepared to accept such practice as normal. It is primarily a Hindu song. The attitude of government servants should be similar to that in the case of Congress flag; in other words, they should try to avoid being put in a position of having to stand up while "Vande Mataram" is sung. But if they have got into that position, they had better conform to what others are doing.

3. If this is view of government as to what government servants should do, the important question is whether these views are to be communicated to government servants and if so how. If they were communicated in writing, it would, in my opinion be necessary to inform ministers what was being done and indeed to consult them. They would doubtless raise objections. We might have matters ventilated in press and situation which Your Excellency wishes to avoid, and which I agree should be avoided, would probably arise, namely, that these questions might develop into a somewhat important political issue.

4. On the other hand, if instructions in writing are not given to government servants, it may take some time before they appreciate what we should regard as right course of action, some of them may deliberately prefer to do what they think to be agreeable to ministers rather than to Governor, and in any case there may be a good deal of lack of uniformity in their behaviour. On the whole, however, I think this disadvantage is to be preferred to other and by talking to Commissioners I have no doubt it would be possible to get the general idea round without issuing any orders in writing.

5. I do not think my ministry is likely to go out of their way to raise these questions if we do not force issue upon them.

78

HAIG TO LINLITHGOW
Telegram
MSS.EUR.F. 125/126

No. 54-G *August 25th, 1937*

Pant had given me clearly to understand that he did not anticipate demonstrations on release of Kakori prisoners. On seeing Press reports that reception was to be organised for them in Cawnpore (and it would now appear also in Allahabad and in Lucknow) I communicated with

Pant and urged him to use all his influence to stop this, pointing out that such demonstrations would create precisely the impressions we want to avoid, and would also make it much more difficult to release any more prisoners. He replies that he fully realises this, that he had already made every effort to prevent these demonstrations but has failed. I have no doubt that his attitude in this matter is perfectly genuine, and that he has done his best, but has definitely failed to hold the extremists.

2. It will be necessary to see effect of these demonstrations, but at present I am inclined to think that we can agree to no more releases.

79

HAIG TO LINLITHGOW
R/3/1/2

Personal and Confidential

Camp,
August 30th, 1937

My dear Lord Linlithgow,

Many thanks for Your Excellency's personal and confidential letter of 28th August and your very useful comments on my tenth fortnightly report. I think I ought to let you know at once that though I have nothing to say in modification of my general picture of the attitude and policy of the ministry, the general situation in the Province seems to me to be definitely deteriorating. In my last two fortnightly reports I have drawn attention to the fact that while we are naturally much occupied with the various problems at headquarters which arise in connection with the relations with the ministry, it is vital to consider what is the actual state of the Province, and in my last letter I indicated certain disquieting features. Since that letter was written the adverse factors have become more pronounced, or at any rate more evident to me. The accounts which I have received of the Kakori prisoners demonstrations, though not yet complete, are most disturbing, and it is evident that I must take a strong pull on the situation. It seems to me clear that I cannot agree under present conditions to any more releases of violence prisoners whatever may be the individual merits of the cases, and I shall very likely have to reverse my decision about Dublis, the prisoner in the Andamans. I shall be telegraphing to Your Excellency on this whole subject as soon as I have had a talk with Pant. At present unfortunately he is laid up; but I have already made it clear to him in writing that I regard the recent developments in connection with the release of prisoners as grave. The situation at Cawnpore, which I visited on Friday in order to get some first-hand impressions, is more disquieting than I had supposed, and I think it is unlikely that we shall eventually escape a serious general strike there, which will certainly be accompanied by disorder. However, that is a situation which no doubt can be dealt with, if and when it arises. I have had two recent talks with the Inspector-General of Police, who has returned from extensive tours in the Province, and the account he gives me of conditions is far from satisfactory. Finally, the Chief Secretary told me this morning that the latest fortnightly reports[42] from Commissioners are decidedly less favourable than the last. I have not changed my view at all about the attitude and policy of the cabinet, but it remains to be seen whether they will, in view of the Left Wing pressure on them and their own liberal theories of how the government should be conducted, be able to keep control over the Province. I do not say that I anticipate any immediate crisis, but there are a number of matters which I must press on Pant, and I am not sure how far he will find himself able to accept them. The next month with the Assembly in session will probably show clearly whether the present cabinet is able and willing to take necessary measures to retain control of the situation.

Yours sincerely,
HARRY HAIG

80

HAIG TO LINLITHGOW
MSS.EUR.F. 125/127

Secret

Camp,
September 4th, 1937

My dear Lord Linlithgow,

I am writing in reply to Your Excellency's secret letter, dated 1st September 1937, about the speech made by one of the Kakori prisoners at Lucknow recently.[43] You will since have seen that this man, Manmathnath Gupta, sent a special letter to the *Pioneer* declaring that what he said had been deliberately misrepresented and generally disclaiming his belief in terrorism. At the same time the Kakori prisoners as a whole issued a somewhat more elaborate statement on the same lines. I enclose copies[44] of this statement and the letter. I do not know that much reliance can be placed on these repudiations, and I have little doubt myself that the original reports of what they said were substantially accurate. At the same time from the point of view of public opinion the repudiations are of some value, and I think it is clear that the object which Your Excellency and I myself have very much in mind, that their utterances should be restrained within appropriate limits, has in all probability now been attained. I have not the slightest doubt that this result was brought about through pressure exercised by Pant.

2. I think Your Excellency's letter must have been written before you had received my letter of August 30th, which makes clear my own reactions to these demonstrations in connection with the Kakori prisoners. I trust that you are in agreement with my general views. I think that really the most important point is that which I have referred to in that letter and also in my telegram No. G-54, dated August 25th, about future releases. Under present conditions I think that any more releases would have a very bad effect on the public mind and would suggest that the government had no real control over the situation. Pant's illness has prevented me from having a really effective talk with him, but I saw him a day or two ago in bed and referred to the very clear indication of my views which I had already given him in writing. It was decided that we would defer further discussion of the matter until he was well. But in the meantime he is well aware of my attitude, and the question of further releases is at the moment in abeyance.

3. Pant himself I think from the language he used was as much upset as anyone by the demonstrations in connection with these prisoners and their utterances. He told me that they had entirely at their own request come to see him and that he had spoken to them pretty straight. He gave it as his personal opinion that whatever they might say, they were in fact rather broken men and that they had no intention at all of running the risk of getting themselves into trouble with the police again. I am not sure that I trust his judgement on this point very far. This is what he has always wanted to believe, and what he told me before the release he was convinced was the case. At the same time my own feeling is that they probably have no intention of resuming terrorist methods, but I should judge that they are still convinced revolutionaries and may very well take up the revolutionary communist policy.

4. While Pant's attitude, I feel sure, is perfectly genuine, it looks to me as if Kidwai may have been in sympathy with these demonstrations, and it was reported in the papers that two of the Parliamentary Secretaries were present at the demonstrations in Lucknow. I will take up these points with Pant when I have my talk with him.

Yours sincerely,
HARRY HAIG

81

HAIG TO LINLITHGOW

R/3/1/2

Strictly Confidential *September 6th, 1937*

My dear Lord Linlithgow,

The business of the government has been considerably hampered during the fortnight by the unfortunate illness of the Premier. After a very heavy time preparing the budget, he went to Naini Tal for a few days and immediately on his return went down with a troublesome boil which eventually had to be cut out. Since the operation his health has improved, but he is still confined to bed and has had to be relieved of a good deal of his work. He proposes, however, to come to the Assembly today for his Budget speech. As I have explained before, the ministry is very much dependent on the Premier, and his illness just at the time the Legislature is meeting and when in addition some very difficult administrative problems have arisen, was unfortunate. I hope, however, he will be about again in a few days. I have myself seen him once, but I have been anxious not to trouble him unnecessarily.

2. The Assembly met on the 2nd September and the Legislative Council on the 3rd. The Budget is being introduced on the 6th. I have decided to address the Houses jointly on the 9th. My proposal to do this was welcomed by the Premier. I granted an interview recently to the Speaker, Babu Purshottam Das Tandon, who has the reputation of belonging to the more extreme wing of the Congress. His attitude in conversation was very friendly and reasonable, and he seemed quite pleased at the idea that I should be addressing the Assembly.

3. In general the fortnight has been a troublesome one, and I feel we have reached a somewhat new phase. The various problems arising out of relations with the ministers and their specific policies have been less prominent, while what is coming to the front is really the general conditions in the Province. When I received Your Excellency's letter of 28th August, commenting on my last fortnightly report, I feared that you might be interpreting it in a more sanguine spirit than it was meant to convey. I thought it necessary to send you at once a letter, dated August 30th, which showed how in many respects the general situation was becoming more disquieting. That letter may be regarded as an intermediate report, and I am sending a copy of it to the Secretary of State.

4. The first and most serious turn for the worse in the situation arose from the demonstrations with which the release of the Kakori prisoners was greeted. These demonstrations were undoubtedly organised by the Left Wing of the Congress in spite of the strong opposition of Pant. While nothing much was done at Allahabad, where the prisoners were released, at Cawnpore a procession of an openly revolutionary character was organised, in the course of which terrorists were held up to public admiration. I attach a copy of a letter[45] from the District Magistrate, describing this procession. The next day the Cawnpore Municipal Board gave an address of welcome to the prisoners. The ministers were quite prepared to veto expenditure on this, but when the matter was enquired into, it was found that by orders passed some five or six years ago no sanction of government was required for expenditure on addresses provided it did not exceed a certain amount. In any case nothing could have been done to prevent the Municipal Board presenting an address and the members themselves financing such small expenditure as was required. The next day the prisoners came to Lucknow and were again taken in a very large and impressive procession, though I gather without the extremely objectionable features which characterised that at Cawnpore. They were throughout treated as heroes and patriots. Various utterances by them at Cawnpore and Lucknow implying a belief in terrorism were reported in the *Pioneer*, which dealt with them in a very effective and vigorous leading article. The ex-prisoners subsequently put out statements saying that they had been misrepresented and that they did not in fact believe in terrorism. These disclaimers did something to diminish the impression created by the reported speeches, but I have little doubt that these incidents as a whole have stimulated revolutionary feeling, even if they are not likely to contribute to any recrudescence of acts of violence.

5. Whether the prisoners themselves have been altogether willing agents it is difficult to say. They were undoubtedly seized upon as soon as they came out of jail and were made into heroes whether they wished to be or not. Pant suggests they are not really anxious to risk being brought into conflict with the police again. But I fear they must be regarded as definite revolutionaries and it is not likely that the Left Wing will leave them alone, or will fail to try and make use of them in connection with the revolutionary communist programme. The most disappointing thing is that Pant was clearly unable to control the Left Wing, and as his method of approach to all problems of this kind is to use personal influence rather than exercise the authority of the law, this suggests certain doubts about future developments. As I have already explained separately to Your Excellency,

I feel it is important for the present not to consider any further releases, and this view I have made clear to Pant. But we have not yet got to grips on the subject owing to his illness.

6. The second important problem is the state of Cawnpore. I felt it desirable, as soon as possible after my return from Naini Tal, to go over to Cawnpore myself so as to be able to acquire some first-hand impressions of the situation. I visited Cawnpore on the 27th August and interviewed, besides the Collector[46] and the Superintendent of Police,[47] three representatives of the mill-owners, three of the Mazdur Sabha, the Labour Officer and the Officer Commanding the station. The mill-owners seemed convinced that a strike cannot in the end be avoided. They declared that the Mazdur Sabha is almost wholly under the control of the Communist Wing and that they have promised the labourers an increase in wages, whereas the mill-owners are persuaded that they have an overwhelming case against any increase in wages and that in any event they cannot afford to raise wages. The wage issue is really the big question that must come up for decision as a result of the committee's enquiry, and they think that in the present temper of the workers and of the Mazdur Sabha there can be no settlement on this point. They seem quite prepared to fight it out. If it comes to a strike, there is almost bound to be violence and it will be necessary to take very firm action.

7. Therepresentatives of the Mazdur Sabha whom I saw professed to be very moderate. They said that at present the main issues in the mills were centred round "victimisation", and did not talk a great deal about wages, though it is clear that this is the real ultimate issue. The mill-owners on the contrary stressed the serious state of indiscipline, and it was evident that there was a considerable degree of friction in the working of the mills. It was hoped that there might not be an actual strike as long as the enquiry committee was sitting, which might cover a period of two months. The Collector attributes the trouble in the mills almost entirely to communist elements who, in his opinion, are the people who really count in the Mazdur Sabha, and not the comparatively moderate people who pretend to be at the top. The circular letter, to which I referred in my last report, was perfectly genuine and was issued by Muhammad Yusuf, a notorious communist who is Joint Secretary of the Sabha and seems to exercise far more influence than the nominal heads of the Sabha. Since then the friction in certain mills has developed into definite strikes, and at the moment it is uncertain whether the situation will remain in an unstable condition during the period the committee are engaged on their enquiry, or whether through

some irresponsible action a general strike will be precipitated earlier. Sporadic violence has also developed against mill workers, and it has been necessary to issue an order under Section 144.

8. A further complication in Cawnpore, in addition to the industrial unrest and the excitement about the Kakori demonstrations, is provided by Muslim demonstrations to protest against the Palestine policy. At these some speeches of an exceedingly violent and provocative character were made, and the District Magistrate proceeded to arrest two of the worst speakers and institute proceedings against them under Section 107. Subsequent events were somewhat unfortunate. The day before the opening meeting of the Assembly it was announced that the Muslims were going to move an adjournment motion to protest against these arrests. I got into communication at once with Pant in order to impress upon him the necessity of upholding the action of the District Magistrate. I found that he was quite prepared to do this; but in the meantime it turned out that the two men had already been released. One of the Parliamentary Secretaries to the Premier, a Muslim, had gone a few days before to Cawnpore and had urged the District Magistrate to release these men. The District Magistrate, evidently understood that this was a message from the Premier, and on certain assurances being given that the men would not offend again, he agreed to release them. As a matter of fact the Premier knew nothing about this and was as little disposed as I was to approve it. One of the men since his release has proceeded to make another violent and defiant speech. The District Magistrate wrote that he could not take action for the preservation of peace if what he did was not going to be upheld by the government. The whole affair has been an unfortunate series of misunderstandings, but it has now been made quite clear to the District Magistrate that he is authorised to take what action the situation demands for the preservation of order and that he will be supported. In fact the latest Palestine Day demonstrations in Cawnpore appear to have fizzled out.

9. In Lucknow also the demonstration in connection with Palestine Day assumed a somewhat formidable character. This was I am afraid largely due to lack of foresight by the police. A large and turbulent procession was allowed to parade some of the principal streets with no control. This matter was taken up at once and it has been made clear to the local authorities that they must exercise proper control over such processions. When a day or two ago the second Palestine Day procession was held under strict control, it created very little impression and was I am told a definite failure. The violent spirit of the first Palestine Day demonstrations

both in Cawnpore and Lucknow was somewhat of a surprise. But whatever the precise cause – and it would seem as if the Ahrars were trying to outbid the Congress in extremism – the assertion of authority seems to be having a restraining effect, and it does not at the moment look to me as if the Palestine agitation will continue to be very formidable.

10. Another set of activities which will require serious attention in this Province is undoubtedly communism. The new ministry could not be persuaded that there was any danger in communism and a number of communist agitators and agents of some importance were released. The labour unrest in Cawnpore is certainly the direct result of this policy, and it is communist influence that is at the moment making all chances of a settlement exceedingly remote. I think the Premier is now beginning to realise this, and I keep on pressing upon him the dangers of ignoring communist activities. As you will see the position as between me and the Premier has to some extent changed. Hitherto he has been pressing certain policies on me and I have been counselling delay and caution. Now the situation in many respects has developed to such an extent that I find it necessary to press certain action on him. So far he has shown himself not unreasonable. But as I said in my letter of August 30th, it remains to be seen whether the cabinet will, in view of the left wing pressure on them and their own liberal theories of how the government should be conducted, be able to keep control over the Province.

11. With regard to the agrarian situation, the Zamindars are becoming more and more emphatic in their protests against the action taken by the ministry in suspending further proceedings in suits for arrears of rent. The attack on the legality of the orders has, I am glad to say, produced a real impression and the cabinet have gone so far as to draft a Bill which would give effect to their executive orders in regard to proceedings in revenue courts, as well as a Bill which they had always been meaning to introduce dealing with proceedings in civil courts. I understand it is their intention to introduce the Bill dealing with revenue courts in a few days. With regard to the practical situation there is no doubt that the collection of rents is at a standstill. But it must be remembered that this is the season when very little rent-collecting normally goes on. The greater part of the *rabi* rents have been collected already. The real test will come when the *kharif* rents have to be paid. In the meantime the Zamindars will maintain their pressure on the government, and having really a strong case will very likely be able to secure some modification, particularly as the cabinet themselves are definitely alarmed at the possibility of any widespread

refusal to pay rents. The difficulty is that Congressmen, or those posing as such, are still going about in the villages declaring that rents are not to be paid, and the official organisation seems to have only inadequate control over these local firebrands.

12. With regard to the position of the Services, I am hoping, in spite of the rather gloomy views stated in my letter of August 30th, that the situation will gradually right itself. Certain instructions which the Inspector-General of Police wishes to issue to Superintendents of Police, intended to clear up the position and reassure the police force, are at present under consideration, and I hope will be agreed upon shortly. In general I am inclined to hope that things will gradually settle down. When particular instances of misbehaviour by Congress organisations or individuals are brought to the notice of the Premier, he takes action to call the offenders to account. I visited Rae Bareli last week, a district which has in the past been one of the strongholds of Congress agrarian agitation, and I found that officials there were in quite good heart and not unduly disturbed about conditions.

Yours sincerely,
HARRY HAIG

82

HAIG TO LINLITHGOW
Telegram
MSS.EUR.F. 125/127

No. 57-G *September 10th, 1937*

I had a conversation yesterday evening with Pant regarding release of prisoners. He was somewhat tired after a long day in Assembly and at the end he showed disposition to avoid reaching definite final conclusions. We will have a final talk in two or three days. His general attitude however was very reasonable.

2. I put it to him strongly that demonstrations on release of Kakori prisoners had created a new situation. They had shown that there was more vitality than was supposed in ideas of violence and revolution, and that belief that prisoners on release would keep quiet and not utilise their liberty to promote revolutionary ideas had been proved wrong. I stressed point that while I had considered it reasonable that new government should try their own policy for dealing with these people at a time when no one could be positive what result of that policy would be, now that its results

had made themselves apparent, it would be most damaging to government to repeat an experiment that had clearly failed. From that point of view I said I felt we could not pay attention to individual circumstances of prisoners who had not been released, but that the general situation seems to me to demand strongly that for the present there should be no more premature releases.

3. Pant fully admitted the disappointment of his own expectations and the weakness of his own position. He did not attempt to press for consideration of any fresh cases, but he urged that the two remaining Kakori cases should be considered.

4. The first of these is Dublis. In accordance with normal rules for remissions in Andamans he is for release on November 5th. The late government had refused to agree to these special Andamans remissions in his case, but present government had reversed this order and their order must clearly stand. I had however agreed in addition that Dublis should be sent back from Andamans by boat sailing on September 23rd and should be released as soon as he arrived in the United Provinces. I told Pant that I felt that this decision ought to be now reversed and that Dublis should not be released until November 5th when he would be due for release under ordinary rules. He argued that it would only be a question of a month and that it was quite possible that delay in releasing Dublis would mean that there would be special demonstrations when he was released. I said that this seemed to me a matter of comparatively less importance. If demonstrations were made when he was released in ordinary course, that would involve no reflection on government, but if after example of recent demonstrations Dublis were released prematurely, even by a month, and there were further demonstrations, position of government would be indefensible. I think Pant will accept this position and will agree to my suggestion that orders should be issued that Dublis should be kept in Andamans until normal date for his release.

5. The other case is that of leper Govind Kar. Pant pressed his case on the ground of his pitiable condition. I pointed out, however, that he was probably better off where he is in a special leper jail and that, quite apart from the question of general principle affecting action of this government, it was clearly unfair to Government of Bengal at a time like this to release a man whom they regarded likely to be a definite embarrassment to them. Here again I think he is prepared to accept my view.

6. I said I recognised that he might have difficulty in Assembly and I suggested to him that he should make it clear that change in policy was direct result of demonstrations in favour of Kakori prisoners. I said I thought that this would put government right again with public opinion. He said that he was not afraid of Assembly and always preferred to state his views frankly, and I think perhaps he will be prepared to take this line.[48]

83

HAIG TO LINLITHGOW
MSS.EUR.F. 125/127

Confidential

Camp,
September 12th, 1937

My dear Lord Linlithgow,

Many thanks for Your Excellency's telegram No. 1033-G, dated 7th September,[49] and the very full investigation that you have had made into the points which I raised in connection with the executive orders of my government staying certain proceedings in revenue courts. The legal opinions expressed in your telegram clear up a good many points on which I was doubtful and may well be of value on some future occasion. Fortunately the immediate difficulty which made me refer to Your Excellency has now solved itself. The ministry decided to introduce a Bill providing legislative authority for the orders staying proceedings which hitherto rested only on an executive basis. At the same time they made certain concessions to the Zamindars in connection with the realisation of current rents, which made the position somewhat easier for the Zamindars and in that way they were able to get their Bill through both Houses without amendment and without even a division. So far as my personal position therefore, is concerned, I am now quite happy, for the orders in force have a legal basis. It is too early yet to form any estimate of what will happen when the *kharif* rents fall due for collection, say, in another couple of months. That will be a real test of whether the present government are able to control the tenants and their own Congress workers.

Yours sincerely,
HARRY HAIG

84

HAIG TO LINLITHGOW
Telegram
MSS.EUR.F. 125/127

No. 61-G *September 14th, 1937*

In pursuance of my conversation regarding release of prisoners reported in my telegram No. 57 of September 10th, I saw Pant again on 12th. He still seemed disposed to accept my proposals, but said that he felt it was a matter of such importance that it ought to be discussed with his colleagues who should themselves hear my views. We considered whether a cabinet meeting would be suitable, but we both realised disadvantages of having to record a definite cabinet decision. He suggested that possibly we might have an informal cabinet meeting, and I left it to him to make proposals after discussion with his colleagues. Yesterday he said that he would like an informal cabinet meeting and accordingly I held it at Government House in the evening.

2. I had anticipated that proceedings would be comparatively short. In fact we discussed for nearly two hours. Pant at the outset briefly explained position and I then stated my views at considerable length on the lines contained in my telegram of September 10th. After that all members of the cabinet, with the exception of Pant who kept silent till the end, and Ibrahim who is of little account and seldom contributes anything to a discussion, explained their views in a very temperate and reasonable way. The gist of arguments was this: that they were by their pronouncements more or less committed to releasing Kakori prisoners as a whole and that this was certainly the general expectation. If they now postponed action about the two remaining prisoners and said that they had to reconsider their policy on account of the demonstrations, there would be a continuous and growing agitation for release of these men and their importance would be greatly exaggerated. It would become in fact a first-class issue. On the other hand, they argued that the two remaining prisoners were not particularly dangerous and that, if released fairly soon, they would not acquire any artificial prestige. They maintained further that there had been a general revulsion of feeling as a result of demonstrations, but that to keep these two prisoners back would produce a change in opposite direction.

3. After hearing these arguments I was left with the clear impression that they felt that their political position would be seriously weakened if

action I proposed were taken. There was a Party meeting on Sunday and I suspect that they were strongly pressed on this point. The discussion proceeded throughout on the basis that they would have to accept my decision. The point was never raised definitely, but that was unmistakable tone and there was no kind of suggestion of protest against my having my own views, or even acting on them, but a strong appeal to consider their position and also to weigh carefully whether course I suggested would not in fact be less advantageous than the one they favoured. I should anticipate that if I insisted on my point of view they would not openly dissent, but they clearly anticipate in that event serious and embarrassing trouble with their own followers even, I should suppose, the non-extremists.

4. I deliberately widened discussion and explained to them my general uneasiness and danger of letting law and order position slip too, or creating an impression that they were not prepared to maintain order. We discussed very frankly but in a most friendly way the Cawnpore situation and dangers of communism. On latter point I found them inclined to a superficial optimism, but I think that certain facts and considerations which I put before them had an effect. They fully appreciated in principle the necessity of maintaining order and also recognised readily that my general attitude was inspired not merely by my sense of my own responsibilities but by a real desire to prevent a situation arising which would be exceedingly damaging to them. Their general attitude of course was that a popular government has to use different methods to those of its predecessors and take certain risks which they would not have taken. On the other hand, I stressed point that they must not under-estimate power of repressive action to maintain order and that in last resort that power must be used.

5. At the end Pant spoke. His general attitude both in his previous conversations with me and at cabinet meeting was, I think, influenced by a certain gentlemanly scruple. He felt that he had unwittingly let me down over Kakori prisoners and, therefore, he did not like to press me against my judgement in regard to the two remaining prisoners. This attitude, which I think is rather characteristic of him, made him refrain from arguments of political difficulty which obviously appealed strongly to his colleagues. But I am inclined to think that political difficulty would be serious. With regard to demonstrations he declared with striking emphasis "I not merely regret them, I hate them." Pant asked me to consider very carefully the practical effect of two alternatives. Was it really better to face a troublesome and possibly increasing agitation or to release these comparatively unimportant people?

6. At the end Pant took up a suggestion which had emerged earlier in

the discussion and asked whether it would make any difference to my attitude if the prisoners gave a definite undertaking that they would not take part in any demonstration on their release. I said apart from this there had been previously discussions between us about the desirability of taking from prisoners if they were to be released an undertaking as to their future behaviour. He gave me to understand that in present circumstances he would not have any objection to that policy. He further touched on question of remaining 10 or 12 prisoners whose cases they had promised to consider. Though I have not seen details of these, I consider some of them to be comparatively harmless people, others definitely dangerous. I pointed out that if we proceeded on principle that it was always necessary to give way to an agitation on such matters, we could not refuse to release any of these prisoners. The point was not met very definitely, but it was suggested that case of Kakori prisoners was distinctly more difficult to resist, and that in fact they would be prepared to resist any demands for release of those prisoners whom they did regard as dangerous.

7. By this time it was late and I said that we could hardly reach a final conclusion, but that I would think over what they had said and talk to Pant later. My general conclusion, trying to look at the matter from every point of view and giving due weight to various considerations, is that on the whole the wisest course would be not to insist on my views. As I have said I think if I did insist they would accept position, but if it resulted in serious political embarrassment to themselves, they would naturally feel that I was responsible for that. I am fully alive to danger which I have stressed in my letters of giving way too much to left wing pressure. On the other hand, taking long view it is important that their political position should not be seriously affected, for that would play into the hands of Left Wing. Further if things were to go wrong from their point of view, my position in relation to them in future would be weakened, whereas if I did something now to meet them, I would establish some claim on their gratitude which I think would be a real asset if it comes, as it may, in time to having to press them to take certain action in other connections. The whole tone of our discussion yesterday was excellent and I think both sides at the end of it had a much clearer appreciation of point of view of the other.

8. What I am therefore strongly disposed to do if you agree is as follows:

(*a*) To let Dublis come from Andamans by boat September 23rd and release him on arrival in the United Provinces provided he gives clear undertakings both as to his future behaviour and as to abstention from taking part in any demonstrations.

(*b*) To release Kar on similar conditions at a fairly early date in consultation with Bengal.

(*c*) To take up as an essential part of settlement the question of remaining political prisoners so that matter may be settled once for all.

(*d*) To agree to release of such of them as may be considered comparatively harmless with similar conditions as in the case of Dublis and Kar, and with provision that they will not actually be released for perhaps another month.

(*e*) To get a definite decision from cabinet that in regard to those prisoners who, it may be decided, are too dangerous for release, they will firmly oppose any subsequent agitation for their release and be prepared to face the consequences.

9. Publication of undertakings of kind contemplated above would I think go far to produce the general impression about attitude of government which seems to me to be required.[50]

85

HAIG TO LINLITHGOW
R/3/1/2

Secret *September 22nd, 1937*
No. U.P.-1

My dear Lord Linlithgow,

The last fortnight has been on the whole a period of considerable anxiety and difficulty, though at the end of it conditions in some respects look rather brighter. The main source of anxiety has been Cawnpore. As I mentioned at the end of paragraph 7 of my letter of September 6th, the friction in certain mills had developed into definite strikes, and three mills have been closed throughout this last fortnight, involving about 10,000 workers. Large numbers of additional police have again had to be drafted into Cawnpore, and an order under Section 144 has issued prohibiting assemblies of more than five persons within half a mile of the mills concerned. Meantime Babu Rajendra Prasad, the Chairman of the Enquiry Committee, was away in the North-West Frontier Province and there was some criticism about the failure of the committee to make any start with its work. The Commissioner,[51] who had been visiting Cawnpore, came to see me at the beginning of last week and gave me a gloomy estimate of probable developments. He seemed to think there was little likelihood of accommodation between the mill-owners and the Mazdur Sabha, and he told me that the District Magistrate felt that the general disregard of authority, which has been conspicuous in Cawnpore in the last few weeks, would make it more difficult to maintain order when a crisis arose. I had a day or so before been talking to the Premier about the Cawnpore situation, which seemed to me to be getting very unsatisfactory, and had intended to suggest to him that we should have the District Magistrate in and discuss affairs with him thoroughly. The Premier, however, assured me that in his judgement the temper in Cawnpore had taken a turn for the better, that the workers and even the extremist leaders were beginning to feel that it was unwise to go too far, and that he had every hope that when Babu Rajendra Prasad visited Cawnpore a few days later he would be able to secure some settlement. I therefore made no further move for [?at] the time.

2. On the morning of the 17th, when the Premier was to see me about certain other matters, he came to me seriously shaken about Cawnpore, and for the first time asked my assistance instead of merely giving answers to my enquiries about Cawnpore affairs. He was a good deal upset by Babu Rajendra Prasad's failure to reach any agreement, and the report which Babu Rajendra Prasad had sent in putting on the government the responsibility for doing something in the way of prompt settlement. Pant realised, as clearly as I did, that if the strike were to spread in Cawnpore, there would almost inevitably be serious disorder, and that the chances of avoiding disorder much longer, even if the workers of the three mills alone remained out, were not very bright. His whole policy has been directed to preventing such a development by his own methods of persuasion, and in pursuit of this policy the government have taken considerable risks with the law and order situation. If therefore their policy of conciliation fails and disorder breaks out, they will be discredited on all sides.

3. Pant evidently hoped that I might be able to bring some pressure to bear on the mill-owners. I said that I was not sufficiently acquainted with the actual conditions at the moment in Cawnpore to be able to give any useful advice, but I suggested that we should get over Owen, the District Magistrate, that evening and ascertain from him the attitude of the mill-owners and of the workers and the law and order situation. Accordingly that evening the Premier, Dr. Katju and I had a long talk with Owen, the Chief Secretary and Industries Secretary[52] being in attendance. It was clear that largely through Owen's influence the mill-owners had in fact gone a long way to meet the Mazdur Sabha by agreeing to refer the question of

victimisation of the five or six workers, whose dismissal from two of the mills was the cause of the strikes there, to a judicial officer. The Mazdur Sabha had demanded not only that the issue of victimisation and the question of compensation if victimisation were proved, should be referred to a judicial officer, but that he should also be asked to decide whether these men should be reinstated. This the mill-owners declined to consider, and it was on this point that negotiations with Babu Rajendra Prasad broke down. As it seemed to me quite clear that the mill-owners could not be expected to make any concession on the point of reinstatement, I strongly advised the Premier to bring pressure to bear on the Mazdur Sabha to drop this issue, and it was finally decided that Owen should return to Cawnpore and try to get the mill-owners to agree once more to referring the limited issues to a judge on the assumption that the issue of reinstatement would not be raised. We also decided that though this matter affected only two out of the three mills concerned, we should proceed with it at once, as there would be a better chance of settling the trouble in the third mill if the men of the other two mills could be got back to work. I also suggested that it was very necessary, even if the present difficulty were got over, that some temporary machinery of conciliation should be established during the next two months while the enquiry committee is at work, so that any disputes that arise could be immediately investigated and decided upon by some authoritative officer or small tribunal. This idea was also accepted and will be explored further.

4. Owen returned to Cawnpore and was successful with his part of the mission. The Premier also succeeded with the Mazdur Sabha, and on the 18th it was reported that agreement had been reached that the limited issues should be referred to a judge and that the workers in the two mills would return to work on Monday the 20th. The setting up of an enquiry by a judge was announced by the government on the 19th, and the workers duly returned on the morning of the 20th. It seems likely that the Muir Mills, which now alone remain closed, will be opened shortly.

5. Owen told me that a large majority of the workers in the three mills concerned were getting very tired of being out of work, and that there was growing feeling in favour of return to work and a considerable degree of feeling against the Communist Wing which is keeping up the trouble. This may account for the slightly less uncompromising attitude of the Mazdur Sabha. On the other hand, it seemed to me there was a danger that if the communists felt that they were losing control, they would try and precipitate disorder. There has been a good deal of criticism lately from the side of the employers, vigorously supported by the *Pioneer*, to the effect that

government ought to take strong action against the communist leaders. Though that is certainly the policy which would have been adopted by a government of the old type, it is quite definitely not the policy of the present government, and I do not see how we can expect them to adopt it. Their policy has involved taking very considerable risks, with the chances heavily against success. Nevertheless, it seems to me that there is no choice but to let the ministry try out their policy to the end. It is impossible for me to interfere in the middle by insisting upon action which would be only justifiable on a wholly different line of policy. Owen himself is quite in accordance with this view and is not in favour of taking any action at the present time against the extremist leaders. But he has made very careful plans for dealing with disorder, and if disorder does break out on a serious scale, he intends to arrest the extremist leaders at once. That I think is the time when action of this kind could properly be taken and when the government will have to agree to it. However for the moment things seem to have settled down a bit, and prospects look more hopeful, though relations between the Employers' Association and the Mazdur Sabha are as bad as they can be.

6. Another situation that has caused me a good deal of anxiety, and which I am afraid will be a source of much trouble before I am finished with it, is the general condition of the Gorakhpur district. Some ten days ago I received from the Inspector-General of Police[53] a very disturbing report by the Superintendent of Police, Gorakhpur,[54] about the general condition of the district. The gist of it was that in certain areas and under the influence of certain Congress leaders the authority of the police was being deliberately undermined, that in general a large number of unfounded complaints were being made against the police, and that there were signs of the spread of a feeling of lawlessness, partly due to this and partly to the strained relations between tenants and landlords. On receiving this report I drew the attention of the Premier to it and invited his comments. I found that he entertained extremely strong views on the subject of the Gorakhpur district, and that they were in several directions diametrically opposed to those of the police. He denied emphatically the accuracy of the picture given by the Superintendent, said that he knew conditions in the Gorakhpur district well, that the trouble was due entirely to mishandling of the situation by the local officers, particularly the young officiating Collector[55] who had been put in for three or four months and that the Congress worker, one Baba Raghava Das, whom the official accounts accused of being the main mover in the attack on the police, was a man of the highest character whom Pant regarded as a saint. (I may say that I have

checked up as far as possible the general official estimate of this man and there is no doubt that for some years he has been regarded as a dangerous agitator.) Matters had been brought to a head by the district authorities initiating proceedings under Section 107 of the Criminal Procedure Code against this man and when he had applied for a transfer of the case interim security was demanded from him, with the result that on his refusing to furnish security he was taken to jail. This naturally created a position of great embarrassment, when a very prominent Congress leader whom the Premier knows well and regards with great respect was dealt with in this drastic manner. Orders had been sent by the government directing the withdrawal of the interim security, but the proceedings under Section 107 are still pending. As a result of my conversation with the Premier it was decided that the Commissioner[56] should be asked to come in to Lucknow at once and discuss the situation. I saw the Commissioner for about two hours, and while he admitted that some of the action taken might have been lacking in discretion, he maintained that the general picture of the state of the district as given by the Superintendent of Police was substantially correct. He stressed particularly the ill-feeling between the zamindars and tenants, which he attributed partly to ill-treatment by the zamindars in the past and partly to the orders of the government staying collection of arrears of rent which had encouraged the tenants to a somewhat defiant attitude. The conditions in this district are potentially dangerous. There is a large depressed population which has been stirred up considerably by the agitation of the last nine months, and one cannot forget that it was in this district that the shocking outrage of Chauri Chaura[57] took place at the time of the Non-Cooperation movement.

7. I have arranged, with the approval of the Premier, to post to Gorakhpur as Collector an experienced and capable officer, who is also of a very reasonable temperament, who is due back from leave at the end of this week. The officiating Collector on being relieved will be transferred as Joint Magistrate to Agra. His continuance in Gorakhpur would obviously have been most undesirable from every point of view. But while this will give us an administration in which I shall have confidence, it will not solve the serious situation that has arisen. I had been waiting an opportunity to have a thorough talk with the Premier about Gorakhpur, and I saw him on the 20th. He told me he had written a very full note on the whole subject and suggested that we might defer our conversation till I had read it. I have now seen this note, which constitutes a direct and even vehement attack on the authorities in the Gorakhpur district and contradicts flatly most of their assertions of fact.

8. The case is an extreme illustration of a difficulty that is being felt rather widely. We get a number of complaints from the police and from district authorities as to the behaviour of Congress workers. Though the Premier is always prepared to make enquiries into the more important of these complaints, the result of these enquiries seems usually to confirm him in his general attitude that the complaints are unfounded, and he frankly expresses the view that a great deal of the information which comes up to government either through the Commissioners' fortnightly reports or C.I.D. reports has no solid basis in fact, and ought to be checked much more carefully before it is passed on to government as representing fact. He has of course this much justification for his view, that many of the incidents reported in this way are based on a report from the local Sub-Inspector of Police, or even a Head Constable, and that they are sometimes passed on by the Superintendent of Police to the District Magistrate and find their way through the Commissioner and the C.I.D. to government without any real check having been applied to the original source. This will have to be remedied. At the same time it is evident to me that Pant's attitude towards the police is so prejudiced that he refuses to accept conclusions even when established by a careful and impartial enquiry. This is, I think, the most disturbing feature at the moment in the administration. It is only during this fortnight, when I have had one or two frank talks with Pant about the police situation and police complaints, that I have come to realise his attitude.

9. With regard to complaints of corruption against the police, on which he takes a very strong line and in which he refuses to believe reports exonerating those who have been accused, I hope that matters will improve owing to the appointment of a thoroughly reliable Indian officer of the Indian police to take over the investigation of the more important of these cases. This officer was selected by the Premier himself and is one in whom he has confidence. At the same time he has an excellent reputation in the Indian police and the Inspector-General of Police has full confidence in his character and integrity. With regard to the general complaints and counter-complaints, I am afraid we must trust to some extent to time to cure what is certainly a most difficult situation. I have to watch carefully whether conditions are in certain areas, as is alleged, beginning to prove demoralising to the police, and at the same time to do all that I can to promote, and to prevail on Pant to promote, better relations between the police and the Congress. In many areas as a matter of fact these relations are establishing themselves on satisfactory lines and seem to me to be improving. But considerable friction is undoubtedly being engendered in

certain localities. With regard to Gorakhpur there are so many direct conflicts of assertion on matters which should be capable of being established plainly one way or the other, that I am inclined to think (though I have not yet reached any conclusions) that Pant's final suggestion that there should be a full departmental enquiry into the conditions of the district by a senior executive and senior judicial officer has a good deal in its favour. I think it not unlikely that such an enquiry, while undoubtedly it would reveal certain unwise and possibly arbitrary action taken on the official side, would also explode a great many unfounded allegations which are being put about by the Congress and are firmly believed by Pant, and possibly an enquiry of this kind might prove something of a revelation to Pant and induce in him a more reasonable attitude of mind towards official reports generally. In any case something must be done to change present conditions in the Gorakhpur district which I fear will continue until some of the points of controversy are set at rest authoritatively.

10. The proposed instructions referred to in paragraph 12 of my letter of September 6th which the Inspector-General of Police wished to issue to Superintendents of Police have not materialised. The Premier saw no necessity for issuing such instructions at all, and apart from this objected to the actual terms of the draft. He suggested an alternative which clearly would not be acceptable. On the whole I am inclined myself to doubt whether instructions of this kind would be of much use. But the Premier is himself anxious to send a general letter to all government officers explaining the attitude and policy of government towards the Services, and under his instructions a draft has been prepared by the Chief Secretary which I myself consider to be admirable and which puts precisely the points which I should like to have emphasized. Whether the Premier will be prepared to accept this draft I cannot say. He has at present directed that it should be circulated to his colleagues for comment.

11. I have been in detailed correspondence with Your Excellency about the question of the release of further prisoners convicted of violence, and in particular the two Kakori prisoners who still remain in custody. I am very glad that Your Excellency agrees with the views reported in my telegram of September 14th as the result of the long discussion I had with my ministers. I have since put those conclusions to Pant, and though he has been trying to some extent to whittle down the proposed undertakings to be given by the prisoners before release, and has suggested that Dublis might not be prepared to give such undertakings in order to secure his release one month in advance, I have maintained my position steadily and Pant now appears to accept it. Apart from the two Kakori prisoners, I have

told him that I will now examine the cases of the other prisoners, but that I propose to take a little time over it. He is of course anxious, as always, that anything that is to be done should be done quickly.

12. The Assembly has been in session throughout the fortnight, but the Legislative Council rose on the 10th September and is meeting again on the 29th for a few days to deal with the Bills which will have been passed by the Assembly. The business before the Assembly has been almost entirely the Budget which has been on the whole well received. The members of the Congress party who would no doubt, had the same Budget been produced by their political opponents, have torn it into shreds have maintained an attitude of decorous responsibility. I fancy a good deal of pressure has been brought to bear on them to refrain from embarrassing their leaders. The Opposition have very little which they could reasonably criticise, and in any case their criticism is far from effective. Even so, it has not been an easy time for the cabinet, and the physical and mental strain on them must have been considerable. This should perhaps be borne in mind in judging the Premier's outlook on various problems, for the main strain of the Budget has fallen upon him. I enclose a copy of his Budget speech.[58] My own criticism of the Budget would be that he has taken credit for a good many economies which it may not be possible to realise. On the other hand, a good deal of the new expenditure which looks well and encourages his Congress followers will obviously not be incurred in full during the current year.

13. I have already sent you a copy of my address to the two Houses of the Legislature which I delivered on September 9th. I was very well pleased with my reception. The Chamber was packed and I should judge that none of the Congress members absented themselves deliberately. The galleries were also as full as they could be and my address was throughout listened to with keen attention. It received a full measure of commendation in leading articles in the *Pioneer* and the *Leader*, but the references to the position of the Services, which were intended to be in the nature of some reassurance to them, met with some hostile criticism in the *Hindustan Times*.

14. The government introduced and passed through both Houses without a division a Bill legalising their stay orders in respect of suits for ejectment and arrears of rent in revenue courts. I was myself greatly relieved that the executive orders which seemed to me to have no legal basis have now been put on a legal foundation, and certain concessions were also made to the Zamindars which were both reasonable in themselves and acted as an inducement to the Upper House to pass the Bill. The policy of course

remains unchanged, and the landlords continue to denounce it as unfair and disastrous. But it is having an excellent effect in stirring the landlords out of their normal lethargy. They are now realising that if they want to survive, they must fight for themselves. They probably regard me as a broken reed, though I have for years been continually impressing upon them that under the new Constitution no one can save them but themselves.

15. The position of the government, however, is one of difficulty. Reports from all quarters agree that the collection of rent has come to a standstill, and District Officers and Zamindars generally anticipate that there will be considerable difficulty in collecting rents when the rent collecting season starts again in November. The Premier, who is disposed to discount these like other official reports, is reluctant to believe, what I think however is the case, that large numbers of village Congress workers are telling the tenants in direct contravention of the government policy that they will not have to pay their rent. I have warned the Premier of the dangers of the situation, and indeed he fully appreciates them himself, and I think that during October he will make some renewed efforts to see that his policy really gets home to the villagers. On the other hand, to the extent that it does and that the villagers do pay up their rents, there will undoubtedly be considerable disappointment among large classes of tenants who are still disposed to think that Congress government means a golden age of no rents.

16. The British Indian Association of Oudh held recently an important meeting, and I attach a copy of the speech[59] of their President, the Raja of Jahangirabad, and the resolutions passed. Today the Raja of Jahangirabad came to see me and gave me some very interesting information about the general attitude of the Taluqdars. One of the taluqdars, who is a Congressman, attended one of their meetings and gave them what they believe to be a frank exposition of Congress policy. He said that he had been talking to Jawaharlal Nehru and that Nehru made it clear that he was much less interested in the improvement of the condition of the tenants, which indeed he was disposed to admit was not very bad, as in the destruction of the landlords whom he regarded as one of the main buttresses of the British position in India. I told Jahangirabad that while that might well be the position of Nehru and the extremists, I did not think it was a fair judgement of Pant and the present ministry. He agreed that Pant is really genuinely anxious to improve the condition of the tenants, and that he and Katju have no particular desire to destroy the landlords. Nevertheless, Jahangirabad's view is that the extremists will gradually get the upper hand. He says that some of the more weak-kneed Taluqdars are

anxious on this exposition of Congress policy to try and make terms with the Congress on the basis of joining them against the British connection. But Jahangirabad is absolutely firm in his loyalty to the British connection and so, I understand, are the great majority of the Taluqdars. He is taking a very sensible line and urging the Taluqdars on no account to commit themselves to the Congress at the present stage. They must wait and see how the situation develops and what Congress policy really is. I understand that these views have prevailed. They are nervous that an attack will be made on the Act under which contributions are levied from all Taluqdars and collected with the land revenue, to finance the British Indian Association. If that Act were repealed, the Association would be practically destroyed. There is talk from the more extreme Congress members of proposing the repeal of the Act.

17. There has been an unexpected development in regard to my relations with the ministers on the subject of postings. The general cold weather postings of district officers had been settled with a little give and take with the Premier who had shown himself very reasonable in general, while I had done my best to meet him where he had expressed views in favour of posting some particular officer to any of the more important districts. Suddenly I received a file from the Chief Secretary in which the Premier had passed an order that Kunwar Jasbir Singh, who has been Collector of Saharanpur for the last two and a half years and had taken a couple of months' leave on the understanding that he would return to Saharanpur, should not return there, but that the officiating Collector, who had been brought over from the neighbouring district of Muzaffarnagar, a comparatively junior, though competent European officer,[60] should remain at Saharanpur while Jasbir Singh was to be sent to Muzaffarnagar. As Jasbir Singh was due back from leave in a day or two, the matter was treated as very urgent. I noted on the file that I should like to discuss the proposal with the Premier, and I was not aware why it was suggested that a transfer should be made which would obviously be regarded both by Jasbir Singh and the public as a reflection on his work at Saharanpur. Instead of accepting my suggestion that we should discuss this matter, the Premier wrote a note explaining that he had no cause of complaint against Jasbir Singh and put forward some exceedingly feeble arguments on general grounds in favour of the transfer. I replied pointing out that to change these two officers from their districts without any good cause was wholly contrary to our administrative principles, that whatever the intention of government might be, the public would certainly regard the transfer of Jasbir Singh from a more important to a less important district as a reflection

on him, and that it seemed to me the balance was heavily in favour of allowing the two officers to return to their own districts. Thereupon the Premier said he would like the matter discussed at a cabinet meeting, to which of course I agreed. The meeting took place on the 18th. It soon became apparent, as I had suspected, that this proposal was put forward without any real justification or even knowledge on the part of the Premier in response to suggestions made by certain M.L.As. I also suspect that a certain Parliamentary Secretary, who comes from Saharanpur and has already made trouble in another district with the District Officer, had something to do with this manoeuvre. I explained that I could not agree to this proposal, as the ground seemed to me administratively quite inadequate, and I felt that there was a serious danger of demoralisation of the Services if it were felt that transfers could be made owing to the favour or disfavour of politicians. There was something of a demonstration in force to attack me on the ground of principle and to enquire whether I intended always to exercise my individual judgement whenever I might find myself in disagreement with the ministry. I declined to be drawn into any kind of definition of my judgement, or how I should exercise it, but made it clear that it would be exercised when I felt that circumstances clearly demanded it, as they did in this case. Finally the Premier said that as Jasbir Singh had already rejoined at Saharanpur, he did not wish to press the matter further.

18. The whole affair is rather curious. If it had been intended as an attack on my powers, they would certainly have selected a more convincing case. The real explanation probably is that the Premier, without realising what he was doing, gave certain promises to M.L.As. and then when he found that he could not fulfil the promises, he felt it necessary to put up a fight. I do not think any harm has been done by making it clear to them that I intend to keep a fairly close control over postings of District Officers and Superintendents of Police, a matter which I regard as of the first importance in order to prevent demoralisation of the most essential Services, and that I shall not agree to political jobs. I took the occasion to emphasize the point that had this particular case been discussed with Pant, as I had suggested, I could hardly believe that it would have come to a disagreement of opinion, and I mentioned the importance which I attached to more frequent personal consultation with Pant than had hitherto been possible. We had started under considerable difficulties, as I pointed out, first my own illness, then Pant's, and then this long and difficult session of the Assembly. The administration of this Province is a very big task and raises innumerable problems of some importance, and at the present

moment there are a great many matters that urgently call for discussion between me and Pant which it is really impossible to find time to discuss. I am hoping that in October we shall both be having a bit of a holiday in Naini Tal, and that then we can get to closer grips with a number of our difficulties. I may add that the incident has left no ill-feeling. On the contrary, the next time I saw Pant he was particularly friendly and reasonable in tone on the matters that happened to come under discussion.

19. In paragraph 7 of Your Excellency's letter of 16th September you refer to the question of touring by Governors. I am entirely in agreement with what you say. The matter has been very prominently in my mind ever since my present Ministry came into office. I base the necessity of doing the maximum possible amount of touring during the next cold weather on the following considerations:

(*a*) It will enable me to form a judgement for myself on the general conditions in the Province, about which one gets conflicting views.

(*b*) It will enable me to reassure officers about my own intentions and about conditions in general and to see that they understand policy properly.

(*c*) It will enable me to keep myself before the public and the Services. This I regard as most essential. There is a considerable danger under present conditions, owing to the fact that the Governor inevitably does his main work in the background and unobtrusively, that he should come to be regarded by the public and the Services as something of a cipher. It is essential that that impression should not prevail. My recent official visits to two small districts in the Lucknow division have undoubtedly been valuable locally and had a good effect, besides being distinctly useful in giving me information and points of view which I could not have had otherwise.

20. With these ideas in mind I have already made plans for visiting the Bareilly and Meerut divisions at the end of October and beginning of November and carrying out a few functions. In the latter half of November I hope to visit similarly the Agra and Jhansi divisions. At the end of November I shall be in Cawnpore. In December I shall be based on Allahabad, and I hope to be able to see something of the Benares and Gorakhpur divisions from there. In this way I should have got round almost the whole Province before Christmas. I feel it is essential to cover the whole Province, even though cursorily, as early as possible in the cold weather. Though I may not be able to spare more than four days for a

division and perhaps would not be able to visit more than one of the outlying districts, I can at any rate see all the District Officers and Superintendents of Police at divisional headquarters and get some first-hand general impression of how things are going. It will mean of course a certain lack of contact with the ministry, but I feel so strongly the necessity of touring that I have no doubt that disadvantage will have to be faced. There may be further difficulties arising from a suggestion that another session of the Legislature should be held in November. I shall try, however, to dissuade the ministry from this. In the latter part of the cold weather the Legislature will be in session again when measures of first class importance will be under discussion and I shall certainly find it necessary to remain pretty continuously in Lucknow. I am satisfied that Commissioners are keeping in close touch with their districts and the Inspector-General of Police has been touring extensively.

21. When Hafiz Muhammad Ibrahim, Minister for Communications, introduced his demands in the Budget discussion, the Muslim League staged a walk-out. He had been elected on the Muslim League ticket and had subsequently joined the Congress. This was greatly resented, and when he was appointed minister, there was a strong demand that he should resign his seat and stand again for election. Whether the demonstration had any effect or whether, as the ministry contend, the decision had been taken before, it has now been announced that Muhammad Ibrahim will be resigning his seat at the end of the month, and there will be a bye-election. At the moment I have no view as to what will be the result, but if he fails to secure re-election, there will again be difficulty in finding a Muslim to replace him in the cabinet. There have been no recent Hindu-Muslim incidents of any special importance, but I am told that the undercurrent of feeling between the two communities is far from good, and this is of course inevitable while practically the whole of the Muslims are in opposition in the Assembly.

22. I fear this letter has run to great length; but it is difficult to deal with some of these topics without going into a good deal of detail. I am proposing, if all goes well, to leave Lucknow for Naini Tal on the evening of the 25th, and to spend three or four weeks in Naini Tal.

Yours sincerely,
H.G. HAIG

86

HAIG TO LINLITHGOW
MSS.EUR.F. 125/127

Confidential
No. U.P.-3

Camp,
September 24th, 1937

My dear Lord Linlithgow,

I am writing in answer to Your Excellency's letter of 12th September 1937 about the publication in the *Bombay Chronicle* of certain extracts from the U.P. C.I.D. report for the week ending 21st August 1937.

2. I have made enquiries on the subject from the Premier, and he tells me that these extracts were sent under his authority to the Congress Committee. I have impressed upon him the essential necessity of treating these C.I.D. reports as absolutely secret documents. He expressed sincere regret at what had happened, which was due to an imperfect appreciation of the importance attached to the secrecy of these reports, and he has promised me that he will take very special care in dealing with them in future. On the point of principle I do not think I can do anything more, and I trust there will be no further ground for complaint.

3. With regard to the practical aspects of the particular incident, Your Excellency will observe that the extracts in question are instances of the common complaints that are being made by the police against Congress workers, and that they are based in no way on any secret sources of information. In fact, as I have explained in paragraph 8 of my letter No. 1-U.P., dated 22nd September 1937, the Hon'ble Premier is inclined to complain that these reports have not been checked before being sent up. The Hon'ble Premier has been in the habit, with the full concurrence of the police, of taking action through the Congress organisations in regard to complaints of this kind with a view to such practices being stopped. In many cases these references by the Hon'ble Premier have been useful and have led to a relaxation of tension. Even if the allegations are denied by the Congress workers, the general effect of the references made by the Hon'ble Premier is to show Congressmen that such activities are not approved and should be discouraged. I do not think this procedure has tended to foster the idea of a parallel government. On the contrary, the police complaints are that local Congress workers are doing things which encourage the idea of a parallel government, and the whole object of these references has been to stop such practices if they are found to exist.

Certainly this is the way in which the police have regarded the matter. The Premier in this connection is acting as the head of the party and not as the head of the government. He is using the party machinery and not government machinery, and the object is to meet complaints made by government officers that the party machinery is being abused. Admittedly, the method by which this reference was made was wholly improper, but that a reference in a different form should be made seems to me not in itself improper, and in fact in many cases has proved to be distinctly useful. Latterly, however, these references seem to me to have perhaps exhausted their utility, and to be leading rather to friction than to a good understanding. This is a point which I am going to discuss with the Premier.

4. The root of the difficulty of course is that the supporters of the government in power are in many cases up against the official servants of the government. That peculiar situation does not lend itself to being handled entirely on orthodox lines. I have discussed some of the difficulties in my letter of 22nd September.

Yours sincerely,
HARRY HAIG

87

HAIG TO LINLITHGOW
MSS.EUR.F. 115/9

Private and Personal — *September 25th, 1937*
No. U.P.-4

I am writing in answer to Your Excellency's letter of 17th September, 1937,[61] regarding the possibility of a Royal visit and Durbar. I have not thought it advisable to sound my ministers, as I feel it unlikely that they could give me any definite opinion and certainly could give no assurance, while on the other hand my opening the subject with them might suggest that we were anxious to enter into a bargain which, as Your Excellency points out, would be a very undesirable impression to convey. I have discussed the matter with certain officials, and I have also mentioned it to the Nawab of Chhatari who, as an ex-Governor and ex-Premier, seemed to me likely to give an opinion of value from the point of view of those Indians who believe sincerely in the British connection.

2. I had certain fairly definite ideas of my own on this subject, but without at first indicating them I awaited the views of those with whom I

discussed the matter. I was impressed by the fact that all of them were substantially in agreement with my own views which I give below.

3. I start from the position that unless a Royal visit is to be a real success, it will be a real disaster. I fully appreciate the great advantages of a successful Royal visit, but a Royal visit which was not successful would, in my judgment, do an immense amount of harm and would tend to shake the position of the Crown in India and the traditionally loyal attitude of the masses. I have a vivid recollection of the visit of H.R.H. the Prince of Wales in 1921. I have always supposed that the advice on which that visit was based must have been inspired by a general hope that the popular sentiment in favour of the Crown would overbear political feeling. If so, events falsified that anticipation, and I consider that the visit was unfortunate and did harm. With more than fifteen years of development of political thought and agitation since then, and with the person of the Sovereign himself concerned and not merely the heir to the Throne, I consider that the consequences of failure now would be far more serious.

4. I now come to the general considerations on which we can attempt to base some anticipation as to the nature of the reception that His Majesty would be likely to have and the suitability of the conditions for a Royal visit. No one can possibly foresee what the political conditions in India are likely to be at the end of 1938. It is possible that in this province the present ministry may have consolidated its position on a reasonably moderate policy and that the administration may have settled down and accommodated itself to the new conditions. But there are many grave possibilities of less favourable developments, and the situation would certainly tend to become more difficult if international complications arose. I could certainly not express any anticipation that the conditions in this province at the end of 1938 would be likely to be favourable to a Royal visit. To base policy on any such assumption would to my mind be taking an unjustifiable risk.

5. If, however, we assume that general conditions would not be unfavourable, we are next confronted with the question of the attitude of Congress and the Congress ministries. The declared policy of the Congress is complete independence, and though there may be many in the Congress ranks who do not seriously believe in this as a practical policy and who do not in fact wish to raise the issue in any immediate form, nevertheless it seems to me that we cannot expect the Congress as a body to co-operate in celebrations which, if successful, would undoubtedly have the effect of strengthening the sentiment for maintaining the British connection. I think it likely that the Congress would not go so far as to advocate any active

boycott of celebrations in connection with a Royal visit, but I think it most probable that they would pointedly refrain from taking part in any such celebrations. In this way the issue of loyalty to the Crown would come prominently before the public, and my belief is that the ill effect of Congress abstention would be considerably greater than the good effect of loyal demonstrations.

6. The crucial point would be, as Your Excellency has pointed out, the attitude of the Congress ministers. For the reasons I have developed above, I think it would be difficult for Congress ministers to attend a Durbar. On the other hand, if they did not attend, a situation of a most damaging kind would be created. Ordinary public opinion in India would regard their non-attendance as a public affront to His Majesty, and yet they would see that those persons who had put this affront on the Crown still remained the ministers of the Crown and exercised authority in the provinces. I think myself that this would be a very great blow to the authority of the Crown in India. I would urge that unless there is a definite assurance that the Congress ministers will attend the Durbar, then the Durbar should not be held. This is a view which was expressed to me with some force by the Nawab of Chhatari, and I am myself fully in agreement with it.

7. From the point of view of the ministers themselves, the position would also be one of considerable embarrassment. I do not think for a moment that my present ministers would wish to do anything which could be interpreted as showing disrespect to the person of His Majesty. At the same time if the issue is forced upon them in this way, they may be placed in a position in which they can hardly act otherwise than in a manner that will be misunderstood. It seems to me unwise to create such a situation.

8. I should not myself attach great importance to the argument that there would be much disappointment and some criticism if there were no Durbar next year. Delhi opinion would be likely to be stronger on this point for obvious reasons than opinion in the rest of the country, and though no doubt there would be some disappointment, I should not regard it as being a factor at all comparable in weight with the considerations I have stated above. My own advice would be that the proper course is that described in para. 3(*c*) of Your Excellency's letter, namely, that His Majesty should intimate that the uncertainty of the general international situation is such that he does not himself feel able to visit India next year and he thinks it preferable in the circumstances that there should be no Durbar, but that at some time in the future he would hope himself to visit India. I think it is quite possible that in four or five years' time conditions will have settled down out here to such an extent that a Royal visit could take

place with complete success, but I would certainly take no risks at the present time.

9. With regard to the possibility of the Viceroy holding a Durbar, I think there are strong reasons against this course. Though the issues arising from Congress opposition may not be so serious, the advantages of holding a Durbar, if successful, would not on the other hand be so great, and it appears to me that for the Viceroy to hold a Durbar instead of His Majesty would draw pointed and undesirable attention to the absence of His Majesty. I can see no necessity for holding a Durbar unless His Majesty himself is to attend.

10. On a point of detail, I should like to say that the suggestion in para. 5(*b*) of Your Excellency's letter that the representatives from the provinces should be charged for their seats at the Durbar would in my opinion be wholly out of keeping with Indian feeling and sentiment, and I should myself be most reluctant to have to communicate any such decision to the provincial representatives. I am sure it would cause a great deal of harm. In my view it would be necessary that those who are invited to attend the Durbar should at any rate not be asked to pay for their seats. I agree that they could not expect to receive travelling allowance or free accommodation at Delhi. I think the central government would have to bear the full cost of establishing a stadium. It would I feel sure be impossible to obtain any grant from the provincial government in connection with a Durbar.[62]

NOTES

1. See No. 46, note 68.
2. Lord Linlithgow minuted: 'But you mustn't consult your ministers ! not on their discretion.'
3. The conditions made by Congress for the inclusion of members of the Muslim League in the U.P. ministry in July 1937 have been the subject of much historical controversy. On 15 July Chaudhri Khaliquzzaman met Maulana Azad and Pandit Pant in a Lucknow hotel. Khaliquzzaman records that Azad handed him a two-page typed document which read as follows:

   'The Muslim League group in the United Provinces Legislature shall cease to function as a separate group.

   'The existing members of the Muslim League Party in the United Provinces Assembly shall become part of the Congress party and will fully share with other members of the party their privileges and obligations as members of the Congress party. They will similarly be empowered to participate in the deliberations of the party. They will likewise be subject to the control and discipline of the Congress party in equal measure with other members and the decisions of the Congress party, as regards work in the Legislature and general behaviour of its members, shall be binding on them. All matters shall be decided by a majority vote of the party, each individual member having one vote.

'The policy laid down by the Congress Working Committee for their members in the Legislature along with instructions issued by the competent Congress bodies pertaining to their work in such Legislatures shall be faithfully carried out by all members of the Congress party including these members.

'The Muslim League Parliamentary Board in the United Provinces will be dissolved, and no candidates will thereafter be set up by the said Board at any bye-election. All members of the party shall actively support any candidate that may be nominated by the Congress to fill up any vacancy occurring hereafter.

'All members of the Congress party shall abide by the rules of the Congress party and offer their full and genuine co-operation with a view to promoting the interests and prestige of the Congress.

'In the event of the Congress party deciding on resignation from the ministry or from the Legislature the members of the above-mentioned group will also be bound by that decision.'

Khaliquzzaman adds that Azad appended the following short note to the typed document: 'It was hoped that if these terms were agreed to and the Muslim League group of members joined the Congress party as full members that group would cease to exist as a separate group. In the formation of the provincial cabinet it was considered proper that they should have representatives.'

Chaudhri Khaliquzzaman, *Pathway to Pakistan*. Lahore: Longmans, 1961, pp. 160-1.

The Muslim League rejected these terms but, according to Pandit Nehru, Khaliquzzaman would personally have been prepared to accept them. Nehru to Rajendra Prasad, 21 July 1937. S. Gopal (ed.), *The selected works of Jawaharlal Nehru* (1st series), Vol. 8, New Delhi: Orient Longman, 1976, pp. 165-71.

Further overtures were made following the breakdown although there are inconsistencies in the various accounts as to whether the moves were initiated by Khaliquzzaman or by Azad and Pant. On 24 July Azad gave Khaliquzzaman a revised set of proposals for the League's agreement. The text of this document does not appear to have survived. After more bargaining it would seem that it was on 26 July that Khaliquzzaman told Azad and Pant that the Muslim League would be sitting on the opposition benches when the Legislative Assembly session started on 29 July.

4. Lord Linlithgow minuted: 'P.S.V. – Stiffen him a bit.'

5. Mr A.G. Phillips was officiating Inspector-General of Police at this date.
6. Lord Linlithgow minuted: 'Logic!'
7. Not included in R/3/1/2.
8. Mr L. Owen.
9. Lord Linlithgow minuted at the end of this paragraph: 'P.S.V. – Very satisfactory!'
10. In his letter of 19 July 1937 Lord Linlithgow wrote that in the early years of the new Constitution it was essential that Governors should preside at cabinet meetings even if it involved a breach with Congress. The Viceroy, however, felt that as time went on the Governor might be able in an increasing degree to withdraw from presiding. MSS.EUR.F. 115/13.
11. All the other Governors (including those in Congress provinces) favoured the Governor presiding at cabinet meetings.
12. Lord Linlithgow replied in telegram 174-G.C. of 23 July 1937 agreeing to Sir Harry Haig's proposed course of action. He felt Haig should stress to Pandit Pant that they could not agree to the Congress flag being flown on any public *Government* building since they could not regard Municipal buildings as falling within the prohibition. MSS.EUR.F. 125/126.
13. See No. 65, note 20 for Lord Linlithgow's reply.
14. This telegram informed Governors that the Governor of Bengal intended to discharge his special responsibility to prevent the Bengal ministry from repatriating its Andamans prisoners if the ministry decided on such a policy. MSS.EUR.F. 125/126.
15. These telegrams informed Governors that the Chief Minister of Madras (Mr C. Rajagopalachariar) was contemplating making an appeal to the Services for a voluntary cut in their pay. MSS.EUR.F. 125/126.
16. See note 3 above.
17. Lord Linlithgow minuted: 'I hope the Governor will rub this in to the cabinet. And a lesson read from this experience upon the general question of letting out bad hats.'
18. Lord Linlithgow minuted at the end of this document: 'P.S.V. – I cannot [?but] feel that the existing position in the U.P. raises in rather acute form the position of the Governorship in its relation to the whole machine of government, at times when the Governor himself is removed from his usual activities by illness. The Premier cannot by the Constitution take the G.'s place. Is there a case for a deputy being told off to do the essential work, and to keep the G. informed? It would not appear that the G.'s Secretary ought to do it. In the event of a severe political crisis, this matter may I feel emerge as one of the highest importance.'
19. In telegram 840-G of 7 August 1937, Lord Linlithgow expressed his concern that the U.P. government's communication to the Government of India on the Andamans' prisoners should be official and confidential. MSS.EUR. F. 125/126.

20. This telegram appears to have been numbered 839-G. It replied to No. 60. The Viceroy said that both he and Lord Zetland were agreed that no compromise was possible on the question of Governors normally presiding at cabinet meetings. Linlithgow went on to suggest ways in which Sir Harry Haig might handle the situation. MSS.EUR.F. 115/13.
21. Lord Linlithgow minuted on this letter: 'He [Haig] seems to have got over his first fence very nicely.' MSS.EUR.F. 125/126.
22. The key passage in paragraph 3 of Lord Linlithgow's telegram 845-G of 8 August 1937 read: 'I cannot see why Government should not be prepared to agree to demand any assurance as regards future good behaviour. Could you amplify this point?' Ibid.
23. See MSS.EUR.F. 125/126.
24. Lord Linlithgow replied on 13 August 1947. He said that there was no question of imposing a ban throughout India on the release of revolutionary prisoners. However, the Viceroy agreed that no prisoners could be released if they were engaged on a hunger-strike. He would fully support any artificial feeding of hunger-strikers. (Lord Zetland later sent his full support for such a policy.) If it were necessary to stop the release of political prisoners in the U.P. because of the objections of the Governor of Bengal, the Viceroy would issue an order to Sir Harry Haig under section 126 of the Government of India Act. (Section 12(1)(*a*) was not yet in force.) L/P&J/7/1261.
25. Lord Linlithgow's telegram 906-G of 15 August 1937 is not included in MSS.EUR.F. 125/126 but his telegram 899-G of 14 August is included.
26. In the last sentence of telegram 838-G of 7 August 1937, Lord Linlithgow said he was investigating the legal position on proposed cuts in rates of travelling allowances. MSS.EUR.F. 125/126.
27. In telegram 941-G of 19 August 1937, Lord Linlithgow said he agreed with Sir Harry Haig's views but the Governor would no doubt consider whether a cut of as large as 25 per cent in travelling expenses would not overstep the limit. Ibid.
28. Note by Sir Harry Haig in original: 'But after time for reflection I anticipate criticism will be much stronger in September.'
29. Lord Linlithgow did not send a considered reply to this letter until 7 September 1937. In telegram 1033-G of that date Linlithgow said he was advised: (1) that if the orders were legal, the Governor had no power to require their recall; (2) that even if the orders were illegal, the Governor was not conferred with any power to override his ministers; (3) that Section 300(1) of the Act, though it might apply in particular instances, did not give the Governor any general power to intervene.

    Linlithgow advised Sir Harry Haig to consult his Advocate-General as to whether the orders were legal. The Viceroy pointed out that when legislation was contemplated, the Governor might consider whether provisions in his Instrument of Instructions were attracted. MSS.EUR.F. 125/127.

30. In telegram 910-G of 16 August 1937, Lord Linlithgow said that Mahatma Gandhi had adopted a very uncompromising attitude with regard to social contacts with government. Linlithgow asked the Governors of Congress Provinces for their views on the line to be taken. MSS.EUR.F. 125/126.
31. MSS.EUR.F. 125/126. The date should be 18 August 1937.
32. Sir John Anderson was Governor of Bengal at this date.
33. In this telegram Sir John Anderson said that the release of the two Bengal-domiciled Kakori prisoners would not constitute a grave menace to the Province. However as Bengal-domiciled detenus in Burma were also being released, the cumulative effect would have to be closely watched. Anderson asked that strong efforts be made to obtain an understanding that Bengal prisoners would refrain from taking part in any formal celebration in Bengal of their release. MSS.EUR.F. 125/126.
34. Mr A.C. Turner.
35. Lord Linlithgow's letter of 20 August 1937 is not included in R/3/1/2.
36. Not printed.
37. The communiqué is not printed in R/3/1/2.
38. Mr W.C. Dible.
39. Mr Khurshid Ahmad Khan.
40. Lord Linlithgow minuted at the end of this letter: 'P.S.V.– There is much above that is extraordinarily satisfactory.'
41. In telegram 911-G of 17 August 1937, Lord Linlithgow said that he had been asked by more than one Governor of the way government servants should behave when 'Vande Mataram' was sung or when the Congress flag was hoisted on a formal occasion. Linlithgow asked for Governors' views. MSS.EUR.F. 125/126.
42. Note by Sir Harry Haig in original: 'Which I have not yet seen.'
43. In his letter of 1 September 1937 Lord Linlithgow expressed his concern at the statement by Mr Gupta that in the event of a death in the Andamans 'terrorism would be revived in the country on a much larger scale.' Linlithgow hoped that Sir Harry Haig would bring home to Pandit Pant the difficulties which such statements caused them. MSS.EUR.F. 125/127.
44. Not included in MSS.EUR.F. 125/127.
45. Not printed.
46. Mr L. Owen.
47. Mr G.A. Pearce.
48. Lord Linlithgow replied in telegram 1049-G of 12 September 1937. The Viceroy expressed entire agreement with the line taken by Sir Harry Haig and with the proposal to stand fast over Mr Dublis and Mr Govind Kar. MSS.EUR.F. 125/127.
49. See No. 71, note 29.
50. In telegram 1065-S of 16 September 1937, Lord Linlithgow said that in the circumstances he agreed with the line Sir Harry Haig proposed to take. MSS.EUR.F. 125/127.

51. Mr Panna Lal, Commissioner of the Allahabad Division.
52. Mr P.M. Kharegat.
53. Mr A.G. Phillips was officiating Inspector-General of Police at this date.
54. Mr E.C. Robinson.
55. It has not proved possible to establish the identity of the officiating Collector of Gorakhpur at this date.
56. Mr C.W. Grant.
57. Early in 1922, during Mahatma Gandhi's Civil Disobedience campaign, a mob set fire to a police station at Chauri Chaura, a village in the Gorakhpur district of the U.P. Twenty-two police Constables were killed. It was this incident that led Gandhi to call off the Civil Disobedience campaign.
58. Not printed.
59. Not printed.
60. It has not been possible to establish the identity of this officer with certainty.
61. MSS.EUR.F. 115/9.
62. On 9 February 1938 Lord Linlithgow sent Sir Harry Haig the text of an announcement which was about to be issued. This stated that the King's proposed visit to India in the winter of 1938 had been cancelled. The King still intended to visit India whenever circumstances permitted. Ibid.

CHAPTER 4

Documents for 1 October – 31 December 1937

88

HAIG TO LINLITHGOW
MSS.EUR.F. 125/127

Secret
No. U.P.-6

Camp,
October 5th, 1937

My dear Lord Linlithgow,

I have now examined in detail the case of 13 more so-called political prisoners who are at present serving terms of imprisonment for crimes connected with violence. I have had before me notes by the Hon'ble Minister for Justice and notes by the police, and have also discussed the matter at some length with a C.I.D. officer. I am expecting to go into these cases with the Premier in the course of the next two or three days in Naini Tal.

2. On my own judgment of these cases, there are five who could I think clearly be released without any harm being done. Two of these, Balraj Singh and Sheoraj Singh, were mere boys who fired at and wounded the guard of a train. They were sentenced to seven years' imprisonment and have served 4½ years.[1] The offence was a serious one, but it was very amateurish and the police do not regard them as convinced revolutionaries and do not anticipate any danger from their release. The other three, Babu Ram, Sudama Prasad and Raj Bahadur, were convicted in what is known as the Shahjahanpur case, in which there was undoubtedly a conspiracy to attack by bombs some district board officials. The case is not really regarded by the police as having been of a political character or directed against the government, and they attach little importance to it and consider the matter of purely local concern. One of these men was sentenced to ten

years, the others to seven years' imprisonment. They have served over five years and I have no objection to their release.

3. There are two other men, Puthi Singh and Jageshwar, who were convicted separately of possession of explosives, but appear to be primarily bad characters and not clearly associated with any revolutionary movement. I do not think the ministry will press for the release of these men and there is no real justification for their release, but they are in a different category from the convinced revolutionaries, and their release would not be a danger to the Province.

4. There remain six men who may be regarded as definite, and in some cases dangerous, revolutionaries. One of them, Chandra Man, belongs to Bihar and his activities have been in Bihar. I should be prepared, if the Premier presses the point, to consult the Bihar government about the expediency of releasing him. The remaining five are men in whose case I feel at present it will be necessary to stand fast,[2] and I propose to take a definite line about these in my conversations with the Premier. Being of the undoubtedly revolutionary type, I fear that these are precisely the men in whose release the Left Wing will be interested, and the Premier may on that account press me in regard to two or three of the less dangerous of these. But as I say, my present strong inclination is to hold that I could not consistently with my responsibilities agree to their release, particularly in view of the attitude of mind shown by the Kakori prisoners and their probable future activities, and also the public feeling revealed on the release of the Kakori prisoners.

5. If Your Excellency has any comments on these views I should be grateful if you would telegraph them.[3]

Yours sincerely,
HARRY HAIG

89

DONALDSON TO LAITHWAITE
MSS.EUR.F. 125/127

D.O. No. 644-G.S.P.

Camp,
October 6th, 1937

My dear Laithwaite,

You have probably seen in the newspapers references to the ruling given by the Hon'ble the Speaker of the United Provinces Legislative Assembly about the use of the vernacular by members speaking in the Assembly. I am desired to send you a detailed account of the position.

2. The ruling of the Speaker was delivered with reference to Rule 19 of the United Provinces Legislative Council Rules as adapted and modified for the United Provinces Legislative Assembly under Section 84(3) of the Government of India Act, 1935. Rule 19 is as follows:

> "The business of the Assembly shall be transacted in the English language, but any member who is not acquainted or sufficiently acquainted with the English language may address the Assembly in any recognised language of the Province:
>
> Provided that the Speaker may call any member to speak in any language in which he is known to be proficient."

This rule and proviso were made in 1921 by the Government of India and were applicable to all the Legislative Councils. The rule was approved by the Secretary of State and had statutory force. It was Rule 14 of the United Provinces Legislative Council Rules and was reproduced in the present Rule 19. These rules for the new Assembly were made by His Excellency in his discretion after consultation with the Government of India and with the approval of the Secretary of State, and they largely reproduced the old rules.

3. The only occasion as far as is known, when this matter came under discussion in the old Legislative Council was in 1925, when notice of a resolution to the following effect was given: "that this Council recommends to the Government to take steps to amend Rule 14 of the United Provinces Legislative Council Rules so that it may be optional for a member to address the Council in any recognised vernacular of the Province even if he is fluent in English." This resolution was not moved on the ground that the Legislative Council Rules were not in those days a provincial subject and did not primarily concern the provincial government. The obvious intention of the proviso to Rule 19 is that if a member of the Legislature claims the right to speak in a vernacular language on the ground of his inadequate knowledge of English, he could still be called upon by the Speaker to speak in English if he was known to be proficient in it. It is clear that this was the meaning placed on the proviso by the mover of the resolution mentioned above, and it is also, I think, quite clear that the President in 1925 would have interpreted the proviso in the way which I have stated. This, however, was not the way in which the present Speaker, the minister speaking on behalf of the government, the Advocate-General and a number of the speakers interpreted the proviso in the recent debate.

4. The Hon'ble the Speaker, Babu Purshottam Das Tandon, after indicating his own views, left the decision to the vote of the House. He stated his views as follows:

> "As he interpreted this rule (Rule 19) it was sufficiently comprehensive to enable the Speaker when the situation required to allow the use of Hindi or Urdu by any member of the House including those who were conversant with English. His interpretation of the rule was that he could permit every member of the House, although he might be conversant with English, to speak in Hindustani when he thought that the situation required him to do so. The very object of a separate proviso indicated that the Speaker might not only give this permission when asked for, but that as a matter of fact it might become his duty to call on any member to speak in Hindustani if the situation so required."

In his opinion, if the intention of the proviso had been as stated in paragraph 3, the wording should have been "in any other language" and not "in any language". He referred in his argument to the wording of the rule in the Central Assembly. The Advocate-General apparently thought that as Rule 19 had been framed under Section 84(3) of the Government of India Act, it must be understood to amplify Section 85 and could be interpreted in the way in which it was interpreted by the Speaker. A subsequent speaker, however, Chaudhri Khaliquzzaman of the Muslim League, said that "while he had been one of those who had been violating this rule practically every day, he did not agree with the interpretation that had been placed upon it by the Advocate-General and others. The rule as it stood did not really provide that members should be absolutely free as regards the choice of their language. He thought that the rule was defective and must be broken. They should take courage in their hands and continue to speak in a language which they thought they should speak. If civil disobedience had been suspended in other directions, let them continue civil disobedience in regard to this rule in the Assembly." The Speaker: "I only wanted interpretation of the rule. I shall not allow any civil disobedience here." The gist of Dr. Katju's (Minister for Justice) argument was: "Section 85 of the Government of India Act stated that 'all proceedings in the Legislature of a Province shall be conducted in the English language.' It did not say that the proceedings should be conducted only in the English language. They could not go outside the language of the Section. Why should they out of wisdom substitute words which were not there? Every single member was anxious that they must find a remedy. Then why should they not find a loophole or a gap in the rule?" After numerous other speeches the Speaker then put the question to the House whether under Rule 19 of the Rules the Speaker had power to require or permit any member who was sufficiently acquainted with English to address the Assembly in Hindustani. This was agreed to by 138 to 2. The procedure adopted seems to His Excellency wrong. It is not for the Assembly, but for the Speaker, to interpret the rules. The decision of the House can only be taken as indicating their desire that the rule should be interpreted in a particular way. It does not relieve the Speaker of the responsibility of giving a fair interpretation of the rule.

5. It is clear, I think, that if this had been the correct interpretation of the proviso, it would have been *ultra vires* of the present Government of India Act as being in conflict with Section 85. It remains to be seen what the precise effect of the ruling will be. It is clear, on the one hand, that there is considerable feeling in the House in favour of greater liberty to use the vernacular, and that this feeling exists even among those who are quite competent to speak in English. In a House where some 40 to 50 members, approximately a fifth of the total, are not capable of following a speech in English, the speakers naturally desire to speak in a language in which their arguments will appeal to the whole of their audience. On the other hand, it is clear that the House has already come up against certain practical difficulties both in the matters of reporting and printing; and when dealing with difficult points of legislation, constitutional law, or technical matters, for which the vernacular does not provide an adequate medium of discussion, as speakers have to use recondite Urdu or Sanskritised Hindi terms which are probably as difficult for parts of their audience to follow as the English terms would be. It is therefore possible that in practice, and with the process of time, we shall get back to a situation when the majority of the speeches are made in English, although this remains to be seen. I see that the Hon'ble Premier, in winding up a full-dress debate on the Constituent Assembly question on Saturday last in a long and eloquent speech, spoke in English. The present position at any rate is not in accordance with the law. It seems likely that sooner or later the question must again come to an issue. Section 87 would apparently bar any reference to the courts, attempting to invalidate past proceedings, but it is possible that an attempt might be made to obtain an injunction for the future. It is also possible that an attempt might be made to get the Governor-General to make a reference under Section 213 to the Federal Court. Another way in which the question might come up would be if it was raised in the United Provinces Legislative Council and the President there gave a conflicting ruling. Again the existing rules are only temporary and are to

be replaced by rules framed by the Assembly itself. If such rules contained a provision contrary to Section 85, it might be necessary to ask the Governor-General to make a reference to the Federal Court for a finding whether or not the rule in question was contrary to Section 85.

6. I see that in the Sind Assembly on August 6th, the Speaker[4] gave a ruling that any member who does not know English at all may speak in Sindhi, but that if he knows English well and at the same time cares to speak in Sindhi it is his duty if called upon to give the purport of his speech in English. I quote from a newspaper report in the *Hindustan Times* of August 8th. There was also a similar case in the Bihar Assembly on September 2nd in which the Speaker[5] apparently interpreted the law and rules in the sense which I have indicated in paragraph 3. It is possible that if a conference of Speakers and Presidents of the new Legislatures takes place, about which I have seen some reference in the papers, this question would be discussed.

7. His Excellency considers that it is advisable at present to let the situation clarify and see how the Speaker's ruling is operated in practice; rather then to take any immediate action. He recognises the feeling on the subject and that there is a basis of reason behind it, particularly in a Province such as this which has one vernacular which, on ordinary topics, is universally understood by persons of any degree at all of education. At the same time, he sees the disadvantages of overlooking any deliberate departure from the plain meaning of the Act. He considers that no action is advisable at the moment, but that I should give you a detailed account of the present position.

Yours sincerely,
J.C. DONALDSON

90

HAIG TO LINLITHGOW
R/3/1/2

Secret *October 7th, 1937*
No. U.P.-7

My dear Lord Linlithgow,

The last fortnight has been a much easier period. In Cawnpore conditions appear to have settled down for the time. Both sides seem to me to have realised that they were on the brink of a serious crisis, and I hope they are a little relieved that it has been avoided. An important and surprising factor in this tranquillisation of feeling on the part of the labour elements has been the attitude of Jawaharlal Nehru. He made a statement, a copy of which I attach,[6] in which he spoke very straight and sensibly to the workmen and their leaders. This statement was issued after he had been staying for two or three days in Lucknow in close touch with the ministers, and it seems evident that any inclination he had in the past to stir up labour troubles has, for the present at any rate, been overborne by the necessity of maintaining the authority and prestige of the Congress government which, as I have said before, is closely bound up with avoidance of serious disorder in Cawnpore. With this spirit prevailing even in the Left Wing of the Congress, the chances of a peaceful issue to the Cawnpore troubles are decidedly brighter.

2. With regard to Gorakhpur, there is nothing further to report about the condition of the district. Both I and the Premier have had long talks with the new Collector on his way to take over charge, and he understands the position thoroughly from our point of view. I had some further talk with Pant before leaving Lucknow about the possibility of a departmental enquiry. While we both realise the advantages of ascertaining authoritatively some of the matters of fact which are in dispute, we also realised, as we talked the matter over, that an enquiry of this nature was likely to rouse a considerable degree of local excitement, to keep alive ill-feeling, and perhaps to impair the authority of the district staff. I think he agrees with me that on the whole it would be better to avoid it if we can. Our final conclusion was that Dr. Katju should visit Gorakhpur as soon as he was free from the Assembly and spend four or five days there, making a fairly thorough unofficial enquiry into conditions in close consultation with the Commissioner,[7] and that he should then report his conclusions. Our hope is that he will be able to make suggestions which will enable the administration to make a fresh start.

3. There have been a good many complaints by the authorities of the Jhansi division about the behaviour of Congressmen there, and the Premier has decided with my approval that one of the Parliamentary Secretaries should proceed to Jhansi and make an informal enquiry there of a somewhat similar nature in conjunction with the Collector[8] in charge of the Jhansi division. I think this ought to ease matters.[9]

4. The whole question of the relations between the Congress organisation and the district authorities is still somewhat unsatisfactory, and I am awaiting the arrival of the Premier in Naini Tal to try and carry this matter a stage further. I have made certain definite suggestions to him for instructions to be issued. My general idea is that the district authorities

and the local Congress organisations should, as far as possible, go into complaints locally and try to ascertain the facts and settle them on the spot instead of sending so many complaints to headquarters. But if this idea, which is welcomed by the Premier, is to work satisfactorily, both sides ought to have a clearer conception of their respective relations, and I want to discuss with the Premier the issue of some authoritative statement about these relations. On the whole I hope these difficulties will gradually subside. But there is no doubt that there has been a good deal of deliberate effort on the part of Congress workers to discredit the authority of the police, and that the police to some extent feel that their position has been weakened. My impression, however, is that this process has not gone dangerously far and that from now onwards we ought to be able to arrest it.

5. The students of the Province show signs at the moment of having been carried off their balance by the new political developments. There was in particular a very disgraceful outbreak in Lucknow, when a mob of university students invaded a cinema, behaved in an outrageous manner and resented even the appearance of the police. For a day or two the students were very much out of hand, but their behaviour turned public opinion against them. They have in effect asked that the enquiry which was originally being held at their instance should be dropped, and I am told that a great many of them are ashamed of themselves. Here, again, the mild methods of the ministry seem to be keeping the situation within bounds. There is no doubt that public opinion shows signs of being a real force, and that it no longer flows automatically in a single channel as it used to so often in opposition to the old type of government.

6. I have addressed Your Excellency separately about further developments in connection with the release of the remaining political prisoners who have been convicted of crimes or conspiracies of violence. The case of Dublis, one of the two remaining Kakori prisoners, is causing some difficulty. He has now arrived from the Andamans and has been lodged in the Benares jail. He is due for release in the ordinary course at the beginning of November. He shows signs of not being prepared to give the assurances on which I have been insisting. I am awaiting further conversations with Pant when he comes to Naini Tal.[10]

7. I mentioned some time ago that the reduction in the travelling allowance rates which the ministry were contemplating seemed to me to be reasonable. The examination of these proposals has now been completed and orders are about to be issued. The railway rate has been reduced from one and three-fifths to one and a half, the daily allowance for first class officers from Rs. 5 to Rs. 4-8-0, and the mileage allowance from 6 *annas*

to 4 *annas*. The latter is the most substantial reduction, but on the information at present before me I am disposed to think that 4 *annas* is not an unreasonable rate. Certainly 6 *annas* was appreciably too high.

8. The Legislature has been in session throughout the fortnight. A resolution which attracted some attention was that relating to *khaddar*. In its original form it proposed that all government uniforms should be made of *khaddar* and that the police should be given caps of Gandhi pattern. I discussed this resolution at a cabinet meeting before it was taken up in the Assembly. The ministry proposed to get the resolution modified by saying that uniforms should be of *khaddar* "so far as possible" and eliminating the proposal about Gandhi caps. In this form the resolution was really innocuous and was passed unanimously. The ministry realise so far as police uniforms are concerned: (*a*) that the supply of *khaddar* would probably be inadequate, (*b*) that it would be expensive, (*c*) that it would not be likely to be either in point of wear or of appearance a suitable dress for the police. No one of course contemplated that if *khaddar* were used for police uniforms, it would be any colour but khaki. I doubt myself whether the proposal so far as police uniforms are concerned will go much further.[11]

9. The resolution on a Constituent Assembly has been passed, but the Muslim League registered their protest by walking out. Pant seems to have made an elaborate and very conciliatory and moderate speech. Another matter that has created a great deal of interest is the question of the language in which speeches are to be made in the Assembly. I am sending a separate report of the facts to Your Excellency.

10. At the end of last week a somewhat serious disagreement developed between the ministry and the Upper House. A Taxation Bill (Entertainments and Betting), which is really of a non-controversial character, had been passed by the Assembly and was sent to the Council. The papers were furnished to the members of the Council one afternoon and the government moved for taking the Bill into consideration next morning. Members of the Council objected that they had no time to study the Bill and a motion for postponing consideration was moved. A point of order was raised by Dr. Katju, who contended that such a motion could not be made in connection with a Bill which goes to the Council from the Assembly. The President provisionally ruled the motion in order and the Council thereupon decided that they would not take the Bill into consideration until after the Dussehra holidays. This was an unreasonable period of postponement, but I think the Council had clearly been irritated by the attitude of the government. The government on their part were very indignant with the

Council and pointed out that every day's delay was costing the Province Rs. 2,000 in income. I received a proposal from the ministers that I should use my special powers under the proviso to Section 74(2) of the Government of India Act to summon a joint sitting with the idea of getting the Bill through at once and teaching the Upper House a lesson. I pointed out in reply that this question of giving reasonable notice to the Upper House in the case of Bills passed at the end of a session by the Assembly was one that constantly arose in the Central Legislature, and that it was one which could, I thought, normally be settled by a process of consultation.[12] I said that I could not hold that the Council had adopted a dilatory or obstructive attitude towards the Bill on its merits, and that I could not take the very drastic steps of using my special powers to summon a joint sitting for the consideration of a Bill which the Upper House had not even taken into consideration. I suggested that the practical considerations should be stressed in conversation with the leaders of the Opposition in the Upper House and that as early a date as possible should be fixed for consideration of the Bill by the Council. By the time my note had got down to Lucknow the ministry itself had apparently seen the wisdom of a conciliatory attitude, and the Upper House agreed to take the Bill into consideration on the 5th instead of after the Dussehra holidays, which is a very sensible conclusion. I see from this morning's paper that the Bill has now been passed without amendment by the Council, and that the Premier has made a conciliatory speech to them about their business.

11. There has been no particular development in the rent and revenue position, but from the conversations I have had with Pant I am inclined to be rather more hopeful about the collection of the *kharif* rents which fall due shortly. Some of the landlords are undoubtedly trying to exploit the position in order to embarrass the government, or are adopting an unreasonable attitude. A High Court Judge actually wrote to the revenue authorities of the district in which he has some zamindari and said that as the action of the government had rendered it impossible to collect rents, he must ask that the Collector should attach his zamindari and realise the revenue directly. He declared that he was not prepared to pay the revenue out of his own pocket. To have conceded the principle of this claim would have established a very unsound precedent, and the Collector was therefore directed to realise the revenue by the methods which are ordinarily employed in the case of solvent Zamindars, namely, attachment of moveable property.

12. Pant has stressed in conversation with me his desire to get the tenancy policy of the government settled as soon as possible, as he feels that the

present uncertainty is doing harm. This is undoubtedly true, but the matters under consideration are so complicated that I doubt whether it will be possible to reach conclusions as soon as he is inclined to hope. The committee to consider these matters will start work in the middle of October, but I do not myself see how they can finish before Christmas, legislation being introduced in January. It has been suggested to me that one reason why the ministry is showing a more moderate attitude towards the landlords than might have been expected is that a very considerable number of the Congress M.L.As. are themselves landlords, though no doubt of the smaller type. Meantime, the larger landlords are still somewhat bewildered as to their best policy, and many of them seem to imagine that they may get better terms from the Congress if they join the Congress in opposing the British connection. I have pointed out to those of them who are toying with these ideas that the strength of the Congress rests on the support of the masses, and that they are not going to throw over their principal supporters in order to gain the adherence of the landlords; in other words, that the Congress are bound to carry out their pro-tenant policy as far as they think is reasonable in the general conditions of the Province and that this they will do whatever the attitude of the larger landlords may be. The latter have a much better chance of making their influence felt by organising themselves and carrying out the normal functions of an opposition than by entering into an anomalous and insincere alliance with their political opponents. But one has to remember that some of these landlords are exceedingly timid at heart and are very much inclined to try and make terms with whoever may be in authority.

13. The drastic action that is being taken against the Arabs in Palestine is likely, I fear, to have before long very definite reactions in this Province. The Palestine agitation has shown on the whole more vitality and reality than I had expected, or perhaps it would be more correct to say that it has been made clear that feeling can be worked up in a somewhat dangerous way for a short period when the necessary stimulus is applied. The District Magistrates of Cawnpore[13] and Lucknow[14] who have been staying with me recently are both inclined to think that they may have trouble in the near future over the Palestine agitation. In Lucknow there is the further difficulty that the Madhe Sahaba controversy between the Shias and Sunnis is still unsettled, and the ministry will I fear have to tackle it before long. Muslim opinion seems to me to be very uncertain at the moment and irritable. They are suspicious of the Congress, while there are important elements busy in trying to promote feelings of hostility against the British.

14. I have been in Naini Tal since the 26th September. Pant is due here on the 8th October, and I hope I shall be able to have some useful conversations with him. You mentioned in a recent letter that the Secretary of State would like to be kept informed about Service feelings in the Province. We have just had the Civil Service Week in Naini Tal which is an occasion for the gathering of members of the Services. In the mass they seem to me to be in reasonably good heart and the week certainly went off very well and gave no indication of depression. They undoubtedly have their difficulties, and in many cases considerable difficulties, but I have been very pleased with the reasonable spirit in which they are endeavouring to accommodate themselves to the new conditions. When I start my tour at the end of this month, I shall come into closer individual touch with those engaged in the district administration.

15. I am very grateful for Your Excellency's letter of 30th September, which was most encouraging and of great value to me.

Yours sincerely,
H.G. HAIG

91

HAIG TO LINLITHGOW
MSS.EUR.F. 115/17B

Secret *October 7th, 1937*
No. U.P.-8

I have just received Your Excellency's letter of 4th October[15] about the resolution that the police should be dressed in *khadi*. I had just finished writing my fortnightly report, and you will see that I have dealt with this question in para. 8. I think what I have said there makes the general position clear, but I add a few more comments in the light of Your Excellency's letter.

2. In the first place, the resolution was not a government resolution. It was put forward by a non-official and was only accepted by the government after modification in important particulars. As I have said, the resolution as accepted seems to me to commit the government to very little. In the second place, the resolution as passed does not refer specifically to police uniforms. Thirdly, *khadi* does not necessarily mean the white material which is commonly associated with the Congress. If *khadi* uniforms are supplied to any government servants, it was made clear in my discussion with the ministry that the colour would be the usual khaki. The fact that

the material was *khadi* would not be particularly apparent to the casual onlooker. On the other hand so far as police uniforms are concerned, I consider there are serious practical objections, which I have indicated in my fortnightly letter, to the use of *khadi*, and I think the ministry quite understand that I should stress those objections very definitely if any question of using *khadi* for police uniforms came up. My own anticipation at the moment is that so far as the police are concerned, the proposal is not likely to go much further, but some experimental use of *khadi* might be made perhaps in the case of some other uniforms. The proposal is put forward on the plea of encouraging village industries.

3. I am greatly interested in what Your Excellency tells me in para. 2 of your letter about the attitude of the Secretary of State. It is very valuable to know in general how questions are likely to be regarded at home, and this undoubtedly has a bearing on the question of Dublis and the political prisoners other than the Kakori ones whose cases will now have to be considered.

4. I have referred also in my fortnightly letter briefly to the behaviour of the students in Lucknow. I think Pant himself was very much displeased with them over the cinema incident. The next day he received an enormous deputation of students from all over the province. This had been arranged weeks beforehand, and he told me that there was no kind of reference during the proceedings to the behaviour of the Lucknow students at the cinema. I think, however, some misunderstanding was created owing to the close conjunction of these two incidents. He did of course go out at the time of the cinema trouble on hearing that it was on, and told the students to disperse peacefully, which they did. As you realise, all the Ministers are strongly inclined at present to personal intervention. I have no doubt they will gradually come to realise the proper limitations on this line of action.

92

HAIG TO LINLITHGOW
Telegram
MSS.EUR.F. 125/127

No. 63-G *October 10th, 1937*

You have probably seen statement in Press that Government of the United Provinces have decided to release 10,000 prisoners and that as a result 2,500 will be released at the end of this month. The proposals only reached me yesterday after this announcement had been made. The suggestion for release of 10,000 is of vaguest description and no consideration seems to have been given to practical aspects, which I should imagine would be decisively against it. The actual proposal on the file is for a jail delivery of about 2,500, similar in principle and scale to one we had in 1935 and several which took place earlier. However, even if proposal is confined to this, there are several points that require full consideration and discussion, and I have directed that before action is taken matter should be considered at a cabinet meeting which will probably be held on October 23rd.

93

HAIG TO LINLITHGOW
Telegram
MSS.EUR.F. 125/127

No. 65-G *October 13th, 1937*

Your telegram No. 1183-G., October 12th.[16] I had conversation yesterday with Premier. It was clear that he had known nothing about this proposal and though as I knew he has comprehensive ideas about (group omitted) for jail which would involve eventually considerable reduction in number of prisoners, he did not seem enthusiastic about the scheme for releasing 2,500 prisoners, to which however two of ministers have committed themselves. With reference to paragraph 2 of your telegram the statement in Press was of course not a communiqué though it was obviously inspired. This must have been done by Kidwai the minister. I shall take up matter at cabinet meeting. The Premier has just published a statement in another connection deprecating practice of Press in giving publicity to matters which are still in stage of consideration by government.

2. With reference to paragraph No. 1 of your telegram we may clearly take it in view of my conversation with Premier that suggestion for release of 10,000 prisoners need not be further considered. I deal in this telegram solely with proposal for release of approximately 2,500 prisoners. The general object presumably is, as in previous jail deliveries, to secure economy. With regard to particular points mentioned in your telegram: (*a*) the main basis of proposal is to release prisoners either serving short terms up to one year or shortly due for release. But there would be comprehensive categories of prisoners convicted of various forms of crime who would not be eligible for release. I will send you copy of orders

issued in 1935. These indicate general outline of proposal subject to certain modifications which I intend to discuss in cabinet; (*b*) dacoits and prisoners of this type are specially excluded. Those convicted under this Ordinance of grievous hurt would be eligible for release; (*c*) I have no papers with me at moment, but I understand there were similar jail deliveries for reasons of economy in 1922, 1926, 1930 and 1935. The largest number released was 2,820 in 1926; in 1935 some 2,150 were released.

3. With reference to paragraph No. 3 of your telegram practice in past has been to prescribe that no prisoners should be released without consent of District Magistrate who is appropriate authority for this purpose. I observed that this precaution had been omitted in present scheme and in my order had already drawn attention to this as a most important point.

4. If cabinet press for this scheme, subject to modifications which would bring it into line with what was done in 1935 and on previous occasions, I do not see by what arguments I could hold that what was done with my consent and without harm in 1935 would now be a grave menace to peace of Province, and I feel confident that you will agree on this point. At the same time I shall do what I can to make use of Premier's obvious lack of enthusiasm and try to divert them to consideration of their comprehensive reform policy.

94

HAIG TO LINLITHGOW
MSS.EUR.F. 125/4

Secret *October 15th, 1937*
No. U.P.-9

My dear Lord Linlithgow,

I had a very disturbing conversation yesterday with Pandit Iqbal Narain Gurtu, the Vice-Chancellor of the Allahabad University, about University affairs. Your Excellency will probably have seen in the papers the report that Lord Lothian had been invited to deliver the Convocation address at the big Silver Jubilee celebrations of the University which are being organised for the middle of December, and that owing to agitation by the students the matter has been dropped. I heard of this first a short time ago from Sir Tej Bahadur Sapru, who is greatly distressed at what has happened. It appears that a definite invitation had been extended to Lothian by Sapru at the request of Gurtu, and that Lothian had accepted. No formal announcement had been made, but when the matter came to be known in University circles, an agitation was engineered among the students, and Gurtu came to the conclusion that if Lothian delivered the address, there would be unseemly demonstrations and that the position would be impossible. Sapru has therefore written to Lothian, explaining the position and telling him that it is impossible to maintain the invitation to him to deliver the address. Sapru himself feels the humiliation of this position very acutely. Gurtu feels it equally acutely, and has informed Lothian that as a result he is tendering his resignation from the office of Vice-Chancellor. He told me yesterday that he was intending to place his resignation before the Executive Council as soon as the University opens after the Dussehra vacation.

2. The Executive Council may, as it seems to me, take one of three courses:

(*a*) They may accept Gurtu's resignation and take steps at once for his replacement.
(*b*) They may accept his resignation, but ask him, in view of practical considerations, to continue in office until after the Jubilee celebrations.
(*c*) They may ask him to reconsider his resignation.

He himself seems to be somewhat uncertain as to his course of action. We both agree that course (*b*) would be unwise. At a time of great difficulty he would be filling the office of Vice-Chancellor merely as a stop-gap and with no real authority. As to (*a*) and (*c*), it is a little difficult for me to judge without being in closer touch with conditions in Allahabad. I think that if the Executive Council pressed Gurtu to reconsider his resignation and I added my pressure to theirs, he would be prepared to do so; but whether there is going to be any real advantage in keeping Gurtu in office under present conditions is a point of doubt. I greatly fear he is in no position to control the students. If he resigns, it will probably be a considerable embarrassment to the Jubilee celebrations.

3. The second point of difficulty is that the question of hoisting the Congress flag is being taken up in the Allahabad University with vigour, and undoubtedly on inspiration from outside. A flag hoisting ceremony was recently held at one of the University hostels. This of course was not a government building, and in accordance with our general policy the government could, even if it wanted to, have taken no steps about this. The students are now about to present a demand that the Congress flag should be hoisted on the main University buildings, and I understand

they are likely to press for this ceremony to take place on the 30th October. Gurtu of course dislikes this, and I understand the majority of the Executive Council would dislike it. But they feel that if the request is refused, there may be a strike in the University, and that conditions of controversy will be set up which would impair the prospects of the Silver Jubilee celebrations in December. On the other hand, it does seem to me on general grounds of principle most undesirable that the Congress flag should be formally hoisted and flown on the University buildings. The buildings belong to the University, and in accordance with our general policy we could not interfere. The question is whether I, as Chancellor, should give any private advice to the Vice-Chancellor in this matter. We have of course in this respect swallowed a great deal in allowing the flag to be flown on municipal and district board offices. At the same time we have five Universities in this Province, and with the possible exception of Aligarh, the example of Allahabad is likely to be followed in the others.

4. The flag complication, however, does not rest there. If it did, I think I should have to acquiesce, even though it means really capitulation to a fairly small body of students. But this question of the flag is, I am afraid, likely to receive prominence at the time of the Jubilee celebrations. I had agreed several months ago, as I think was inevitable, to take part in these celebrations. There is to be a special Convocation at which messages will be received from Universities all over the world, and an ordinary Convocation for the conferring of degrees. At both of those I had consented to preside. I raised with Gurtu the question whether the Congress flag would be flown on these occasions. He made it clear that he did not anticipate being able to prevent it. Of course there are various possibilities. There might be a flag hoisting ceremony just before the Convocation, or the Congress flag might be flying over the main University buildings and/or over the pandal in which the ceremony will take place, or the pandal itself might be ornamented with Congress flags, or there might merely be a Congress flag flying outside the pandal. My own strong inclination would be to decline to take part in any ceremony in which the Congress flag was flown in any formal manner. When I indicated this view to Gurtu, while he did not seem surprised at the likelihood of my taking such an attitude, he said that it would be exceedingly damaging to the Jubilee celebrations if I did not attend. This no doubt is perfectly true. Moreover, my absenting myself from these celebrations, when it is already known that I had agreed to take part in them, would raise the issue of the Congress flag in a very prominent manner. I cannot help feeling that Nehru and his people deliberately intend that I should either have to put myself in an equivocal

position at this ceremony, or provoke a first-class controversy about the Congress flag. If, however, we are to maintain the position that government servants all over the Province, and indeed all over India, are not to take part in ceremonies in which the flying of the Congress flag is a formal or conspicuous part, it seems to me that action by a Governor, which would be liable to misunderstanding, would seriously compromise the position, and that it would be better to face the issue and have it out. At present I feel that so far as Gurtu is concerned, and possibly Pant, to whom I had mentioned the matter very lightly before I had seen Gurtu, the threat of my not attending the celebrations is a fairly strong card, and that they might endeavour to do all they can to ensure that the flag question was not obtruded on the Jubilee celebrations. But they may be unable really to control the situation, and from some points of view I feel it might be better for me to break away from the celebrations altogether at the earliest possible date and make some re-arrangement of my programme, though it could not be re-arranged so as not to make it perfectly plain that I should be absenting myself from Allahabad precisely for that week.

5. I have felt it desirable to inform Your Excellency of the position at once, and I shall be very grateful for your advice on the various problems that arise. It is indeed a most difficult and complicated situation.[17]

Yours sincerely,
HARRY HAIG

95

HAIG TO LINLITHGOW
MSS.EUR.F. 125/127

Secret — Camp,
No. U.P.-10 — *October 15th, 1937*

My dear Lord Linlithgow,

With reference to the correspondence ending with Your Excellency's telegram No. 1160-G, dated 8th October,[18] regarding release of political prisoners, I had a fairly long conversation yesterday with the Premier. In regard to Dublis, who, as you will remember, is a Kakori prisoner returned from the Andamans and due for release on 5th November, the Premier did not attempt to controvert the note which I had sent him on the 3rd October explaining in some detail that the result of the conversations with Dublis in jail came far short of what I regarded as the essential minimum in the way of assurances. He has therefore dropped the question of premature release of Dublis. But he anticipates demonstrations when he is released, and he pressed, purely as a matter of administrative expediency and not as any kind of concession, that Dublis should be released a few days before 5th November, as he thinks that this may to some extent disorganise the plans of those who are arranging for a reception for him. I do not myself attach great importance to this one way or the other, but it may be wiser to release Dublis unexpectedly, and I therefore told the Premier that I had no objection to his being released on any day that he thought convenient, not earlier than the 1st of November. I have heard no more about Govind Kar, the Bengal leper; nor I think is the Premier greatly interested in him.

2. We then discussed the remaining prisoners. I explained that I should be prepared to meet him in respect of the five prisoners mentioned in paragraph 2 of my letter No. U.P.-6, dated October 5th; but the other prisoners seemed to me to be too definitely connected with the revolutionary movement to be fit subjects for release. Pant was evidently very ill satisfied with this view. He argued that several of these prisoners were hardly more than youths when they committed the offences for which they have been convicted, and that on that account they deserved consideration. Further he felt that their psychological background was of great importance. I agreed and said that on the information available to me I was afraid that their psychological background was very unsatisfactory. He said that what he would like to do would be to sound them and ascertain whether they really had changed their views and were prepared to give assurances. He declared that Maxwell[19] had made some statement in the Central Legislature to the effect that those political prisoners who gave satisfactory assurances as to their future behaviour would be released.[20] I do not suppose this is an accurate reproduction of what Maxwell said, but perhaps Your Excellency could let me know what the actual statement was.

3. I then asked Pant what his practical proposal was. He said that in the case of Yashpal he recognised that he was too dangerous to be let out now. He is serving two sentences of seven years' imprisonment which were originally concurrent, but on appeal were made consecutive. He has served about 4½ years. He said he proposed that the sentences should be made concurrent, thereby reducing the period to seven years and Yashpal should be kept in jail till then. He also did not wish to make any recommendations about the two prisoners whom I have described in paragraph 3 of my letter of 5th October as primarily bad characters. The remainder he wished to approach, as I have described above. Of course there can be no question

of approaching these men unless we have decided to release them if the response is satisfactory.

4. I told Pant that I saw very great difficulties in his proposals, but that I would naturally consider carefully what he had said and would discuss the matter with him again when I return to Lucknow on October 23rd. He evidently attaches very considerable importance to this matter.[21] But it seems to me that, as Your Excellency has said in your telegram of October 8th, we must stand fast. I presume that in so doing I should not be taking a firmer line than is being taken in other Provinces where somewhat similar conditions prevail, e.g. Bihar, and that Bengal is not contemplating any appreciable release of revolutionary convicts.

Yours sincerely,
HARRY HAIG

96

HAIG TO LINLITHGOW
Telegram
MSS.EUR.F. 125/127

No. 66-G

Naini Tal,
October 17th, 1937

Your telegram No. 301-G.C., October 15th.[22] About statement in Press. I am afraid that my telegram of 13th October must have conveyed to you somewhat misleading impression. The paragraph seemed to me obviously derived from an official source, and I had assumed that source was minister, but it certainly could not be described in terms as a statement to Press by him. Information I have since received suggests that the source may have been the Parliamentary Secretary and not minister. Again there was no question of two ministers having committed themselves publicly to scheme. I was referring merely to views they had expressed on file.

2. I quite agree about the importance of principle, and intend as I stated in telegram of 13th October to take up matter at cabinet meeting. Meanwhile I have suggested to Pant that in view of widespread misunderstanding it is desirable to issue a communiqué to the effect that previous statement had no authority, and that while government intend to consider at an early date a comprehensive policy of jail reform, which might eventually involve a considerable reduction in number of prisoners, no conclusions have yet been reached.

3. Your paragraph No. 5. I fully agree. It has always been my intention to secure these points at the cabinet meeting, and also point referred to in paragraph 3 of my telegram of October 13th.

4. Dates and figures of previous jail deliveries are being telegraphed separately.

97

HAIG TO LINLITHGOW
Telegram
MSS.EUR.F. 125/127

Clear the Line
No. 70-G

October 20th, 1937

Your telegram No. 316-G, dated October 19th.[23] My position is that I propose to release five prisoners of whom three concerned in the Shahjahanpur case are regarded as not political and two were mere boys and are not believed to have any serious revolutionary connections. I intend to refuse release in the case of six prisoners whom I regard as revolutionaries. Several of these seem similar in record and character to the two Madras prisoners.

2. We are faced by an all-India demand for release of all prisoners of this class and we have to meet it with an all-India policy. Pant will certainly be strongly pressed in Working Committee over prisoners whom I propose not to release and to that extent the release of two Madras prisoners will weaken our general position. Working Committee will doubtless press their policy more strongly the more chance they think there may be of its success. But if we are standing fast on general position in other Provinces and particularly Bihar, I should hope that they would not press the matters to a break. I do not think that Pant himself would desire to provoke a crisis. But his action in this matter will no doubt be determined for him by Working Committee. I anticipate good deal of trouble in any case from the decision not to release these prisoners. There may be considerable agitation and possibly hunger-strikes. But I am clear that we should stand fast and not allow ourselves to be coerced into releasing those whom we regard as definite revolutionaries.

3. So far as Madras prisoners are concerned, I realise they may not be an actual danger in Madras, whereas further releases of this class of prisoners in the United Provinces seem to me definitely dangerous in view of behaviour of Kakori prisoners. It is possible therefore to distinguish

the United Provinces position from Madras, and I recognise that having the intention of releasing five others, though they are not dangerous, it would be difficult for me to press that Madras should not take action which on their local situation is justifiable. I am more concerned in having united front with Bihar where conditions seem to me much more close to ours. Main point is that it should be clear to Congress Working Committee that we intend to stand fast at any rate in Northern India on general position of not releasing those terrorist prisoners who may be regarded as definite revolutionaries.

Repeated to Secretary of State.

98

HAIG TO LINLITHGOW
MSS.EUR.F. 125/127

Secret *October 24th, 1937*
No. U.P.-11

My dear Lord Linlithgow,

With reference to the correspondence ending with my telegram No. G-66, dated October 16th [17th], 1937, about the jail delivery, the matter was discussed yesterday evening in the cabinet. I asked in the first place on what basis the proposal was put forward. Was it simply a proposal based on a desire to secure economy, and might it be taken as a self-contained proposal and not intended to lead to further releases? I was told that it was, like the previous jail deliveries, intended to secure economy, and that it was to be regarded as a proposal standing by itself and not leading to any further jail delivery. On this basis, we discussed the matter, and decided that releases should be made very closely in accordance with the principles laid down in 1935. I enclose a note[24] which indicates the orders that will be issued. It is anticipated that the number to be released will come to something between 2,500 and 3,000. I insisted that prisoners convicted under the Explosive Substances Act and the Arms Act must be definitely excluded from release. We had some discussion about persons in jail for failing to give security under Sections 107 and 109. With regard to the former, it was agreed that they need not be excluded provided they furnish a personal bond for the remainder of the period. With regard to those under Section 109, it was decided that they should be eligible for release if they have served half their term and provided that they have not been previously convicted. There are no prisoners now in jail under Section 124-A, I.P.C. or Section 108, C.P.C., so that their cases do not arise.

2. With regard to previous reference to the District Magistrate, I found the ministers were very definitely opposed to this on the ground that in the case of a jail delivery of this kind, in which all the really dangerous classes of criminals have been excluded, it was extremely unlikely that there would be any adequate ground for the District Magistrate to object, and that in fact in past cases there had been practically no objections raised by District Magistrates. On the other hand, the procedure of scrutiny by the District Magistrate in these very ordinary cases lent itself to possible malpractices on the part of the subordinate staff. There was some force in this view, and as I found that in previous cases it had not invariably been laid down that the District Magistrate's consent was required, and as the jail delivery is being made on certain quite precise principles, and no prisoner whose release is likely to be in any way seriously undesirable would come within these principles, I did not press the matter further.

3. I drew attention to the very undesirable nature of the publicity that had taken place in connection with this proposal, and said that I hoped we should hear no more talk about the release of 10,000 prisoners. The Premier had already a day or two ago issued a communiqué (a copy of which I enclose[25]) which at any rate made it clear that the previous press reports were unauthorised.

4. It was decided that having got this question of jail delivery for the purposes of economy out of the way, the ministry would devote itself now to working out a comprehensive and well-considered policy of jail reform dealing with such matters as probation, Children's Act, Borstal system, more intelligent and humane treatment of prisoners, &c. The hope is that means may be found to reduce very considerably the number of short-term prisoners detained in our jails. If so, this will be done in pursuance of a properly thought-out policy and not merely in an arbitrary way. The Premier fully realises that the system of these jail deliveries, though it may have something to be said for it from the point of view of economy, cannot in any way be regarded as a contribution to the problem of reform of the jail administration.

Yours sincerely,
H.G. HAIG

99

HAIG TO LINLITHGOW
MSS.EUR.F. 125/127

Secret *October 24th, 1937*
No. U.P.-12

My dear Lord Linlithgow,

With reference to the correspondence ending with Your Excellency's telegram No. 341-G.C., dated October 21st,[26] about the release of terrorist prisoners, I had a further talk with Pant this morning. I told him that after giving careful attention to the views he expressed at our last interview, I still felt it was unsafe to agree to the release of more than the five prisoners indicated in paragraph 2 of my secret letter No. U.P.-6, dated October 5th, 1937. We went over the old ground again. I made it clear that I regarded the terrorist-communist development as a serious menace, and that I felt it was most important not to give it further encouragement or accretion of strength. I said that from the information I was getting it seemed that the Kakori prisoners were showing considerable activity in this group, and that they had no means relapsed into quiescence or insignificance which Pant had told me he anticipated would be the case. We discussed the matter quite amicably, and I indicated that as my judgment was based on a particular situation which was not static, I should be quite prepared to review my conclusions six months hence, when the situation would have become clearer and it would be more easy to see whether his anticipations or mine had proved correct. Eventually he said that he felt it was necessary in a matter of this importance to put the case before the cabinet. I said I quite agreed that this was reasonable, but asked him what would be the position if after discussion in the cabinet the views on both sides remained as at present. He said that that depended on whether I considered that my special responsibilities were concerned, and I said that that was the case. He then said that in that event it would presumably have to be made plain that the action was taken on my responsibility and not on that of the cabinet. I said that that again was a perfectly reasonable position, but it would give rise to certain embarrassments and it would be desirable to think it over carefully. His reply was to the effect that he fully realised my position, that his own inclination was very much to accept the responsibility for a decision if he was unable to convince me of the rightness of his view, but that this was a matter of such public importance and principle that he felt it might not be possible to do what he would himself have preferred. He finally told me that he would discuss the matter at the coming Congress meeting in Calcutta, putting the whole situation before the Working Committee. There was not the slightest suggestion in anything he said that he would have to consider resignation.

2. He then asked me whether he could take immediate steps about the release of the five prisoners to whose release I was agreeable. I said that from some points of view it would have been more convenient to postpone this until after the release of Dublis at the beginning of November which might lead to some further demonstrations. It is not that either of us anticipate any demonstration in connection with the release of these five prisoners, but that their release just about the time of some demonstrations taking place might lead to comment. He gave me to understand that, though so far as the Working Committee is concerned, it would be just as effective to inform them that these five persons were going to be released as to tell them that they had been released, this would not be the case with regard to the All-India Congress Committee, and that with a view to meeting their criticisms it would certainly help him if these five persons were already released. I therefore authorised him to take steps at once to sound these five men in jail as to their present attitude and the question of assurances.

3. In the course of conversation Pant mentioned to me the case of Bihar and said that when he was in Bihar recently he had understood that a large number of prisoners of this class had been released. I said that I knew a certain number had been released just as we ourselves have released a considerable number, but that I understood that there were still an appreciable number of prisoners of this class in Bihar who had not been released. He said he was not very sure of the facts. Nor indeed am I. But the point is clearly of importance. He evidently felt that our position would be distinctly more difficult if we appear to be the only Congress Province standing out against the release of this class of prisoner. This is precisely the point I had already taken in my telegram No. 70-G., dated 20th October 1937.

Yours sincerely,
H.G. HAIG

100

HAIG TO LINLITHGOW
R/3/1/2

Secret *October 24th, 1937*
No. U.P.-13

My dear Lord Linlithgow,

I am writing my fortnightly report under conditions of rather heavy pressure on my time, as I am in Lucknow for three days only, after having been away from my ministers, except the Premier, and my Secretaries for nearly a month. Naturally, there is a great deal to be done in the way of work and interviews. I hope therefore Your Excellency will understand if I do not in this report deal as fully as I should like with some of the very interesting points referred to in your letter of 15th October, and in particular the question of the relations between the Congress organisation and the district authorities, though that is a matter to which my attention is continually directed. With regard to the *khaddar* resolution, what I had in mind was that the government might possibly put forward proposals for experimenting with a *khaddar* uniform for jail officials and possibly in some cases chaprasis.

2. I have been in correspondence separately with Your Excellency about the question of a jail delivery of some 2,500 prisoners on the lines of the jail deliveries which have frequently taken place in this Province in recent years, and on the more crucial question of the release of the remaining political terrorist prisoners. I have written today to Your Excellency on both these matters. I also explained in a recent letter my anxieties about the Allahabad University and its Silver Jubilee functions in December. With regard to that the situation has not further developed, but I have heard from Gurtu that he intends to place his resignation before the Executive Council on the 26th October.

3. I have not been able yet to have a full talk with Katju about Gorakhpur affairs, but he has told me that he had a very successful visit and that he hopes satisfactory relations have now been established. I heard in very much the same tone recently from the Commissioner;[27] and there is no doubt that the posting of Pedley as Collector to Gorakhpur has been a great success, and that there has been a very marked change of feeling all round. I am told also that the joint enquiry by the Collector[28] in charge of the Jhansi division and Kher, one of the Parliamentary Secretaries, has

been successful and has gone a long way to remove the causes of friction there. They have sent in a joint report, which, however, has not yet reached me. Trouble has again developed in one of the Cawnpore mills, resulting in stoppage of work, but the present anticipations are that the men will go back to work again on Monday. It is a reminder, however, that the situation in Cawnpore is still most unstable.

4. Important progress has been made in the consideration of the government's tenancy policy and the procedure adopted is, I think, very encouraging in regard to the attitude of the government. They decided that as a preliminary to convening the parliamentary committee, which is to consider the problem, a strong official committee should meet and place their views before the government. This committee has been sitting for the last week or so and has reached conclusions which state very clearly the reforms which from the official point of view would appear suitable and safe. The committee included all the principal revenue authorities in the Province and in addition two Parliamentary Secretaries. It is not intended that the report of this committee should be published; it is merely for the information of the government and to act as a basis of solid facts and sober opinion which I hope will guide them when it comes to the deliberations of the parliamentary committee. This will start work about the 5th November, and the Premier is determined to finish this stage before Christmas. He intends to pursue a similar procedure with regard to debt relief and to convene shortly an expert official committee to make a preliminary survey of that problem. The Premier has also been very busy with sugar problems, and so far as I can judge the policy at present outlined is reasonable and likely to be beneficial.

5. While I was in Naini Tal I had a good deal of discussion with the Premier about the question of retaining the services of Sir William Stampe[29] for a longer period. He reaches the age of 55 at the end of this month, and in accordance with the principles very strictly laid down by the Secretary of State there can be no question of giving him a further extension. It had been my intention, however, to re-employ Stampe for a limited period on contract. He himself has shown an unwisely urgent desire to be kept on and has in this way created against himself a good deal of prejudice both in political and service circles. After full consideration Pant was not prepared to re-employ Stampe, and though from some points of view I regret this, I cannot regard him at this stage as being quite as indispensable as he regards himself. At the same time there have been some very unfair political attacks made upon the hydro-electric scheme and the tube wells. I propose shortly to take part in a ceremony marking the practical

conclusion of these great schemes, and I intend to explain them and express my confidence in them, seeing that it was Lord Hailey's government and my own which initiated and carried them out, and at the same time to express my appreciation of Stampe's work. I have told the Premier that I propose to speak on these lines, and though he is himself inclined, through lack of information as I believe, to share some of the doubts about the schemes, he seems to have no objection to my stating my views, which I think I am bound to do both in justice to my former government and to Stampe.

6. Another important matter affecting the Irrigation administration has just been decided. Some months ago the ministers expressed a strong desire that a Civilian Secretary should be substituted in the Irrigation Department for the Chief Engineer Secretaries. Since then, the matter has been examined carefully, and I must confess that my own view, which to begin with inclined to maintaining the existing system, has now changed. I think under the present political conditions and with the extension of the Irrigation Department to take charge of the hydro-electric scheme and the tube-wells, and with a large number of possibilities of new development, it is definitely desirable that there should be a Civilian Secretary. At present the government is really too much in the hands of the Chief Engineers, and very important matters of policy and administration will be coming up in which it would be advisable for the ministry to have the assistance of secretariat opinion. There is some doubt whether technically the sanction of the Secretary of State to this change is or is not required. In view of the doubt, I expressed the desire that the matter should be referred to the Secretary of State, but I trust that there will be no difficulty about giving effect to the wishes of the government, and allowing the new arrangement to be introduced as early as possible. A seventh Secretary will also give some very urgently needed relief to some of the other Secretaries.

7. You will have seen very full accounts of the Muslim League meeting in Lucknow. In my letter of October 7th I said that Muslim opinion seemed to me to be very uncertain at the moment and irritable. The Conference discharged its irritation in full measure against the Congress, and less markedly against the British in regard to Palestine policy, federation and the ultimate goal of full independence. But the sense of uncertainty has for the time being at any rate been removed, for the Muslims have now been given a very strong and definite communal lead which seems to have inspired great enthusiasm, and will obviously have a most important bearing on political developments in the near future. War has been declared unmistakably between the Congress and the Muslim League. The Shias had

a few days earlier decided to join the Congress, but I think a great many of them will in fact follow the lead given by the Muslim League. The first great trial of strength is in progress at present over the bye-election in which Hafiz Muhammad Ibrahim, one of my ministers, is standing. No one is prepared to give a very confident opinion as to the result of the election, which will be most hotly contested. But if Ibrahim is beaten, I think the ministry will be placed in a position of some considerable embarrassment in connection with filling his place.

8. I am glad that you were able to get away for a little into the hills. I have also just been enjoying a week walking through the hills near Naini Tal in lovely country and have returned feeling very well. I have quite got rid of the effect of my illness during the summer. Tomorrow I start on the first stage of my tour round the Province.

Yours sincerely,
H.G. HAIG

101

DONALDSON TO LAITHWAITE
MSS.EUR.F. 125/132

D.O. No. 716-G.S.P. Camp,
October 31st, 1937

My dear Laithwaite,

Section 84 of the Government of India Act provides that a Chamber of a Provincial Legislature may make rules for regulating, subject to the provisions of this Act, their proceedings and the conduct of their business.

2. A committee of the Legislative Assembly has been engaged for some time in drafting rules and has, I understand, produced some, which we have not yet seen. The question arises what happens if those rules are plainly contrary to the provisions of the Act or appear to be so? What authority can invalidate them? The particular point on which we think that the Assembly might make rules inconsistent with the Act is the language question, about which I wrote to you in my D.O. No. 644-G.S.P. on 6th October. His Excellency has asked me to write to you and to ascertain the views held by the Government of India about the correct course of action if the Chamber insisted on making a rule which appeared to be manifestly *ultra vires*. Would a reference be made to the Federal Court

under Section 213, or should the matter be left for the opposition or some member of the public to take up in the courts?[30]

Yours sincerely,
J.C. DONALDSON

102

HAIG TO LINLITHGOW
R/3/1/2

Secret
No. U.P.-16

Camp,
November 8th, 1937

My dear Lord Linlithgow,

I have just returned from my ten days' tour in the Bareilly and Meerut divisions. The tour has, I think, been valuable in itself, and it has given me some extremely useful information about administrative conditions and the state of feeling. Three main topics are uppermost in the minds of district officials:

(1) relations between the Services, particularly the police, and the Congress;
(2) relations between landlords and tenants; and
(3) relations between Hindus and Muslims.

With regard to the first, though conditions naturally vary from district to district, it was clear to me that while on the whole the general administration is running on fairly smoothly, there are in most places clear signs of depression and nervousness in the police. The common features are these:

(*a*) Interference by Congressmen in police investigations. This ranges from busy-bodies going on ahead and taking down statements before the police arrive, or inviting statements to Congress committees before they are made to the police, to an irritating form of shadowing the police and making it impossible for the investigating officer ever to have any private conversation with a witness. These conditions are not universal, but they are prevalent to a greater or less extent in many districts, and undoubtedly they make the task of the police more difficult and lower their authority.

(*b*) Complaints of corruption. Not very many individual cases have been taken up seriously, but I came across two which have created a considerable sensation in the districts concerned. In both cases the police officer, from the police point of view, has an admirable record. In one case it is exceedingly probable, and in the other possible, that the officer has been making money in various ways. These cases are very difficult. The police view is that while similar charges could be brought against a large number of officers, particular officers who have done very good work for the government and who happen to have incurred the enmity of the Congress are singled out for attack. It is difficult to say that there is no element of truth in this. On the other hand, it is not possible to say that there is no justification for investigating the complaints brought. I may add that there is general agreement that owing to fear of complaints corruption has been greatly reduced.

(*c*) Apart from specific charges of corruption which, as I say, are not very numerous, the police feel that any action they take is liable to call forth complaints. They have been accustomed to using somewhat rough and ready methods, and to a large extent know no other way of getting results; but if they use the methods to which they are accustomed, they know that they may get into trouble. Consequently, it is inevitable that they should tend to take less interest in carrying out their work and more interest in saving themselves from attack. There is a definite feeling of nervousness and lack of confidence, particularly among Sub-Inspectors, and the tendency is to take the line of least resistance.

(*d*) Bad characters are less under control. It is more difficult to get evidence against them, and they are often able to enlist the sympathy and support of the Congress if the police try to deal with them.

As a result of (*c*) and (*d*) there are indications in many districts of the number of smaller crimes increasing. Superintendents of Police do not suggest that there are any signs of failure in discipline, or that their men would not respond to leadership, or that they would not deal with serious emergencies and crimes. But in the day-to-day administration there is some slackening and they have lost authority with the public, and consequently have lost some confidence in themselves.

2. With regard to landlords and tenants, conditions vary to some extent from district to district, but on the whole district officers think there will be decided difficulty about collecting the *kharif* rents, and that relations between landlords and tenants are unsatisfactory. Most officers do not anticipate any serious disorder arising out of these conditions, but if the short collection of rents is extensive, the government will be faced with a difficult problem as to their attitude in the collection of land revenue. I was also told in various places of a tendency on the part of tenants who had been ejected some time ago from their holdings to reoccupy them

forcibly. As it is known that the conferment of hereditary rights will certainly be one of the features of the government tenancy programme, there is an obvious temptation for tenants to try and secure possession before the rights accrue. This movement may lead to trouble if it spreads.

3. With regard to Hindu-Muslim relations, there is a general feeling in these two divisions that they are becoming markedly more strained. As one Collector put it to me, the general mass of Hindus consider that they have now got a Hindu Raj and are inclined to presume on this fact and to be much less accommodating to Muslims than they used to be. The Muslims have the same impression and naturally resent it strongly. If on top of this position the Muslim League propaganda is strongly pressed, we are bound to have trouble developing to an increasing extent. Another cause of friction of course is the direct appeal of the Congress to the Muslim masses, which is strongly resented by Muslim Leaguers. This comes to a head in the course of bye-elections, and we have two more bye-elections in Muslim constituencies pending in addition to the Bijnor election which has just finished.

4. In Bijnor I understand that the Congress succeeded to a large extent in avoiding the issue of Hindu versus Muslim being raised. I am told that at a very early stage all Congress flags were suppressed and that the Congress candidate pursued his campaign under a green flag similar to that of the Muslim League. Moreover, he was supported by a very influential body of Maulvis, particularly the Deoband Maulvis. This, combined with superior organisation, superior personal influence (for the Muslim League candidate was a man of no importance) and the power which the holding of office always confers may be regarded as responsible for the decisive success of the minister, Hafiz Muhammad Ibrahim. It does not follow that other elections will go the same way; but naturally the result of this election has been a great encouragement to the Congress and a cause of depression to the Muslim League.

5. Towards the end of my tour I sent a note[31] to the Premier with a request that it should be discussed at an early cabinet meeting, and we are going to consider it tomorrow. The note deals with certain developments to which I am inviting their serious attention. The first is the campaign of revolutionary and violent speeches which has been in progress recently in the eastern districts by members of the Youth League and particularly some of the ex-Kakori prisoners. The worst speaker is an ex-revolutionary prisoner from the Punjab named Parmanand. Many of these speeches as reported have been of a very bad type, and it is necessary to bring the cabinet up against the situation and find out what they are prepared to

do. I fear it may not be possible, in the first instance, to induce them to do more than issue a severe warning; but even if I can secure this, it will, I think, facilitate further action should that become necessary. In the second place I have invited attention to the outrageous attacks on the police at Cawnpore delivered at an anti-police day demonstration which seems to have been organised by prominent Congressmen. Nothing could be more unjustifiable or more dangerous than to attack the authority of the police in Cawnpore at the present moment, and though I am sure the cabinet fully realise this, I want to bring them formally up against it and see what they propose to do. In the third place, I am inviting their attention to the conditions in the police which I have described above. I have had some general talk with the Premier on this subject since I returned, and it seems to me that he is beginning to show a better appreciation of the dangers of weakening the police, and I think he may be genuinely anxious to do what he can to remove the less desirable features of Congress activity and to promote a better understanding between the district authorities and the Congress organisations. As a matter of fact in many districts the relations between the district authorities and the leading Congressmen are reasonably satisfactory. The mischief is done by the smaller fry who are continually trying to enhance their own importance and are under very little control.

6. I have just seen the joint report made by the Collector in charge of the Jhansi division and the Parliamentary Secretary who enquired into conditions in the Lalitpur sub-division. Their report reveals a state of affairs which was a good deal more serious than any one at headquarters had appreciated. It is a very backward tract, and undoubtedly in the past the landlords have ruled over their tenants in a most autocratic way. They have fought the Congress vigorously and, for a long time, successfully. But at the last election Congress swept the board and ever since then the situation has been deteriorating rapidly. It is as if a dam had given way and the accumulated volume of discontent and grievances has spread over the whole area. Congress has been busy stirring up the tenants in every way, the landlords have been resisting very often by methods of violence. The enquiry seems to have had a very salutary effect. A situation like this can only be cured by a change of outlook on all sides, and there is no doubt that the conjunction of the Collector with the Parliamentary Secretary, who is himself a man of considerable influence in Bundelkhand, has produced a steadying effect, and the counsels of conciliation which are being addressed both to the landlords and to the tenants, and will be pursued by the administration and the Congress, afford some reasonable hope of better things. But it was certainly high time that the situation was faced.

7. An important Zamindars' conference was held recently in Lucknow, the main feature of which was that the smaller Zamindars attended in very large numbers, and efforts are now to be made in every district to organise the smaller Zamindars in support of the general Zamindar interests. I enclose a copy of the resolutions passed.[32] So far as words are concerned, the Zamindars showed a considerable degree of determination, and indeed whatever may be the attitude of some of the larger and more decadent landlords, I think there are a very considerable number, particularly perhaps among the smaller men, who are not going to see themselves deprived of their rights without a fight. I do not mean to suggest that they wish to oppose reasonable reforms, but there are certain matters under consideration which might affect their position vitally. Doubts, however, are expressed, in view of the constant failures of the zamindars to translate their words into action, how far the latest move will be successful, and they themselves seem to be somewhat doubtful as to whether they will be able to raise any appreciable funds.

8. The situation in Cawnpore is at the moment rather obscure. A week ago it looked as if the long threatened general strike was almost upon us. But again the parties seem to have stopped on the brink. Jawaharlal Nehru has once more been enlisted by the cabinet to try and control the labour elements. They were reported a week ago to be entirely out of control by the Congress or by the Mazdur Sabha, and there have been suggestions that the latest trouble was instigated by Muslims with some intention of causing embarrassment to the government. In the present state of feeling in Cawnpore it is difficult to see how this strike can in the long run be avoided.

9. I have been faced with some difficulty about the new rural development scheme which the cabinet contemplate. They are proposing to appoint as their rural development officer Mr. S.K. Paliwal, whom Your Excellency probably knows by reputation, as he is a member of the Central Legislature. I raised with the cabinet the question whether it was not necessary to refer such an appointment to the Public Service Commission, and at the same time pointed out the probable effects both in the administration of the scheme and in respect of their reputation as a government if a politician of that type were appointed to be in control. Since I returned from tour I have had a long discussion with the Premier about this. He himself appears to have committed himself completely to Mr. Paliwal, and strangely enough seems genuinely to believe that Mr. Paliwal will be able to be of real assistance in organising the scheme they have in mind. At the same time he assures me, and I cannot but regard the assurance as

genuine, that he is anxious to run the scheme really for the benefit of the public and not in the interest of his party. I pointed out what appeared to me to be various weaknesses in the scheme, particularly the apparent elimination of the district officer. He gave me to understand that he was quite prepared to see that the district officer played a reasonable part. He also seemed prepared to meet me in regard to establishing a reasonably impartial method of appointing the subordinate staff. He also maintained that Mr. Paliwal was not likely to remain in this post more than six months, so that strictly speaking a reference to the Public Service Commission would not be required under the rules. We are to discuss the whole matter in the cabinet tomorrow. But on the whole, subject to some reasonable understanding about the main outlines of the scheme, I think I must agree to the appointment of Mr. Paliwal much as I dislike it from many points of view. It seems to me to be one of those cases in which the ministry must be allowed to learn by experience. I think Pant will find that he has chosen the wrong man, that the appointment will be regarded with suspicion, and that his scheme will not progress. But the discredit for that will fall on him, and he is a man who, I think, is prepared to learn by his mistakes.

10. The Allahabad University situation has been causing me a good deal of anxiety. I am very grateful for Your Excellency's letter of 25th October[33] on this subject, which confirms my own general view. While I was on tour I sent my Secretary, Donaldson, to Allahabad to discuss the whole matter with the Vice-Chancellor,[34] the Commissioner[35] and others. I indicated to him some pretty stiff conditions in connection with the Congress flag and asked him to find out whether the Vice-Chancellor was prepared to guarantee them. The Vice-Chancellor made it clear that he really could guarantee nothing, and that though the attitude of the Executive Council with regard to the hoisting of the flag is unexceptionable, if it is challenged by the students they will almost certainly give way. I am myself pretty clear that the wise course now is for me to change my tour programme and not visit Allahabad at all in December. I discussed this with Pant. It seems that Nehru's assistance has been sought with a view to getting the students not to raise the flag issue until after the Jubilee. But though Nehru seems prepared to give some assistance in this direction, I do not think anything is likely to come out of it which I could regard as really satisfactory. I told Pant yesterday that unless he had anything strongly to urge to the contrary I proposed to inform the Vice-Chancellor that my tour arrangements were changed. Pant has begged me to wait until Dr. Katju returns today and postpone a decision until I have talked to him, and I

have felt bound to accede to this request. My own feeling is this, that at present I can get out of what might prove an exceedingly embarrassing situation without bringing right into the forefront the controversy about the flag which Pant himself is most anxious to avoid. It is true that my absenting myself might lead to the Jubilee functions being given up altogether, but there are many in Allahabad who would welcome such a development. My absenting myself need not be attributed entirely or even mainly to the flag trouble but to the general state of indiscipline among the students. On the other hand, if I go to Allahabad and at the last moment difficulties arise about the flag, then we shall have a really serious and direct controversy over this issue, and Pant is as little anxious as I am that this should happen. On my judgment of the situation therefore it seems to me decidedly more wise to cut adrift now. But Pant is still hankering after the possibility of some sort of arrangement. At present I do not feel that I could base myself with any assurance on such an arrangement. In the Allahabad University situation there is no solid ground.

11. I made an elaborate speech at Chitaura to mark the practical conclusion of the Ganges Canal Hydroelectric Scheme, and paid a farewell tribute to Stampe which, I think, was greatly appreciated. The speech, which faced all the main criticisms that have been made recently, seems to have been well received, and Pant, though he was inclined from lack of information to think there was a good deal of substance in some of these criticisms, does not seem to have any kind of objection to what I said or the line I took. I quite agree with Your Excellency about Stampe. His absorbing interest is in the work and in the schemes which he has fathered. But on the whole I think he has now reconciled himself to the present position. He is staying on in India, and I feel sure that if occasion arises my government will be very ready to consult him and take the benefit of his experience. Meantime, in some ways, it is not a bad thing that some one else should take administrative charge. I enclose a copy of my speech.[36]

12. Though I have had two long interviews with Pant since I returned from tour and he returned from the Calcutta meeting, we have neither of us made any further reference to the question of release of prisoners. From this I am inclined to draw the conclusion that there is no intention of pushing matters to a definite issue with me – a possibility which he had indicated very plainly at our last interview – and that he has been able to get the Working Committee to agree to postponement for the present and acquiescence in my views. I hope at any rate that this may be so. I find Pant's attitude particularly friendly since my return.

13. I am very glad you had such a pleasant interlude in Kulu. I leave here again on the night of the 11th to visit the Jhansi and Agra divisions.

Yours sincerely,
H.G. HAIG

103

HAIG TO LINLITHGOW
MSS.EUR.F. 125/127

Secret
No. U.P.-17

Camp,
November 9th, 1937

My dear Lord Linlithgow,

With reference to paragraph 10 of my fortnightly report, No. U.P-16, dated November 8th, I think I ought to let you know at once the result of my conversation with Dr. Katju about the Allahabad University Jubilee celebrations which has opened up certain new possibilities. In the first place, Dr. Katju made me realise more fully than I had before the very great importance which is attached by those who are interested in the Allahabad University and its Jubilee to my presence on the occasion. He said that if I had to absence myself, either the Jubilee celebrations would be given up altogether, or, if held, they would be a practical failure. There is thus a very strong inducement to those who wish the University well to secure my attendance. In the second place, he said that he thought the issue had never been put plainly before the students, namely, that they must either drop the flag question for the period of the Jubilee celebrations, or else do without me and thus damage the celebrations seriously. He feels that Gurtu has not been in sufficiently close touch with the students, and this fits in with what I have heard of his attitude, for he clearly regards the students as a somewhat menacing and incalculable force in the face of which he is powerless. Indeed, Katju said that in his opinion if Gurtu had handled the matter differently, it would not have been necessary to give in to the students over Lothian's address.

2. The third point that arises is that if the students, when the matter is placed plainly before them, show themselves reasonable, what assurance is there that they will observe any undertaking given. Katju's answer to this is, that if they give a promise to Jawaharlal Nehru they will not depart from it. Nehru himself seems anxious to co-operate in seeing that this

issue is avoided at the time of the Jubilee celebrations; and if the students are in a reasonable mood, and Nehru as well as Pant and Katju are committed to maintaining the situation, it seems probable that the solid ground for which I have been looking in vain will be there.

3. I put my position very plainly before Katju and explained to him the conditions which I had conveyed to Gurtu. One of these conditions was that no flag hoisting ceremony should take place on the University buildings between now and the Jubilee celebrations:

(*a*) because I thought it exceedingly improbable that if the flag were once hoisted it would be taken down again;

(*b*) because the Executive Council have expressed themselves as opposed to flag hoisting, and therefore any flag hoisting would appear to be in defiance of the wishes of the Executive Council.

Katju suggested, and I had already heard this before, that the flag might be put up for a day now, with the definite understanding that it would be taken down after a day and would not be displayed during the Jubilee celebrations. This suggestion apparently proceeded from Nehru, and Katju said that if this understanding was reached, he was absolutely confident that Nehru would see that it was observed. I did not commit myself one way or the other about this, and stressed the difficulty that would arise in connection with the Executive Council's resolution recording their disapproval of any flag hoisting on the University buildings. But provided that that difficulty had been got over, I do not in fact feel that I could reasonably insist on no flag hoisting beforehand, provided it was quite clear that the flag issue will not be raised in any way during the celebrations.

4. Katju takes a very great interest in this matter as an old member of the University, and he also clearly feels that if some settlement can be reached, it will avoid very considerable future embarrassments in the attitude of the students and is likely to promote a much better feeling in the University. I am quite in agreement with him and I do not want to go out of my way to cause trouble. Successful celebrations in which I take part may produce a generally sedative effect.[37] At the same time he fully appreciates that there can be no question of any Congress flags being in evidence during the Jubilee celebrations, if I am to attend. On this clear understanding I have agreed to wait for a week, till the 15th November, before reaching a decision. In the meantime Katju himself is going over to Allahabad and will talk the whole thing over with Nehru and Gurtu and definitely ascertain the attitude of the students. With regard to my view

that I might possibly get out of the situation now without much comment, he said that that was not so and that it would really make no difference whether I withdrew now or a week hence, for in any case the withdrawal would be very marked, have important results and attract the maximum of attention. There may be force in this view. In any case I feel bound to give Katju the chance of effecting a settlement.

5. The recent intervention of a Bihar minister who came to Allahabad and urged the students to insist on hoisting the flag has not been helpful, and I am told that Nehru is very far from pleased about it and considers that it was an unwarrantable interference in a situation which did not concern the minister.[38]

Yours sincerely,
HARRY HAIG

104

HAIG TO LINLITHGOW
MSS.EUR.F. 125/127

Secret
No. U.P.-18

Camp,
November 10th, 1937

My dear Lord Linlithgow,

The Premier on his return from Calcutta raised with me the question of the grant of titles. He reminded me that when he had last mentioned the subject to me, he had explained that the ministry wished to have nothing to do with recommendations for titles, and that their attitude would be one of indifference. He explained that this was no longer the case in view of decisions taken at the All-India Congress Committee. The attitude of the ministry now instead of being one of indifference must be one of active opposition to the grant of titles. He mentioned the case of various dominions where the grant of titles has, at the request of the dominion governments, been discontinued, and suggested that the provincial Legislature and/or the ministers would wish to make a formal representation for the consideration of His Majesty that the grant of all titles in this Province should be discontinued. I said that it seemed to me difficult to deal with a matter like this on a provincial basis, and that if any representation were to be made to His Majesty, I considered that it ought to proceed from the Government of India. In the course of further conversation the Premier indicated to me that if it were not found possible to meet the wishes of the Council of Ministers in this matter, they might direct officers of government serving in the Province not to assist me by sending in any recommendations for titles. I said that that raised a constitutional issue of some importance on which I was not prepared at the moment to express a final opinion, though it seemed to me that the Governor would have the power to obtain from officers of the Crown assistance in making recommendations for the consideration of the Crown or the Governor-General.

2. Another point made by the Premier in the course of the conversation was that it would be an anomalous position if titles were conferred on government servants in a Province in direct contravention of the wishes of the government. To that my answer was that if the ministers were prepared to express any views about particular officers, I should be pleased to consider them, but that government servants must be regarded not as the servants of the ministers but as servants of the Crown.

3. The Premier said that he wished to raise the matter formally at the next cabinet meeting which was taking place a day or two after this conversation. I said that it was evidently necessary that I should communicate with Your Excellency on this subject, and that being so, it would probably be more convenient if the matter were not raised formally at a cabinet meeting while I was in no position to give any definite reply. The Premier agreed to this, but said that he would take the occasion to mention the matter informally. Accordingly at a cabinet meeting yesterday evening he raised the question informally, and we had a short general discussion much on the lines indicated in paragraphs 1 and 2 above. The ministers seemed to be anxious to have their views on record and communicated to the Governor-General. I said I would certainly communicate their views to Your Excellency. I fancy also this will be followed up by a resolution in the provincial Assembly.

4. With regard to policy, I imagine there is no question of discontinuing the system of granting titles. Apart from members of the Services, who naturally value these distinctions, great importance is attached to them by a large section of non-officials.

5. With regard to the method for dealing with this request, which will no doubt also be put by the other Congress Provinces, I think, as I have indicated above, that possibly the most convenient course would be to hold that it could not be dealt with on a provincial basis.

6. With regard to the threat of active opposition, and in particular any attempt to forbid government officers to send recommendations to me, I should be glad to know what the constitutional position is. The grant of

titles is a prerogative power and outside the sphere of the executive authority of the Province. It might therefore be held that I had no right in such a matter to issue orders to government servants as my authority is only co-extensive with the executive authority of the Province. But I cannot help thinking that there is probably some legal way out of this difficulty; and even if I were not legally in a position to issue instructions in this matter to government servants, equally the ministry would be unable to issue orders to them in a contrary sense. In practice I should request them to help me, and as the ministry could not issue orders to the contrary, my request would naturally be acted upon.

Yours sincerely,
H.G. HAIG

105

HAIG TO HALLETT
Telegram
MSS.EUR.F. 125/127

Clear the Line *November 11th, 1937*
No. 71-G

Addressed to Governor of Bihar [repeated to Governor-General]. Your telegram No. 1804-G.S., dated the 10th November.[39] My letter, October 1st, placed you in possession of situation here up to the time of the Calcutta Congress meeting. Since meeting I have had two long interviews with Premier in neither of which he made any further allusion to release of prisoners. Yesterday at end of cabinet meeting he mentioned the matter informally and said that in view of decisions in Calcutta he hoped I would be able to agree to his proposals for release of prisoners. I said that we had had many discussions and he knew my views and that for the present I felt that we ought to postpone the matter. The topic was not further pursued. I formed the opinion that he felt bound to raise it in cabinet, but did so deliberately in an informal manner and not with intention of pressing it to an issue as he had previously warned me he might have to. There was no suggestion that any departure should be made from practice we have hitherto followed of examining each individual case. In the case of our worst terrorist prisoner the ministry themselves had not proposed his immediate release.

106

HAIG TO LINLITHGOW
MSS.EUR.F. 125/127

Secret
No. U.P.-19

Camp,
November 11th, 1937

My dear Lord Linlithgow,

With reference to Your Excellency's telegram No. 385-G.C., dated 8th November,[40] I am afraid I have little information to give you in connection with the All-India Congress Committee meeting at Calcutta. My ministers have not been communicative on the subject, and I have not pressed them for information. I have written to Your Excellency separately about the question of the grant of titles, which has definitely emerged as an issue from the Calcutta meeting. My telegram No. G-71 of November 10th to Hallett, which I have repeated to you, gives what I know of the present position in regard to the release of prisoners. On this subject I find it a little difficult to judge what the situation really is. But so far as we are concerned in this Province, it appears to me that Pant is not intending to press the matter publicly to an issue, as he had suggested before might be necessary; and if that is so the conclusion must be that he has persuaded the Working Committee that that would be unnecessary and unwise. I should judge that the general policy is to do everything possible by pressure to get prisoners released, but that they are not prepared to face an open breach with the Governor on this subject.

2. The ministers show no signs of being depressed about their position, and appear to be pursuing their policies precisely as before. I should judge that in spite of a good deal of criticism they have emerged with their position substantially unshaken, and they have probably been able to make clear to the Working Committee the practical limitations inevitably imposed on their action.

3. Jawaharlal Nehru seems to be working in close co-operation with the Ministry in certain matters. They asked him to come to Cawnpore to try and relax the tension there, though I gather he has not been successful. He also, as I have explained in another letter, shows signs of wishing to avoid trouble in connection with the Allahabad University Jubilee functions.

Yours sincerely,
H.G. HAIG

107

HAIG TO LINLITHGOW
MSS.EUR.F. 115/12

Secret *November 17th, 1937*
No. U.P.-21

My dear Lord Linlithgow,

I have received Your Excellency's secret letter of 15th November.[41] It discloses that you take a very grave view of the administrative position in the United Provinces. It also discloses what seems to me to be a very misleading impression of my relations with my officers and the administration generally. I have kept Your Excellency constantly in touch with our situation; for some months now I have been impressing on you the view that what really matters in this province is the administrative position and conditions in the districts, even more perhaps than the policy of the ministry in particular matters. You will understand therefore that I have no wish to minimise the importance of these aspects. Indeed it was for the purpose of getting in personal touch with conditions and with my local officers that I have arranged the extensive tours I am carrying out this cold weather, for my experience is that interviews and reports at headquarters are not enough and that it is difficult to form from these a balanced picture. I gave you in my letter of November 8th my considered judgment on the situation in the first two divisions I visited. That judgment was based on a large number of conversations with the officers who are actually handling these problems every day. It is a situation that requires very careful consideration, and I discussed it before I left Lucknow with my permanent I.G. of Police,[42] who, I am glad to say, has just returned from leave, and have been turning it over in my mind constantly since. It is not a situation that lends itself to short cuts or dramatic solutions. It requires patience and persistence. I had hoped that my letter would elicit Your Excellency's views, and I welcome the opportunity you give me of talking out with you not only this situation, but a number of other fundamental points on which I wish to be perfectly clear about Your Excellency's policy and that of the Secretary of State. I say this because, possibly through my closer contact with the facts and personalities in this province, certain solutions do not seem to me quite so simple as perhaps they do to Your Excellency.

2. I shall not attempt in this letter to deal with the various specific points made in your letter, for to deal with them adequately would involve

somewhat elaborate presentation, and they are essentially matters in which a discussion will be of great value. One general reflection, however, I think I may permit myself. I see the reports which Your Excellency sees about my province. I assess their value in the light of many other reports and conversations, and I arrive at a general estimate of conditions which I communicate to you and the Secretary of State. I do not set up my judgement as infallible. In the difficult conditions with which we are confronted, I have to form my opinion as to the relative importance of the various factors and the expediency at any given moment of the various possible courses of action, taking into consideration the character and mentality of the ministry with which I am dealing. Other men might reach other conclusions on individual issues, or might choose to follow a different general line. These are all matters which I should like to talk out with Your Excellency in the fullest possible manner. But I do have an opportunity, better I think than anyone else possesses, of putting facts into a reasonable perspective, and that is, as it seems to me, the essential preliminary to formulating policy.

3. As regards the speeches at Lansdowne, mentioned in para. 6 of your letter, I have only just now received some very brief references to them, as it appears that neither the Deputy Commissioner[43] nor the Commissioner of Kumaun[44] considered them to be of such importance as to deserve a special report. I gather that the audiences were not large. In the Commissioner's fortnightly report which reached the Chief Secretary in Lucknow yesterday, I understand that he made only a brief reference to these speeches and he did not forward the letter of the Assistant Commissioner,[45] dated the 25th October, which has reached Your Excellency through the military. The speeches were mentioned in para. 501 of the Police Secret Abstract No. 155, dated November 13th, on which the Chief Secretary at once asked for the police papers and a further report. I am having immediate inquiries made into the full details and will report further when I have them. In the case of these hill districts, when the Commissioner and district officers are on tour, communications are often rather slow. The Commissioner, I may add, is a very capable and experienced officer, who has served for many years in Garhwal, and knows Lansdowne and the Garhwalis thoroughly.

4. As you have sent a copy of your letter to the Secretary of State, I should be grateful if you would also send him a copy of this letter, so that he may have a general idea of my attitude.

Yours sincerely,
H.G. HAIG

108

HAIG TO LINLITHGOW
MSS.EUR.F. 125/127

Secret *November 17th, 1937*
No. U.P.-22

My dear Lord Linlithgow,

I notice that in Hallett's fortnightly report to you, dated November 11th, he refers to a remark of mine in my report, dated 8th November, to the effect that "the police have been accustomed to use somewhat rough and ready methods and to a large extent know no other way of getting results; but if they use the methods to which they are accustomed, they know that they may get into trouble". Hallett quotes this in connection with some incident in which it appears that a Magistrate gave an order and the police carried it out somewhat drastically.[46] I should like to make it plain that my remarks were not written with reference to any such situation. What I had in mind particularly were the processes of investigation, or possibly somewhat irregular methods of controlling bad characters. I think it is well to make this clear.

Yours sincerely,
HARRY HAIG

109

HAIG TO LINLITHGOW
L/P&J/7/1059

Secret Governor's Camp,
No. U.P.-24 *November 18th, 1937*

Dear Lord Linlithgow,

With reference to para. 3 of my secret letter No. U.P. 21, dated November 17, 1937, I have just received fuller papers about the Lansdowne speeches contained in a letter from the Commissioner, dated 14th November. Both the Commissioner and the Deputy Commissioner would like to see prosecutions instituted. I am taking the whole matter up with the Premier.

Yours sincerely,
H.G. HAIG

110

HAIG TO ZETLAND
Telegram
MSS.EUR.F. 125/127

No. 80-G *November 27th, 1937*

With reference to your telegram No. 2796 of November 25th addressed to Governor-General,[47] available figures for United Provinces are as follows for third quarter of 1937, July 1st to September 30th, and corresponding quarter of 1936. Prisoners prematurely released by order of government on account of sickness, old age or infirmity, or on recommendation of a revising board, 305 in 1937, 130 in 1936. Released by order of government on other grounds, e.g. having served 14 years' life sentence, 63 in 1937, 62 in 1936. No later figures or further classification available and can only be had by lengthy enquiries from individual jails. Total number of convicts for crimes of so-called "political" motive released in Province before expiry of sentence since July 1st to date is 14. In regard to jail delivery this is proceeding according to rules reported to Governor-General. Exact numbers affected by those rules cannot yet be stated, but now thought likely to be about 3,000. Releases are to be completed by December 1st and exact figures will not be available until some days later.

Addressed to Secretary of State; repeated to Governor-General with reference to his Secretary's telegram No. 1366, dated November 26th.

111

HAIG TO LINLITHGOW
Telegram
MSS.EUR.F. 115/15

No. 81-G *November 27th, 1937*

On my return to Lucknow I found that further tour in west of the province had been undertaken by Parmanand and the ex-Kakori prisoners and that further speeches of a dangerous kind were being made. In particular I have received details of an outrageous speech made by Parmanand at Dehra Dun inciting to violent revolution and revolt against the British and seducing of troops. I decided that it was necessary to prosecute Parmanand without further delay. I put my views to the Premier yesterday evening, but he pleaded in accordance with his general policy for a preliminary warning, which unfortunately owing to Parmanand being constantly on the move had not been conveyed to him in accordance with cabinet decision taken about a fortnight ago. I told him that it seemed to me that warning was useless in such a case as this and that immediate prosecution was necessary. It was decided to bring the matter up at a cabinet meeting this evening. I put the whole case for prosecution both in detail and in principle very fully before the cabinet. They listened with great attention to my general arguments but eventually felt that they might be considerably embarrassed by taking such action and that public opinion would be against them, and urged again that a warning should be given in first instance. I told them that with a full sense of my responsibility and their position I urged them strongly to take this action. They said that they felt they could not do it. I then said that my own special responsibilities placed a definite obligation on me to see that this action was taken. They did not demur to this and an order was issued that subject to the necessary legal examination, result of which I think may be taken for granted, the District Magistrate at Dehra Dun will be ordered immediately to institute prosecution. They did not indicate what will be their line before the public, though we did just touch on this point. I do not think they have yet made up their minds. But we parted on friendly terms.

112

HAIG TO LINLITHGOW
R/3/1/2

Secret *November 28th, 1937*
No. U.P.-28

My dear Lord Linlithgow,

My fortnightly letter is late, as at the time when I should ordinarily have been writing it, I had the advantage of discussing fully with Your Excellency at Delhi the whole situation in the United Provinces, and I thought it best not to write to you until I had had some days in Lucknow and had been able to take up certain matters with my Ministers.

2. I will not attempt to recapitulate our conversations which were, as far as I was concerned, of great value. But I explained to Your Excellency that while it seemed to me that the general policy should be to give the Congress ministry every chance of working the constitution (which indeed

they are clearly anxious to do) and not to produce conditions which might make Pant reluctant to continue in office, a contingency the result of which at the moment would almost certainly be a complete breakdown of the constitution, this general policy must be subject to two conditions:

(*a*) that we should not allow dangerous revolutionary feeling to develop;
(*b*) that the administration, in particular the police, should be kept intact.

3. In paragraph 5 of my report, dated November 8th, I drew attention to the campaign of revolutionary and violent speeches which had been in progress in the eastern districts of the Province by members of the Youth League, in particular Parmanand, and some of the ex-Kakori prisoners, and I said that I had sent a note to the Premier inviting the serious attention of the cabinet to this among other features of the situation. This note, dated 3rd November, I showed Your Excellency in Delhi. As a result of the cabinet meeting held about the 9th November, it was agreed that Parmanand should receive a warning in regard to his speeches. Parmanand, I may mention, was sentenced to transportation for life in the Conspiracy case of 1915, which involved tampering with the troops. He was released by the Punjab government in August last, and immediately returned to the United Provinces which is his home. Subsequently while I was on tour I received further reports which emphasised the harm that these speeches were producing in the east of the Province, and I told Your Excellency in Delhi that as soon as I got back to Lucknow I proposed to take this question of the speeches further with the cabinet. When I returned I found further information about a tour which the same men were making in the west of the Province. I found also that owing to Parmanand having been constantly on the move the warning approved by the cabinet had not actually reached him. It seemed to me necessary to press further action at once on the cabinet, and just at that time I received a report of an outrageous speech which Parmanand had made at Dehra Dun about November 15th. The nature of his speech, which I have referred to in my telegram No. 81-G., dated November 27th, made it in my opinion essential to prosecute Parmanand at once. I have explained in my telegram of November 27th what happened, and I need not repeat this. The position is that I have ordered the prosecution of Parmanand in exercise of my special responsibility. The cabinet were definitely not prepared to take this action on their own initiative, but I think it is possible that they may in public assume responsibility for it. In any case there is no suggestion that they would make this a ground for breaking with me. They themselves recognise to a large extent that this action is called for, but they shrink from taking it. It

was also decided at the cabinet meeting of November 27th that five or six of the more important speakers who have been taking part in this tour should also receive a serious warning. My own hope is that this action will suffice to put a stop to speeches of this kind. If they had been allowed to go on, the effect might have been serious. There will of course be a great deal of political criticism, and the cabinet will be heavily attacked by the left wing. But, as I said to them, the trouble arises from the inescapable facts of the situation. It is of course necessary in my opinion to maintain the position of not releasing any more revolutionary prisoners for the time being. This decision, as Your Excellency knows from my previous correspondence, has already been conveyed to the Premier.

4. I also took up with the Premier the question of revising our existing orders about the reporting of speeches which were definitely experimental. I found that he himself was not very well satisfied with the existing arrangement. He is somewhat worried at hearing that violent communal incitements are being made in speeches by the Muslim Leaguers. It was agreed yesterday at the cabinet meeting, without any opposition, that all District Magistrates should be authorised, without any reference to government or any reporting of their action to government, to order reports to be made of speeches whenever there was reason to suppose that they would be likely to tend to encourage violence or dangerous communal feeling. I am disposed to think that this will give the police all the power they require. The District Magistrate of Cawnpore has recently been authorised to order the reporting of any speeches he chooses and these Youth League speeches have also been reported in detail for sometime. For the moment the new orders seem likely to be sufficient, but I shall await the promised communication on the subject from Your Excellency.[48]

5. The other main matter which was causing me anxiety, as explained in some detail in my letter of November 8th, was the indication of some lack of confidence among the police. My tour in the two divisions of Jhansi and Agra confirmed the general picture which I gave in paragraph 1 of my letter of November 8th, though on the whole the tone was brighter. I told Your Excellency in Delhi that I intended, partly owing to these conditions in the police generally and partly owing to the special attacks made on them in Cawnpore, to speak fairly plainly at the annual police parade which was being held in Lucknow on November 27th. I enclose a copy[49] of the speech I made on this occasion. The Inspector-General of Police writing yesterday to thank me for what he called an inspiriting address said that it would go far to reassure all ranks. The effect of course of a speech of this kind can only be limited, but I hope at any rate that it will have done some good.

6. I have been a good deal encouraged since my return to find that the permanent Inspector-General of Police, Mr. Horton, who has only recently returned from long leave, has been able to establish satisfactory and indeed promising relations of confidence with the Premier which were markedly lacking in the case of his predecessor.[50] The Premier is essentially susceptible to personal handling, and if he acquires real confidence in Horton, as seems to me likely, a great deal of the suspicion which is at the root of many of our difficulties in connection with the police administration will be removed. The Premier by way of making amends for the attacks on the police in Cawnpore made a long speech to a police parade in Cawnpore about a fortnight ago. Though the speech might have dwelt a little less on the shortcomings of the police and the complaints against them, the general tone was decidedly better than any previous utterances of the Premier on this subject, and the Inspector-General is definitely of opinion that it will do good and he is taking steps to have copies of the speech widely circulated among the police.

7. Another matter to which I attach importance in connection with the working of the district administration is a circular letter[51] which we issued on November 10th to all District Magistrates, of which I showed a copy to Your Excellency in Delhi. The main point about this letter is that I hope it will mark the end of a phase which has undoubtedly been somewhat demoralising the district administration, in which every one seemed to think that complaints can be taken over the head of the district authorities straight up to headquarters.[52] Henceforth the intention is that these complaints should be handled and settled in the districts. The district officers with whom I have discussed the matter are generally confident that they will be able to handle the local Congress leaders effectively. Indeed in most districts they have already established relations which they have found to be useful. There is no question at all of the authority of the District Magistrates being diminished by such relations. On the contrary in all districts which I have visited the district officers are quite satisfied about their own authority, save in so far as things are taken over their heads to headquarters. At the same time I hope that district officers will now be in a position to take up definitely with local Congress leaders conduct by Congressmen for which no legal remedy exists, and which is contrary to the expressed policy of the Congress organisation. If the present occasions for friction are diminished, there is no doubt that the general result will be very beneficial to the district administration and particularly to the authority of the police.

8. I was relieved to find when I visited the Jhansi division, that the

conditions which I reported in paragraph 6 of my letter of November 8th were confined to the limited area of Lalitpur sub-division of the Jhansi district. Conditions in the other three districts of the division appeared to be perfectly quiet and normal, and the rest of the Jhansi district, excluding the Lalitpur sub-division, also seemed to be on the whole satisfactory. The Collector in charge of the Jhansi division[53] told me that in Lalitpur conditions had improved immensely as the result of his enquiry, and that the previous trouble was now confined to one or two villages; and this also appeared to be the view of the Superintendent of Police.[54] The area will want watching, but I have no doubt that the steps taken have been very beneficial. In the Agra division I found a general impression that the administrative conditions were decidedly better than they were two months ago, and that the attitude of the people in general towards government servants was friendly and respectful. I do not expect to find the situation as satisfactory as this in the east of the Province; but the reports for some weeks from Gorakhpur, which, as Your Excellency knows, at one time gave me cause for a good deal of anxiety, have been decidedly more reassuring.

9. In the Jhansi and Agra divisions there is no very widespread complaint of bad feeling between Hindus and Muslims, though in Aligarh there had recently been a communal outbreak. This was dealt with effectively and further trouble is not anticipated there. Cawnpore seems to me from what I hear to be the place where communal feeling is perhaps most dangerous at the moment. I have just had reports, however, of certain outbreaks in the Ballia district in the extreme east of the Province, which reveal a situation that will have to be watched very carefully. Hindu feeling seems to have been worked up against cow killing, and in consequence assaults were made on a number of butchers who had been buying cattle for slaughter at a big fair. Two butchers were killed and a number of cattle taken away forcibly. Two or three incidents of this character occurred within a day or two. The situation is reported now to be quite in hand and conditions quiet. This is an area in which the Hindus are peculiarly susceptible to appeal to sentiment about cow killing, and disorder might spread rapidly and seriously. Precautions are therefore being taken to strengthen the police and to see that the situation is kept well in hand.

10. The Parliamentary Committee which is examining the tenancy questions is pursuing its enquiries steadily. So far, I understand, the proceedings, though naturally not agreeable to the landlords are not seriously disturbing to them. It will not however be possible to judge until the conclusion of the proceedings what line the government are likely to take.

11. I have since my return to Lucknow had further discussions with Dr. Katju about the government's rural development scheme, and I have pressed on him the importance of keeping our existing scheme, which has been carried on with the Government of India grant, intact and working on its own lines at any rate until the 31st March, and until there has been plenty of time to see what the new scheme looks like in operation and to address the Government of India if it is desired to modify the old scheme so as to bring it into line with the government's new scheme. I think it is possible that when the work is launched, it may be found to approximate pretty closely to what we have been doing already. But I told Dr. Katju plainly that the arrangements about staff and some of the suggestions in connection with organisation had given rise to a good deal of suspicion, which it seemed to me necessary should be completely removed in the course of the working.

12. When I was at Agra I attended the annual convocation of the Agra University. There had been rumours that there might be trouble about the Congress flag or that the students might make some demonstration. The principals of the Agra colleges however assured me that there was no kind of foundation for these apprehensions, and that the spirit of their students was in fact very satisfactory. This turned out to be correct. The whole proceedings at the convocation went off admirably and nothing could have been better than the spirit shown by the students. Altogether I had a very satisfactory reception in Agra, a place where I have myself served for some four years. In Allahabad and Lucknow, however, the students seem to be very much out of hand, and though I am definitely going to be in Allahabad during the second half of December, I shall not take part in the University convocation if there is any reasonable apprehension of trouble.

13. Cawnpore continues to escape the long threatened strike. Indeed the workers in two mills who had recently been out have just returned to work again. I go to Cawnpore tomorrow and shall then be able to judge better the actual position. The enquiry committee has made a rather disappointing start. Babu Rajendra Prasad has for various reasons been unable to attend and it is not at all certain that he will not have to fall out altogether. Dr. Katju consulted me about the possibility of a successor if it is necessary to replace Babu Rajendra Prasad as Chairman, and I shall consider this matter while I am in Cawnpore.

Yours sincerely,
H.G. HAIG

113

HAIG TO LINLITHGOW
Telegram
MSS.EUR.F. 115/15

Express (By Special Messenger) *November 29th, 1937*
No. 82-G

In continuation of my telegram No. G-81, dated November 27th, I should explain that when we reached an impasse I had suggested that the Premier should consider the matter further and that we should discuss it once more as soon as we were able to meet. The difficulty was that we were both going on tour at once. But I said I was willing to discuss again on the 2nd December when I returned to Lucknow and that I could even wait till the 4th December when the Premier would be back without disturbing his tour programme. He said however that it appeared that neither of us was likely to change his mind and that as I attached importance to early action he did not think he would be justified in asking me to wait for further discussion. It was at that stage that I said that I felt my special responsibility placed on me an obligation to see that the action was taken.

2. On the night of the 28th when I arrived at Cawnpore I found the Premier at the station as he was also passing through and he had specially arranged to see me. He brought me a letter dated November 28th which he had intended to send me, but having an opportunity of speaking he was anxious to explain personally so that I should not get any wrong impression. After referring in courteous terms to our discussion and failure to reach a conclusion acceptable to both of us, the letter proceeds: "I did not consider it fair to hamper you in carrying out the decisions at which you had finally arrived, as we were not prepared to share the responsibility for that decision. We are anxious not to precipitate a crisis or embarrass you, but your decision gives rise to issues of a far-reaching character. The matter is naturally engaging our attention. We are however not in a position to take or anticipate any final decision in the matter at this stage and have to consult others to whom according to our constitution a reference will have to be made on occasions like these."

3. Pant explained that he was anxious that I should not regard this letter as a threat, and it is perhaps significant that he made no request that action should be postponed pending the consultation about his own position. His attitude was perfectly friendly as before. He explained to me that normally they would have wished to consult Nehru, but he is away. Under

the circumstances they feel bound to consult the Committee which is charged on behalf of the Working Committee with the supervision of U.P. affairs. This consists, I understand, of Vallabhbhai Patel, Abul Kalam Azad and Rajendra Prasad, and he is asking them to come to Lucknow as early as possible so that he could consult them personally. He preferred not to write. On the other hand he did not think they would be able to come very soon. He would if necessary return to Lucknow before the 4th December to meet them, but he seemed to think they might not arrive much before then.

4. My own reading of the situation is that the cabinet feel they could not acquiesce in this action without getting sanction of the Working Committee. But I feel sure that the last thing they would desire to do would be to resign and that they would only take this step if it were forced upon them by the Working Committee. No attempt has been made by Pant to ask me to reconsider my position and he clearly does not intend to use the threat of resigning as a weapon. Subject to your instructions I propose to maintain my position unaltered, and though the issue of actual orders for prosecution may in any case take a few days, I should propose to take that action when the case is ready and not wait for the result of the consultation with the Working Committee members. Indeed one could not resile on a threat of resignation and this Pant clearly recognizes.

114

HAIG TO LINLITHGOW
Telegram
MSS.EUR.F. 115/13
No. 84-G [?83-G] *November 29th, 1937*

On arrival at Cawnpore last night I heard that previous night an important worker at the Elgin Mills who had been prominent in bringing the men back to work had been set upon and murdered. No definite clue has yet been found, but it seems certain that this has been done at the instance of the extremist section of workers. I have discussed the whole situation with the D.M.[55] and S.P.[56] and also Commissioner.[57] The action already taken includes arrest on suspicion of the seven members of the Mill Committee in this mill, searching of several houses and of the office of Mazdur Sabha. I understand so far these steps have not yielded much in the way of evidence. The D.M. is also issuing orders under Sec. 144 on some 10 communist leaders, prohibiting them from making any speeches or issuing any pamphlets for the next two months. He is also running in Muhammad Yusuf under Sec. 107 Cr.P.C. in respect of his past activities as he is convinced that this situation is mainly the result of Yusuf's actions.

The D.M. mentioned his intentions yesterday to the Premier who made no comment. I have told the D.M. to go ahead and he will be supported. The murder has brought matters to a head in Cawnpore and firm action is required immediately. There is a good chance that it will produce a marked change for the better. But even if it should lead to further trouble for a time this should now be faced.

2. There was some anxiety yesterday lest the situation should take a communal turn. Hindu Muslim feeling is distinctly bad in Cawnpore and the fact that the murdered man was a Muslim was being used to rouse Muslim feeling against Hindu Congressmen. Full precautions were taken by the police and the military stood by. Communal feeling today does not seem to have developed and position generally is reported quiet.

115

HAIG TO LINLITHGOW
MSS.EUR.F. 115/13

Secret *December 2nd, 1937*
No. U.P.-31

[Dear Lord Linlithgow,]

With reference to Your Excellency's telegram No. 1409-G, dated November 30th, 1937,[58] I fully agree about the general constitutional position and the importance of observing it strictly. The position in Cawnpore in my judgement, which agreed with that of the local officers, was that there was a grave menace to the peace of the city, which is the most turbulent and dangerous city in the province. The recollection of the 1931 riots is still fresh in everybody's memory, and it seems to me very difficult to risk deliberately by inaction the possibility of a serious outbreak in Cawnpore. Public opinion would certainly, I feel, hold us very strictly to account if this happened. It is true that we have for some months past been running considerable risks in Cawnpore. This was in pursuance of a policy which the government were committed to try out, and which I think everybody, including themselves, is beginning to feel now has been a failure. But it has always been my view that if violence develops, it will have to be suppressed very firmly and quickly. The recent murder set up conditions which might very easily have led to disorder spreading rapidly. There was the possibility that the violence party would be encouraged by immunity to further violence. There was the possibility that in some cases the loyal workers might retaliate. There was in any case a sense of great uneasiness which often leads to an outbreak. Apart from this, the communal situation was such that there might have been a clash at any moment. Some of the Hindu Congressmen who saw me were obviously very nervous and I think it likely that if the district authorities had not shown definite signs of gripping the situation firmly, the Muslims might have worked up dangerous feeling. I have no doubt that the action taken by the District Magistrate, though drastic, has produced a general sense of relief in the city, has restored confidence which was shaken, and has greatly minimised the likelihood of disorder breaking out.

2. With regard to the position of the ministry, the District Magistrate's action was of course entirely within his powers, and he was not bound by any orders to refer to government before taking action. It so happened that the Premier was in Cawnpore. This I think was fortunate, for I hope that the Premier, though he will undoubtedly be subject to considerable pressure by a section of Cawnpore Congressmen, will feel that he cannot well modify the action taken by the District Magistrate. If he were to wish to modify it, I feel I should have to bring the strongest possible pressure to bear on him not to do so, for to go back on these orders now would be so damaging to the authority of the District Magistrate and the police that it would create, in my opinion, a most dangerous situation in which we should have no right to acquiesce. It was in the light of these views that I told the District Magistrate that he would be supported. But this was of course merely for his private information, and I entirely agree with Your Excellency that I must in this matter keep in the background as long as possible.

3. I should think it likely that the Premier was not reluctant that the District Magistrate should take the action on his own responsibility. Had the matter been referred to the government, apart from the delay which would have been dangerous, the government might have found it exceedingly difficult to pass the orders which the District Magistrate has passed. Indeed, they would almost certainly have shrunk from any such action, and I should have been placed in a very difficult position in judging what I should do. It is, however, far easier for the Premier to support the District Magistrate's action on the ground that it has been taken and that it is impossible to go back on it. It is also far easier for me to prevent the

government now issuing an order modifying what has been done, which I should regard as dangerous, than to force them to issue an order which they were not prepared to pass. It is unfortunate that the *Pioneer* inserted an embarrassing and untrue telegram yesterday to the effect that these orders had been passed with the full concurrence of the Premier. I am afraid this may upset him and he may think that an attempt is being made to force his hand. It is not known how such a message was sent from Cawnpore, and I have asked the Chief Secretary to take up the matter with the editor of the *Pioneer* and explain to him how very embarrassing these things are, and that he really ought to refer to some responsible officer before inserting telegrams of this kind.

4. In general I fear that the cabinet in taking the minimum action necessary to preserve order will be up against serious difficulties from their followers. I think I mentioned to Your Excellency in Delhi that I did not believe that the trouble came directly from the Working Committee. It is rather the influence of the provincial Congress Left Wing. I am told that their strength and confidence have appreciably increased in the last few weeks, and I think this is the cause of the hesitating line taken by the cabinet over Parmanand's prosecution, which may well be repeated in the case of Cawnpore. They must, however, face the situation. I believe the Working Committee want the cabinet to remain in office, and if that is so, the cabinet ought to be able to act against the views of the left wing. But at present it looks as if they are not prepared to do this without some species of compulsion.

5. I left Cawnpore this morning. Before I left the District Magistrate told me the latest position. Muhammad Yusuf was arrested yesterday morning. So far there has been no serious reaction. The city is quiet, and there seems to be a general feeling of relief and restoration of confidence. Some efforts were apparently made yesterday to suggest a general strike, but the District Magistrate told me that the women were asserting themselves and saying they wanted no more strikes, but they wanted food and money. It is reported in the papers this morning that the communists, on whom orders have been served under Section 144, propose to disobey them. In that case the District Magistrate's intention is to run them in at once. Some evidence is now coming in as to a definite conspiracy to commit violence and in particular to assault the man who was murdered, and the District Magistrate thinks that gradually a good deal more evidence will come in. In connection with this evidence there will be a considerable number of arrests.

6. I had talks with people of all kinds while I was in Cawnpore, and I

am proposing to press strongly on my ministers the view that if once the law and order situation is restored there is a very considerable chance that a vigorous handling of the labour difficulties by the ministry at this moment may produce a real improvement, and indeed some prospect of a solution. Everyone, both employers and labour, is tired of the present conditions, but at the moment there is no policy. If it were possible to reorganise the Mazdur Sabha on sound lines and at the same time to reconstitute the Inquiry Committee, form it into a court of inquiry under the Trade Disputes Act with a strong Chairman and get it really working, I think a considerable improvement might result.

Yours sincerely,
H.G. HAIG

116

HAIG TO LINLITHGOW
Telegram
MSS.EUR.F. 115/13

No. 84-G *December 5th, 1937*

Many thanks for Your Excellency's telegram No. 1428-G dated December 5th.[59] Pant returned to Lucknow yesterday and I discussed Congress [?Cawnpore] situation with him. His attitude seems to me satisfactory, and he realises that firm action was required. He does not like the Section 144 orders, but seems to have no objection to the proceedings under Section 107. I do not think he has any intention of proposing to over-rule action of District Magistrate.

117

HAIG TO LINLITHGOW
Telegram
MSS.EUR.F. 115/15

No. 86-G *December 7th, 1937*

Pant raised yesterday at a cabinet meeting question of Parmanand's prosecution. He suggested that fact that he had been arrested at Delhi and would presumably be sentenced to several months' imprisonment altered situation in that he would be restrained for some time from making any more speeches. I pointed out that his period of imprisonment was likely to be comparatively short and that my object was not merely to have Parmanand in jail, but to make it clear to people generally that speeches of this kind would not be tolerated. I also pointed out that plaint had already been filed in the District Magistrate's court at Dehra Dun and that a warrant against Parmanand had issued. We did not take the matter any further at the cabinet meeting; but he raised it again in the evening in an interview with me, stressing the point that the arrest in Delhi introduced a new complication, if the prosecution was to proceed. He pointed out that quite apart from the possibility of more serious trouble, by which presumably he meant resignation, which he did not wish to bring into the conversation, he was placed in a position of great embarrassment. On the one hand if he accepted the responsibility for what was done, he rendered himself liable to serious attack for a course of action which he did not really approve. On the other hand if he made it clear that the decision was mine and that he did not agree with it, he felt that much of the advantage which the administration has hitherto enjoyed from the general belief that he and I work together in friendly relations would be lost and he feels that this would be an unfortunate development.

2. I quite recognize Pant's difficulties, but of course they have been inherent in the position from the beginning. It is however the case, though I have not admitted this to him, that the arrest of Parmanand and the ex-Kakori prisoners in Delhi, if they are all put away for some substantial period, will greatly ease our situation in the province, for these are precisely the men who have been going round making these revolutionary speeches. On the other hand it is in my view of importance that it should be known, as in fact it must now be known, that orders have been issued for the prosecution of Parmanand.

3. In course of conversation the idea came up that if cabinet publicly accepted responsibility for having ordered Parmanand's prosecution for sedition, and if he received a substantial sentence at Delhi, then it might not be necessary to proceed with our prosecution. The practical difficulties involved in such a suggestion would be considerable. There is no assurance that Parmanand would be sentenced to six months, which would be about the minimum which might justify our not proceeding, or that if sentenced the period would not be reduced in appeal. On the other hand if proceedings were suspended at this stage on hypothesis that he would receive substantial sentence and this hypothesis were not realised, the difficulty from popular point of view in proceeding would be intensified by the delay and hesitation. On the other side one thing to which I attach special importance is that it should be made clear to people in general that the government do not

propose to tolerate speeches of this kind. If the cabinet themselves accepted responsibility for having actually ordered prosecution, that is to my mind a more effective warning to the public than if the prosecution were carried through on my order and with the opposition of the ministers. Further if Parmanand and the other ex-Kakori prisoners were in fact put out of the way for six months, the practical situation would be greatly improved.

4. These ideas were discussed only in a very tentative way. I made it clear that as I had not given the matter any considered thought, he must not assume that I should be prepared to agree to any such course of action even if he found himself agreeable to it, which again on his part seemed doubtful. But we decided that we would both think over the whole situation further in the course of the next few days. Patel I understand is arriving tomorrow and he will no doubt discuss thoroughly with Pant the whole question of what attitude the cabinet should adopt in the circumstances.

5. I should be grateful for Your Excellency's views and those of the Secretary of State on the possibility which I have indicated above. I think there might be considerable advantage in a solution of this kind, but the practical difficulties of basing any action on a supposition of what might be the Delhi sentences are so serious, that I doubt whether it would be justifiable to proceed on any such basis. Of course if the ministers were not prepared to accept publicly the responsibility for prosecution, then I am clear that the prosecution should proceed. On the whole it looks to me as if the Delhi incident must be disregarded, the prosecution must proceed and ministers be left to decide on their own course of action.[60]

118

HAIG TO LINLITHGOW
MSS.EUR.F. 125/127

Confidential *December 7th, 1937*
No. U.P.-34

My dear Lord Linlithgow,

A proposal came before the cabinet yesterday that the Bill for control of sugar factories, which it is intended to introduce here at our next session in January, in precisely the same form as it is being passed in Bihar, should, as soon as the Bihar Bill is passed, be issued as an ordinance under Section 88 of the Government of India Act. I pointed out that it seemed highly undemocratic to resort to such procedure in the case of a complicated measure of this kind unless some real emergency existed, and I was not clear what the emergency was that would justify this procedure. After some discussion it was accepted that there would be no question of issuing an ordinance except to cover points for which it was really vital to make provision before legislation could be passed. On examination of the points which it was suggested might come within this definition they reduced themselves to two.

2. In the first place, provision for licensing of factories. The contention is that unless all factories can be forced into the sugar syndicate and thus made to agree to a uniform selling price, prices of sugar will be forced down by uneconomic competition to a rate at which it will become impossible to pay the minimum price fixed for sugar cane. It is contended that even a month's delay in bringing all the factories into the sugar syndicate might have disastrous effects on the sugar market. I do not comment on the economic policy here indicated, though I have explained to the ministers my own grave doubts about certain features, but they are committed to the policy in agreement with Bihar, and the question is whether the issue of an ordinance for this limited period would or would not be justifiable. Some of the ministers are obviously doubtful whether it would be justifiable, and the proposal for the issue of an ordinance on this point will not go forward unless a reasonably good case can be made out. If the ministers do press for this, I do not think I could raise any objection.

3. In the second place, it is suggested to include in the ordinance the provision in clause 29 of the Bihar Bill for a tax on the sale of cane, or the levy of a cess on entry of cane into a local area. I pointed out the strong objections in principle to imposing taxation by ordinance.[61] These were I think appreciated, and the arguments in favour of proceeding with this provision by means of an ordinance appeared to me to be rather slight and, I hope, on further examination, will not be pressed. Admittedly, it would give a month's more revenue, but this hardly seems an adequate ground for proceeding by ordinance. An argument based on the difference in cost price of cane between Bihar and the United Provinces, if this tax were in force in Bihar and not in the United Provinces, seems to me to have very little substance in it.

4. Apart, however, from this general question of whether there is really any justification for dealing with this matter by ordinance, I pointed out that it appeared to me that under Section 88 (1), proviso (*b*) of the Government of India Act, I could not agree to such an ordinance without instructions from the Governor-General. My argument was that the legal validity of the proposed tax seemed to be a matter of doubt, and it was not

clear whether the Government of India would hold that it was in effect a trespass on their right of levying excise. In those circumstances it seemed to me that I might have to reserve the Bill when passed for consideration of the Governor-General in respect of this point, and that therefore I could not without his instructions agree to the issue of an ordinance. It was agreed that though in the Bihar Bill the rate of tax is described as not exceeding 6 pies a maund, as the intention at present is only to levy 3 pies a maund, the provision in the ordinance would be for only 3 pies a maund.

5. I undertook to write to Your Excellency informally on this matter at once and ascertain whether it was likely that objection would be taken by you to the issue of an ordinance covering the provisions of clause 29 of the Bihar Bill, but providing for a tax of 3 pies and not 6 pies a maund.[62] My own feeling is that there would be no real justification for proceeding by ordinance in this matter. But of course the point which Your Excellency will have to consider is whether you would object on legal grounds. Possibly the matter is already being taken up with Hallett in connection with the Bihar Bill.[63]

Yours sincerely,
HARRY HAIG

119

HAIG TO LINLITHGOW
MSS.EUR.F. 125/127

Secret *December 7th, 1937*
No. U.P.-35

My dear Lord Linlithgow,

With reference to my secret letter No. U.P.-18, dated November 10th, 1937 on the subject of the grant of titles, the Premier informed me yesterday that he wished to raise the matter formally at our next cabinet meeting which will be taking place in Allahabad possibly on the 13th December, but more probably on the 18th. I should be grateful if Your Excellency could let me have any preliminary indication of your views before the cabinet meeting.[64]

Yours sincerely,
H.G. HAIG

120

HAIG TO LINLITHGOW
R/3/1/2

Secret *December 9th, 1937*
No. U.P.-37

My dear Lord Linlithgow,

I returned from Cawnpore to Lucknow on the morning of December 2nd, and I have given Your Excellency in my letter No. U.P.-31, dated 2nd December, a full account of my judgement of the position at Cawnpore and the steps which might be taken to produce a real improvement. As I have since informed you by telegram, Pant's attitude to the action taken by the District Magistrate seems to be satisfactory, and he appears to be prepared to support it, though I have since heard that he is likely to be heavily attacked on this subject at a party meeting which is being held on the 9th December. I fear the Left Wing will attack him at this meeting on a number of points.[65] On the other hand, I think a good many Congressmen themselves have been rather shaken by the recent developments in Cawnpore and particularly the dangerous communal feeling. I have been a little dis-appointed in his attitude to my suggestions for trying to produce a real improvement in labour conditions. He admits that in principle I am right, but he seems to be proposing to set about things in a very tentative and gradual way.[66] He recognises the necessity of strengthening the committee of enquiry, but prefers not to reconstitute it at present. For some reason, which has not been apparent to me, he seems to shrink from having a judicial officer of standing at its head. Nor is he inclined at present to convert it into a definite court of enquiry under the Trade Disputes Act.

2. I have kept Your Excellency in touch with the developments in the matter of the prosecution of Parmanand, and particularly the complications introduced by the arrest of Parmanand in Delhi. The ministers have not yet made up their minds what attitude they are going to adopt towards the prosecution. A warrant for the arrest of Parmanand has already been issued by the District Magistrate of Dehra Dun. The Premier mentioned to me again two days ago the question of the release of our remaining political prisoners, but I think he did so more with the idea of obtaining a reiteration of my views than of pressing me to reconsider them. I told him that my opinion remained as before, and that I felt that the question of releasing

any more political prisoners should not be considered in present conditions. He did not press the point.

3. I continue to be hopeful that the police situation will gradually improve. Both the Premier and Dr. Katju in recent speeches have adopted a far more friendly attitude to the services generally and the police in particular than has been the case before, and I think they are genuinely anxious that there should be no weakening of the police. I think this development is in part due to the views I have been pressing on them ever since my note of the 3rd November[67] was written, and in part to the much more cordial relations which now exist between the Premier and the Inspector-General of Police. When a conference of Deputy Inspectors-General of Police was taking place recently in Lucknow, the Premier came there and addressed them, and I understand that the feeling on both sides was satisfactory. The Premier altogether seems to be now realising much more definitely his responsibility for the police and their welfare.

4. The time for collection of rents has now arrived. Collections appear to be starting very slowly, but the ministers still maintain a generally optimistic view about their payment.[68] We discussed the whole question in some detail recently at a cabinet meeting. In the west of the Province I myself think it is probable that the rents will normally be paid. In the east there may be more difficulty. In any case there is likely to be some holding back of rents until the tenancy policy of the government has been declared. There are still many of the smaller Congress workers who are assuring the villagers that they will not have to pay their current rents in full. The ministers are very anxious to conclude as early as possible the work of the tenancy committee and to be able to reach their conclusions and announce them. I hope they will be able to announce conclusions early in January.

5. I forgot to mention in my last letter that I had actually had one of my ministers informally to a meal. This was Mrs. Pandit, who really appears to show no kind of reluctance in this matter. She had been attending a Red Cross meeting at Government House which went on till nearly lunch time, and at the end of the meeting I asked her whether she would stay on to lunch and she agreed quite readily.

6. I have just issued a statement about Her Excellency Lady Linlithgow's Anti-Tuberculosis Appeal, of which I enclose a copy.[69] The ministers agreed to the terms of this, which I think are satisfactory. I had some talk with Pant about it. I asked him in particular whether he would have any objection to district officers forming local committees for collection of funds. He said that normally he did not like the idea. But I think in fact he

will agree. I also suggested to him that possibly Mrs. Pandit might become President of our appeal committee. This idea seemed to him quite suitable, and he promised to speak to her on the subject. I have also mentioned it to her, and I think she will probably be prepared to undertake it, if the ministers generally agree. If so, it will be an excellent arrangement. She is of course the Minister In-charge of Medical and Public Health.

7. At the last cabinet meeting some very comprehensive proposals for making a start with prohibition were put up.[70] They were stated to involve a possible loss of revenue of some 32 lakhs, but the estimates were little more than guess-work and the actual loss might even be appreciably greater. As there were various points that really required some further and closer consideration, I got the cabinet to agree to postpone the matter till our meeting next week in Allahabad. It seems to me clear, however, that they are determined to embark on a very definite policy of temperance, enforcing a number of general restrictions and tightening up the conditions of sale generally, and at the same time to try an experiment of prohibition in several districts. The Premier evidently feels that owing to this policy and to a number of other adverse factors, our financial position, even with the aid of the income-tax receipts which we are hoping to get, will not be satisfactory, and he mentioned to me two days ago that he might have to consider once more the question of a cut in the pay of the services. He has not got any definite ideas in mind at present, but merely told me this for my information. I told him that it was clearly a matter which would require my[71] very anxious consideration, and we left it at that.

8. I am sorry to say that the cabinet have made up their minds practically to terminate the functions of the existing honorary magistrates and honorary assistant collectors. The matter has been under consideration for some time. With regard to honorary magistrates, certain new rules have been framed laying down qualifications, methods of appointment, and so on. I had hoped that they would agree to continue without a break those honorary magistrates who fulfilled the conditions they desired, which would not, I think, have been a negligible number. But they are determined to have a complete break and then reappoint men under the new conditions. Consequently they are issuing orders that both in the case of honorary magistrates and honorary assistant collectors no more work should be sent to them after a date about the end of the year, and they will then take steps as early as possible to appoint a much smaller number. There has no doubt been a great deal of public criticism of the work of honorary magistrates, and one cannot say that the action that is being taken is

altogether without justification. But of course it will be a great further cause of depression to the old-fashioned loyalists, and the landlords.

Yours sincerely,
H.G. HAIG

121

HAIG TO LINLITHGOW
R/3/1/2

Secret *December 10th, 1937*
No. U.P.-38

My dear Lord Linlithgow,

In continuation of my letter No. U.P.-37, dated the 9th December, the fortnightly D.O. letter from the provincial government which ordinarily accompanies my report was not ready, and I send it now.[72] In accordance with standing orders, I do not see the draft when I am on tour. I think I ought to let you know that the following passage in paragraph 4 of the report on the agrarian situation seems to me very much too optimistic: "The agrarian situation has perceptibly improved. There are still some apprehensions among the Zamindars in some places about rent collections, but it is now expected that on the whole there will be no serious difficulty." The whole of this paragraph was inserted by the Premier to replace a somewhat alarming paragraph drafted by the Chief Secretary which started with the words: "The reports from Commissioners show a growing anxiety about rent and revenue collections." My own position is rather midway between the two. I think, as I have said in my letter of December 9th, it is probable that in the west of the Province rents will normally be paid. In the east, however, I think there may be very considerable difficulty. In the Gorakhpur district, which I have just visited, it is clear that the payment of rent is going to be a serious problem, and in the Allahabad district also official anticipations are gloomy. The critical time will be in January when the government policy about tenancy reform and arrears of rent has been announced.[73]

Yours sincerely,
HARRY HAIG

122

HAIG TO LINLITHGOW
Draft Telegram (Not Sent)[74]
MSS.EUR.F. 115/15

December 10th, 1937

Addressed Governor-General repeated Secretary of State. Reference my telegram G-86, dated December 7th. At party meeting on 9th December Pant made it clear that he intended to support action of District Magistrate of Cawnpore, and after much discussion the party accepted his view. This is to my mind a development of great importance, for it shows that the ministry are prepared to take firm action and can get the party to support them.

2. The case of Parmanand was also discussed though somewhat briefly. Pant has sent me a message through Chief Secretary who has just arrived in Allahabad. He says that the members of the party agreed that the speech was very bad and that if anything of the sort were repeated prosecution must be undertaken. Pant's own position is that he is very strongly impressed by the undesirability of any open disagreement between himself and me which he thinks would have a most damaging effect from the point of view of administration, the services and the public generally, and might make his own position very difficult. In order to avoid such a position he would be prepared to accept responsibility for having ordered Parmanand's prosecution provided use is made of the Delhi arrest not to proceed with the sedition case. His suggestion appears to be that a communiqué should be published saying that the government had ordered this prosecution but in view of the Delhi prosecution they did not propose to proceed. At the same time they would wish to make it clear that the fact that prosecution had been ordered constituted a serious public warning and they were not proceeding with the prosecution only on the definite understanding that if similar offence were repeated the prosecution would be carried out. He is confident apparently that the party would back him up on this and would like to make a public statement to this effect.

3. The advantages of this course of action are very great, as indicated in later part of para. 3 of my telegram of December 7th. I am myself satisfied that this would be adequate to control our situation and indeed that a very great point will have been gained by such a public announcement by the government coupled with their firm attitude in regard to Cawnpore. The only difficulty would be the practical ones indicated in my telegram of

December 7th. If there is any reasonable assurance that Parmanand will be sentenced even to three months' imprisonment I think it would be possible to issue orders for suspension of sedition case and then immediately on his sentence in Delhi issue the communication withdrawing the sedition charge. Position has been complicated by press telegram of which I have just heard alleging in detail disagreement between myself and Premier over this matter and probability of Premier's resignation. This is being contradicted. Pant will come to Allahabad tomorrow to see me and I should like to be in a position to settle matter with him.

123

HAIG TO LINLITHGOW
Telegram
MSS.EUR.F. 115/15

Clear the Line *December 12th, 1937*
No. 89-G

Addressed Governor-General repeated Secy. of State. Reference your telegram 1453-G dated December 10th[75] and Secretary of State's telegram No. 2927 dated December 11th. On December 10th the Chief Secretary who had arrived in Allahabad for investiture brought me a message from Pant. It was to the effect that the case of Parmanand had been discussed somewhat briefly in the Party meeting on the 9th. I understand that the members of the Party agreed that the speech was very bad and that if anything of the sort were repeated prosecution must be undertaken. Pant's own position is that he is very strongly impressed by the undesirability of any open disagreement between himself and me from every point of view and that it might make his own position very difficult. In order to avoid such a position he would be prepared to accept responsibility for having ordered Parmanand's prosecution provided use was made of the Delhi arrest not to proceed with the sedition case. He was apparently prepared to state publicly in explicit terms that if similar offence were repeated prosecution would be carried out, and he was confident that the party would back him up on this.

I wrote to him on December 11th with reference to the message that I had been considering the whole position very carefully but the difficulties in any solution on those lines appeared to me very serious. There would be no public justification for not proceeding with the prosecution unless it was clear that Parmanand was receiving a very substantial sentence in

Delhi. Of that there was not much probability and it could not be known for a considerable time what the final sentence on him would be. This made it to my mind almost impossible to withdraw or suspend proceedings against Parmanand on the ground of the Delhi case. I said I quite appreciated that he would regard the effect of a serious and public warning of this nature as being considerable. I feared however that the public judgment would rather fasten on the point that the government had ordered the prosecution and then on grounds which seemed inadequate had withdrawn from it; in other words that the impression produced would be one of vacillation rather than determination, and I said in conclusion that the more I thought over the matter the more I felt that the only safe course was to go through with the prosecution.

2. I have received this morning a reply from Pant in which he says that the case is causing him great anxiety. As he had indicated at Cawnpore the matter involves several far-reaching issues of great importance. He goes on: "I have also since consulted some of the leading members of the Congress Working Committee and they take a serious view of it. The ministers have in the interval been trying to discharge their duties without giving any cause for public concern, but I am afraid serious developments are likely to ensue if no way out of the difficulty is found. I shall be grateful if you will give further thought to the matter."

3. Pant is coming to Allahabad for the convocation tomorrow and I shall see him in the morning. I intend to maintain my position which I agree is the only course possible. It looks to me as if Nehru may have stiffened him up considerably.

124

HAIG TO LINLITHGOW
MSS.EUR.F. 115/15

Secret *December 13th, 1937*
No. U.P.-40

[Dear Lord Linlithgow,]

With reference to correspondence ending with your telegram No. 408-GC, dated December 12th, on the subject of Parmanand's prosecution, I had a long conversation with Pant this morning. Regarding the merits of the question we went over much of the old ground, and he stressed once more his objection in principle to prosecuting without giving a previous warning. He said that if a previous warning were given, he would not shrink from prosecution, and considered that he would have no difficulty in justifying his position to his followers. He definitely repudiated the suggestion that while a system of warning would put off action, there would be the same difficulty and reluctance to take that action when a warning was disregarded. He pressed again the opportunity afforded by the Delhi case to confine action against Parmanand to a warning which, in his view, in the light of the fact that prosecution would have actually been ordered, would be taken as a serious indication of the intentions of the ministry.

2. I indicated that I did not see any possibility of a solution on these lines, and I invited him to discuss the possibilities of the situation in the event of my insisting that the prosecution must proceed. He said that there were three possibilities:

(1) that he would accept responsibility for the action;
(2) that he would disclaim responsibility and make it clear that the responsibility was mine and that the ministers did not agree;
(3) that the ministry would resign.

3. He felt very strong objection to course No. (2). He said that it would have a most damaging effect from the point of view of the administration, the services, and the public generally, and would make his own position very difficult. Though he did not refer to the general policy of the Congress and put his views entirely on the basis of his own personal convictions in this matter, it does seem to me likely that the Congress would regard it as damaging to their position to have to admit that a Governor had used his special powers and that they had accepted the situation. In any case it seemed to me clear from what he said that he ruled this alternative out.

4. As between the other two, I put to him very definitely the effect of the termination of all the fruitful activities which were now being pursued by the Congress ministers, and the incalculable results on the province of a breakdown of the constitution which would presumably follow from his resignation. He said that he fully realised all these things, that he had been thinking about them constantly, and that he would not take any rash decision. But he left me with a very clear impression that this possibility is certainly not one to be ruled out. I do not think that if he took this action he would be taking it at the instance of the Working Committee, but as a result of his own convictions and policy. I had thought before I saw him that he might be bluffing, but I formed a very clear view from our conversations today that he was not bluffing nor threatening and that he

might, in spite of all the consequences, finally decide on this course of action.

5. I put it to him that the occasion for producing such far-reaching consequences seemed quite out of proportion to the results that would ensue, and I tried to get from him his real objection to proceeding with the prosecution. I asked him definitely whether he anticipated serious trouble with his followers. He said that if this meant, would they pass a vote of no-confidence in him, the answer was No, but that there was a large body of fluid opinion between the right and left wings that would be influenced against him by this prosecution, and that his position for the future would become decidedly weaker and that later on the results would make themselves apparent. He also referred to the action which he has publicly supported in Cawnpore, which of course has been most satisfactory and has definitely improved the general situation and produced a much needed impression that the ministry are prepared to deal with a serious menace to order. He said that while his followers would swallow one thing, they would be naturally reluctant to swallow two. I could not make up my mind whether his difficulty about accepting responsibility for the prosecution is primarily one of his own personal convictions, which are undoubtedly very strong and on which he seems prepared to act with some disregard of consequences, or whether he is worried about his followers, and even at the end of our conversation I could not fully realise why he shrunk so much from a prosecution without warning. He told me he had had all these things in his mind when he saw me at Cawnpore, but that it was a weakness of his to understate his position.

6. I did not absolutely and finally tell him that I could under no circumstances agree to the case being withdrawn in the event of a substantial sentence at Delhi, though I gave him clearly to understand that I did not see any possibility of doing so. He is staying here till the 16th and I shall have to have a further conversation with him before he leaves. I asked him whether he had talked all these things out with the other ministers. He said he had consulted them in a general way, but had not put the issues to them quite as starkly as they were discussed between us. Nehru arrives in Allahabad tomorrow evening, and undoubtedly he will consult him on the 15th and 16th. I thought it desirable to let Your Excellency know the position in as full detail as possible at once. I do not think I am misjudging the situation when I say that it seems to me there is a very definite possibility that he will resign, even though to us the grounds would appear most inadequate. One of the points that seemed to worry him was the possibility of being landed in other prosecutions. I told him that in my judgment if

this prosecution were carried through and certain other warnings were given, we should create an impression which would discourage further speeches of this type, and that was one of the reasons why I felt it was so important to take firm action at this stage, as otherwise the situation might steadily deteriorate. He was, however, I think, definitely nervous that bad speeches might continue to be made, and that he would be gradually drawn into a policy of extensive prosecutions. I do not myself anticipate such a development.

7. As there is a possibility that within a week or ten days the ministry may resign I must consider at once with Your Excellency the action required in that event.

Yours sincerely,
H.G. HAIG

125

HAIG TO LINLITHGOW
MSS.EUR.F. 115/15

Secret
No. U.P.-41

Governor's Camp,
December 14th, 1937

My dear Lord Linlithgow,

With reference to para. 7 of my secret letter No. U.P.-40, dated December 13th, I put down certain ideas which have occurred to me regarding action in the event of the ministry resigning.

2. *Issue of Statement.* I shall have to issue a full statement as quickly as possible explaining the course of events which have led up to the crisis. I should propose to start from the release of the ex-Kakori prisoners and the general policy of relaxation of control followed by the ministry, with its effects on the province generally. As the statement would be of great importance, I should like, if Your Excellency thinks it would be advisable, to send you the draft in advance for any comments or suggestions you may have.

3. *Attempt to Form Alternative Government.* Apart from the Congress Party[76] there are two other parties in the Legislature:

(*a*) a miscellaneous party headed by the Nawab of Chhatari;
(*b*) the Muslim League party.

I am not familiar with the exact strength of these, but I think Chhatari's party is probably slightly the larger. I do not think there is the least possibility of either of these or the two in combination being prepared, or able, to form a ministry, but I presume it would be right for me to send for the leaders of each of these parties separately and ask them whether they are prepared to form the government.[77]

4. *Issue of Proclamation.* On the failure to form an alternative Government, it will be necessary for me to issue at once the Draft Proclamation under Section 93(1) assuming all powers to myself.

5. *Advisers.* As I intimated to Your Excellency when the matter was under discussion before, I should propose to appoint two Advisers on a salary of Rs. 4,000/- each.

6. *Draft Ordinance.* It is not clear what line the Congress would take immediately in the event of the ministry resigning. There will probably be some lull during which they would be deciding on their policy and making preparations for carrying it out. It would, I think, be very inadvisable for us during this period to take action which could justly be criticised as provocative. If they are to go into extreme courses, it must be clear that their action was voluntary and has not been forced upon them. Moreover, the Ordinance presupposes, I understand, the existence of an emergency, and it would not be justifiable to issue it until a definite situation had arisen. I should, however, propose to proceed at once with the consideration of the practical steps that would be required if a situation arose justifying the issue of the Ordinance.

7. *Immediate Dangers.* Even without a definite decision on the part of Congress to launch a revolutionary movement, the situation might require special action under the following heads in particular:

(*a*) *The Activities of Communists.* I am inclined to think that though we have no special legislation enabling us to detain such persons we could probably deal with them effectively under our existing powers. This, however, is a view which will require to be considered very carefully with my officers.

(*b*) *A No-Rent Campaign.* There is already a very general reluctance of tenants to pay rent and in some parts of the province even the exhortations of my present government may very possibly not be fully effective in securing that rent will be paid. If the ministry resign, it seems to me almost certain that the Congress workers in villages will, without necessarily any direction from above, intensify their exhortations to the villagers not to pay rent, and a serious situation might develop rapidly. Indeed this is probably the way in which the conflict with Congress would start. We have under our Special Powers Act of 1932 certain powers for dealing with a no-rent campaign. Whether these would be fully adequate, I cannot at the moment say. But as soon as there were clear signs of the development of a no-rent campaign on a large scale, I think it is likely that the Draft Ordinance would be required at once.

8. *General Policy Towards Congress.* There are likely to be considerable embarrassments in deciding on the attitude to be taken towards Jawaharlal Nehru, and all India considerations of importance would be involved. But it is clear that trouble with Congress cannot be handled without involving Nehru vitally.

Yours sincerely,
[H.G. HAIG]

126

HAIG TO LINLITHGOW
Telegram
MSS.EUR.F. 115/15

Clear the Line *December 15th, 1937*
No. 92-G

Addressed Governor-General repeated Secy. of State. Reference your telegram 414-GC dated December 15th.[78] I see Your Excellency bases your view about action to be taken on the general situation in the U.P. I feel I must make my view about this quite plain. When I took the responsibility of ordering the prosecution of Parmanand the situation in my opinion was definitely alarming. Parmanand and the ex-Kakori prisoners had been for a month touring in the east of the province making violent speeches which were said to be producing appreciable local effect. They had then transferred their activities to the west of the province and the speeches were continuing in one district after another with apparently increasing virulence, for the Dehra Dun speech was the worst that had been reported. In addition the speeches on anti-police day at Cawnpore had been of a most dangerous character and the fact that no action was being taken against all these speeches was in my judgement producing an impression that the ministry would not take any effective steps to stop these dangerous developments. It seemed to me essential to remove that impression before it went too far. My discussion with the cabinet left me with the belief that they were not prepared when it came to the point to take any effective action on their own responsibility. You may remember that in para. 4 of my letter No. U.P. 31, dated December 2nd about the Cawnpore situation, I indicated my general view that it looked as if the cabinet were not prepared to act against the views of the Left Wing without some species of compulsion. It was on the basis of this estimate of the situation and those conditions that I felt it essential to insist on the prosecution of Parmanand.

2. Since then the situation has very markedly changed for the better. So far as the revolutionary speeches are concerned I made my view of this clear in para. 2 of my telegram No. G-86 dated December 7th. The arrest of Parmanand and the other ex-Kakori prisoners who were precisely the men who had been going round making these revolutionary speeches immediately put a check to one of the most dangerous features of the situation, namely, the unchecked continuance of these speeches. If they are sentenced even to three months imprisonment the effect on our general situation is bound to be decidedly good.[79]

3. Another very important development has been the Cawnpore situation. This arose after I had taken my action about Parmanand. I was clear that the situation which developed at Cawnpore after the murder was one which had to be gripped firmly at once. I was not sure what attitude Pant would take and I felt it might be necessary to bring the strongest pressure to bear on him in this matter. His attitude however proved to be on this point far more satisfactory than I had anticipated. Without direct pressure from me he determined to support the action of the District Magistrate. He faced his party meeting on December 9th on this point and in spite of a good deal of criticism carried them with him. As indicated in my letter No. U.P. 40, dated December 13th, I regard this action as having definitely improved the general situation in the province and produced a much needed impression that the Ministry are prepared to deal with a serious menace to order.

4. It is against that background, which is substantially different to the general situation prevailing at the end of November when I took my action about Parmanand, that we have to consider the justification for allowing matters perhaps to proceed to a crisis the full effects of which cannot be foreseen. Admittedly, the ministry would seem to be on very weak ground in resigning on a point that would appear small compared with the issues involved. On the other hand the argument could equally be turned against us, and it might be said that, in view of the general improvement in the

situation and particularly the indication that the ministry had given in the case of Cawnpore that they were prepared if necessary to take firm action, we by insisting on our original position were premeditating a crisis on inadequate grounds.

5. With regard to Your Excellency's anticipations about Pant's attitude to any future prosecutions he assured me positively more than once that he would be prepared to prosecute an individual if a warning had been given and was disregarded. I certainly do not think he would agree to prosecution following on a general warning, but at the present time I do not think it would be necessary to insist on that. It was decided that subject to detailed examination individual warning would be given to about six of Parmanand's companions who had been making intemperate speeches, and if this band of speakers is effectively curbed I do not think that the general situation in the province at present would call for any more drastic action.

6. Bearing all these points in mind the question is what would be the effect of withdrawal of Parmanand's prosecution on the general situation in the province. As I indicated at the end of para. 3 of my telegram No. G-86, dated December 7th, I attach special importance to it being made clear to people in general that the government do not propose to tolerate speeches of this kind, and if the cabinet themselves accepted responsibility for having actually ordered prosecution and coupled this with a plain statement that while the Delhi case removed the immediate necessity for action against Parmanand, they were not proceeding with the prosecution only after reaching a definite decision that if a similar offence were repeated prosecution would be carried out, this combined with their firm attitude about Cawnpore would have a definitely reassuring effect on the situation, and I am inclined to think would not produce that impression of vacillation which I suggested to Pant, vide my telegram G-89, dated December 12th, might be produced by a withdrawal.

7. If you agree that this course of action could be contemplated it would be possible to stop proceedings in the sedition case being initiated in Court until after the 22nd December, and if then Parmanand were sentenced to three months imprisonment the prosecution might on that basis be withdrawn.

8. I have not had any further conversation with Pant since I wrote my letter to you, No. U.P. 40, dated December 13th. He and certain other members of the cabinet will be considering their position today with Nehru who has now returned to Allahabad. I do not expect to see Pant again till tomorrow. It is possible they may not be prepared to face the extreme

course of resignation. In that case I could of course hold them to the prosecution. At the same time if I were to judge that they feel their position acutely and attach really vital importance to not proceeding I should be glad to know whether you would agree to my meeting them on this point. The matter might have a very important effect on my general future relations with my ministers. If on the other hand Pant indicates that their objection is so strong that they are prepared to face resignation I feel I could still agree to a withdrawal of the prosecution on the conditions indicated above without loss of face so far as he is concerned and without letting him feel that my action is a direct result of his decision if necessary to resign. I have still kept my final attitude open as shown in my letter of December 13th.

9. I should be grateful if it were possible to let me have by tomorrow your views on this telegram.

127

HAIG TO LINLITHGOW
Telegram
MSS.EUR.F. 115/15

Clear the Line *December 17th, 1937*
No. 94-G

Many thanks for your telegram No. 424-GC, dated December 16th.[80] I shall see Pant morning 18th and handle situation to best of my judgement in accordance with general line of our correspondence. I do not rule out possibility of being able to hold him to prosecution, but I feel it necessary to have alternative line as discussed between us.

2. I have of course always been very conscious of practical difficulties of withdrawing proceedings on basis of Delhi case and I am aware that developments in Delhi might make such a course practically impossible.

3. With reference to para. 1(*b*) of your telegram what I said in my telegram G-86 of December 7th was that six months was about the minimum which might justify our not proceeding. In writing to Pant, vide my telegram G-89, dated December 12th, I naturally stressed the difficulties and stated the position more strongly. On merits I still consider that sentence of six months would ease the position greatly, but in a matter which is out of our control I feel that difference between six months and three would not be sufficient to justify facing a serious crisis.

4. It is not the case that warnings have actually been given to Kakori prisoners. I hoped I had made this plain in para. 5 of my telegram G-92 of December 15th. Papers about contemplated warning have just reached me. They would not seem to justify action in more than four out of six cases, but I should propose to hold Pant to this as part of any settlement.

5. I quite appreciate advantages of getting public assurance from Parmanand that he will not repeat his offence, and I will certainly take this up with Pant. I have considerable doubt whether Parmanand would give such an assurance and of course, if we demand it and he refuses, it would hardly be possible after that to withdraw proceedings. I feel therefore I have to go a little cautiously about this. I would of course sound Pant as to his attitude if Parmanand refuses to give such an assurance – vide your para. 3.

6. As proceedings in Delhi are down for December 22nd case against Parmanand would naturally not be taken up in Dehra Dun till after Xmas holidays. This gives us a little spare time which may be useful.

128

HAIG TO LINLITHGOW
Telegram
MSS.EUR.F. 115/15

Clear the Line *December 18th, 1937*
No. 95-G

My telegram G-94, dated December 17th. I saw Pant this morning. He has barely recovered from his fever and possibly on that account seemed in a state of considerable mental perturbation. He said he felt he had been wrong in not making his position plain at a much earlier stage. It was clear that he is not prepared either to accept responsibility for going through with the prosecution or to disclose difference of opinion and remain in office. He says he has discussed the position with very few people and I get the impression again that his attitude is primarily his own.

2. He would be quite prepared to put out a statement on following lines which are satisfactory to me, making it clear that the government have been disturbed for some time about these speeches, that they had taken action on the 9th November to give a warning which miscarried, that they decided on the 27th November that a stop must be put to the continuance of these speeches and that prosecution against Parmanand should be instituted, that the sentence in Delhi automatically puts a stop for a time

to his activities and they do not feel in the circumstances it is necessary to proceed with the case against him, but that they make it clear that they cannot tolerate a repetition of such speeches and if Parmanand repeats a speech of this nature they will have no hesitation in ordering his prosecution. They would also emphasise their realisation of the necessity of preventing the creation of any atmosphere of violence. This is not to be taken as a definite draft, but he said he would have no difficulty about agreeing to a statement on these lines. He is also prepared to administer warning to about six speakers whose speeches have included definite incitement to violence and would be prepared if necessary to prosecute them if they subsequently offended. He is quite properly anxious to make sure that the material justifies the warning, but he is prepared to go outside the original list of six names as he says that there are one or two speakers who in his opinion have made more dangerous speeches than those whose speeches have been hitherto examined.

3. I put to him the great advantages of getting an assurance from Parmanand. He is clearly of opinion that Parmanand would not give such an assurance, which in the circumstances would be regarded as showing lack of courage when faced with prosecution. He said that Parmanand might possibly give an assurance under different conditions but not in these circumstances. He felt it would not strengthen his position in going on with the prosecution if Parmanand had refused to give such an assurance, for the demand would be felt by the public he has to consider to have been an unfair one. I returned to this point more than once, but he was firm about it.

4. His information is that Parmanand has made no application to the High Court and is not defending himself and that each case is being taken up separately. He is therefore under the impression that Parmanand will be sentenced on the 22nd. It would of course be an essential part of a settlement on these lines that Parmanand should be sentenced to not less than three months imprisonment.

5. If Parmanand is sentenced on the 22nd to three months imprisonment or more, then a statement could be put out withdrawing proceedings against him in the sedition case. I strongly recommend that this course should be adopted. I have given the most anxious consideration to the points made in Your Excellency's telegram 424-GC of December 16th. But so far as the general situation in this province is concerned I am prepared to take the responsibility for holding that it does not in present circumstances necessitate action beyond what I propose. So far as Parliament is concerned I think it is relevant to remember that the constitutional position as emerg-

ing from such a settlement would be that the cabinet have accepted responsibility for ordering the prosecution, that they have now advised me not to proceed with it on certain conditions and that I have to decide whether I am justified in refusing to accept that advice. It is not as if I am directly on my own responsibility withdrawing the proceedings, which obviously I could not do.

6. I should be grateful for earliest possible instructions in this matter. Pant's state is such that it is clearly most desirable to put him out of suspense as early as possible, and in any case the prolongation of the crisis is very embarrassing. Action of course cannot be taken till after 22nd December. But I should be glad if I could tell Pant that assuming the anticipated sentence in Delhi the matter could be settled on these lines.

129

HAIG TO LINLITHGOW
MSS.EUR.F. 125/132

No. U.P.-42 *December 19th, 1937*

My dear Lord Linlithgow,

I have read with great interest Your Excellency's letter of November 26th and its enclosure about the position of Parliamentary Secretaries.[81] It arrived at an opportune moment. Pant in a recent note to the Chief Secretary has shown some desire to entrust to Parliamentary Secretaries certain delegations of ministerial authority. I understand that the Parliamentary Secretaries have also been agitating for greater powers. Pant's object is to relieve ministers of some of the heavy burden of work which falls on them. The Parliamentary Secretaries naturally want to increase their own importance. The Chief Secretary has pointed out to him the constitutional obstacles to delegation, and the practice in England about the duties of Parliamentary Secretaries. Pant is still considering the question, but it is bound to come up in the cabinet before very long. The real answer to Pant's difficulties of course is that the number of ministers should be increased, but the dearth of Congress Muslims renders this no easy matter, quite apart from possible political embarrassments involved in altering the existing composition of the cabinet.

2. Ministers may be perfectly willing to accept in theory the proposition that a Parliamentary Secretary exercises no authority independent of his minister and that the minister can only delegate his administrative duties

to the permanent officials of his department. In practice, however, faced as they are with a very heavy legislative programme and at the same time a large number of reports and applications chiefly from their political supporters about alleged abuses, disputes, local calamities and various other matters which appear to demand local investigation, ministers tend to use their Parliamentary Secretaries as their deputies for any task which crops up which they cannot undertake themselves. They still lack confidence in their local official subordinates, and when an enquiry of any importance has to be made, they wish to associate with it someone who will look at the point in issue from the standpoint of their own political ideas.

3. The real difficulty has so far been found not in the relations of Parliamentary Secretaries with the Departmental Secretaries, but in those of Parliamentary Secretaries with local officials when the former have gone out on some roving commission of a political nature and have started enquiring into complaints locally. One early case was in the Gorakhpur district where the Parliamentary Secretary was sent down by his minister to enquire into complaints that flood relief was not being properly tackled by the district authorities. The case of the Jhansi enquiry mentioned in paragraph 3 of Your Excellency's letter of October 15th was a different one, as that was a formal joint enquiry set up by arrangement between Pant and myself into a serious situation in which political and administrative considerations were both involved. The enquiry had satisfactory results. A recent case has been reported to me where a Parliamentary Secretary visiting a district received complaints through the President of the District Congress Committee that adequate relief had not been allowed for damage to crops by failure of the monsoon and enquired into these locally in the presence of the S.D.O. and Tahsildar.

4. With the type of men we have chiefly got in this position, younger men than the ministers and with less experience, less contact with administration and a narrower view, it is difficult to establish sound conventions. Their ministers may be reluctant to call them to account, and in most cases their actions will not come to notice till some time after the event. It is often not known until some time afterwards whether they have been away on purely political and party business or on matters which concern the administration. The Departmental Secretaries who understand their position and who have immediate access to the minister, and who carry weight by reason of their ability and experience can keep them to their proper sphere, but local officials have more difficulty. I therefore hope to get the cabinet to agree to the issue of some instructions for the

guidance of the Parliamentary Secretaries themselves and of ministers and secretariat and local officials.

5. I hope that it may be possible to reach a satisfactory agreement about their functions, but should this not be possible, I have been considering whether there would be any power under Section 59(3) to issue suitable additions to the Secretariat Instructions made under the Rules of Executive Business, even though Parliamentary Secretaries are not mentioned in the Government of India Act. The expediency of doing so is another matter, but I should be glad of Your Excellency's advice on this point, as it might affect the tactics of the discussion.[82]

6. I attach a separate note which shows the existing position about Parliamentary Secretaries in this Province.

Yours sincerely,
H.G. HAIG

ENCLOSURE TO NO. 129

NOTE ON PARLIAMENTARY SECRETARIES IN THE UNITED PROVINCES

Undated

The position in this Province about Parliamentary Secretaries is at present as follows. They are 13 in number. Of these 12 are paid at the rate of Rs. 250 per mensem with Rs. 100 car allowance, while one does not accept any salary. Two are Muslims and two belong to the Scheduled Castes which are not represented in the ministry itself. Three Parliamentary Secretaries are attached to the Hon'ble Premier's departments. These include the Chief Whip of the Government Party. Three are attached to the Hon'ble Minister for Revenue, and two to each of the other Hon'ble Ministers, with the exception of the Hon'ble Minister for Communications and Irrigation who has only one. Two Parliamentary Secretaries are members of the Upper House and take a prominent part there in conducting government business as no minister is an elected member of that House. The remainder sit in the Legislative Assembly. At the time they were appointed the orders of the cabinet were that they were to perform administrative and legislative duties. They would help ministers in dealing with departmental cases, and call for information, but would not be in charge of a department or part of a department or intervene between the

Departmental Secretary and the minister. In practice, their duties have been as follows, although they have not as yet been laid down by rules:

A. LEGISLATIVE

(*i*) Questions. – They frequently read out the answers, already approved by Hon'ble Ministers, to questions asked and answer the supplementary questions arising from those answers. They therefore have to make themselves thoroughly familiar with the files dealing with the subjects raised in the questions so as to be able to answer supplementary questions adequately and in accordance with the policy of the Government.

(*ii*) To introduce or speak on Bills which are introduced by the government or to deal with Bills which may be introduced by private members.

(*iii*) To speak on resolutions. For this purpose it is essential that they should see official files so as to be aware of the policy of the government and the previous history of the case. They also have to keep in touch with feeling inside the House and keep their ministers well posted with information. They also assist the government whips in lobbying for support.

(*iv*) They have served on a number of Committees either appointed by the Legislature to enquire into matters of public importance or set up by the government and containing members of the Legislature. In particular several of them have taken a prominent part in the work of the Rent and Revenue Laws Amendment Committee and the Local Self-Government Laws Amendment Committee.

(*v*) In certain cases a Parliamentary Secretary has been employed to take up some general problem with which the ministry propose to deal and to study it in consultation with the administrative officials to see how far the general policy of the government can be applied to the actual facts and conditions prevailing so that definite proposals can be formulated. For example, the question of jail reform which the government wish to take up is at present being examined by the Parliamentary Secretary in consultation with the I.G. of Prisons. In this case the Parliamentary Secretary is to some extent acting as a substitute for the minister who has not time to devote to prepare his own proposals. There will thereafter be full departmental examination of the proposals made and the decision on them will be a decision of the cabinet.

(*vi*) Parliamentary Secretaries have done a good deal of visiting constituencies, especially those in which bye-elections are proceeding.

They have occasionally addressed public meetings and have also published contributions to the press on matters of public importance. They have also conveyed to the Congress organisations in certain districts the instructions of the ministry that rents must be paid; and have been used to attempt to settle communal and other disputes by use of political influence and organisation.

B. ADMINISTRATIVE

(*i*) Members of the present government receive a very large number of petitions every day direct from the districts. These are sent, for the most part, by members of the Congress party or members of District Congress Committees. They are received by Parliamentary Secretaries on behalf of the minister concerned, sorted out by them and passed on by them to the Secretariat, or to the authority concerned, for necessary action. A Parliamentary Secretary sometimes makes suggestions for action and sometimes intimates the Hon'ble Minister's order or opinion. He does not finally dispose of the cases.

(*ii*) A large number of visitors throng to the Secretariat every day in the hope of interviewing the Hon'ble Premier or other ministers. Many of these are now sent to a Parliamentary Secretary who in this way considerably relieves his Minister.

(*iii*) Occasionally the Parliamentary Secretary helps the minister with a file where the minister asks for his views. As a rule, the Parliamentary Secretary writes what would be described in the Secretariat as a routine note which is not placed on the file.

(*iv*) Parliamentary Secretaries have been used by the ministry in some cases for conducting local enquiries. This is a practice which appears undesirable, and needs full discussion with the cabinet.

C. RELATIONS WITH DEPARTMENTAL SECRETARIES

The relations of Parliamentary Secretaries with the Departmental Secretaries have on the whole been satisfactory, and their relative spheres are understood, although not so well understood by the public. A Parliamentary Secretary cannot authenticate the orders of the government. These must be communicated by Secretaries to government or officers similarly empowered, or in purely executive matters by the Heads of Departments. A Parliamentary Secretary is not entitled to correspond with the Executive Officers of government informing them what the policy of government is or giving them orders or stating the conclusions of government. Parliamentary Secretaries are perhaps at present inclined to take too much upon themselves, partly through ignorance of secretariat procedure and partly because they regard themselves as minor members of the government. They have, however, undoubtedly been able to relieve their ministers of a considerable burden of work with which it was absolutely necessary that they should have assistance.

D. RELATIONS WITH DISTRICT OFFICERS

In the case of District Officers the difficulties have been more apparent; and it is desirable that the position of Parliamentary Secretaries in regard to them should be more clearly defined. When Parliamentary Secretaries visit districts, they do so as envoys on behalf of the ministry with no power to issue instructions, to give orders, or to hold enquiry into the conduct of government servants. Their specific functions are to carry out the instructions given to them by the minister, and particularly to bring about settlements of disputes. The utmost that a Parliamentary Secretary might do by way of direct correspondence with a District Officer is to inform him of a proposed visit and the time of his arrival and to ask for his assistance and co-operation which should always be forthcoming.

130

HAIG TO LINLITHGOW
Telegram
MSS.EUR.F. 115/15

Express *December 21st, 1937*
No. 97-G

Your telegram 462-GC dated December 20th.[83] I will certainly try to get Pant to make as strong a general statement as possible about speeches advocating violence. On the other hand I think it is clear that in his present mood he would not be prepared to prosecute an individual following merely on a general warning. The crucial point in his present position is that the individual must have had a warning, and he is prepared as we see to go even to the length of resignation on this principle. On the other hand I am not seriously disturbed at present at the resulting situation. We are dealing with a comparatively small body of speakers acting on their own responsibility and not directed by any powerful organisation. I hope the measures now contemplated will result in effectively restraining the group. We need not look too far ahead, for Pant's views undoubtedly develop. For instance, two months ago he would not have agreed to the action at Cawnpore which he has recently endorsed.

131

HAIG TO LINLITHGOW
Telegram
MSS.EUR.F. 115/15

Clear the Line *December 23rd, 1937*
No. 99-G

Reference your telegram No. 488-GC of December 23rd.[84] I discussed briefly with Premier yesterday and at greater length this morning situation arising out of Delhi sentences. I told him that shortness of sentence passed on Parmanand made it difficult to go on with the compromise we had been contemplating. I urged him strongly to go through with the prosecution, pointing out that it was a very strong case, that he would be faced with difficulties at any time if he had to order a prosecution, and that having gone so far it seemed much wiser to take the final step. With reference to an indication which he had given me that his insistence on a previous warning was based on conclusions reached at the Calcutta meeting of the Congress Committee I said I could hardly believe that the Working Committee would desire to precipitate a crisis on such an issue.

2. I found him however quite firm in declining to go through with the prosecution. He argued that the government had originally decided to give a warning. When that miscarried and speeches were still being made in one district after another it might be held that there was justification for ordering immediate prosecution as only means of stopping the speeches. But Delhi arrests and sentences had effectively stopped them for time being and enabled warning to be given safely. In these circumstances he could not justify prosecuting without warning. In further discussion he made it clear that his primary objection was that this would be the first time that section 124A would be used by Congress ministry in this province, that it was not expected that the Congress ministry would use this section

and that to use it for the first time without any kind of warning was a position to which he could not reconcile himself. When I pressed him on the point which Your Excellency has raised several times that he might find himself in difficulty about agreeing to a prosecution even after warning, he expressed some resentment and said that if his word could not be trusted it was hardly possible for us to work together. I made it clear that I did not in any way distrust his word. But altogether he was showing a considerable degree of prickliness regarding his position as being primarily responsible for law and order. He pointed out that in today's paper it was announced that two students had been sentenced in Lucknow to two years' imprisonment on a charge of communism and that he had gone on with this case in spite of considerable pressure to withdraw it. He also referred to the action that is being taken in Cawnpore. It is clear to me that he is definitely not prepared to take responsibility for continuing prosecution against Parmanand and if I insist on this it looks to me as if his resignation would be inevitable.

3. I then explored possibility of going on with the compromise in spite of the small sentence. I said that any discussion on this point must be tentative, but that it seemed to me clear that if the case were now to be withdrawn the statement would require to be a very firm one. In particular I put it to him that it might help a good deal if it included a general warning that speeches of this kind would not be permitted and that government would hold themselves free to institute proceedings without further warning against any individual who offends in this manner. He did not reject the idea and appears prepared to consider it. We decided to meet again tomorrow.

4. I did not press him further about obtaining an assurance from Parmanand for it seems certain that Parmanand would not give such an assurance. Nor am I proposing at this stage to meet the cabinet. They would merely support the Premier's arguments. It would only be if we had definitely decided to insist on prosecution and I could tell them this, that there might be some very remote chance of influencing them against resignation.

5. With regard to my own views as distinct from case I put to Pant, (*a*) I would repeat that so far as any actual menace to the peace of the province at the present time is concerned I am satisfied that this would not arise, if a statement is published on lines of para. 2 of my telegram G-95 dated 18th December with such additional provisions about warning for the future as Pant can be got to accept, coupled with the assurance, which he has

already given me, that if speeches of this kind start again he will be prepared to prosecute. The main argument in the statement for dropping prosecution would be that immediate danger from continued repetition of speeches has been checked by these sentences, and this argument can still be used even with six weeks sentence on Parmanand; (*b*) this would be a particularly inopportune moment to break with the ministry on such an issue. They are right up against a first class issue on a vital administrative point (the payment of rent) between themselves and the Left Wing or their undisciplined followers. They are tackling this vigorously, for they know it affects the foundations of the administration. It would be a calamity if instead of this struggle between Right and Left, arising inevitably from their own policy and likely to have most far-reaching effects, we substitute a struggle between the Governor and the Congress on an issue which would be generally felt to be much smaller, and at a time when we should certainly be landed instantly in a no-rent campaign. We have reached a point at which the reaction of political forces to the system of responsible government is beginning to show itself vigorously and the main interest in the province is centred on economic issues and general problems of policy rather than on the old antagonisms between ruler and ruled, though certain elements are trying to stimulate the latter. The Congress use at once the language of revolution and reform, but there is a reasonable and I think growing chance that reform will predominate and the constitution justify itself.

6. I should be very grateful if I could have your views on this as early as possible tomorrow. I was leaving for Xmas camp this evening but have postponed my departure till evening of 24th. If I cancelled my camp it would give rise to widespread comment and everyone would conclude that there was a serious constitutional crisis. If there is any chance of a peaceful solution this would be a very great embarrassment. I am due back in Lucknow morning of 31st, but could of course if necessary come in without exciting undue comment a day or two earlier. Actual decision need not be taken till beginning of January. But obviously if there is to be settlement the earlier it is announced the better. If you agree to my attempting settlement on lines indicated in para. 5(*a*), which I am personally convinced would be much the wisest course, I should anticipate being able to get the matter to all intents and purposes settled before I leave on evening of 24th.[85]

132

HAIG TO LINLITHGOW
Telegram
MSS.EUR.F. 115/15

Clear the Line *December 23rd, 1937*
No. 100-G

Reference para. three my telegram G-99 dated December 23rd. Pant has informed me that he is prepared to include in statement following passage which I had suggested. *Begins.* "The Government wish to make it clear that the action taken in this matter must be understood as constituting a general warning that speeches of this kind will not be permitted, and having thus stated their position the Government hold themselves free to institute proceedings without any further warning against any individual who offends in this manner." *Ends.*[86]

133

HAIG TO LINLITHGOW
R/3/1/2

Secret Camp,
No. U.P.-44 *December 24th, 1937*

My dear Lord Linlithgow,

The main preoccupation of the last fortnight has been the crisis over Parmanand's prosecution about which I need say nothing in this letter. At the same time I think it may be useful if I give Your Excellency certain impressions about Pant's general position and attitude as arising from these difficulties. As I have explained previously, he has exceedingly strong personal convictions about democratic principles, and actions which circumstances force upon him which are in conflict with his general ideas of the liberty of the subject are extremely repugnant to him. His reluctance should not be attributed merely to fear of criticism; it represents in large part his convictions. In the second place, he has an exceedingly vigorous and troublesome Left Wing opposition. He is prepared, when in his judgement conditions require it, to face this opposition, and at present he can, when he faces it, beat it. This was shown in the attack made on him over his action taken at Cawnpore. But I think he had to exert all his authority on that occasion. I do not think therefore that there is any question, as Your Excellency suggests in your letter of 15th December, of his being heartened by this result.[87] He did not get, I should imagine, a great deal of willing support. He made the question one of confidence, and no one is prepared at present to try and displace him. But it would be unwise to suppose that he is not confronted with a very strong opposition, and one must realise that he cannot view with equanimity continual attacks upon his position. Finally, one has to consider his physical condition. The strain of the crisis over Parmanand taxed him severely, and when he went down with fever in Allahabad I was somewhat apprehensive that he might break down completely. He was in an emotional state. He has pulled himself together now, but he is still not the man he was a few weeks ago. He has been consistently overworking himself, and is faced with an almost endless series of difficulties. He has been standing up to it all in a way which commands admiration, and he is sustained by his generally optimistic temperament. But if he once begins to despair and feels that the task is too heavy for him, I fear he might collapse rapidly. That would produce a grave situation in the Province. It is the general opinion, and I share it, that there is no other right wing leader who would have the ability and authority to control the situation. I should probably before long find myself with a left wing cabinet and that would lead very rapidly to a breakdown.

2. While I was at Allahabad I had many discussions about Jawaharlal Nehru's attitude with those who come in contact with him not infrequently. There is no doubt that he is taking considerable pains to support Pant's government, even though it means contradicting a good many of his own previous activities. He threw in all his weight at Cawnpore to discourage further labour agitation. It was his action which brought the Allahabad University students under control, and enabled the jubilee celebrations to go through successfully. While I was in Allahabad he attended a very large gathering of peasants near there and, I understand, told them that they must pay their rents. The proceedings started with a resolution declaring that the zamindari system should be abolished and concluded with a resolution saying that rents must be paid. Even in the case of Parmanand his public reference to the matter was clearly intended to save the government from embarrassment. The reason for these activities appears to be that Nehru is convinced that the continuance of the Congress government in office is strengthening the hold of the Congress on the Province, and there I think he is quite right. Congress prestige stands very high and is all-pervasive. It may be that Nehru looks upon this as a preliminary stage to a revolutionary situation. On the other hand, I do not

think we ought to be afraid of this situation. We are playing for high stakes and we must take certain risks. We need not assume that Nehru's judgement is necessarily correct and that the situation in fact will work out as he may wish. The longer the Congress government remain in office, the more deeply does it become involved in administrative problems and policies and the more do the ordinary reactions of political forces come into play. Dissensions will arise, disillusionment in many respects will spread, and my own view is that a year hence, if the Congress government remain in office, the Congress will not command the same degree of popular support which it does at present.

3. The question of payment of rents remains the crucial issue in the Province at the moment, and during the fortnight the ministry have come to realise more clearly the necessity for vigorous action on their part. The communiqué[88] which they have issued and to which the widest publicity is being given is attached to the demi-official fortnightly report. The clash of policy between the official Congress organisation and the Kisan Sabhas is becoming more pronounced. I have no doubt at all that the ministry fully realise how vital this matter is for them and that they are by their own methods making every effort to secure that rents are paid. With reference to Your Excellency's suggestion in paragraph 5 of your letter of December 15th about progress reports, the system is being introduced which prevailed during the no-rent campaign, in accordance with which the available figures are reported by Commissioners more promptly than usual once a fortnight, but I do not think it would be feasible to introduce a weekly report.

4. Conditions in Cawnpore seem to have been fairly quiet during the fortnight, but today I hear that a new strike has developed. With regard to labour conditions and what Your Excellency says about them in your letter of 15th December,[89] there is no failure on the part of the ministry to realise the importance of improving these and of establishing better relations generally between the employers and the workers. It is only in regard to the methods of achieving these ends that they are inclined to be less vigorous than I should wish. Undoubtedly they have a very difficult tactical situation to handle in Cawnpore and they have their hands so full with other things that there is an inclination to let matters run on there for a bit without taking any very effective steps. But this is a matter which I shall keep before them.

5. Another place where labour trouble, of course on a much smaller scale, might develop is Gorakhpur. Trouble is being worked up in the railway workshops by Dr. Bishwanath Mukerji, M.L.A., a fairly well-known communist. The Premier is doing what he can to bring influence to

bear on Dr. Mukerji, but I fear the latter is out for his own advantage which he sees in stirring up a strike. I spent two days in Gorakhpur before visiting Allahabad. There is no doubt that conditions there both agrarian and administrative are decidedly worse than in any other district of the Province. I discussed the whole situation fully with the Commissioner[90] and the Collector.[91] The Congress have a very strong organisation in the district, and it is unfortunately in some parts of the district being directed by extreme left wing men. There is a considerable history of oppressive treatment by Zamindars. There is an enormous and very poor population. Relations between landlords and tenants are very unsatisfactory and it looks to me as if when the government policy is announced in January, special efforts will be required to get rents paid. There are also a good many disputes about possession of land, and there may be trouble at the time when the *rabi* crop is harvested. Administratively the existence of a large number of Congress *panchayats* is a danger, and after discussion with me the Commissioner has issued instructions which I hope will improve the situation considerably. There has also been some recrudescence of trouble in a few villages of the Jhansi district, but this is being dealt with.

6. The Allahabad University jubilee celebrations went off very well in a general atmosphere of good-will which could hardly have been anticipated a few weeks before. I see that our Police Secret Abstract says that: "The proceedings passed off smoothly except for an incident when His Excellency the Governor was greeted by some students shouting *Inqilab zindabad*." This conveys a very misleading impression of the facts. On the first day when the special convocation was held, as the head of the long procession of which I was at the end appeared in the *pandal*, some rather rowdy shouts were raised from the back of the *pandal*, where an audience of about 5,000 was seated. These shouts continued while the procession was marching up on to the dais. I had to open the proceedings with a speech of welcome. The moment I rose absolute silence descended and my speech was listened to with great attention and considerable applause. Your Excellency's message was much appreciated. Throughout the two and a half hours there was not the slightest misbehaviour on the part of the students. On the next day when the ordinary convocation was held, much the same thing happened. Shouts were raised as the procession walked in. As soon as the proceedings started they were absolutely orderly. When I closed the proceedings with a short speech, it was again very well received. At a garden party following on the ordinary convocation I exchanged a few words with Jawaharlal Nehru, whom I

had never seen before. I was sitting with Mrs. Naidu when he arrived. Mrs. Naidu called him up and introduced him to me, and though he did not sit down, we had a few minutes' three-cornered talk. This incident apparently created a good deal of interest at the party. Politically the atmosphere at Allahabad throughout my visit was very friendly, and I am definitely glad that I attended the celebrations.

7. In a cabinet meeting at Allahabad we had a useful discussion about prohibition policy. The ministers agreed eventually to confine the actual prohibition experiment to two adjoining districts of no particular importance. The main policy really consists in extensive restrictions and administrative changes throughout the Province. These will I think certainly make for temperance, but will also involve considerable loss of revenue. The proposals however are to be worked out in full detail before any action is taken.

8. The three Muslim bye-elections have all gone in favour of the Muslim League, and it is possible that this may lead to some reconsideration by the Congress of their attitude towards the League. If the policy of absorbing Muslims in the Congress is not going to succeed, they may feel inclined to come to terms with the League, which I fancy the League would be very pleased to do. This, however, would involve far-reaching adjustments, and a re-shuffling of the cabinet. I have no definite information that anything of the sort is under contemplation.

9. The troublesome dispute in Lucknow between Sunnis and Shias over the Madhe-Sahaba question may have to be faced before long. We had a discussion in the cabinet recently and efforts for some compromise between the parties are still being made. But the ministry may have to make up their minds about the matter early in January, and any orders issued are likely to lead to trouble.

10. The Legislature will meet on the 17th January, and it is anticipated that it will be in session more or less continuously till about the end of March. I am proposing to remain in Lucknow throughout January, as there will be a great number of crucial questions under consideration. I have visited now every division in the Province during this cold weather except Fyzabad and Benares. These I think will have to be left. I have found my tours of very great value to myself and I think they have been heartening to the administration.

Yours sincerely,
HARRY HAIG

NOTES

1. Lord Linlithgow minuted: 'This constitutes a very heavy remission for such cases, but worth it if the toughs in paragraph 4 can be kept in gaol.'
2. Lord Linlithgow minuted: 'Stand, and count on my support.'
3. In telegram 1160-G of 8 October 1937, Lord Linlithgow said he agreed with the general line of Sir Harry Haig's proposals. The Viceroy reported that at a recent student conference at Benares, the released prisoners Sachan Sanyal and Sachin Bakshi had appealed to students to do all in their power, including resort to violence if necessary, to achieve the release of their communist comrades. MSS.EUR.F. 125/127.
4. Mr B.G. Pahalajani.
5. Mr R. Sinha.
6. Not printed. Pandit Nehru's letter of September 1937 to the Mill Workers at Cawnpore was written in Hindi. It is reproduced in English in S. Gopal (ed.), *The Selected Works of Jawaharlal Nehru* (1st series), vol. 8, New Delhi: Orient Longman, 1976, pp. 328–34.
7. Mr Panna Lal.
8. Mr H.S. Ross.
9. Lord Linlithgow minuted: 'I don't much like the sound of this plan.'
10. Lord Linlithgow minuted: 'One would have thought the solution as at 7th October was pretty obvious!'
11. Lord Linlithgow minuted: 'What class of officer is left if the police are omitted?'
12. Lord Linlithgow minuted: 'It would, at a pinch, be quite in order for the G[overnor] to suggest to his P[remier] a conference, under the G[overnor]'s chairmanship, of the leaders and deputy leaders of both front benches in both Houses to adjust matters of this kind.'
13. Mr L. Owen.
14. Mr H.J. Frampton.
15. In his letter of 4 October 1937 Lord Linlithgow expressed his concern at a Press report that police in the U.P. would in future be dressed in *khadi*. Linlithgow wondered whether any real economy would result and also stressed that the police should have a distinctive uniform which could be easily recognised.

    Later in the same letter Linlithgow reported that Lord Zetland was very apprehensive that serious difficulty would arise with Parliament on the ground that Governors had not taken a sufficiently strong line with Congress ministries on such matters as the release of prisoners, communist propaganda and the like. MSS.EUR.F. 125/127.
16. Lord Linlithgow's telegram 1183-G of 12 October 1937 replied to No. 92. The Viceroy was disturbed by the very large numbers of prisoners involved. He asked: '(*a*) on what basis or principle selection is to be made for release, (*b*) what type of prisoner is involved? Do these figures include persons convicted of violent crime? (*c*) I would be glad of further particulars of release

which took place in 1935 and earlier releases referred to by you.' L/P&J/7/1261: ff. 186-90.

17. Lord Linlithgow replied on 25 October 1937. He felt that: 'When a representative of the Crown in India appears in public in circumstances in which it is physically appropriate that a flag be flown, that flag must be the Union Jack.' The Viceroy suggested Sir Harry Haig should lay down his terms quite definitely with the Allahabad University authorities and if they were unable to meet his requirements then the Governor should not attend the Jubilee Celebrations. Arrangements should be made for the flagstaff to be adequately guarded to prevent a last minute substitution of the Congress flag. MSS.EUR.F. 125/4.
18. See No. 88, note 3.
19. Mr R. Maxwell was Secretary to the Government of India, Home Department at this date.
20. Lord Linlithgow minuted: 'I do not recall this.'
21. Lord Linlithgow minuted: 'It is probably only a question of standing out till after Congress' Calcutta meeting. After that meeting I dare say Ministers will be in less of a panic about releases. It is, I suspect, mainly a matter of funk.'
22. In his telegram 301-GC of 15 October 1937, Lord Linlithgow said that he trusted Sir Harry Haig would impress on Pandit Pant the very serious nature of ministers speaking to the Press without consultation or prior intimation to the Premier. In paragraph 5 Linlithgow listed points they should be able to state about the jail release such as that there had been frequent jail releases before and persons released were of little importance. L/P&J/7/1261: f. 179.
23. In telegram 316-G of 19 October 1937, Lord Linlithgow reported that the Governor of Madras (Lord Erskine) was being pressed by his Prime Minister (Mr C. Rajagopalachariar) to release two terrorist convicts recently repatriated from the Andamans. The two prisoners were not due to be released until the end of 1939. Linlithgow asked for an estimate of reactions in the U.P. to the prisoners' early release. MSS.EUR.F. 125/127.
24. Not printed.
25. Not included in MSS.EUR.F. 125/127.
26. Lord Linlithgow's telegram 341-GC of 21 October 1937 was a reply to No. 97. The Viceroy said he was agreeing to the release of the two Madras prisoners subject to certain conditions and to Lord Zetland's concurrence. Linlithgow agreed that the U.P. position could be distinguished from that of Madras. He was asking Sir Maurice Hallett (Governor of Bihar) to keep in touch with both the U.P. and Bengal. MSS.EUR.F. 125/127.
27. Mr Panna Lal.
28. Mr H.S. Ross.
29. Sir William Stampe had been Professor of Engineering at Roorkee College 1925-31. Between 1931 and 1937 he was Chief Engineer and Secretary to the U.P. government Irrigation Branch.

30. Mr Laithwaite replied on 9 November 1937. He said he was advised that the effect of Section 87 of the Act was to make the Speaker or President, as the case may be, the sole judge of a rule of procedure made under Section 84. Section 87 completely protected the proceedings from being challenged in any court of law.

    The Viceroy's advisers felt that the Federal Court would be likely to report that any opinion of theirs would be useless in the face of Section 87. On the same ground the ordinary courts might be expected to refuse to make any declaration of invalidity. MSS.EUR.F. 125/132.
31. Appendix 8.
32. Not printed.
33. See No. 94, note 17.
34. Pandit Iqbal Narain Gurtu.
35. Mr Panna Lal.
36. Not included in R/3/1/2.
37. Lord Linlithgow minuted: 'And even soporific.'
38. Lord Linlithgow minuted: 'P.S.V.– The G[overnor] should insist upon a written undertaking from the highest authority in the University undertaking that the G[overnor]'s wishes in all matters (each specifically mentioned) will be respected in their entirety.

    He is winning. Let him stick to his game 110 per cent.'
39. Sir Maurice Hallett was the Governor of Bihar at this date. He had evidently asked for information on developments in the U.P. regarding the question of the release of political prisoners.
40. MSS.EUR.F. 125/127.
41. See Appendix 10.
42. Mr R.A. Horton.
43. Mr Philip Mason, D.C., Garhwal.
44. Mr A.W. Ibbotson.
45. Mr R.M. Saner.
46. Sir Maurice Hallett had been commenting on an enquiry which had just concluded into a riot at Sitamarhi, Bihar the previous September. Hallett said the Bihar police were watching the case closely. He added: 'put rather crudely, the question at issue is whether the police should use "velvet" gloves in carrying out an order given to them. In this particular case, possibly the order given by the Magistrate was not entirely justifiable, but it would clearly be disastrous to the morale and discipline of the police if they were dropped on for carrying out a legal order somewhat drastically.' L/P&J/5/169: ff. 68-9.
47. Lord Zetland had reported that a question was to be asked in the House of Commons seeking information on the numbers of prisoners released in India since 1 July 1937 and how this total compared with the corresponding months in 1936. Zetland sought information from the Provinces. MSS.EUR.F. 125/127.

48. Lord Linlithgow minuted: 'That remains to be seen and I do not doubt that the G[overnor] with the I.G.P. will most carefully watch the position; there must be no hesitation in insisting upon any change that experience may show to be necessary to obtain the required result, viz., reporting of all dangerous speeches.'
49. Not included in R/3/1/2.
50. Lord Linlithgow minuted: 'V[ery] g[ood].' Mr Horton's predecessor was Mr A.G. Phillips.
51. See Appendix 9.
52. Lord Linlithgow minuted: 'P.S.V. – I feel the G. must have a reasoned criticism of that document.' See Appendix 16.
53. Mr H.S. Ross.
54. Mr. E.F.G. Chapman.
55. Mr L. Owen.
56. Mr G.A. Pearce.
57. Mr Panna Lal, Commissioner of the Allahabad Division.
58. In this telegram Lord Linlithgow agreed that it was necessary to take a firm line in Cawnpore in view of the circumstances described in No. 114. The Viceroy felt they must 'aim at fixing primary responsibility either for action or inaction on Ministry, on whom of course it properly falls.' The Governor should not have to come in until the case for his doing so was clearly decisive. Furthermore when the Governor came in, he should be in a position to say that he had been forced to do so by the failure of the Ministry to deal with a situation affecting his special responsibilities. MSS.EUR.F. 115/13.
59. This telegram replied to No. 115. Lord Linlithgow said he understood Sir Harry Haig's position. The Viceroy's remarks about trying to bring Ministers up to taking responsibility (see note 58 above) were made at large. He entirely supported Haig over Cawnpore. MSS.EUR.F. 115/13.
60. Lord Linlithgow replied in telegram 1453-G of 10 December 1937. In the course of the telegram Linlithgow said: 'The real point is clearly whether or not Parmanand shall be prosecuted, the question whether your Cabinet shall take responsibility or not being a secondary one. My own view is quite definitely that we should allow prosecution to go forward.' MSS.EUR. F. 115/15.
61. Lord Linlithgow minuted: 'The objections are overwhelming.'
62. Lord Linlithgow minuted: 'P.S.V.– We shall soon be in difficulties if we answer hypothetical questions of this kind!'
63. Lord Linlithgow replied in a lengthy letter dated 22 December 1937. He said that he considered the purposes for which the proposed Ordinance was suggested, lay within the ministerial field. No special responsibility of the Governor was attracted but the Ordinance would be open to challenge in the U.P. Legislature.

    As regards the proposed Bill, Linlithgow explained that the 1935 Government of India Act had wholly changed the Governor-General's responsibilities with respect to conflicts between Provincial Governments and the Centre. The Viceroy 'would not ordinarily use the power given to me in Section 54 to issue directions to a Governor to reserve for my consideration a Bill passed by a Provincial Legislature simply because I thought the Bill might trespass on the central field.' It was open to the Government of India or any affected individual to challenge the Bill in the courts.

Finally, Linlithgow said that Sir James Grigg (Finance Member of the Viceroy's Executive Council at this date) had sent Sir Harry Haig proposals for a grant from central revenues which might lead the Ministry to review its taxation proposals. MSS.EUR.F. 125/127.

64. Lord Linlithgow replied on 10 December 1937 enclosing a copy of the telegram he had sent Lord Zetland on this subject. MSS.EUR.F.125/127. In the telegram (No. 1311-G of 15 November 1937) Linlithgow pointed out that although responsible ministers could instruct Departments not to make recommendations for honours, the Governor was entirely free as to whom he consulted. A Governor could consult officers directly on an informal basis as to whom deserved recognition. Linlithgow proposed to instruct Governors in this sense. MSS.EUR.F. 125/26.
65. Lord Linlithgow minuted at this point: 'Is he made of sugar?!'
66. Lord Linlithgow minuted: 'Keep pressing him – over and over again.'
67. Appendix 8.
68. Lord Linlithgow minuted to his P.S.V. (Mr Laithwaite): 'I hope the G[overnor] will insist on being fully and immediately posted with the revenue system [?collections]. Ask a U.P. officer whether their system admits of (say) a weekly progress report to the G. – the point is cardinal.'
69. Not printed.
70. Lord Linlithgow minuted: 'Fight for as small and as intensive an area of experiment as possible.'
71. Lord Linlithgow minuted: 'It certainly will.'
72. Following the usual practice in these volumes, the Chief Secretary's fortnightly reports are not printed. See Editor's Introduction.
73. Lord Linlithgow minuted to Mr Laithwaite: 'You will remember my note on a previous letter from the G[overnor] as to expediency of his calling for periodic reports on revenue collections.'
74. This telegram was not sent. Evidently Sir Harry Haig received Lord Linlithgow's telegram No. 1453-G (see note 60 above) and this was one reason why he decided to alter the tone of his message.
75. See note 60 above.
76. Lord Linlithgow minuted: 'He must look out for any possibility of a new Congress leader.' MSS.EUR.F. 125/127.
77. Lord Linlithgow minuted: 'Right.' Ibid.
78. In telegram 414-GC of 15 December 1937 to Lord Zetland (repeated to Sir Harry Haig), Lord Linlithgow summarised the latest developments in the Parmanand case. The Viceroy felt 'in view of general situation in the U.P.

I see nothing for it but to stand firm and to face risks involved.' MSS.EUR. F. 115/15.

79. In his telegram of 15 December (see note above) Lord Linlithgow said he understood that the Chief Commissioner of Delhi felt it most unlikely that Pandit Parmanand would be sentenced to more than three months for the Delhi offence and if the case went to appeal the High Court might reduce the sentence to the period already served pending their decision. Ibid.

80. In his lengthy telegram 424-GC of 16 December 1937, Lord Linlithgow explained his considerable migivings over the course of action which Sir Harry Haig was suggesting in No. 126. However 'with very great doubt', Linlithgow had 'reached the conclusion that in the interests of general situation we shall be justified in taking the risks involved in withdrawing the Dehra Dun prosecution if (*a*) Pant can get from Parmanand an assurance that he will not repeat his offence; (*b*) your cabinet in addition to accepting responsibility for having ordered the prosecution make a public statement.' Ibid.

81. With his letter of 26 November 1937, Lord Linlithgow forwarded a copy of a letter of 9 November from Lord Zetland which enclosed a memorandum prepared in the India Office on the duties of Parliamentary Secretaries in Britain. L/P&J/9/327.

82. Lord Linlithgow replied in a letter of 6 January 1938. The Viceroy felt there would be no constitutional objection to the use of the Secretariat Instructions to define the functions of Parliamentary Secretaries. However he felt that this would be unwise tactically. 'I gather,' he wrote, 'from your letter that part at least of the difficulty which your Ministers are experiencing in agreeing upon the functions of their Parliamentary Secretaries is that they realise that if those functions are made too specific, their own position may be weakened or threatened by rivals pressing upon their heads without carrying any of their responsibilities.' The Viceroy felt it would be unwise for the Governor to try to cut the Gordian knot by the use of statutory powers. R/3/1/73.

83. In telegram 453-GC of 19 December 1937 to Lord Zetland (repeated to Sir Harry Haig), Lord Linlithgow expressed his continued misgivings over the proposed settlement with Pandit Pant but concluded that on the whole he would be prepared to accept Haig's proposal.
In telegram 462-GC of 20 December to Haig, Linlithgow put forward some additional points needing consideration. The Viceroy attached great importance to breaking away from the idea of an individual warning before prosecution. 'Obviously,' he wrote, 'if that is accepted as a principle, agitators would find it easy to devise means of evading service of warning, etc.' MSS.EUR.F. 115/15.

84. Lord Linlithgow's telegram 488-GC of 23 December 1937 to Sir Harry Haig read: 'I shall be grateful for your comments (which please repeat to the Secretary of State) in the light of the sentence of 6 weeks passed on Parmanand at Delhi yesterday.' L/P&J/7/1059.

85. In telegrams sent on 24 and 25 December 1937 Lord Linlithgow and Lord Zetland agreed to Sir Harry Haig proceeding on the basis of his proposed compromise. MSS.EUR.F. 115/15.
86. In a telegram sent on 25 December 1937 Sir Harry Haig informed Lord Linlithgow that the matter was settled and that the agreed statement was being issued. L/P&J/7/1059. See Appendix 17 for the text of the communiqué as issued by the U.P. government.
87. The relevant sentence in Lord Linlithgow's letter read: 'Pant seems to have got away from his party meeting on the 9th more successfully than you had reason to anticipate on the date of your letter now under reply [No. 120], and I should have thought that the fact that he had been able to stand up to criticism ought to have heartened him a good deal.' R/3/1/2.
88. See Appendix 14.
89. In his letter of 15 December 1937, Lord Linlithgow said that he felt an improvement in labour conditions in the U.P. might well materially reduce the difficulties with which its government was confronted. R/3/1/2.
90. Mr C.W. Grant.
91. Mr J.E. Pedley.

83 [illegible] 1 and 23 December [illegible]
[illegible]
[illegible]
84 [illegible] December [illegible]
[illegible]
[illegible]
[illegible]
[illegible] any [illegible]
[illegible]
reason to complain of the case of your leader and [illegible]
should have brought [illegible] the fact that he had been able to stand up to
[illegible] from your work [illegible]
85 [illegible] April [illegible]
86 In his [illegible] until [illegible]
[illegible]
[illegible] your command was [illegible]
VII [illegible]
VI [illegible]

Appendices

APPENDIX 1

LINLITHGOW TO ZETLAND
MSS.EUR.F. 125/161

Secret

The Viceroy's House, New Delhi,
March 17th, 1937

My dear Lawrence,

After much thought, I take the view that I had better tell you that I am not happy about Haig. The result of the elections in the U.P. have left him worried, pessimistic and dazed. He is on the defensive on every front, and shows signs of having very little stomach for the contest. I have done all in my power to comfort and support him. I got him up to Delhi to this house for a few days, and gave him as much of my time as I possibly could. He was in better shape when he left me, and I gather from the signs available that this improvement persists.

I have no hesitation in writing that he has never had hold of his province, nor acquired the initiative in anything approaching the way in which Anderson,[1] Brabourne[2] and Emerson[3] have achieved these things. Indeed, I feel pretty confident that his gifts lie more in the field of the Secretariat than in that of a governorship. Nevertheless he is quite good enough for ordinary times, in which his wide experience would largely compensate for any inherent lack of power. But the present is not an ordinary time, and the circumstances of the moment have exposed shortcomings which, in other days, might well have gone unobserved. The mischief of the position is that this weakness has been widely noticed, and not only by our friends. Thus I may tell you that Ewart, my D.I.B., has made a discreet and perfectly proper approach through Laithwaite to ask if I am happy about Haig in his position in the Province. And, from another angle, the *Hindustan Times* published the other day a cartoon depicting an enormous Congress rat in juxtaposition to a tiny, emaciated, and miaowing cat labelled "Haig". The cartoon dealt with an all-India aspect of contemporary politics, and the inference – therefore – was unmistakable.

Haig's position has been rendered very difficult by the extent to which he had associated himself throughout the pre-election period (and not always entirely discreetly), with the efforts – or want of them! – of the landlord party in the U.P. to get together on a programme and conduct its propaganda. I gave him, before the election, my view that according to my reading of electoral prospects, he would have been more usefully employed in paving the way for a Congress ministry; but both he and the landlords were confident they would command a majority. I rather think that Haig in some measure inherited this tendency to act as party organiser to the landlord party from Hailey,[4] as Hailey, though never the Taluqdars' man that his predecessor was, inherited it from Harcourt Butler.[5] The great landed proprietors of Oudh have seemed a valuable shield against the spread westwards of subversive tendencies from Bengal through Bihar. But the new franchise was bound to undercut the Taluqdars' position. It has done this in no uncertain fashion, and so far as the 'gadi' of the U.P. has been underpinned by the favour of the local aristocracy, its foundations have been sensibly weakened by the election results. Inevitably, the propertied classes have felt deep resentment against "Government", which – they think – has let them down. Haig is conscious of some share of their displeasure, and this adds to his discomfort.

The U.P. is very important at this time because of its tendency towards agrarian disquiet, and since it is Jawaharlal Nehru's home province, and is destined to have Pant, an able and forceful person, as its first Chief Minister.

I will do my best to get Haig through the remainder of his time as Governor (he is due to hand over in December 1939), but I must tell you quite frankly that I am not sure that this will prove possible. My anxiety as to Haig's sufficiency for his post under existing conditions has moved me to suggest Hallett's name for the "Dormant Commission" for the U.P.[6] If it becomes clear to you and me that Haig has to go, I would strongly recommend, unless you have other views, that Hallett be moved immediately to the U.P., and confirmed in the governorship of that province so soon as you are able to get the King's consent. Bihar is not, I think, likely to prove anything but an easy place to run, since Congress have in the province no men likely, or even capable, to make trouble. A successor for Hallett should not, therefore, present much difficulty.[7]

Yours ever,
[LINLITHGOW]

APPENDIX 2

PANT TO DONALDSON[8]
L/P&J/5/264: ff. 518–19

April 8th, 1937

When I was last at Lucknow I heard a report that the first meeting of the Provincial Legislative Assembly had been fixed for the 12th of this month. I have, however, not received any summons yet and there are some indications in the press that the meeting is not likely to come off for some time yet.

It is true that under Section 62(3) of the Government of India Act 1935 a period of six months from the date of the inauguration of the new constitution is provided for this purpose. But this is the extreme maximum limit. According to Section 61(2) the term of five years prescribed for a Provincial Legislative Assembly begins to run only from the date of their first meeting and not earlier. The implication of this rule is plain enough – the first session of the Assembly should be summoned immediately after the election or the coming into force of the new Act, as the case may be. Section 65 is quite definite and leaves no doubt as to the intentions of the framers of the Act. Sub-section 1 of the aforesaid Section lays down that every Provincial Legislative Assembly shall, as soon as may be, choose two members of the Assembly to be respectively Speaker and Deputy Speaker thereof. This language is unambiguous and mandatory. The words *as soon as may be* are significant and do not admit of any intentional delay. Arrangements for the election of Speaker and Deputy Speaker by the Assembly should be made at the earliest moment possible so that its structure may be completed and it may begin to function. The Punjab Assembly has just elected its Speaker and the new assemblies in several other provinces have similarly been summoned for this purpose. Such was, probably, the intention in our province. It is a general belief that the session is being delayed in order to avoid any embarrassment likely to be caused to the present ministry which does not enjoy the confidence of the Assembly or the electorate. These considerations should be, however, strictly ruled out, as the law requires that these officers of the Assembly "shall be chosen as soon as may be", and for the purpose of this section it is absolutely immaterial whether the Council of Ministers does or does not possess the confidence of the House. The likelihood of any embarrassment to the ministers cannot be a valid ground for putting off the first meeting. Any discrimination on such grounds would be inconsistent with the oft-repeated declaration of the governors about their determination to remain above party politics and to act in a detached and impartial manner as the sole representative of the Crown in the province.

There need not be any difficulty in the way of a meeting of our Provincial Assembly being convened forthwith. The summons can reach every member within a week and the Assembly can meet any time thereafter. If such a session is not held within a fortnight I should regard it as a deliberate breach of Section 65.

I should feel obliged by your communicating to me His Excellency's decision in the matter on or before the 11th on which date our party will be meeting at Lucknow.[9]

APPENDIX 3

PANT TO DONALDSON
L/P&J/5/264: ff. 521-2

April 11th, 1937

I have just received your letter[10] and I exceedingly regret to note that His Excellency has no immediate intention of summoning the Legislature and proposes to do so when his ministers are in a position to place their budget proposals and programme before it. I am of opinion – and I am saying this on behalf of the largest party in the Assembly – that the course contemplated is in contravention both of the letter and the spirit of the Government of India Act. The Legislature under the Act is the only agency through which the elected representatives of the people can effectively voice opinion on public questions, redress the grievances of their constituents and draw attention to the defects in the administration. As mentioned in my last letter there are numerous provisions in the Act itself which indicate that it was considered imperative that the Legislature should be summoned as early as possible after the inauguration of Provincial Autonomy. I particularly emphasize that under Section 51(3) "the salaries of ministers shall be such as the Provincial Legislature may from time to time by Act determine". Presumably the ministers desire this indefinite postponement of the first session. I wonder if it has struck them that questions affecting them personally in regard to their emoluments ought according to the scheme of the Act to be placed by the ministers before the Assembly at earliest moment possible. This is the course adopted in other provinces such as the Punjab where bills fixing ministers' salaries have been already finally considered. The anxiety of the ministry in the U.P. to put off the evil day when they will have inevitably to face a hostile Assembly is easily intelligible, but, apart from other matters, delay in the submission to the Legislature of a bill about ministerial salaries involving as it may financial loss to the province amounts to an abuse of the Law and is deplorable. I should have thought that honourable ministers themselves would have taken the initiative for summoning the Legislature immediately for settlement of the embarrassing question of their personal emoluments by the elected representatives of the people of this province.

I am amused, though not surprised, to know that one of the reasons assigned for not summoning the Legislature is that the ministers have at present no programme to place before the Legislature. I should have thought that it is the duty of any party or individual who accepts office to have a well-defined programme before he does so. But evidently this interim ministry has not at the moment even an interim programme and they require time, no one knows how much, to evolve one. Till then the ministry will probably govern by the light of nature, keeping the public entirely in the dark of what they do. It is clear that the ministry is anxious to prevent, so long as it can, through the agency of the Governor, the Assembly having an opportunity to express its opinion of their conduct.

N.B.: I have laid this correspondence before my party and am releasing it to the press as it covers a matter of great public importance.

APPENDIX 4

STATEMENT ISSUED BY U.P. CABINET
L/P&J/5/264: ff. 523-6

April 13th, 1937

The Congress party in the U.P. Legislature met on Sunday and passed several resolutions approving of the decision taken by its leader not to form a ministry in these provinces, condemning the action of the Governor in appointing a minority ministry and denouncing us in unmistakable terms. We are charged with having betrayed the real interests of the country, shown an utter want of self-respect and common decency and degraded public life in India. It is further stated that any act of ours would be a clear usurpation. The meeting also criticised the Governor and the ministry for not convening a meeting of the Legislature immediately.

These charges necessarily demand a clear and unequivocal statement from us.

The Congress went to the electorate with a definite programme which forms part of the manifesto issued at the time. This programme was amplified by the various Congress candidates and others in the course of their election speeches. The Congress secured an absolute majority in the Legislature. The A.I.C.C. decided in favour of office acceptance subject to certain conditions. The leader of the Congress party was invited by the Governor to form a ministry but he expressed his inability to do so failing an assurance from the Governor that he would not exercise his special powers. It has since been explained that it was not the intention of the Congress to secure an abrogation of the constitution in any sense. That is to say, the Congress believed among other things that the constructive part of its programme could be worked within the four corners of the Constitution. Nevertheless the Congress refused to accept office.

We would place before the public the consequences of Congress refusal to form a ministry, despite the fact that Congressmen were aware that there were certain urgent problems which cried for solution and which could be solved by assumption of power. The refusal of the Congress to accept office was a virtual refusal to address themselves to such problems, the consideration of which cannot in any circumstances be postponed without great hardship to the sufferers. Without a ministry the provinces would have been reduced to a system of autocratic government which would not have been responsible to the people.

We are elected members of the Legislature representing certain constituencies of these provinces. It is our intention to the best of our ability to further the interests of the rural and urban masses, ameliorate their condition and devise such measures as will conduce to their comfort and well-being.

If this conception of our duty is interpreted to mean that we are lacking in self-respect and common decency and that we are the tools of British Imperialism, then we can only say that our future action will be the best refutation of these charges. As regards usurpation of power we emphatically repudiate the charge and declare that we have been placed in this unenviable position as the result of refusal of the majority party to shoulder the responsibility.

Our answer to the charge is, as was made clear in our first statement, that if the Congress is willing to come back and accept office we shall be only too glad to make way for them.

We have been charged with deliberately refusing to advise the Governor to convene a meeting of the Legislature immediately and that by taking full advantage of the period allowed in the Constitution for calling a session of the Legislature we are in fact flouting the spirit of the Constitution. It is indeed surprising that those whose sole object it is to wreck the machinery of government should be so anxious to preach constitutional morality. If it had been the intention of Parliament that the Legislature should be summoned "as soon as may be", this would have been stated plainly in Section 62 which deals with the summoning of the Legislature. But Section 62 merely provides that the Legislature shall be summoned not later than six months after the commencement of the Act. The words "as soon as may be" which occur in a different section – Section 65 – clearly refer to the proceedings to be taken when the Legislature has been summoned, and provide for the steps necessary for the Legislature after meeting to start functioning.

It is as well to consider in this connection the intention of the Congress when the Legislature is summoned to create a deadlock. We submit that a deliberate attempt to wreck the Constitution and in short to put the Legislature out of action is in fact a betrayal of the real interests of the country.

As to our programme, it would be easy to put out at once vague and fantastic promises if we had no intention of trying to carry them out. But our programme will be one of detailed measures which, if we get the support of the Legislature, we intend definitely to carry out. We shall put forward things that can be done, and not things that cannot be done.

If the Congress is really keen about their programme, why do they not take office and try to carry it through? By refusing office they are running away from their responsibilities. The villager knows that promises of a most attractive kind have been made to him. He knows that the Congress could only carry them out by taking office. And he knows that the Congress refuse to take office. When he sees the Congress passing resolutions instead of taking action, he will realise that these promises were never meant and that the Congress want to continue to criticise others instead of doing things themselves.

We appeal to the public to judge our programme and actions in the spirit in which we have undertaken them and not to condemn us out of hand on the strength of charges made by persons whose chief complaint against us is that we have stood in the way of a complete breakdown of the system of representative and responsible government in the country.

APPENDIX 5

EWART TO LAITHWAITE[11]
MSS.EUR.F. 125/4

Secret and Personal

Intelligence Bureau, Home Department,
Government of India,
April 19th, 1937

Discussions in Lucknow indicate that there is considerable uncertainty in Secretariat circles about the practical working of the new system of government, and that much remains to be evolved. This is inevitable, but there seems to me to be a lack of co-ordination and direct consultation between the different people concerned in working out plans; the result seems to lead to undue improvisation and to the obscuring of vital principles. I do not think enough consideration has been given to the fact, which officials admit when it is put to them, that officers in districts, including Commissioners, will not be able to report frankly as in the past, not merely in regard to actual occurrences, but even more in regard to tendencies of which they may be conscious and which may cause them some apprehension. If general standards are to be preserved from serious deterioration, it is the close watching of tendencies before they develop to an active stage, that is almost more necessary than anything.

2. In the United Provinces, all sections of public opinion, which have in the past been opposed to Congress and dependent on government support, are badly demoralised. Competent observers have noticed that, particularly in educated circles, the open expression of feelings of strong nationalism is very noticeable, even among people who are not particularly keen supporters of Congress.

3. Under the best of conditions it must be unusually difficult for the headquarters of the United Provinces government to keep in real touch with what is happening in the districts, owing to the exceptional number (46) [48] of these districts and, particularly on the police side, the lack of intermediate co-ordinating machinery (Deputy Inspectors-General[12]). I have heard it freely stated that the staffing of the districts is in many cases poor in quality and that, in Oudh in particular, the standard of administration has already deteriorated, particularly in consequence of the heavy blow which the election has dealt to the Taluqdari system and to the exposure of the really bad agrarian conditions.

4. All these factors tend towards a falling off in standards in a slow and

insidious way, making it very difficult for the Governor to say at exactly what moment deterioration has passed beyond the danger point. In the Police Department shortage of District Officers is partly accounted for by the fact that an unusually large number of good British Superintendents of Police have been allowed to go away on deputation to Indian states and the efficiency of the Police administration of the Province seems to be suffering in consequence. The staff of the Special Branch of the C.I.D., on which both the government and the Governor must depend for Intelligence, is most inadequate for the work which it has to do. This has been represented to the Governor.

J.M. EWART

APPENDIX 6

NOTE BY EWART
MSS.EUR.F. 125/157: ff. 230–8

Secret

Intelligence Bureau, Home Department,
Government of India,
August 20th, 1937

My stay at Lucknow was curtailed as H.E. the Governor was in Naini Tal and wished to see me there.[13] In Lucknow I saw the Premier, the Chief Secretary,[14] the I.G. Police[15] and other police officers, the Commissioner, Lucknow,[16] and a few other officials, and the Manager of the Allahabad Bank; in Naini Tal I had several long conversations with H.E. the Governor and his Secretary.[17]

2. Considering the special and numerous difficulties of the situation in the United Provinces, I have gained a more reassuring impression than I had expected.

3. The strength of the ministry rests in the Premier and Dr. Katju, but Mrs. Pandit is looked upon as likely to prove quite competent when she has gained more experience and confidence. The favourable impression which Mr. G.B. Pant has created is quite remarkable. Including the Governor, everyone speaks highly of him, and those who have direct dealings with him, including the I.G. Police and D.I.G., C.I.D.,[18] both like him personally and feel considerable confidence in him. The Premier has a very heavy burden of work and personal responsibility, but all are agreed that he has considerable strength of character and sincerity of purpose;

the view which I have heard frequently expressed in the past few months that he lacks the strength to resist pressure from Nehru and others, does not seem to be borne out by the manner in which he has been acting since he became Premier. Mr Gwynne, the Chief Secretary, feels that he is now getting on terms of mutual understanding with Mr. Pant and finds considerable ground for guarded optimism as regards the future. In his opinion, Mr. Pant still suffers from suspicions based on the usual inferiority complex of the Congress politician, and is obstinate in respect of certain strongly held theories, but is full of sturdy common sense and is very ready to listen to advice and to opinions contrary to his own. There is general agreement that the Premier came very creditably out of the Cawnpore strike situation, and that the experience he gained has given him a more realistic appreciation of some of the problems of his position. He had serious difficulties to contend with; he made a clear appreciation of the situation, formed clear ideas as to the appropriate action and, having made up his mind, worked hard and successfully in securing his object. The relations between him and the District Magistrate of Cawnpore[19] were excellent and creditable to both of them. The police behaved admirably under very trying conditions and received full support. In public (including official) estimation, the Premier had much the best of his exchanges with the Cawnpore employers, both on merits and in respect of dignity.

4. The favourable estimate of the Premier personally and of the chances of the new government settling down, which are being formed at headquarters among those in the best position to understand, are more important because, in the province at large, there is, very justifiably and naturally, widespread and serious anxiety. If the present hopeful feelings at headquarters prove justified, their spread outwards to the districts and the evidence of events and the action of the ministry will, in course of time, allay this anxiety and re-establish confidence. Meanwhile, the situation in the districts gives cause for some anxiety and needs most careful watching. The Inspector-General of Police has just returned from a tour in the eastern part of the province with material for considerable anxiety as regards the police. H.E. the Governor is very much alive to the delicacy of the situation in the districts and has received confidential reports from Commissioners which, in some cases, disclose somewhat disquieting conditions. The danger is that the authority and prestige of the district administration may be undermined by uncertainty and lack of clear direction as to the policy of government and the methods to be followed in carrying it out, and by the truculent and hostile activities of local Congress organisations. In my estimation, the ministry, and, in particular,

the Premier, given time and a period of tranquillity, will develop and make clear to the public and to officials a reasonable policy, and will, in his own way, curb the excesses of his less responsible supporters in the districts so as to prevent Party political activities from interfering with administrative activities. But the balance is delicate, and there is certainly a risk that administrative efficiency may be seriously affected before the necessary adjustments are made. From the information gathered by the I.G. Police on tour and from what the Governor has heard from Commissioners, it is clear that in many districts the local Congress organisations are being deliberately provocative and are endeavouring to set themselves up as a parallel administration. Notices have been posted in Congress offices encouraging the public to make complaints against the police which, the notices state, would be forwarded direct to the Premier. Congress Committees and individual workers are putting themselves forward as intermediaries and representatives before the authorities in respect of complaints and reports which should be handled direct between the parties concerned and the appropriate officials. In the absence of clear directions, which it is difficult to convey in the present elementary stage of the new Government's development, and in view of the inexperience and pre-occupations of the ministers, officials in districts are confronted with much difficulty in determining their attitude in many matters and their relations with local Congress functionaries. In this connection the Governor feels that the question of the Congress flag and the *Vande Mataram* song is likely to create difficulties. He is not concerned so much with possible attempts to fly the Congress flag on government buildings but thinks that officials will be placed in a difficult and unfair position if, at functions which they may be attending in their official capacity, the ceremonial hoisting of the flag or singing of the song, during which all present are expected to stand up or salute, are included in the programme.

The impression of weakening the authority of local officials has been encouraged by orders issued by the government restricting the liberty of officials to exercise their authority under the law, e.g. restricting the initiation of prosecutions and suspending all litigation connected with the realisation of rents. In this atmosphere it is but natural that many officials, especially Indians in the provincial and subordinate services, should see the hand of malice and political prejudice everywhere, even in actions which are a part of normal administration and which have passed without comment hitherto. I found this form of anxiety very prominently displayed in a conversation which I had in Lucknow with a Deputy Superintendent of Police. He quoted two or three cases in which inquiries have been started into the conduct of police officers, and took it for granted that Congress prejudice was responsible. Actually, his own description of the incidents, and inquiries which I later made from the I.G. Police and others about them, showed that they were perfectly normal matters of departmental control, and no case has yet occurred in which a police officer has actually suffered any injury whatever from any kind of victimisation. I am told on good authority that the knowledge that actual malpractices are much less likely than in the past to remain unobserved, owing to the readiness not only of Congress organisations but of the general public to bring them to the notice of the ministry, has had the effect of causing subordinate police officers to curtail considerably the petty exactions to which, particularly in large towns, the police are addicted. The loss of this illicit income is a cause of some resentment among the sufferers. This is an aspect of the influence of public opinion on police behaviour which is altogether welcome, but it has a bearing on the question of possible cuts in pay which is another of the causes of anxiety among officials. Where scales of pay are in some cases so low as almost to amount to an encouragement to illicit supplements, the reduction of salaries coming on top of curtailment of illicit gains, would be particularly bad policy. I mentioned this point to H.E. the Governor.

5. Though rumour is busy, as in other provinces, about the intention of the Ministry to reduce salaries, H.E. the Governor does not himself think that the Premier intends to take this action. The ministry is, however, anxious to affect appreciable economy by the reduction of expenditure on travelling allowance. They believe that the existing rules are abused to a considerable extent. There is no intention to make hasty decisions in this matter, and there could be no objection to the subject being thoroughly examined.

6. Several of those whom I have met comment on the difficulties in the United Provinces of maintaining personal contact between headquarters and the districts, of which there are 48 in the province. Personally, I am convinced that the only way in which the present difficulties and anxieties of District Officers can be mitigated is by the fullest possible development of means for conveying to them personal reassurances as to the reality of the protection which they can count on and as to the broader developments of the situation which are beyond their field of view. I feel, therefore, that it is of the greatest importance that Commissioners, heads of Departments, and others who can keep [in] touch both with headquarters and with districts, should themselves be thoroughly well informed of the broader features of the situation and should take every possible opportunity of

helping those officers who are in a more isolated position, to put their comparatively petty troubles and annoyance into the correct focus, and to realise that the general position is not deteriorating to the extent which local conditions may sometimes indicate, and that, in the event of any real deterioration, the means exist, and will be used, to restore the position. The Governor fully realises the importance of what I may call the district situation, but it is one which is probably more difficult to deal with in the United Provinces than in any other province.

7. As regards the Secretariat and the ministry, there is general satisfaction as to the way in which things are developing. The Premier's task is extremely onerous. In addition to his own heavy departmental duties, all his ministers, except Katju, constantly bring their cases to him for advice. The Governor tells me that in cabinet not only is the Premier completely master of his colleagues but the majority hardly venture to express an opinion of their own. Secretaries are extremely hard worked and are responding to the demands of ministers with noteworthy devotion. In the enthusiasm of ignorance ministers are apt to call for elaborate notes and returns at entirely inadequate notice, and Secretaries are working literally day and night to meet such requests. As regards the functions of Parliamentary Secretaries, the Premier has accepted the advice of the Governor and the Chief Secretary limiting very strictly their intrusion into departmental procedure. The Chief Secretary told me that Mr. Pant had readily appreciated one point which he put to him in this connection that Parliamentary Secretaries are not part of the ministry and have taken no oaths of office or secrecy, and that if they were allowed to make decisions in the name of the government, the Premier might find himself badly compromised. The Premier has been showing some inclination to accept and pass orders on allegations about the police without inquiry through the proper channel, but the Chief Secretary is finding him responsive to advice in this connection also.

8. There is at present absolutely no organised opposition to the ministry but the suspension of rent recovery litigation has to some extent aroused the landlords, and it is probable that, when the Assembly meets, the formulation of specific proposals by the government will evoke opposition from individuals, and from that some organisation may develop.

9. The recent troubles in Cawnpore afforded some test of the police reserve organisation. It was possible to concentrate some 600 extra police fairly rapidly, but I gather from the Inspector-General that such concentration is effected by somewhat haphazard means, by scraping together contingents in other districts at the expense of normal duties. A recent

reorganisation on a provincial scale with a view to economy in the police budget has resulted in a considerable reduction of the total police strength but in a redistribution of reserves giving better concentration in centres where trouble is likely. The present arrangement would be inadequate if there were widespread trouble or serious trouble in several places simultaneously, but skeleton arrangements exist for raising additional forces at short notice since, as a result I believe of recent correspondence between the Governor and H.E. the Viceroy, the I.G. Police has compiled lists of men ready to accept temporary police service at short notice.

10. My interview with Mr. Pant showed him to be much interested in the nature of C.I.D. and Intelligence work in the province and at the Centre. He clearly imagined that the C.I.D. did little more than watch the activities and intercept the letters of Congressmen, but he is quite friendly, reasonable and realistic in his outlook. He indicated a point of view which was not possible to develop fully in the time available but which seemed to be that a popular government should, and could, develop methods of handling its own and its opponents' policy which would, to some extent, take the place of the activities for which a bureaucratic government had to depend on its Intelligence service. He illustrated his point by suggesting that Nehru's recent unequivocal statement that any government must meet force with force, gets wider hearing and has a greater effect than either government publicity or widespread C.I.D. activity.

J.M. EWART

APPENDIX 7

GWYNNE[20] TO PHILLIPS[21] AND ALL
U.P. DISTRICT MAGISTRATES
MSS.EUR.F. 115/12

Confidential
D.O. No. 534 P./VIII

Lucknow,
September 15th, 1937

My dear Phillips,

Will you please refer to your D.O. No. O.-878, dated August 6th, 1937.[22] In this letter I am replying only to the last paragraph of your letter on the question of sending shorthand-reporters to report speeches at meetings. Speeches at ordinary political meetings need no longer be reported. The Hon'ble Premier has promised to discontinue the practice of reporting political speeches and orders should be issued accordingly. There is however nothing to prevent you from directing the police to attend such meetings on special occasions in *mufti* or deputing agents to observe the general drift of the speeches delivered.

2. Government recognise however that in special cases or in special conditions it may be necessary to report speeches. This would only be when there was good reason to suppose that a speech or speeches would be made calculated to arouse feeling likely to lead to acts of violence or dangerous communal excitement. In such circumstances the procedure would be as follows:–

The District Magistrate should pass a special order that the speech of some individual or speeches at some particular meeting should be reported. In this order the District Magistrate should record his reasons for considering this course necessary. If there is time, the District Magistrate should make a reference to government before issuing his order, and if there is no time he should report to government without delay the fact that he has issued such an order together with the contents of his order and the reasons justifying it and at the same time a copy of the speech.

3. In cases where the Criminal Investigation Department consider it desirable that government should issue an order, a similar reference should be made to government direct.

Yours sincerely,
C.W. GWYNNE

APPENDIX 8

HAIG TO PANT[23]
L/P&J/5/264: ff. 53-5

Confidential *November 3rd, 1937*

Hon'ble Premier,

I take a serious view of certain developments which seem to me to be occurring in the province, some of which are illustrated in the three papers below,[24] and if the Hon'ble Premier agrees, I should like this note of mine to be laid before an early meeting of the cabinet and discussed.

2. In the first place, it is reported that unrestrained revolutionary speeches are being made chiefly, I understand, by the recently released revolutionary prisoners. In the second place, speeches are reported by this same group

of persons, and also in various other connections (e.g. during the recent elections in Bijnor) making violent racial attacks on the British. Thirdly, there has been an outrageous campaign against the police in Cawnpore. Fourthly, it has become plain to me since I have been on tour that in some districts the activities of Congressmen in interfering with police work and in establishing a regular system of complaints against whatever the police do are producing some deterioration in the morale of the police force and are beginning to affect their authority and to be reflected in some weakening of control over crime. There also seems to be growing mention of attempts by Congress workers to establish parallel institutions of their own in rivalry to government institutions in the nature of courts and machinery for inquiring into criminal cases.

3. So far as concerns the first two points, I am well aware of the general reluctance of the cabinet to set the law in motion in respect of speeches or writings. Nevertheless, I am sure they would agree that there must be some limit to this policy of tolerance, and that when speeches are really producing dangerous effects the government may be forced by the essential nature of its responsibilities to the province as a whole to take action.

4. With regard to the position of government servants, and particularly the police, I am quite sure that the Council of Ministers will be as much concerned as I am to see that developments which work against an ordered system of government are discouraged in every possible way. The authority of the provincial government is exercised through the government services, the machinery of which is at their disposal. Party organisations and machinery have their own functions, but they are quite distinct, and it seems to me exceedingly important that they should not appear to be usurping the functions of the government services, and should not be worked in such a way as to impair the authority of the government machinery.

5. It is very evident looking ahead that conditions are in any case likely to put some considerable strain on the government machine in the coming months. The difficulties for instance at Cawnpore are grave and do not seem to be diminishing. Nowhere in the province is it more obviously necessary to see that the authority of the police is not impaired. Relations between landlords and tenants may become very strained in the next few months, and it may be necessary for the district authorities to act with promptitude and resolution, if the situation is not to get out of hand. There are also indications that in many places relations between Hindus and Muslims are becoming more strained. Here again firm action by the district authorities gives the best chance of avoiding trouble.

6. We have to remember that the foundation of order is respect for authority. If that is destroyed, and there seem to me to be clear indications that it is being weakened, no government can in the long run expect to preserve order without finding itself under the necessity of employing force. That is a contingency which a government cannot regard with equanimity. There is still plenty of time to correct these tendencies, and that is why I wish to invite the attention of the Council of Ministers most seriously to the situation, so that steps may be taken to prevent it deteriorating.

7. What seems to me to be required in the main is:

(*a*) to check open incitements to revolution and violence;
(*b*) to check attacks on the police, such as those recently at Cawnpore;
(*c*) to make it clear that the Ministry desire to maintain the authority of their own services, and particularly of the police.

H.G. HAIG

APPENDIX 9

GWYNNE TO ALL U.P. DISTRICT MAGISTRATES
MSS.EUR.F. 115/12

No. 712 (1)/III

U.P. Civil Secretariat, Lucknow,
November 10th, 1937

Dear Sir,

In the course of three months since the present government assumed office frequent reports have been received from government servants in which Congress supporters are stated to have adopted an embarrassing attitude towards the district authorities, and a very large number of complaints have similarly reached government from Congress workers against the behaviour specially of the lower grades of government officials. The government are of opinion that such complaints and counter-complaints only tend to engender and crystallise an attitude of mutual suspicion, which is in every way opposed to the public interest. They feel therefore that the time has come when determined efforts should be made by the officers of government to establish relations of mutual confidence with the district leaders of the Congress organisation. A letter will be addressed to you shortly on the position of Government servants vis-à-vis the general public, and a second letter on the measures contemplated by government to check corruption in the public services. All these letters read together will give a synoptic view of the government policy in regard to the position of the services generally. In this letter I am to emphasise the importance of the establishment of relations of mutual confidence between the district authorities and the leaders of the Congress organisation. Government officials, whether revenue or police, are the executive of government. They have certain statutory powers and responsibilities and various other functions to perform. They are the agents through whom the orders or the policy of government is given a concrete shape and there is no question of substituting any other agency for this purpose. The Congress on the other hand represents a large body of public opinion and is the party on the support of which the present government rests. The Congress is naturally anxious to secure the maximum benefit for the members of the public out of the public institutions and functionaries. It is also interested in seeking all relevant information and bringing to the notice of the authorities appropriate cases and facts for redress and relief and in seeing that malpractices and neglect of duty on the part of public servants should be enquired into and corrected. It is the duty of the government servants concerned to deal with complaints of this nature which are brought to their notice, and to make it clear that they are giving due attention to them. The object of the government and of the Congress alike must be that the official agency functions with the maximum of efficiency and with the full confidence of the public, and this result will be facilitated if relations of mutual confidence and harmony are established between the district authorities and the leaders of the Congress organisation in the districts. How best to set about establishing more friendly and co-operative relations in each district is a matter primarily for the district officers themselves to consider, but I am to point out that any successful method in this direction presupposes tact, sympathy, accessibility and impartiality, and that it is important that the district authorities should be in touch with the representatives of the Congress organisation in their respective areas. The Congress Committees are being addressed in a similar sense by the United Provinces Congress Committee.

Yours sincerely,
C.W. GWYNNE

APPENDIX 10

LINLITHGOW TO HAIG
R/3/1/2

Secret

The Viceroy's House, New Delhi,
November 15th, 1937

My dear Haig,

I have read your secret letter of 8th November, No. U.P.-16,[25] with very great interest; but I confess also with a very considerable uneasiness of mind. That uneasiness of mind represents a condition which has I fear been growing in intensity for some weeks past, for I am as I read your very clear and interesting reports increasingly impressed by the unsatisfactory condition, as I cannot but regard it, of matters in the United Provinces. I think I have made it clear in the past that in my judgement the United Provinces situation is the key-point, the handling of which is of critical importance in relation to the all-India position, and I cannot feel, in the light of the full information which I receive from you, and from police reports and the like, that the state of things as it now stands is such as to warrant me in taking any but a grave view. To put it in a word I cannot avoid a general impression of what I may describe, not to put too fine a point on it, as drift on the part of the administration, and if I am correct in that judgement (and I would welcome your comment on it) I must clearly regard it as a most serious matter. There are in effect in the situation with which you and I are now confronted two main factors. The first is the special responsibilities. On the Governor's position in regard to them I need not enlarge. But a second responsibility, as you will agree, which falls upon the Governor personally (Section XX of his Instrument of Instructions is of course relevant) is that of keeping in touch with every detail of the administration, of leaving nothing undone to maintain its efficiency at the highest pitch, to bring pressure to bear on ministers whenever there is any sign that the effect of their policy is likely to be detrimental, of watching with the utmost and most constant care the trend of events and the signs of development of tendencies which may be dangerous or embarrassing, and of making it quite clear to the ministers without a moment's delay that while the Governor is dealing here with matters which do not directly affect his special responsibilities, he feels it his duty to make it plain to his ministers, and to place it on record, that if they pursue a certain course, that course cannot but have certain consequence[s] of a detrimental character and may bring about a situation of a really serious type. And, in the different circumstances of their position, there is of course a very clear responsibility on the higher officials of the administration to keep the Governor in the closest touch, and to see him at frequent intervals.

2. I will proceed later in this letter to indicate certain of the recent papers (I deliberately propose to take those only which have come before me in the last month or so) on which my growing uneasiness at the United Provinces position is based. Let me also explain that when I speak, as I have in the concluding sentences of the preceding paragraph, of the duty of officials in this matter, that duty as I conceive it is the duty of the Chief Secretary,[26] of the Inspector-General of Police,[27] and of the Deputy Inspector-General, C.I.D.,[28] not to fail to bring to the notice of the Governor tendencies which they may regard as dangerous or likely to become embarrassing. The situation is much too important to justify us in running any risks on matters of this character; and as I see it there is nothing improper, to put it at its lowest (I would indeed myself regard it as the specific duty of the officials concerned), in their drawing the Governor's pointed attention to movements or tendencies which they regard as fraught with danger to the morale of the services, to the maintenance of law and order in the Province, to the maintenance of the morale of the troops, with a view to the avoidance of anything calculated to undermine that morale, and in particular to the avoidance of anything which might be regarded as constituting the establishment of a parallel government.

3. Before I proceed to the detailed instances to which I have just referred, let me say a word on the importance I attach to the maintenance of personal contact. The tours in which you are now engaged represent I need not say a most valuable contribution to this. But with a situation such as now confronts us it would be a relief to me to know how frequently you see your Inspector-General of Police (in your letter of 17th February last you referred to a fortnightly interview), and the Deputy Inspector-General, C.I.D., and whether in particular the Inspector-General is kept in close contact with all decisions affecting the police and consulted before they are taken. I would like, too, to know how frequently, in the light of the experience of the last seven months, you now interview your Secretaries? I assume that the Chief Secretary is in constant touch? These points arise only because some of the matters which have come to my notice seem to me to be such that it is clearly essential that the Governor should not only be given the earliest information about them but be kept in constant touch with their development, and because (I have in view particularly the

position in relation to the troops at Lansdowne) I am not in fact clear that such information has been made available to you. The question of contact with ministers is on a different footing; but here again it seems to me essential that it should be as close as possible, and that the Governor should be in constant and immediate touch with all that is going on – for it is axiomatic that it is only if he is so equipped that he can lay his own plans, and if necessary consult with the Governor-General, sufficiently ahead. I could not help noticing in this connection that in paragraph 1 of your secret letter U.P.-13 of 24th October you mentioned that you were then in Lucknow for three days only, having been away from your ministers, except the Premier, and your Secretaries, for nearly a month. I would ask you to consider whether steps could not be taken to ensure even closer contact with your ministers (individual ministers as well as the Premier) and your Secretaries, for I feel no doubt whatever that it is only by constant and intimate contact with individual ministers that that close acquaintance will be engendered which breeds confidence: and it goes without saying that the more personal support is available to officials the stronger their position will be, and the more likely the Governor to hear everything that is in the wind.

4. Let me now turn to the various specific matters which are in my mind. I will deal first with this question of a parallel government, for that issue has come prominently before me as the result of your Secretary's letter of 8th October, No. 654-G.S.P., a copy of which I am sending to the Secretary of State, commenting on certain recent references to this in the Dominions Report.[29] I am I fear entirely unable to accept the view suggested in that letter that there are no signs of a parallel government. I regard indeed the signs to which you refer, and the other evidence available to me, as of a very grave character; and while it may well be that, as your Secretary's letter suggests, we have not yet reached the stage at which there is any question of establishment of a parallel government throughout the Province, the "fairly numerous instances reported" referred to in your Secretary's letter, and the other matters referred to in that letter are such as in my view entirely to justify the statement made in the Dominions report, and to call for the most serious notice. Donaldson's letter mentions that the ministry have taken certain steps, and in a number of cases with success. But the general impression left on me is disturbing, and I would be grateful if you would on this specific point let me know in still greater detail to what extent you have found it possible to maintain pressure on your ministry, and to bring them to a full realisation of the fact that in no circumstances shall we be prepared to agree to any endeavours of this

type to establish parallel organisations, or to tolerate deliberate attempts to undermine the authority of the District Officer or of the other legitimate authorities of government. Let me in this connection mention one or two of the cases which have struck me. I do not propose to take instances of longer standing, though the extracts enclosed[30] from the United Provinces Police Reports Nos. 35 (week ending 11th September) and 36 (week ending 18th September) are directly relevant. But I enclose an extract from the Report on the Political Situation in the United Provinces, No. 41, for the week ending the 16th October 1937, which you will have seen at the time. I would comment on this that I see no objection to endeavours to settle cases of adultery or cases of defamation or the like through *panchayats*. But I see the strongest objection to independent enquiries under sections 148 and 324 of the I.P.C. I take equally strong objection to the fact, if correct, that persons in the Kishanganj circle of Lucknow have been asked to make reports first at the Congress Office. Nor can I regard with equanimity instances such as that reported in the village of Jeegon. These are all significant signs, and it is our duty to deal with them without delay and at the earliest possible moment.

5. In the same connection I enclose an extract from the report on the Political Situation No. 42 for the week ending 23rd October 1937, received from your Special Branch with their letter 9/S-3 dated 27th October. Surely it is exceedingly significant that in the capital of the Province there should be a suggestion for the establishment of a Congress Thana where reports should be made before people go to the regular Police Station. The statement made in this report as regards Azamgarh is equally unsatisfactory; I cannot but take seriously the speeches summarised in paragraph 1 of the extract; and I find it difficult to reconcile the statements made in it in regard to Shahjahanpur and Hardoi with the suggestion that there are no serious efforts on the part of Congress to establish a parallel organisation. I would like to know what steps have been taken to check activities of this nature and the extent to which they have formed the subject of representations by you to ministers? The speeches recently made at Cawnpore, and the disgraceful and most dangerous attacks contained in those speeches on the police call again, in my judgement, for the severest notice; and I am glad to see from your letter of 8th November, No. U.P.-16, that you have drawn Pant's attention to this. But you will feel with me that it is not sufficient merely to draw attention to such cases – it is necessary I am certain to bring constant and strong pressure to bear on Ministers to remedy the situation. It is essential if the position is to be held together that that pressure should be sustained, and, too, that the Governor should

keep in the closest touch with the Inspector-General of Police; that he should require to be shown all reports bearing on activities of the nature now under consideration; and that he should not be content merely with discussing the matter in the cabinet, but should bring pointedly and in the sharpest language to the notice of his ministers, collectively or individually as may be appropriate, his own views of the situation which will arise both from the point of view of the ministry and of the Province if immediate and decisive action is not taken to deal with a position which he regards as threatening. There is a definite and specific obligation on the Governor, to which I have referred above, under paragraph XX of his Instrument of Instructions, for maintaining the general level of administration: and to find from the valuable report contained in your secret letter of 8th November, No. U.P.-16, that in your judgment, in the area you have recently toured, there is in the case of the Police "in the day-to-day administration some slackening, they have lost authority with the public; and consequently have lost some confidence in themselves" is disquieting. I would like to ask what steps you have in view to remedy that condition of affairs?

6. I now turn to the question of endeavours to subvert the loyalty of the troops. With this letter I send you a copy of reports recently received about Lansdowne. No reference has been made to this situation in any of the reports I have received from you. I regard them as of the gravest possible significance, both as affecting the loyalty of the troops, and, on the grounds advanced by Mr. Saner in his letter of 25th October,[31] of their possible effect in inciting racial feeling against Europeans, and I would be glad to have your observations on them with the minimum of delay. I have spoken to the Commander-in-Chief on the subject, and you will not be surprised to hear that he takes a view even more serious than my own. It seems to me intolerable that, even given the special geographical position of the station at Lansdowne, activities such as those described in these reports should be permitted; and I must ask you to raise the matter immediately with Pant and to let me know his reaction. We cannot, as you will agree, allow a situation in which responsibility will fall either on the Governor or the Governor-General for allowing a deterioration of administration and of control in a Province of such vital importance as the United Provinces to arise through any lack of activity on the part of either of us.

7. Nor I confess had I fully appreciated the precise extent of the orders which have been issued by your government in regard to reporting political meetings, etc. I propose to return to this subject in a later letter, for I regard it as of very great importance. For the moment I will only say that I quite recognise that ministers may take exception to Police reporters

being present at their meetings, and that is a feeling to which I would naturally defer. But to close down reporting of this type to the extent shown in the orders of your government of which copies are now enclosed is to take a very serious responsibility, and I need only invite your attention to the speeches of the ex-Kakori prisoners and the speeches made at the anti-police demonstration at Cawnpore on 24th October, to which I have referred above, and of which I enclose a copy, to show how strong a case exists on general grounds for the maintenance of a closer watchfulness on meetings and on speeches – a watchfulness the case for which I would have hoped that Pant could himself easily have been brought to realise. Nor can I but regard the instructions in your Chief Secretary's letter of 15th September as tying the hands of the local authorities to a most dangerous degree. I would like to know in this connection what action was taken on the proposal of the Assistant Collector, Lansdowne, made in his letter of 25th October referred to in the preceding paragraph, to warn all intending speakers that the law would be enforced, and that verbatim reports of manifestly illegal passages in speeches should be made?

8. It is with great reluctance that I have to approach you on this subject; and, as you will have seen, I have taken the utmost care to sift the material available to me, and personally to isolate the points which in my judgement call for particular attention and on which I must address you. I am sure that you are, if possible, more concerned than I am that the situation in your most important Province, on local as well as on general grounds, should be well in hand; but you will I feel agree with me that, on the material to which I have referred above, we can neither of us feel that we can with conviction claim that that is the case; and the consequences of any further deterioration may well be very serious indeed. You will share my view that in the situation with which we are now faced, it is essential that the Governor and his principal officers should take a direct, an immediate, and an active interest in every aspect of the administration which may have any reaction such as those to which I have referred in paragraph 1 of this letter, and that there can be no hesitation in raising doubtful cases with ministers and bringing the maximum pressure on them. The cumulative effect on me of the reports, including your own very valuable personal reports to me, on the situation in the United Provinces is, I must frankly confess, disturbing to a degree; and it is for this reason that I felt bound not only to address you on the situation generally, but to send a copy of my present letter to the Secretary of State. I think that the most satisfactory thing will be that you should come up to discuss the situation generally with me, and I shall, I need not say, be delighted to see

you at the earliest possible opportunity. Perhaps when you have had this letter you will telegraph to suggest a date. I shall be absent from Delhi from the 19th to the 22nd, but any other time that will be convenient to you will suit me perfectly well; and I think you will probably agree with me that, given its great importance both locally and in its wider reactions, the sooner we can examine the general position personally in discussion with one another the better.

Yours sincerely,
LINLITHGOW

APPENDIX 11

LINLITHGOW TO ZETLAND (EXTRACT)[32]
MSS.EUR.F. 125/4

Private and Personal — The Viceroy's House, New Delhi,
November 19th, 1937

10. I have telegraphed to you[33] about the United Provinces position, and you will have had the copy of my letter to Haig which Laithwaite sent to Clauson by the air mail which left here on the 17th November. By the time this reaches you, you will probably have had a telegram from me giving the gist of my discussion with him. I have, as you know, never felt quite easy as to his handling of that most important Province; though (as I think I mentioned to you at the time) there seemed to be signs of a definite improvement during August, and I thought then that my earlier forebodings might have been unfounded, and that unfamiliarity with the new position and the fact that he was not a very fit man for some time during the summer, might be the trouble. But I again find myself confronted with a series of incidents which, even though individually they are not very important, cannot but make me feel grave doubt as to his success in his handling of the situation. I give the fullest weight to the facts that the situation is one of the most difficult in the country; that the United Provinces is a very large Province with 48 districts; that the ministry has at its head a Premier who is a prominent character in Congress circles and who may on occasion be far from easy to handle; and, finally, that Jawaharlal Nehru has his headquarters in the Province and is most unlikely to be anything but an additional embarrassment. For all that I cannot help contrasting Haig's approach to the situation which confronts him with the approach of Hallett[34]

and Hyde Gowan;[35] I say nothing of Lumley,[36] who, with no experience whatever in this country, has in my judgement in the last couple of months handled the situation, by no means simple, in Bombay with eminent success and resolution. Haig, in his fortnightly personal letters to me over the last two or three months, frequently refers to indications of deterioration, or mentions that the situation in his view is taking a turn for the worse, or comments on a lowering in service morale or the like; but I do not think I am being wholly unfair to him when I say that, while he does report all these indications, I have not seen any very marked evidence of resolution on his part to grapple with the situations arising out of them. It is probably a question of temperament, and it may well be that he would be better as a secretariat officer than as a Governor. Much must depend on his reaction when I see him; and I must do my utmost to hearten him and try to make him pull himself together rather more than he does. And I must also endeavour to impress upon him the necessity for adopting an active and not merely a supine attitude in dealing with the situation and for standing up to his ministers behind the scenes; and – when necessary – saying things to them that they may not altogether relish. But I shall certainly not fail to make it clear to him that I regard my own responsibility in the matter as a very heavy one given the critical importance of his Province in the general scheme of things.

APPENDIX 12

LINLITHGOW TO ZETLAND
MSS.EUR.F. 125/161

Secret

The Viceroy's House, New Delhi,
November 25th, 1937

My dear Lawrence,

I have, as you are aware, been for some time anxious about the condition of things in the United Provinces. I got Haig to come to New Delhi, and had long talks to him on Tuesday and Wednesday last. I send you an account of our conversations.[37] The report is a full one, but I think it worth while troubling you to read it. The position is to be measured not so much by the importance attaching to one incident or to another, as by the impression made upon the mind by a conspectus of all the relevant incidents and by Haig's reactions to these, and by his approach to the questions of policy involved. I felt it necessary to speak with all directness, and it was clear that the first interview distressed him severely. On Wednesday he was more at his ease, and I think the general effect of the two talks I had with him was to hearten him. I wish I could say as much for myself. I am left with the feeling that Pant is very much on top. I dare hope that my talks with Haig may stiffen him for a while; but I fear that their effect may be no more than temporary.

I shall be greatly interested to hear from you the impression that these papers make upon your mind. You are better able to take a detached view than I. I have done my best to give you a fair and balanced presentation of the facts.

Haig is, I think, tired and much in need of leave. But while weariness may account for some lack of grip and drive, it should not (his health being apparently good) give rise to serious shortcomings in terms of judgement. In this connection, I draw your attention to the circular[38] to District Magistrates issued over the name of the Chief Secretary. To my mind this is a dreadful document. Yet the fact is that Pant consulted Haig as to its preparation and that Haig amended it and approved its issue. Moreover when I criticised it, Haig was most ready to defend its terms, and to canvas the wisdom and expediency of the policy it advocates. I showed it to Craik[39] and Maxwell,[40] and its effect upon them was no less shattering than upon myself. Maxwell, a most experienced officer, and a model of caution and restraint, observed that had he, as a District Officer, received such a document, he would have at once sent in his papers! They both thought it the worst circular they had ever seen. Since Haig left, this document has got into the Press. I only hope it may not be a nuisance to you in the House of Commons.

You will also find attached to my report a copy of a paper[41] sent round by Haig to his Cabinet in the early days of November. This, as you will see, is a well-intentioned effort; but nothing much of substance has so far followed its circulation.

You are entitled, I feel, to know my present mind upon this most awkward difficulty. I do not think that Haig will be found able to hold together the United Provinces for the next two years – he is due to go on Dec. 6th, 1939. At the same time, I am well aware of the difficulty of removing a Governor. There is a risk of scandal; of difficulties with his ministry if we are suspected of having put him out for being too soft with Congress; of misunderstandings in the Service; of a row in Parliament and the Clubs over the dismissal of a senior Service Governor. Again, I am sure Haig is doing his best, and I know that you will feel with me that he is entitled to every consideration. What then, may best be done?

He is anxious to take leave from next May, which would bring him back to his charge in September 1938 with about 14 months still to run. I am inclined to suggest to you that unless matters improve greatly over the next few months, we had better let him go home on leave and then persuade him to retire at the end of his leave, with, if necessary, a decoration. I sincerely hope that he *may* improve and that I may be able to get him through his full term, but I greatly doubt it.

Subject to your views, I would be disposed to suggest that I should in due course tell Haig:

(*a*) that I have fully reported to you my discussion with him, and the fact that he felt my criticism more severe than was justified. Also that I have reported to you the suggestions I had made to him for the improvement of the position in the province; and that I had told him, as we parted, that while I felt reassured as to his attitude, I still took a grave view of the position in the province.

(*b*) that you have informed me that you too took a grave view; that you attached the first importance to the adoption by him of a stiffer attitude towards Pant; that it was essential that the Police should have full support, and that Service morale should be maintained, and that you could not but regard Pant's and his circular to District Magistrates as an error of judgement which it was important to repair; that you and I would clearly have to keep a very close watch on the U.P. situation, but that you had hoped, in the light of his talks with me, that an improvement would manifest itself without delay which would reduce our present apprehension.

Should it become necessary to make a change of Governors in the near future, I would suggest Hallett, if indeed the selection is to be made out here. For many reasons, I would much prefer to see a Brabourne[42] or a Lumley[43] at Lucknow. But I realise of course the difficulties of upsetting existing conventions in that regard, more particularly in view of the narrowed opportunities open to the I.C.S. on account of the recent constitutional changes.

I fear, Lawrence, that I have had to write you rather a disturbing letter. But the U.P. is too important a province, and my own responsibility too heavy and too direct to make it possible for me to disguise from yourself as Secretary of State the very grave apprehension I feel as to the condition of the province, or my doubt as to the capacity of Haig to set right the things now amiss, or to prevent further deterioration.[44]

Yours ever,
HOPIE

APPENDIX 13

NOTE BY EWART[45]
MSS.EUR.F. 125/4

Secret

Intelligence Bureau, Home Department,
Government of India,
November 28th, 1937

NOTE ON VISIT TO LUCKNOW AND CAWNPORE

I have spent a day in Lucknow and a day in Cawnpore during which I have discussed the position in the United Provinces, both in general and in particular aspects, with His Excellency the Governor and his Secretary, the Chief Secretary, the I.G. of Police, the Central Intelligence Officer, a Range D.I.G of Police, an officer of the C.I.D., the Collector and Superintendent of Police, Cawnpore, a group of eight leading Europeans of the Cawnpore mill industry, and several other persons. I have seldom found it more difficult to draw clear conclusions from such a series of interviews. Nevertheless, I am quite clear in my mind as to the main features of the problem which the United Provinces present.

2. Everybody agrees that the government is not governing and that, as a necessary consequence, the administrative Services are deteriorating. Everyone also agrees that the burden of ministerial responsibility is carried by Pandit Pant alone (with some increasingly useful assistance in her own sphere from Mrs. Pandit). Everyone agrees that it has not yet been possible to induce the Premier to face up to realities and to take action to control subversive and demoralising influences, and that the resulting situation is dangerous. It is further agreed that the strength of the police force, especially in the matter of centrally controlled reserves (which are practically non-existent) is inadequate for dealing either with widespread agrarian unrest or with simultaneous disturbances in several large towns. Opinions differ as to whether there is reasonable ground for expecting that the Premier can ever be induced to make a positive declaration of his intentions to maintain law and order and to take necessary action in support of such declaration, and as to how much time can be allowed for the instructional process without deliberately risking an acceleration of the processes of deterioration to the point of loss of control. This division of opinion is, with the exception of His Excellency the Governor, fairly clearly marked as between the Secretariat and the Executive. In between come the Central Intelligence Officer and the Provincial Special Branch who

are cognisant of both points of view. I have tested the information and opinions of the latter officers by a particularly searching interrogation and I find that, with a full realisation of the Secretariat point of view, they are still so convinced of the dangers to the administration of the Province at large of the present indefinite state of drift that they quite positively support the point of view taken by the Executive Officers of districts. The Secretariat view, which is shared by the I.G. of Police (very recently returned from leave and with no up-to-date knowledge of the actual events in districts) and the D.I.G., C.I.D.,[46] who is somewhat notoriously cranky, is that Pandit Pant is a sincere and estimable man, honestly trying, in face of great difficulties, to be fair to everybody and to administer according to ideals which are variously described as those of the Gladstonian Liberal or of Mr. Lansbury, and that if he is handled carefully and given plenty of time he will become increasingly amenable to official advice, while at the same time keeping control of his heterogeneous party. The view taken by District Officers of proved ability in the persons of Mr. Owen, the Collector, and Mr. Pearce, the Superintendent of Police, of Cawnpore, and shared by the European businessmen of that city, who, whatever their defects, have had considerable opportunities in recent months of forming first-hand opinions of the Premier's character, is that Pandit Pant is an incorrigible visionary and that there is little or no hope of time, persuasion and experience causing him to act according to the demands of realities. It follows logically from the latter view that the sooner the universally admitted deterioration is arrested by, however, drastic means, the better, but this logical view is qualified, in the case of such responsible opinion as that of Mr. Owen, by recognition of the fact that there is no alternative to the Premiership of Pant except the assumption of complete control by the Governor. The latter alternative might have the extremely serious effect of driving both the dangerous revolutionary wing and the present ministry and its supporters into opposition on a common front of mass action. I have mentioned earlier that His Excellency the Governor is an exception to the clear cut division between the two schools of thought. The reason is that which I have just stated. His Excellency realises fully the grave effects of a breach with Pant. He feels, and he has general support in the opinion, that Pant can perhaps be led, but certainly cannot be driven; he has formed a careful estimate, as a result of extensive touring, of the extent to which administrative deterioration has gone, and I think that I interpret him correctly as feeling that it is in all the circumstances both safe and wise to allow more time for efforts to bring the Premier into a more assertive frame of mind.

3. On the side of time and persuasion the chief argument really is the extremely serious consequences of a break, which those most intimately associated with Pant think bound to result from unyielding pressure at this stage. In support of the belief that he may be brought to face up to his responsibilities, the facts which I have been able to gather are that Mr. Horton, the present I.G. of Police, who has known Pandit Pant for many years, seems to have got on very much better terms with him than Mr. Phillips who was acting in Mr. Horton's absence, and will thus be able to apply his course of instruction in realism with better hopes of success. Also, Pandit Pant appears to have given a distinctly favourable impression in an informal talk and discussion which he had with a conference of the I.G. and D.Is.G. of Police on November 26th; in the course of this discussion he stated that he was learning every day more of the conditions under which the police had to work and of the value and importance of that work. I was impressed by the opinion of Mr. Weymouth, the D.I.G. of the Allahabad Range of some 15 districts, and of a Muhammadan Deputy Superintendent of Police, that police officers are feeling on the whole less apprehensive than they did in August. Mr. Weymouth expressed the view that the loudest complaints about Congress interference from the police came often from bad officers, and that the better officers, both in the higher grades and subordinates, were adapting themselves to changed circumstances with considerable success and were getting help instead of hindrance from responsible Congressmen. Further consideration and enquiry regarding these opinions somewhat qualifies their significance. I feel little doubt that such lessening of apprehension as has occurred among the various grades of police officers in districts is due mainly to relations being less bad than they had at first expected, when anticipation of widespread victimisation of individual officers was much more prevalent than experience has justified; moreover, the fact that police in rural areas are now getting help from the local Congress M.L.As. and other prominent Congressmen is potentially an element of danger; for it may safely be assumed that such assistance is given for a *quid pro quo*, viz., the support of police influence at the next election.

4. In support of the view that administrative deterioration is widespread and serious and that nothing has been done to check it or to control the demoralising influences, the array of facts presented to my notice is far too lengthy to enumerate in this note. There is no doubt that the prestige, but not the loyalty and hitherto not the morale of the police, has everywhere been affected. In the case of the Revenue establishment, there seems

justification for thinking that politics have actively influenced deterioration. Mr. Owen mentioned that in his own district (Cawnpore) very recently a tehsildar had had to be removed at a few days' notice to another district for having fragrantly falsified the crop assessment of his tehsil in favour of tenants with the clear object of winning favour in Congress circles, and the patwari establishment has made direct representations to the ministry regarding their conditions of service and demanding increases of pay. I was not favourably impressed with the representatives of the European industrialists whom I met, but they have undoubtedly gone through difficult and discouraging times during which they have gained concrete experience of the new system of government and of individuals connected with it. They are impressed by the fact – admitted by the District Magistrate to be a deliberate policy necessitated by present circumstances, though thoroughly distasteful – that the police are holding back from interference in the activities of unruly crowds so long as they stop short of violence, and talk of being forced to take the protection of themselves and their property into their own hands by raising bodies of armed guards or special constables. Dominating their views is a distinctly critical opinion of the attitude of His Excellency the Governor and a firm conviction that nothing practical can be expected of Pandit Pant. Mr. Pearce, the Superintendent of Police, Cawnpore, is a very level-headed officer who has done splendid work; he is very far indeed from being disheartened, and everyone acknowledges that he has kept the efficiency and morale of his Force at a high pitch. Nevertheless, he sees little that is encouraging in the situation and, like others, can give no answer to the question: How long can the present methods be allowed to prevail without disastrous consequences? Mr. Owen speaks with an obvious sense of responsibility as well as with an outlook founded on practical experience. He is supporting a burden which nothing but direct contact enables one to appreciate. He is taking on himself responsibilities which should be those of the provincial government, but which the latter refuse to shoulder, and he is going against all his training and instincts as an administrator in order to give the maximum chance to the ministry to make good. Under these almost intolerable conditions he is administering a charge which, in addition to the town and industrial area of Cawnpore, comprises a rural population of one and a half millions among some of whom scarcity conditions are assuming ominous proportions. He has preserved remarkable serenity in the circumstances, but admits that conditions may well arise under which he would find it impossible to continue to serve; among other things he quite seriously fears the victimisation by insidious means of certain of his most loyal and efficient police subordinates. I cannot avoid qualifying what I have said earlier in this note about the good relations which Mr. Horton, the I.G. of Police, is establishing with the Premier by the opinion, which I have derived largely from others, that he is unwarrantably optimistic and insufficiently sympathetic towards the position and difficulties of officers and men of his Force working in the districts; unfortunately Mr. Horton is to an exceptional extent a "headquarters" man with very little district experience. This is an example of the general position and is illustrated by the fact that so responsible a person as Mr. Owen expressed the view that officers in the comfortable detachment of Secretariat posts had no appreciation of the conditions under which officers in the districts were working.

5. Influencing all these impressions is one more impression which I have clearly gained; that is, that Pandit Pant instinctively avoids any action which might offend anybody and that he has not hitherto been amenable to the influence of intensive instruction by his official advisers as has been the case, for instance, in Bombay, with the notable effect of compelling the Bombay ministry to face realities. It is very noticeable that the utmost which Pant has done is to remonstrate privately with individual extremists. He has neither made any public demonstration of an intention to control extremist activities, nor has he published any condemnation of undesirable actions, e.g. the Anti-Police Day. Just as he tries to secure a simple passage for himself among the extremists by privately placating them, so he allays official apprehensions by occasional sympathetic talks, but he rarely, if ever, commits himself to a formal or public statement by which he could be held to his pledges. In this connection there is no doubt that the Premier's speech to a police parade at Cawnpore, and the circular letter[47] issued by the Chief Secretary to all officials regarding the attitude which they should adopt towards the Congress, have proved very distasteful, especially as, while the letter to officials has been published in the Press, no such publicity has been given to the letter "in a similar sense" to the Provincial Congress Committee, the issue of which was promised in the official letter. I did, indeed, hear some appreciative views in regard to the Premier's speech to the Cawnpore police, but this amounts to no more than a feeling that the speech is somewhat better than what might have been expected from Pant.

6. I must add that my own observation, so far as it goes, supports what others tell me, that no general spirit of lawlessness or hostility is apparent, though many examples have been given me of signs that a slackening of control is widely assumed. Gandhi caps and *khaddar* are comparatively

rare, and the Congress flag is hardly seen at all, e.g. in the course of my journey by road from Lucknow to Cawnpore – except on District Board schools and similar buildings.

J.M. EWART

APPENDIX 14

COMMUNIQUÉ ISSUED BY U.P. GOVERNMENT[48]
L/P&J/5/264: f. 19

Undated

Government have recently received representations that tenants in some areas are withholding payment of the current rental demand and of the *rabi* (1344) arrears in the mistaken belief that if they pay they might at some future date lose all or part of the benefits which may accrue to them when legislation reforming the tenancy and rent law comes into force.

Government desire to make the position clear. The recovery of arrears due for *kharif* 1344 or earlier *kists* has been stayed under the Stay of Proceedings (Revenue Courts) Act, and tenants are entitled to have all payments they now make credited towards the current rent or the arrears, if any, of *rabi* 1344 Fasli. But the rents of *rabi* 1344 and *kharif* 1345 are recoverable in the ordinary courts of law; and, if a tenant withholds payment, a landlord may take action for the recovery of those sums, or for the ejectment of the tenant in default of payment in one or other of the ways laid down in the Agra Tenancy Act and the Oudh Rent Act. The tenant who now pays in full the arrears of the last *rabi* and the rent of the current instalment need have no fear that he will be deprived of the benefits of the coming legislation; but a tenant who fails to pay up and thereby renders himself liable to ejectment and is subsequently ejected, will of course lose its benefits. The government wish to impress upon tenants generally the advisability of paying up these demands punctually and fully, in their own interests.

A.A. WAUGH
Secretary to Government,
United Provinces,
Revenue Department

APPENDIX 15

LINLITHGOW TO HAIG
Telegram
MSS.EUR.F. 115/15

Clear the Line *December 20th, 1937*
No. 467-GC

Following received from Secretary to Governor-General Public. *Begins.* "D.I.B. has received secret information that Babu Rajendra Prasad has received a letter of which extract follows from Vallabhbhai Patel, Bombay. *Begins:* 'Returned here yesterday morning. Met Bapu [Mahatma Gandhi]. Told him about Lucknow visit. He was sorry to hear all that had happened. He felt that they have allowed themselves to be entangled on a wrong issue. I got a message from Jiwat [J.B. Kripalani] on telephone. He says he met J. [Jawaharlal Nehru] at Benares and travelled with him to Lucknow. As expected he does [?not] agree with our views. He feels it is of [?a justifiable] reason why they should resign. Probably he may feel that they have done well.'" *Ends.*

APPENDIX 16

LINLITHGOW TO HAIG
MSS.EUR.F. 115/12

Secret Viceroy's Camp, India (Calcutta),
December 24th, 1937

My dear Haig,

In the course of our conversations at Delhi last month you showed me a circular letter (D.O. No.712/III of 10th November 1937)[49] which your government had issued to all District Magistrates on the subject of their relations with the Congress. I then indicated to you that I was far from happy about this letter and I think it only fair to you now to indicate in more detail the reasons why I feel continued uneasiness at the thought that all government servants in the United Provinces must in the meanwhile be regarding these instructions as binding upon them.

2. It was apparent to me at the time of our talk on this subject that you

did not view the circular in the light in which it immediately struck me when I saw it. But I am sure you will agree with me that the success of the constitutional experiment on which we have embarked depends in a very large measure on the extent to which we can preserve the integrity of the public services, that is to say secure their immunity from political influences or interference and, in the unfamiliar circumstances in which they are working, build up as early as possible a firm tradition of complete detachment from Party organisations and policies. It is only so that they can be taught to regard themselves as the instruments of the Governor in his exercise of the executive authority of the Province and not merely as the servants of whatever Party happens to be in power.

3. It is because it shows no trace of a realisation of this cardinal principle that I regard the circular letter issued by your ministry with grave misgivings. Officers are told that the time has come when they should make determined efforts to establish relations of mutual confidence with the district leaders of the Congress organisation. One may well ask, why should the burden be placed on the district officer and why in relation to the Congress organisation only? The answer comes later, and it is a very dangerous one – "The Congress . . . represents a large body of public opinion and is the party on the support of which the present Government rests." This fact is apparently held to give a privileged position to the party organisation of the Congress in the districts including not only a right to supervise the conduct of public servants but a claim to decide which complaints or other matters shall receive their special consideration. The explanation is given that "the Congress is naturally anxious to secure the maximum benefit for the members of the public out of the public institutions and functionaries" but unless (as I am afraid we must conclude) "public" means only "Congress supporters" there is no reason why this anxiety should be attributed to the Congress rather than to the District Officers addressed. To speak quite frankly, if I were a District Officer I should regard the whole circular as an uncalled for and rather offensive lecture. Its underlying assumption is that no government servant can be trusted to do his duty unless he is told to do it by Congress busybodies, to whom he is enjoined to show special deference because they happen to be the adherents of the political party in power. The same tone appears in a circular letter which I have seen reproduced in one of the newspapers and which purports to have been issued by a Mr. Seth, Secretary of the U.P. Provincial Congress Committee, to District Congress Committees and other subordinate Committees. I suspect that this may be the communication foreshadowed in the last sentence of the circular we are discussing, and I

notice that it imposes no corresponding obligation on Congress supporters to seek to bring themselves into "relations of mutual confidence and harmony" with government officials. This, as the present circular says "is a matter primarily for the district officers themselves to consider".

4. Apart from the false perspective in which this circular presents the relationship between the public services and the party in power, there is one other tendency which it signifies, the dangerous import of which will I know be familiar to you from your experience of the methods used in past civil disobedience movements, and that is the tendency to impress on the public that the Congress are their sole intermediaries in securing fair treatment or redress of grievances from the officers of government. Congress, as you know, have always aimed at establishing themselves in this position and thus discouraging direct access of the public to district officers and there is no doubt that this method is one of the devices intended to prepare the way for parallel institutions. The same tendency to represent the Congress as intermediaries appears in the newspaper report of the circular letter of the Secretary, U.P. Provincial Congress Committee, to which I have referred above, and a position of this kind is not, as I am sure you will agree, one which we can even by implication accept.

5. I recognise the difficulty of your position in relation to this circular, in that although it was prepared on the instructions of your ministry it did at one stage pass through your hands, and the best method of dealing with it is clearly one which must be dictated by circumstances. I am sure however that given the apprehensions which I have expressed above and which you and I in fact discussed in some detail during our conversation at Delhi, you will appreciate my anxiety that if a suitable opportunity offers such steps may be taken for its withdrawal or modification as may be practicable, and that to such extent as it may lead to a misunderstanding on the part of the Services, again any appropriate reassurances should be given in such manner as you may judge to be the wisest and most suitable to the circumstances.[50]

Yours sincerely,
LINLITHGOW

APPENDIX 17

COMMUNIQUE ISSUED BY U.P. GOVERNMENT
L/P&J/7/1059

December 27th, 1937

The United Provinces government have for some time past been disturbed about the nature of speeches that have been made on numerous occasions, especially in connection with the movement for the release of political speakers. A band of speakers consisting, to a large extent, of ex-prisoners and including several of those convicted in the Kakori case to whom clemency had recently been extended by the government, have been touring all parts of the province, making speeches which, as reported, amount to incitement to violence. The most prominent among these speakers was Pandit Parmanand who was released by the orders of the Punjab government in August last. By the 9th November the U.P. government had decided that some steps must be taken to check these speeches. They had accordingly directed that Pandit Parmanand, whose speeches, as reported, were the worst should be sent for by the Chief Secretary and should be warned that the government would be unable to permit a repetition of such speeches. A letter was accordingly sent to Pandit Parmanand but as he was continuously touring from place to place, it was not delivered and the speeches continued. Towards the end of November the government received details of a speech of a particularly objectionable nature delivered by Pandit Parmanand at Dehra Dun. Immediate steps were necessary to stop this flow of speeches and the government decided that action should be taken to institute a prosecution against Pandit Parmanand for his Dehra Dun speech and to warn certain of the other speakers. Shortly after this decision was taken, Pandit Parmanand and some others of this group of speakers were arrested in Delhi for breach of an order for which they have just been sentenced there to different terms of imprisonment. The U.P. government are inspired by no feelings of vindictiveness nor by any desire to interfere with the legitimate freedom of speech. They are, however, deeply concerned to prevent conditions developing which will lead to the spread of a spirit of violence. They are pledged to a policy of non-violence, and speeches which promote an atmosphere of violence are in conflict with the fundamental principles of the present ministry as well as with their responsibilities to the public for maintaining peaceful conditions. They cannot, therefore, allow speeches of this kind to continue.

It was necessary to take action against Pandit Parmanand without loss of time. But the immediate danger arising from the continued repetition of these speeches has now been checked. The government also feel that the step taken by them to institute the prosecution against Pandit Parmanand, which was the first case of its nature, will serve as a public warning to him as well as to others that they will not tolerate a repetition of such speeches. In view of the changed situation and the events in Delhi the government have decided that it is not necessary to proceed with the case against Pandit Parmanand in respect of his Dehra Dun speech. It is needless to add that if Parmanand repeats a speech of this nature there will be no hesitation in ordering his prosecution. The government have also administered a warning on the same lines to some of the other speakers. They wish to make it clear that the action taken in this matter must be understood as constituting a general warning that speeches of this kind will not be permitted, and having thus stated their position the government hold themselves free to institute proceedings without any further warning against any individual who offends in this manner. The government hope that the generous course they have adopted will be fully appreciated and all will join hands to maintain and promote a peaceful and non-violent atmosphere which is the essential foundation of ordered society.

APPENDIX 18

NOTE BY EWART[51]
MSS.EUR.F. 125/5

Secret

Intelligence Bureau, Home Department,
December 29th, 1937

I send, herewith, two interesting letters from the C.I.O., Lucknow. P.U.C.-I is in reply to a letter in which I advised him to keep in touch with His Excellency the Governor while the latter was in Allahabad. P.U.C.-II answers an enquiry from me about the relative strength of Right and Left Wing views in the United Provinces cabinet.

2. I have had personal opportunities in the past few days of obtaining information about the state of the United Provinces as I have visited Agra by road and, while there, saw the Collector (Mr. Mudie) and the Superintendent of Police; the latter is a very experienced and able officer who has been in the Agra District for nearly three years. I have also had a talk with Khan Bahadur Muhammad Mazhar of my office who is now on

leave and is a resident of the United Provinces, and in conversation yesterday with Mr. Butler of the International Labour Office heard his impressions of his visit to Cawnpore and Allahabad.

3. Mr. Butler found Nehru a very different and less impressive person than he had been led to expect. He appreciates Nehru's pleasant personality and sincerity, found him fairly well-informed on world problems, but could not picture him as an effective leader of a big movement. Nehru impressed on Mr. Butler that, for the Congress, the cause of the peasants was their most important commitment, and that industrial problems took a very minor place. Like others, Mr. Butler got the impression that Nehru's constructive ideas are very few and undeveloped.

4. The Agra district has been less affected than other parts of the Province by violent speaking and subversive agitation. Nevertheless, there are grounds for apprehension of trouble in two directions; Mr. Measures[52] considers that there is growing disappointment over the non-appearance of the millennium which Congress promised at the time of the elections, coupled with growing hostility to Congress on the part of both small and big landowners and others whose interests are in stability and the security of property rights; secondly, communal animosity is very bitter and outbreaks of trouble in this connection are definitely apprehended.

5. Both Mr. Measures and Mr. Mudie described experiences on tour in the rural areas, which show that so far from there being any hostility among the common folk towards officials in general and British officials in particular, friendliness and confidence are shown to a quite remarkable extent; for instance, in the fact of shopkeepers and their customers in village bazaars spontaneously, and without exception, rising to show respect to officers passing through a village; even Mrs. Measures riding alone past a village received recognition on the same scale. Mr. Measures says that throughout his time in the district he has never experienced such cordiality, and cannot escape the impression that there is a definite feeling that the District officers are the one permanent and reliable element in a confused and unstable situation. Both my own observation while driving through the Muttra and Agra districts and what I heard in Agra bear out what Mr. Blunden has written about the Province being generally quiet. There is no sign whatever, either in towns or villages, of Congress truculence, and Gandhi caps and Congress flags are rarely seen.

6. As has been reported before, the apprehensions of subordinate police officers when Congress first took office were mainly due to fears of victimization, and these have been allayed, but I hear from more than one source that there is, among police officers, considerable annoyance and even bitter resentment in regard to the officiousness of petty Congress

followers who intrude and try to interfere in normal police investigations and other activities. A Deputy Superintendent of Police told Khan Bahadur Muhammad Mazhar that if there were a constitutional break-down followed by an unlawful movement by Congress, there would be no such thing as a "mild lathi charge", but lawless crowds would be dispersed with full vigour.

7. My own impressions, supplemented by Mr. Blunden's letters, fit in with the impressions which I gained when on tour last month. At that time I felt that any continuance of the policy of drift which had begun to cause deterioration would be extremely dangerous, but that quite a minor show of determination would have a heartening effect on officials and a sobering effect on subversive agitators. The recent public examples of a stiffening attitude may, I think, be expected to improve the situation all round very considerably.

8. The most disquieting information which I was given was the quite positive statement by Mr. Measures that land in the Agra district has practically no value now as a security. He went further and said that even urban property was a very much poorer form of security now than in the recent past. We have had reports of the same nature before, confined, I think to Bihar and the United Provinces. The implication is one of the greatest seriousness. I am hardly in a position to obtain more than desultory and superficial reports in this connection, but the subject seems to require serious investigation. It would appear that the Financial and Revenue authorities in Provinces on the one hand, and Banking interests on the other, should be in the best position to give authoritative and specific information as to the extent to which the sale and security value of land has been affected by the anti-landlord policy of Congress governments.

J.M. EWART

ENCLOSURE 1 TO APPENDIX 18

BLUNDEN TO EWART

Secret

Camp, Allahabad,
December 23rd, 1937

My dear Sir John,

Your No. 1-J.E.-37 of the 20th was handed to me this morning; my Deputy had however to show it to Donaldson in Lucknow, and I hope it duly reached His Excellency before his departure for his Xmas camp – the party left here a day earlier than was originally proposed.

You will have seen from my tour programme that I had already come across to Allahabad, leaving Lucknow on the 19th; His Excellency sent for me here before I had time to apply for an interview – as usual at my interviews, His Excellency went over the whole field of politics, after going through my last fortnightly and asking for a few more details. His Excellency was very interested in your note on Bombay and he thought it showed that the Bombay ministry have developed more than his own government, but here too there seems to be a definite stiffening up in their attitude though up to the moment they have not done very much to combat subversive activities.

His Excellency also discussed J.L. N[ehru] at length, and went through all the latest indications of his constitutional position – I said that all my information to date showed that he wants to support the Pant ministry, for the time at least, though many think it is expediency rather than conviction of the essential durability of the constitution. J.L.N. is a man of knowledge and experience and he is keenly interested in world affairs and their repercussions on India. (I have been told that he has no definite plans for combating Federation at present.)

His Excellency went on then to discuss the Kisan Sabba – it is unlikely that serious trouble will take place while the cultivators are busy with their *rabi*, and this year's poor monsoon makes them busier than usual with irrigation; but the people who thought that voting for Congress meant complete freedom are definitely disappointed with the present official party advice to pay up their dues, and tempers may I think easily become frayed when the landlords, who have probably paid up their revenue from capital in most cases, try to realise their rents. We went over the case of the ex-prisoners, and His Excellency indicated extreme annoyance with Parmanand especially – I thought His Excellency has stiffened up considerably in his own views and also in his attitude towards the ministry.

I have found Allahabad very interesting; having served here so much in various capacities, including Superintendent of Police, I met a number of people of interest, including some subordinate policemen who definitely do not feel that the proper attitude of the best Congressmen really serves to control the riffraff who shelter behind Congress and who still annoy and insult the subordinate police officers not infrequently. An old Muslim friend actually delivered to me a really fighting speech, declaring that they are going ahead with the League and they have not the least intention of becoming mere appendages – they want to hoist their own flag if

Congress hoist theirs. If possible I shall try to spend a few days here frequently – it is in a less provincial atmosphere than Lucknow – and your letter indicates that you will approve of my doing this? A very reliable informant told me that the Bengal released detenues have not the least intention of following the straight path, so Benares will be a place to watch, as I have mentioned before.

On the 21st I was about to pack up to return to Lucknow when I got a letter from Murray saying that his Governor would like to see me before Xmas, so I fixed things up by telephone and went off to Patna the same night – I had the pleasure of meeting Brett and Johnson there, and we had a profitable discussion of affairs.

His Excellency Sir M. Hallett was good enough to give me a long interview; I was able to show him that against all the various unfortunate incidents which are duly reported from here, the great fact remains that generally speaking the United Provinces are still quiet, and very different from 1921 and 1930, when I personally had enough bad experiences of the effects of agitation on ignorant people. We are certainly a long way from that sort of thing on a wide scale at the moment, and every peaceful month is probably something to the good, while the ministry are learning to be servants of His Majesty rather than followers of the principles laid down by Congress as the refuge of irresponsible criticism and discontent with few means of doing anything to carry out their programme.

Sir M. Hallett ran through the whole field of current politics, and if my replies were of any use to him I shall feel more than repaid for the journey [to] Patna. I will not extend this letter, as no doubt Murray reports fully on his provinces; but if there are any points you would like me to try to clear will you kindly let me know.

I must add that before going to Patna I asked Sir Harry Haig through his Military Secretary if he would like me to go and he kindly approved. From my point of view it was a very instructive trip.

I have been on tour most of this month, and so have not had time to write much beyond my brief diary notes; but I may have a few things in mind which if you will let me know what you require can be sent up when I get back to Lucknow.

With all good wishes for Christmas.

Yours sincerely,
A.C. BLUNDEN

ENCLOSURE 2 TO APPENDIX 18

BLUNDEN TO EWART

Secret

Lucknow,
December 25th, 1937

My dear Sir John,

Your personal letter of the 21st reached me on my return to Lucknow.

The United Provinces ministry is not an impressive body – we have not really had good ministers for some years, and so the present ones in some ways shine by contrast with their predecessors, but that does not mean that they make a good cabinet.

Mr. Pant is doing well in a way; he is over-worked and does not like anything which causes him extra trouble; so he is annoyed with the Left; but he is a real Congressman rather than a servant of His Majesty.

Mrs. Pandit is a real Nehru, and she is quite a character; but she is probably a sympathiser of the Left rather than the Right.

Peary Lal [Sharma] counts little but is a Leftist.

Ibrahim also counts little and is said no longer to be very pleased with his job.

R.A. Kidwai is rather inclined to the Right; but he is a friend of Jawahar.

Katju is regarded as a disappointment; he has Left inclinations.

Thus there is really no strong Right influence in the ministry, and several of the members are definitely Left in their sympathies.

The last election in the United Provinces was not really won by "Congress" in the old sense of the word; there is still but little strong feeling outside certain circles for pure Congress principles; the mass of voters supported Congress candidates in hopes of getting something; the opposition failed dismally in their campaign, and their trust in privilege and influence let them down badly in view of the strictly impartial attitude of the Officials on whom they have always depended; Jawahar's lightning tours and hard work, Gandhi's mysterious influence and religious prejudice, had a great effect, but the ignorant masses were chiefly swayed by the false promises put forward by the Left Wing.

The ministry therefore got in through Left Wing influence, and they are not in too strong a position apart from Left support; and when they look back to the election promises and forward to the next appeal to the country they must feel inclined to the Left. So much was talked of wrecking the Constitution and so little of constructive work that they began with false ideas of their duties and powers, and there has not yet been time for them to be brought round by responsibility.

Now that the Congress higher command has more or less clearly indicated that they want to retain office for the present, it is possible that we may soon see more of a stiffening up; but the ministers individually are old Congress talkers and critics rather than administrators, and personally I doubt if they can improve much without pressure from outside. This matter of outside influence is of great importance, and very recently it has tended to be slightly Right; hence as I reported in my last fortnightly Mr. Pant won a minor victory by threatening resignation which is now becoming generally known to be against the All-India leaders' policy.

Our ministry is believed to have learnt a lot but its members still retain their old inclinations and prejudices. Also none of them is in any sense of the word first class; Mr. Pant and Mrs. Pandit are as administrators the best men of the lot, but the latter is not specially interested in law and order; therefore Mr. Pant has to bear a very heavy burden with little help from his own colleagues.

Yours sincerely,
A.C. BLUNDEN

NOTES

1. Sir John Anderson was Governor of Bengal at this date.
2. Lord Brabourne was Governor of Bombay at this date.
3. Sir Herbert Emerson was Governor of the Punjab at this date.
4. Lord Hailey was Governor of the U.P. 1928-30 and 1931-4.
5. Sir Spencer Harcourt Butler was Governor of the U.P. 1918 and 1921-3.
6. Sir Maurice Hallett was Governor of Bihar at this date.
7. No reply to this letter has been traced in the India Office Records.
8. This document and the documents in the following two Appendices were sent to Lord Zetland as enclosures to Sir Harry Haig's Fortnightly Report of 7 May 1937 (No. 28). Haig also sent copies of correspondence between Mr Jinnah and Chaudhuri Khaliquzzaman and the text of resolutions passed by the Working Committees of the Indian National Congress and the Muslim League.
9. Mr Donaldson replied on 10 April 1937. He said that Sir Harry Haig had no immediate intention of summoning the Legislature. He proposed to do so when his ministers were in a position to place their budget proposals and programme before it. L/P&J/5/264: f. 520.
10. See previous note.
11. Sir John Ewart was the Director of the Intelligence Bureau at this date. This letter was enclosed in the letter of 13 May 1937 from Lord Linlithgow to Lord Zetland.

12. Note in original: Only three.
13. It is clear from other papers on the file that during the second half of 1937, Sir John Ewart visited all the Provinces with Congress ministries and also Bengal.
14. Mr C.W. Gwynne.
15. Mr A.G. Phillips was acting Inspector-General of Police at this date.
16. Mr G.M. Harper.
17. Mr J.C. Donaldson.
18. Mr E.G.B. Peel.
19. Mr L. Owen.
20. Mr C.W. Gwynne was Chief Secretary to the U.P. government at this date.
21. Mr A.G. Phillips was acting Inspector-General of Police at this date.
22. Not printed.
23. Sir Harry Haig sent a copy of this letter to the India Office.
24. The three papers mentioned are not on the file.
25. No. 102.
26. Mr C.W. Gwynne.
27. Mr R.A. Horton.
28. Mr E.G.B. Peel.
29. The various enclosures to Mr Donaldson's letter are not reprinted with the exception of the letter of the Chief Secretary dated 15 September 1937 (Appendix 7).
30. The various enclosures to Lord Linlithgow's letter are not reprinted.
31. Mr R.M. Saner was Assistant Collector, Lansdowne. His letter of 25 October 1937 was addressed to his immediate superior, Mr Philip Mason. Saner gave accounts of speeches made at a Congress meeting in Lansdowne in aid of the Congress candidate in the Bijnor bye-election. He felt: 'there is no doubt that the intention of the speakers was to excite hatred and contempt against Europeans and this was done in the very centre of a Cantonment inhabited by British Officers and their wives and where large numbers of Indian troops are stationed'. R/3/1/2.
32. Only the paragraph of Lord Linlithgow's letter reproduced here relates to the United Provinces.
33. Lord Linlithgow's telegram has not been traced.
34. Governor of Bihar at this date.
35. Governor of the Central Provinces at this date.
36. Governor of Bombay at this date.
37. Unfortunately it has not proved possible to trace in the India Office Records Lord Linlithgow's account of his conversations with Sir Harry Haig in November 1937.
38. Appendix 9.
39. Sir Henry Craik was Home Member of the Viceroy's Executive Council at this date

40. Mr R.M. Maxwell was Secretary, Home Department, Government of India at this date.
41. Appendix 8.
42. Lord Brabourne was Governor of Bengal at this date.
43. Sir Roger Lumley was Governor of Bombay at this date.
44. No reply to this letter has been traced.
45. This note was enclosed in the letter of 3 December 1937 from Lord Linlithgow to Lord Zetland.
46. Mr E.G.B. Peel.
47. Appendix 9.
48. This communiqué was enclosed in the Chief Secretary's Report of 18 December 1937.
49. Appendix 9.
50. Sir Harry Haig did not reply to this letter until 12 February 1938 (No. U.P-55). The reply will be printed in the next volume.
51. Evidently sent to Mr Laithwaite (P.S.V.). A copy of the letter and enclosures was forwarded to Lord Zetland.
52. Mr P.H. Measures was Superintendent of Police, Agra.

Index

Certain terms, such as Hindus, Muslims and United Provinces, occur in almost every document and have therefore not been indexed. For the same reason there are no index entries for Lord Linlithgow as Viceroy nor for Sir Harry Haig as Governor of the United Provinces. Footnotes are indexed under the document to which they are attached. References to documents in the Appendices are preceded by the letter 'A'.

The index entries refer to document numbers